Gunboats, Empire and the China Station

Gunboats, Empire and the China Station

The Royal Navy in 1920s East Asia

Matthew Heaslip

BLOOMSBURY ACADEMIC
LONDON • NEW YORK • OXFORD • NEW DELHI • SYDNEY

BLOOMSBURY ACADEMIC
Bloomsbury Publishing Plc
50 Bedford Square, London, WC1B 3DP, UK
1385 Broadway, New York, NY 10018, USA

BLOOMSBURY, BLOOMSBURY ACADEMIC and the Diana logo are trademarks of
Bloomsbury Publishing Plc

First published in Great Britain 2021

Paperback edition published 2022

Copyright © Matthew Heaslip, 2021

Matthew Heaslip has asserted his right under the Copyright, Designs and Patents Act,
1988, to be identified as Author of this work.

For legal purposes the Acknowledgements on p. viii constitute an extension
of this copyright page.

Cover image © British Insect-class gunboat on the South Bank of the Yangtze River at
Nanjing, China circa 1929. Chronicle/Alamy Stock Photo

All rights reserved. No part of this publication may be reproduced
or transmitted in any form or by any means, electronic or mechanical,
including photocopying, recording, or any information storage or retrieval
system, without prior permission in writing from the publishers.

Bloomsbury Publishing Plc does not have any control over, or responsibility for, any
third-party websites referred to or in this book. All internet addresses given in this
book were correct at the time of going to press. The author and publisher regret any
inconvenience caused if addresses have changed or sites have ceased to exist, but can
accept no responsibility for any such changes.

Every effort has been made to trace copyright holders and to obtain their permissions
for the use of copyright material. The publisher apologizes for any errors or omissions
and would be grateful if notified of any corrections that should be incorporated in
future reprints or editions of this book.

A catalogue record for this book is available from the British Library.

Library of Congress Cataloging-in-Publication Data
Names: Heaslip, Matthew, author.
Title: Gunboats, empire and the China Station : the Royal Navy in 1920s
East Asia / Matthew Heaslip. Other titles: Royal Navy in 1920s East Asia
Description: New York : Bloomsbury Academic, 2020. |
Includes bibliographical references and index.
Identifiers: LCCN 2020023031 (print) | LCCN 2020023032 (ebook) | ISBN 9781350176188
(hardback) | ISBN 9781350176195 (ebook) | ISBN 9781350176201 (epub)
Subjects: LCSH: Great Britain. Royal Navy. China Station–History. |
Great Britain. Royal Navy–History–20th century. | East Asia–History–20th century. |
Great Britain–History, Naval–20th century. | British–East Asia–History–20th century.
Classification: LCC VA457.C47 H43 2020 (print) | LCC VA457.C47 (ebook) |
DDC 359.40951/09042–dc23
LC record available at https://lccn.loc.gov/2020023031
LC ebook record available at https://lccn.loc.gov/2020023032

ISBN: HB: 978-1-3501-7618-8
PB: 978-1-3502-1356-2
ePDF: 978-1-3501-7619-5
eBook: 978-1-3501-7620-1

Typeset by Newgen KnowledgeWorks Pvt. Ltd., Chennai, India

To find out more about our authors and books visit www.bloomsbury.com
and sign up for our newsletters.

Contents

List of Illustrations	vii
Acknowledgements	viii
Introduction	1

1.	Joining the China Station	15
	Looking beyond the battle fleet	22
	The Royal Navy's role in Britain's interwar foreign policy	25
	Britain's China conundrum	30
2.	Between China and Japan, the China Station's strategic balance	41
	The right warships in the right places?	45
	China: Friend or foe?	51
	Surplus to requirements: The China Station ashore	53
	The Hong Kong question	59
	The cooperation challenge	63
	Europe's retreat and an emergent 'special relationship'	71
3.	Adapting to a new China in a violent peace	95
	Britain's changing interests in China	100
	The Royal Navy's growing piracy challenge	105
	An exceptional deployment: The Shanghai task force	115
	Britain's global struggle against communism	121
	A changing role in protecting British civilians	126
4.	Technological development and imperial policing	149
	Maintaining imperial prestige	152
	Hermes the trickster	160
	Understanding China	169
	Responding to crises	178
	Naval gunfire at Wanxian and Nanjing	182
	Controlling the violence	191

5. Changing attitudes, ideas and approaches	205
Late-Victorian gunboat diplomacy in East Asia	208
A failed attempt at returning to pre-war ways	213
The impact of the May Thirtieth Incident	218
A double crisis: Gunboat diplomacy living up to its reputation	224
The gunboat retreat	228
Sailing to war	237
Conclusion	261
The Royal Navy's peacetime front line	272
Appendix 1 Examples of key warship types	275
Appendix 2 Timeline of senior officers	279
Bibliography	281
Index	299

Illustrations

Figures

1	Shanghai Bund in 1928	18
2	HMS *Hawkins* at Shanghai in 1927	19
3	Royal Navy 'stations' during the 1920s (simplified)	23
4	China Station command structure in the 1920s	24
5	Official Royal Navy storage facilities 1900–14	54
6	International warships anchored at Shanghai in April 1927	72
7	Foreign defensive lines for the Shanghai International Settlement 1927	81
8	Damage to HMS *Bee* 8 September 1926	157
9	Shanghai Volunteer Corps membership 1920–7	159
10	Movements of HMS *Carlisle* 1920–3	172
11	Map of Socony Hill and the surrounding area in 1927	187
12	Merchant vessels and the upper Yangtze rapids in 1928	209
13	Patrols by HMS *Moorhen* 1919–24	216
14	Shamian Island in the 1920s	220
15	Officers of the 'cutting-out' group taken on the morning of 5 September	227
16	Extent of official Royal Navy protection on the Yangtze	236

Tables

1	Royal Navy global deployments	5
2	Population of the Shanghai International Settlement 1915–20	104

Acknowledgements

In the process of writing this book I have been fortunate to have received guidance and assistance from so many friends and colleagues, among others. I appreciate and would like to acknowledge all of those who have helped me get to this point but want to highlight a few whose support has been instrumental over the years. To begin with, I am extremely grateful to Professor Richard Overy, Dr Laura Rowe and Dr Tehyun Ma for their expert supervision while I worked on my doctoral thesis – the basis for this book. It was an honour to have been mentored by such a respected group of historians and their advice has proven invaluable on many occasions. On a similar vein, I would like to thank Professor Joe Maiolo and Dr Hao Gao for their insightful comments and constructive feedback on my research.

When conducting overseas research in new locations, securing local assistance is of immeasurable value. In my case, I am indebted to Professor Dai Gao and Dr Gaoli Wei of Peking University, for their kind assistance during my enjoyable and fruitful research trips to China. Such research can prove expensive and so I would also like to thank the Western Front Association's Wessex Branch and Santander UK for their kind support. Throughout the research process I received friendly and professional assistance from countless archivists in London, Portsmouth, Shanghai and beyond – to all of them I owe a debt.

By the nature of the task, historical writing can sometimes be a lonely path. The support and encouragement of my friends has so often helped me navigate through the setbacks and challenges I encountered on that journey. Some have gone so far as to take time reviewing various unpolished draft copies, notably Justine Lei and Brynn O'Connell, and their helpful feedback at key moments has been very much appreciated. To all of you – thank you.

Publishing my book against the background of the COVID19 pandemic could have been quite a stressful process, but I am thankful for the kind assistance of Maddie Holder and Abigail Lane at Bloomsbury, along with the patient guidance of my copy editors. If you will excuse a hint of Patrick O'Brian - excellent navigators really prove their worth in rough seas.

None of this would have been possible without Alla's encouragement and patience and whose support helped me draw the writing process to its conclusion, without losing too much of my remaining sanity. Finally, I dedicate this book to my parents Terry and Angela, whose love and hard work, particularly through what must have seemed like endless years of study, enabled me to climb to where I am today.

Introduction

In recent years we have seen growing discussion about the changing global balance of power. China's economic and military challenges to the United States, questions about the relevance of post-1945 multilateral conventions and renewed gunboat diplomacy all feed into those debates. This is not the first time the world has seen this kind of tumultuous transition. Comparisons have already been drawn with the interwar period as a key phase in the previous changeover between superpowers.[1] British economic dominance was usurped by America's rise. The British Empire hit its peak in size and influence, after which it began a slow decline that led to increasingly desperate attempts at maintaining the status quo, often using Britain's key global power asset: the Royal Navy. With a curious twist it is to the home of today's ascendant superpower that we must go to explore that previous process, the epicentre from which Britain's imperial system started to crumble. In doing so, we will explore the changes and challenges that affected the Royal Navy's China Station, as it worked to maintain the British Empire's interests in and around East Asia, over the course of that chaotic decade. Amid pirates and revolution, with events pushed to the verge of war, Britain's seamen fought to hold back the changing tides of fortune.

There have been some excellent studies of the two contrasting elements to developments in 1920s East Asia. A recent flurry of accounts, for example, has explored specific elements of the economic, sociological and diplomatic aspects of Britain's relationship with China.[2] This has given us a far better understanding of the 'diplomacy of imperial retreat', as Edmund Fung once described it.[3] On the military side, discussion has long been framed by debate over the Admiralty's naval strategy in relation to Japan, and to a lesser extent the United States.[4] Those two stories run almost entirely separately, despite both featuring the Royal Navy's China Station, one of the British Empire's two main institutional cogs in East Asia and its third-largest fleet. That will be addressed in this book. Britain's 'Far Eastern' fleet had a significant impact on its furthest outposts of the Empire and its relationship with China. In return, events in China had an important bearing on the way the Admiralty developed its strategy for East Asia in a rapidly changing world. In the process, the region saw one of the largest ever peacetime deployments of British naval force during the forgotten 1927 Shanghai Crisis. Exploring those developments helps us understand Britain and the Royal Navy's place in modern East Asia, and the evolving struggle between the United States and China.

Bridging the decades between two of the most destructive conflicts the world has seen, the interwar period is sometimes treated as little more than a pause in which the major powers recovered their strength, before almost inevitably resuming hostilities.[5] The very title 'interwar' highlights the extent to which the 1920s and 1930s are defined by the wars at either end of the period. David Reynolds went so far as to describe the pre-war and interwar eras as being 'punctuation marks' in our understanding of the early twentieth century.[6] In the context of the Royal Navy, that idea of an interwar interlude has been a core theme in discussion of the power struggles with the other major players of the period: the United States, the Soviet Union, Germany, France, Italy and Japan.[7] Naval operations during the 1920s have often been neglected, with a tendency to view the period just as background to the major power struggles in the 1930s. As a result, the decade is largely viewed as one of peace.[8]

Little research has gone into the potential for Britain to have been drawn indirectly into a war through existing commitments involving armed conflicts, such as the civil wars in China, or how those wider developments helped shape British defence policy. Perhaps the exception to that rule has been the discussion of the 1922 Chanak Affair, when Mustafa Kemal Atatürk's nationalist movement challenged some of the conditions laid down in the Treaty of Sèvres.[9] Atatürk ordered the reoccupation of Istanbul and Eastern Thrace, culminating in a stand-off between Turkish troops and the Allied forces stationed to hold the Çanakkale (Chanak) region, controlling the strategically important Dardanelles Straits. Ultimately war was only narrowly avoided.[10] The fact that outright war did not result from such interventions in the 1920s does not mean that the events were peaceful, or that the threat of force by a major power was sufficient to ensure the peaceful capitulation of a lesser power. In the Chanak Crisis, the lesser power, Turkey, was seemingly willing to fight and it was Britain that eventually backed down. The 'Great War' may have ended, but the world had not moved on to a 'Great Peace'.

Discussion of this 'violent peace' has been largely limited to events in Eastern Europe and the former Ottoman Empire, particularly between the Russian

Revolution and the Chanak Crisis.[11] Otherwise areas such as the Mediterranean have been described as having seen occasional crises, but were mostly 'relatively quiet'.[12] This peaceful narrative is particularly true of naval developments east of Suez. The risk of British forces being drawn into a sustained war due to events in 1920s China has only been acknowledged as a 'thinkable', if undesirable, explanation for why the Admiralty felt it vital to build up a major naval fortress at Singapore.[13] This may reflect British naval history's long-running hangover from Arthur Marder and his tendency to continue fighting Herbert Richmond's battles over preparations for a future major conflict. This has come at the expense of discussing what the mainstream Royal Navy was actually doing in the 1920s.[14]

There have been a few tantalizing references to events that highlight how the 1920s were far from peaceful for Britain's Royal Navy, particularly in East Asia.[15] In dealing with a range of state and substate threats the Royal Navy and other branches of the British imperial establishment were involved in violent clashes in China, throughout most of the decade. Indeed, the country was the scene of the Navy's most sustained active deployment over the entire interwar period, and events in China came very close to ending Britain's peace.[16] Along the way, new developments in technology, tactical and strategic thinking, and changing attitudes to the British Empire all affected the China Station's disposition and behaviour. Through all this the Royal Navy played a significant role in Britain's interwar foreign policy, beyond the major power struggles. Preparations for 'big wars' took place in parallel with the Navy fighting the Empire's 'little wars'.

Our knowledge of the interwar Royal Navy has been, and to some extent still is, dominated by a few key overarching topics, notably the disarmament and arms limitation conferences, and associated cruiser arms race between Britain, the United States and Japan.[17] Core to these has been the debate over the seriousness with which Britain treated the Ten Year Rule. Conceived by the British government in 1919, that 'rule' effectively guided the armed services and the Treasury to assume that no war would occur in the following decade. Assessments of the rule have become more nuanced, noting that it only really applied to major wars requiring an expeditionary force to be sent to mainland Europe but not to minor expeditions and policing operations elsewhere around the world.[18] However, there was a much broader spectrum of strategic deployments and challenges that affected the 1920s Royal Navy.

Chief among these was the Royal Navy's role dealing with potential localized conflicts as Britain's 'imperial gendarmerie', particularly in response to the escalating violent outbursts in Palestine between Arab nationalists, British garrison forces and Zionists.[19] While considering the broader context of the

British Empire as a whole, the treatment of the Royal Navy has often been relatively one dimensional, as a tool of the Empire. There have only been brief mentions of new developments, such as faster ships, and how changes to the Navy related to those in the Empire, and vice versa.[20] In effect, this has become a hallmark of how imperial histories of Britain's relationship with China treat the Royal Navy's role.[21]

If histories of the British Empire in East Asia take a simplistic view of the 1920s Royal Navy, naval historians have been guilty of almost completely forgetting China. For example, while Christopher Bell provides a convincing argument about the importance of Hong Kong as a forward operating base in the developing power struggle between Britain and Japan, he makes no mention of the relationship between the naval base and events in China itself.[22] Most histories of the 1920s Royal Navy east of Suez focus heavily on tracing the path to the Second World War and explaining the shift in strategic focus from Hong Kong to Singapore,[23] in particular, how Japan was almost certain to end up at war with one or both of the United States and Great Britain, given its 'Asia for Asians' rhetoric and expanding commercial interests.[24] Concentrating on Japan is logical and valuable when debating the origins of the Second World War, in terms of East Asia, but when examining the interwar period itself such a focus risks ignoring events that did not ultimately result in conflict.

The interwar Royal Navy comprised three sections: (1) the main fleet – centralized in order to destroy an enemy battle fleet, (2) detached cruiser forces – to protect the sea arteries of the Empire and (3) local defence forces – performing the day-to-day work of the Empire.[25] Due to the focus on major power conflicts, we have many excellent naval histories that follow a similar course of concentrating almost exclusively on the first two segments of the fleet.[26] John Linge's fascinating examination of the Royal Navy's policing of Ireland's coastline, during the establishment of the Irish Free State in 1921–2, provides one of the few notable exceptions.[27] Given that over 400 of the Royal Navy's roughly 475 armed, sea-going vessels in commission in the mid-1920s were types used for regional defence and policing, this represents a notable oversight.[28] In contrast, historians of the late Victorian and Edwardian Royal Navy almost all make far greater reference to the global deployment and use of smaller warships for trade defence and imperial policing.[29]

Examining the day-to-day work of the ordinary fleet, during moments of calm and crisis, is crucial to understanding the Royal Navy's role in shaping the British Empire's interwar foreign policy. The ordinary fleet was spread across the entire world, in contrast to the battle fleet, which by the 1920s was concentrated in the 'Home' theatre and the Mediterranean. It was through the mainstream Navy, the bulk of Britain's fleet, that Britain was able to wield significant influence over global developments.

Perhaps a result of the focus on the battle fleet, the interwar China Station itself has also featured in surprisingly little historical literature, despite having been Britain's third-largest naval deployment over a period of decades. Those that do exist tend to skip over events in the 1920s to focus on the major conflicts in the Station's history.[30] In doing so they have largely missed the pivotal moments where the China Station was on the frontline in the turn of the Empire. On a day-to-day basis the China Station was involved in policing and defending the furthermost stretches of the British Empire in China's littoral regions (Table 1).[31]

During the 1920s, the British Empire had considerable interests in China, built up after Britain forced open China's borders to Western merchants through the Opium Wars of 1839–42 and 1856–60.[32] In purely nominal terms, British firms had investments totalling roughly £200 million in China in 1927, equivalent to almost £13 billion in 2019 when adjusted for inflation.[33] Going into the 1920s those peripheral areas came under sustained pressure from the growing economic dominance of the United States and a more assertive Japan. As a result, those assets and trade routes were not critical, but they were

Table 1 Royal Navy global deployments

	Capital Ships	Cruisers	Destroyers	Minor Warships	Submarines	Total
1920						
Home/Atlantic	14	12	78	7	22	133
Mediterranean	8	6	22	7	–	43
China	–	5	–	21	12	38
East Indies	–	3	–	3	–	6
Other	–	10	–	7	–	17
1929						
Home/Atlantic	10	6	22	46	19	103
Mediterranean	10	9	38	7	7	71
China	1	6	9	25	6	47
East Indies	–	3	–	4	–	7
Other	–	8	–	10	–	17

Note: Only includes warships in active commission (i.e. not in reserve or at training schools).

important enough for the British government to risk localized conflict. China was not just an economic concern for the British Empire, however, with the country representing a vital tile in the jigsaw of Britain's global grand defensive strategy. In addition to the well-known imperial outpost at Hong Kong, the Royal Navy also maintained another formal base at Weihai (Weihaiwei) in northern China and saw the country as both a potential trigger for a future conflict with Japan and also a source of victory in such a war. British policy for East Asia was therefore largely one of trying to maintain existing business arrangements and trade flows, to keep hold of its strategic outposts, all the while avoiding being drawn into a larger military commitment. Diplomatic and economic policy decisions tended to fall under the Foreign Office, grand strategic planning was largely guided by the Admiralty and imperial policing was by the China Station itself. As we shall see, however, in practice things were never that simple and many decisions fell to the officers and officials on the scene, whether working in collaboration or in isolation.

Exploring how the China Station dealt with its full range of responsibilities will centre around the generally young, men that were sent out to the other side of the world and the people they encountered. As a result, it is fitting to begin with what they experienced during those first days and weeks and how that shaped their views of East Asia. During that formative period, they met men and women from around the world, some of whose lives would be changed by the events detailed in this book. Featuring heroes and antiheroes, tragic and comedic moments, this is a human tale where Britain's steel castles were a floating community that built and sometimes broke bonds with those they encountered.

At a higher level, the book will go on to consider the China Station within the wider geostrategic climate. After the First World War the Admiralty retained a gunboat force on the Chinese coast and a string of naval bases to support them, despite significant pressures on the naval budget. This section will therefore, in part, consider what relationship those resources had to the wider strategic concerns about defending against Japanese expansion in the region and the threat that posed to British imperial interests. In doing so, it will highlight the key interrelationship between Britain's strategy for China and its corresponding one for Japan, particularly in terms of the viability of defending Hong Kong.

Many of the challenges faced by the Royal Navy in peacetime along China's coastline and rivers were also dilemmas for the other major powers operating in the region, as well as for China's local and regional authorities. With almost all the countries affected having worked together previously as allies during the

First World War, continued cooperation in peacetime could prove beneficial for all concerned. The following section will focus on the China Station's interactions with America's Asiatic Fleet and Japan's First Expeditionary Fleet. While the problems faced by the three powers were often identical, government policy frequently dictated different responses. Moreover, service personnel in East Asia sometimes acted in contrast, rather than in parallel, to those at the top level. It is important therefore to consider what frontline cooperation occurred and why naval personnel sometimes chose to go against their nation's official policies. We should not assume that officers, trained in following orders, always acted obediently and exactly in line with their instructions. This is all crucial in order to understand more precisely the role of navies in interwar international relations, when they often served as extensions of their nations' diplomatic corps. The conduct of naval officers on deployment could shape foreign policy and define how countries were perceived worldwide.

With that strategic position established, part three will consider the China Station's peacetime role in interwar British foreign policy, along with the challenges posed by the revolution and subsequent civil wars in China. It will look at what Britain sought to influence, control and protect and how those priorities translated into requirements for the Royal Navy. The lightweight sloops and gunboats that formed two-thirds of the China Station's standing force were clearly not there to counter the Imperial Japanese Navy (IJN), which regularly sent battlecruisers and cruisers to China's ports.[34] The peacetime work against piracy and banditry, and the efforts to keep Britain's imperial outposts in China secure during a period of turmoil, must therefore be considered to fully understand Britain's naval presence in East Asia developed. This will explain why so many local defence vessels were posted to China and how that force evolved over the 1920s – in particular, how a new piracy problem forced the Royal Navy to work with both British imperial and Chinese authorities in an attempt to counter it.

An evolving crisis in China from 1925 relegated piracy to a secondary concern as events pushed the Royal Navy's stretched resources to breaking point. What happened in and around Shanghai in 1927 features heavily in histories of the British Empire's relationship with China, but it also triggered the most significant peacetime deployment of naval power by the Admiralty in the period. Addressing the near-complete absence of that task force from existing naval accounts, this section puts the events into context and takes another step further away from the 'Road to 1939' narrative of interwar developments. Developments in China were considered important enough to elicit a pronounced military response, not only in their own rights but also against a background fear in Whitehall of a global Soviet plot to undermine the British Empire.

With the 1920s Royal Navy required to respond to such significant operational and financial challenges, technology was proposed as a source of solution to the emergent problems. Wireless communication, faster vessels and effective military aircraft offered the potential to transform how the post-First World War Navy went about its role in supporting the British Empire. Technology played an important role in reinforcing the international prestige of both the Royal Navy and the wider British Empire, and yet once again most research on military innovation during the period has focused on major power conflicts, to the neglect of its role in Britain's 'little wars' and in peace.[35] To rectify this, part four examines how new technology influenced the 1920s China Station in three key areas. First, it considers the role technology played during the decade in reinforcing imperial prestige, 'waving the flag', to strengthen Britain's influence in the region. Secondly, exploring the roll-out of wireless equipment demonstrates how technology affected the Navy's ability to both understand and control how its warships went about their peacetime work at the periphery of the Empire.[36] In doing so, we will need to be mindful that not all outcomes were intentional, as a result of deliberate efforts by the Royal Navy to address the challenges it faced in East Asia. Finally, we will consider the role technology played in the outcome of key flashpoints.

The deployment of HMS *Hermes* to the China Station offers a significant case study in exploring the extent to which the exploitation of new technology was really intended to improve the efficiency of peacetime operations. Public announcements from the time explaining why Britain's first purpose-built aircraft carrier was being sent to China for imperial policing purposes obscured the Admiralty's real, secret motivation behind the move. Events in China simply provided Britain with an excuse to contravene the terms of the Washington Treaty to strengthen its strategic position in the region. As we shall see, those findings are of great significance to existing discussions about the later 'Allied' nations' attitudes towards the Treaty.

Technological factors have always been a feature of naval history, if sometimes discussed ad nauseum to the point of being unable to see the wood for the trees. However, technical details have played a significant role in key events. The bombardments conducted by British warships at Wanxian (Wanhsien) and Nanjing (Nanking) were two such pivotal moments in Britain's relationship with China. Wildly varying claims over the number of casualties have been thrown around over the years, but no one has attempted objectively to weigh those estimates or consider the naval factors behind the casualties. The outcomes were not decided by what calibre of guns were available on Britain's warships, but similar details help draw together evidence about how many people died and what factors led to their deaths. This analysis does not change our core understanding of the consequences of those events, but it provides significantly greater depth to our knowledge of what happened and why.

Countering the challenges facing the China Station was not just a matter of technology and finance but also the willingness and ability of naval officers to develop and adopt new methods. We therefore also need to consider three key questions: Did the China Station proactively adopt new ideas and tactics? What impact did the presence of new ideas, or continued use of outdated approaches, have on the work done by the China Station? Lastly, were the tactics used chosen by junior officers in the course of their work, the commander-in-chief of the China Station, or were they imposed by the Admiralty? The final part of this book will therefore feed into discussions about anti-intellectualism in the Royal Navy and the speed with which centralized command and control was adopted.[37]

Central to this will be a review of when the Royal Navy's attitude towards using Victorian 'gunboat diplomacy' tactics in China changed and how. To what extent did Austen Chamberlain's much discussed 1926 December Memorandum really influence the China Station's operating procedures? This is integral to understanding how tangible the link was between the changing diplomatic and military approaches to China, across all three levels involved: Whitehall, the Royal Navy's senior command and junior officers on the scene. While many imperial histories treat the Royal Navy as a uniform entity, there was considerable variety in officers' attitudes and behaviour, influenced by human and institutional factors. As we shall see, those factors produced a gradual shift in the Navy's approach before the official change in policy from London, and for different reasons to that top-level pivot. The variety of approaches came to the fore during the surge in warships arriving on the scene in 1927. The introduction of so many ship captains who were unused to the local circumstances, with minimal knowledge of Britain's strategy for China, was highly influential in the outcome of key events and has previously been overlooked.

In addition to changes in strategy and mindset, this book will also consider structural developments such as the planned reorganization of the Royal Marines, discussed by the Madden Committee in 1924, to turn the marines into a rapid response force.[38] The Madden Committee reviewed the structure of the Royal Marines, to assess whether their duties could be fulfilled at a lower cost by the mainstream Navy or alternatively whether greater value could be secured from the existing force. The committee proposed to modernize and adapt the Royal Marines into a rapid response role, allowing a few carefully located units around the Empire to settle swiftly most threats to imperial stability. Ultimately those recommendations were dropped due to concerns about the upfront costs of such a reorganization. Nonetheless there has been some debate about whether the Royal Marines developed into the proposed force by the time the 12th Battalion was despatched to Shanghai in January 1927.[39] We shall see that the benefits of a true rapid response force would have been beneficial during major incidents, but it may have also proven counterproductive on a day-to-day basis.

Together all these strands weave a story involving tens of thousands of British service personnel and the hundreds of thousands, if not millions, of people they encountered while serving on the China Station. Posted far from home and away from the prestigious fleets that measured the balance of global power, their experiences and actions framed a key period in the slow transition from British to American hegemony. Their mission was to maintain the status quo against the growing military reach of key rivals, amid regional upheaval and violence, and backed by a state struggling to cope with fiscal challenges. While events in China did not precipitate the ultimate collapse of British imperial power, they saw Britain's final confident display of the naval mastery secured by Nelson. A century on from that transformative decade, it is worth appreciating the complexity of those past events before we look forward to what might prove an equally dramatic phase in world history.

Notes

1 John Maurer and Christopher Bell, 'Introduction', in *At the Crossroads between Peace and War: The London Naval Conference in 1930*, ed. John Maurer and Christopher Bell (Annapolis: Naval Institute Press, 2014), pp. 1–6.
2 E.g. Robert Bickers, 'The Colony's Shifting Position in the British Informal Empire in China', in *Hong Kong's Transitions 1842–1997*, ed. Judith Brown and Rosemary Foot (Basingstoke: Macmillan, 1997); Robert Bickers, 'Shanghailanders: The Formation and Identity of the British Settler Community in Shanghai 1843–1937', *Past and Present* 159 (1998), 161–211; Robert Bickers, *Empire Made Me: An Englishman Adrift in Shanghai* (London: Penguin, 2004); Robert Bickers, 'Ordering Shanghai: Policing a Treaty Port, 1854–1900', in *Maritime Empires: British Imperial Maritime Trade in the Nineteenth Century*, ed. David Killingray, Margarette Lincoln and Nigel Rigby (Woodbridge: Boydell, 2004); Ian Phimister, 'Foreign Devils, Finance and Informal Empire: Britain and China c. 1900–1912', *Modern Asian Studies* 40/3

(2006), 737–59; Zhang Jianguo and Zhang Junyong, trans. Alec Hill, *Weihaiwei under British Rule* (Jinan City: Shandong Pictorial, 2006); Zwia Lipkin, *Useless to the State: 'Social Problems' and Social Engineering in Nationalist Nanjing 1927–1937* (Cambridge, MA: Harvard University Press, 2006); Zhongping Chen, 'The May Fourth Movement and Provincial Warlords: A Reexamination', *Modern China*, 27/2 (2011), 135–69; Isabella Jackson, 'Expansion and defence in the International Settlement at Shanghai', Sherman X. Lai, 'Nationalistic enthusiasm versus imperialist sophistication: Britain from Chiang Kai-shek's perspective', and Chen Qianping, 'Foreign investment in modern China: An analysis with a focus on British interests', which are all in *Britain and China, 1840–1970: Empire, Finance and War*, ed. Robert Bickers and Jonathan Howlett (Abingdon: Routledge, 2016).

3 Edmund S. K. Fung, *The Diplomacy of Imperial Retreat: Britain's South China Policy, 1924–1931* (Oxford: Oxford University Press, 1991).

4 Christopher Bell, '"Our Most Exposed Outpost": Hong Kong and British Far Eastern Strategy, 1921–1941', *Journal of Military History* 60/1 (1996), 61–88; Christopher Bell, '"How Are We Going to Make War?" Admiral Sir Herbert Richmond and British Far Eastern War Plans', *Journal of Strategic Studies* 20/3 (1997), 123–41; Christopher Bell, *The Royal Navy: Sea-Power and Strategy between the Wars* (Basingstoke: Macmillan, 2000); Christopher Bell, 'The "Singapore Strategy" and the Deterrence of Japan: Winston Churchill, the Admiralty and the Dispatch of Force Z', *English Historical Review* 116/467 (2001), 604–34.

5 John Ferris, 'The Greatest Power on Earth: Great Britain in the 1920s', *International History Review* 13/4 (1991), 726–50.

6 David Reynolds, 'The Origins of the Two "World Wars": Historical Discourse and International Politics', *Journal of Contemporary History* 38/1 (2003), 29.

7 E.g. Brian Bond, *British Military Policy between the Two World Wars* (Oxford: Oxford University Press, 1980), pp. 36–40; Brian Bond, *War and Society in Europe, 1870–1970* (Stroud: Sutton, 1998), pp. 142–50; Lawrence Butler, 'The British Empire, 1918–1945: Interwar Change and Wartime Pressures', pp. 18–21, in *Crises of Empire: Decolonisation and Europe's Imperial States, 1918–1975*, ed. Lawrence Butler, Bob Moore and Martin Thomas (London: Bloomsbury, 2008), 17–46; Barry Watts and Williamson Murray, 'Military Innovation in Peacetime', in *Military Innovation in the Interwar Period*, ed. Williamson Murray and Allan Millett (Cambridge: Cambridge University Press, 1996), pp. 371–3.

8 Jeremy Black, *The British Seaborne Empire* (Yale: Yale University Press, 2004), p. 290; Bell, *The Royal Navy*, pp. 60–9 and 184.

9 Stephen Roskill, *Naval Policy between the Wars. Vol. 1, The Period of Anglo-American Antagonism 1919–1929* (London: Collins, 1968), pp. 188–200; Joseph Moretz, *The Royal Navy and the Capital Ship in the Interwar Period* (London: Frank Cass, 2002), p. 162.

10 John Darwin, 'The Chanak Crisis and the British Cabinet', *History* 65/213 (1980), 32–48.
11 Robert Gerwarth, *The Vanquished: Why the First World War Failed to End, 1917–1923* (London: Penguin, 2017), pp. 4–9; Duncan Redford and Philip Grove, *The Royal Navy: A History since 1900* (London: Tauris, 2014), pp. 109–11.
12 John Grainger, *The British Navy in the Mediterranean* (Woodbridge: Boydell & Brewer, 2017), pp. 225–35.
13 James Neidpath, *The Singapore Naval Base and the Defence of Britain's Eastern Empire 1919–1941* (Oxford: Clarendon Press, 1981), p. 15.
14 E.g. Arthur Marder, *From the Dardanelles to Oran: Studies of the Royal Navy in War and Peace 1915–1940* (London: Oxford University Press, 1974); Arthur Marder, 'The Influence of History on Sea Power: The Royal Navy and the Lessons of 1914–1918', *Pacific Historical Review* 41/4 (1972), 413–43.
15 Roskill, *Naval Policy between the Wars*.
16 Moretz, *The Royal Navy and the Capital Ship*, pp. 258–9.
17 E.g. Andrew Field, *Royal Navy Strategy in the Far East 1919–1939: Preparing for War against Japan* (London: Frank Cass, 2006); Greg Kennedy, 'Britain's Policy-Making Elite, the Naval Disarmament Puzzle, and Public Opinion, 1927–1932', *Albion: A Quarterly Journal Concerned with British Studies* 26/4 (1994), 623–44; Carolyn Kitching, *Britain and the Problem of International Disarmament: 1919–1934* (London: Routledge, 1999); Joe Maiolo, *The Royal Navy and Nazi Germany, 1933–1939* (Basingstoke: Macmillan, 1998), pp. 5–19; Philips P. O'Brien, 'The Washington Treaty Era, 1919–1936: Naval Arms Limitation', in *The Sea In History: The Modern World*, ed. N. A. M. Rodger (Woodbridge: Boydell & Brewer, 2017); Bell, *The Royal Navy*; Roskill, *Naval Policy between the Wars*.
18 Elizabeth Kier, *Imagining War: French and British Military Doctrine between the Wars* (Princeton: Princeton University Press, 1997), p. 93; Bond, *British Military Policy*, pp. 26–38.
19 Anthony Clayton, 'Deceptive Might: Imperial Defence and Security 1900–1968', in *The Twentieth Century: Oxford History of the British Empire*, ed. Judith M. Brown and William R. Louis (Oxford: Oxford University Press, 2001), p. 289.
20 Anthony Clayton, *The British Empire as a Superpower 1919–1939* (Basingstoke: Macmillan, 1986), pp. 80 and 141–227.
21 Jürgen Osterhammel, 'China', in *The Oxford History of the British Empire: Volume IV: The Twentieth Century*, ed. Judith M. Brown and William R. Louis (Oxford: Oxford University Press, 1999), pp. 647–9.
22 Bell, 'Our Most Exposed Outpost', 61–88.
23 E.g. Orest Babij, 'The Royal Navy and the Defence of the British Empire: 1928–1939', in *Far Flung Lines*, ed. Keith Neilson and Greg Kennedy (London: Cass, 1996), pp. 171–86; Kent Fedorowich, '"Cocked Hats and Swords and Small, Little

Garrisons": Britain, Canada and the Fall of Hong Kong, 1941', *Modern Asian Studies* 37/1 (2003), 111–57; Boyd, *The Royal Navy in Eastern Waters*, pp. 4–29; Bell, 'Our Most Exposed Outpost', 62; Bell, 'The "Singapore Strategy"', 604–63; Field, *The Royal Navy Strategy in the Far East*; Neidpath, *The Singapore Naval Base*.

24   Greg Kennedy, 'British Sea Power and Imperial Defence in the Far East: Sharing the Seas with America', in *Sea Power and the Asia-Pacific: The Triumph of Neptune?*, ed. Geoffrey Till and Patrick C. Bratton (London: Routledge, 2012), p. 206; Field, *Royal Navy Strategy in the Far East*, pp. 5–11.

25   Moretz, *The Royal Navy*, pp. 156–8.

26   Andrew Boyd, *The Royal Navy in Eastern Waters: Linchpin of Victory* (Barnsley: Seaforth, 2017), pp. 4–29; Eric Grove, *The Royal Navy* (Basingstoke: Macmillan, 2005), pp. 149–62; Dan Van der Vat, *Standard of Power – The Royal Navy in the Twentieth Century* (London: Pimlico, 2000), pp. 143–55; Bell, *The Royal Navy*, pp. 15–77; Marder, 'The Influence of History on Sea Power', pp. 413–43; Roskill, *Naval Policy between the Wars*.

27   John Linge, 'The Royal Navy and the Irish Civil War', *Irish Historical Studies* 31/121 (1998), 60, 69–71.

28   Report of Sub-committee on Staffs of Admiralty Office, War Office and Air Ministry for the Cabinet Committee on Reduction of National Expenditure, January 1923, TNA, CAB 24/160/72, p. 9; Robert Chesneau (ed.), *All the World's Fighting Ships 1922–1946* (London: Conway, 1992), pp. 7–85. Large numbers of vessels in the Royal Navy's fleet were held in reserve during peacetime, particularly destroyers and minesweepers. The overall proportions remain broadly similar, however, given that many fleet cruisers were also held in reserve.

29   Nicholas Lambert, 'Strategic Command and Control for Maneuver Warfare: Creation of the Royal Navy's "War Room" System, 1905–1915', *Journal of Military History* 69/2 (2005), 376–86; Lidgren, 'A Station in Transition', 468–73; O'Brien, 'The Titan Refreshed', 150–6; Padfield, *Rule Britannia*, pp. 209–22.

30   Mark Felton, *China Station: The British Military in the Middle Kingdom 1839–1997* (Barnsley: Pen and Sword, 2013); Jonathan Parkinson, *The Royal Navy, China Station: 1864–1941* (Kibworth: Matador, 2018); Malcolm Murfett, *Naval Warfare 1919–1945: An Operational History of the Volatile War at Sea* (London: Routledge, 2009), pp. 7–8.

31   NLS, Navy List (December 1920), NMM, Navy List (February 1929).

32   See Julia Lovell, *The Opium War: Drugs, Dreams, and the Making of China* (London: Picador, 2011); Robert Bickers, *The Scramble for China: Foreign Devils in the Qing Empire 1832–1914* (London: Penguin, 2012).

33   Fung, *Diplomacy of Imperial Retreat*, p. 4. Calculated using the Bank of England historical inflation converter: http://www.bankofengland.co.uk/education/Pages/resources/inflationtools/calculator/.

34 As noted in the ship's log of HMS *Diomede* 1924–5, TNA, ADM 53/75887 and ship's log of HMS *Hawkins* 1923–4, TNA, ADM 53/78593.
35 E.g. Sumida, 'British Naval Procurement', pp. 129–43; Lautenschlaeger, 'Technology and the Evolution of Naval Warfare', 3–51; Watts and Murray, 'Military Innovation in Peacetime', pp. 371–3.
36 Daniel Headrick and Pascal Griset, 'Submarine Telegraph Cables: Business and Politics, 1838–1939', *Business History Review* 75/3 (2001), 573–4.
37 Lambert, 'Strategic Control', 362; Marder, *From the Dardanelles to Oran*, pp. 34–8. Marder, 'The Influence of History on Sea Power', 413–43. See also Bell, 'The King's English', 685–716; Kier, *Imagining War*, p. 149.
38 Charles Madden, 'Function and training of Royal Marines' commonly referred to as 'The Madden Report', 1924, TNA, ADM 1/8664/134; Donald Bittner, 'Britannia's Sheathed Sword: The Royal Marines and Amphibious Warfare in the Interwar Years – A Passive Response', *Journal of Military History* 55/3 (1991), 345–64.
39 War Diaries of 12th RMB on service in China, 1927, TNA, ADM 1/8709/102; Bittner, 'Britannia's Sheathed Sword', pp. 345–64; Julian Thompson, *The Royal Marines* (London: Pan, 2000), p. 229; Kenneth Clifford, *Amphibious Warfare Development in Britain and America from 1920 to 1940* (New York: Edgewood, 1983), pp. 18–19.

1

Joining the China Station

By the early 1920s, knowledge in Britain about China, its history and its culture was improving. Paintings, books, newspaper articles, photographs and even early cinematic depictions all served to enlighten the British public to what life was like in the world's most populated country at the time. Not all of this was accurate, fair or complimentary, but it did increase awareness about life on the other side of the planet. Nonetheless, for those who travelled out to the region on service whether in Britain's armed forces, in the Foreign Office or as civilians, the experience was both exciting and profoundly disorientating. For many, perhaps even most, of those who set out to East Asia it was not their first experience outside of British waters. Indeed, the journey itself required short halts at regular intervals at harbours along the way, notably Singapore. While those port calls provided an opportunity to gain insights into other cultures, the impact was often quite limited. For Royal Navy crewmen the stops were normally quite brief before departing on the next leg of their journey, involving social and sporting events with other naval vessels, as well as the chance to 'blow off steam' in bars ashore. Those pauses were busy affairs, but some individuals did find time to explore and encounter experiences that started to change their view of the world. Leading Seaman William 'Robby' Roberts, for example, started to question his pride in the British Empire, after witnessing the brutality of some of his fellow countrymen, which was not in keeping with what he 'expected of an Englishman'.[1]

When first arriving into Hong Kong's harbour the crews were confronted with a band of three- and four-storey buildings in an Edwardian Baroque colonial style, framed against the backdrop of the imposing, mist-enclosed Victoria Peak. Sometimes even before the men made it to shore, they were 'swarmed' by an array of Chinese tradesmen offering to repair boots, make suits and mend clothes and selling various other items.[2] Initial impressions of all this were varied. Some later recounted how they were drawn to the vibrancy of the city and embraced the unusual new culture. Others complained about dirty conditions and the heat. Sweltering in high humidity, even those buildings that underwent regular cleaning struggled to compete against the near ever-present mildew and mould.[3] When the sun set, attention shifted from shore to sea, as Britain's warships lit up the bay with an electrical glow.[4] To many British visitors the contrast between the calm, clean, bright white-painted warships, illuminated by the latest technology, and the conditions in some areas ashore reinforced their belief in the British Empire's supremacy and their own mission as its representatives.

Hong Kong was a hybrid city combining local culture and architecture with a pronounced British imperial influence. As a result, it eased British service personnel into life in East Asia with a degree of familiarity. A variety of English-language newspapers with common titles – the *Telegraph*, *Mail* and *Sunday Herald* – featured news from home, advertisements for British brands and all the latest sporting results from far and near. A growing array of cinemas showed films and news reels from Britain and the United States, although from 1922 there was a budding array of locally produced Chinese films too.[5] Many of the Hong Kong Chinese population spoke a 'surprising' amount of English, making day-to-day interactions much easier for the new arrivals.[6] Even the now-iconic trams had been manufactured in Preston and were little different from those still perambulating around Britain's towns and cities. It was strange and different, daunting to some, exotic to others, but one in which they felt secure.

For those who remained in the city over the following weeks, months and even years, life retained that feeling of familiarity, with a degree of homeliness. In contrast to Victorian times when there was an unwillingness to study what was regarded as the 'beastly' local language, many officers, seamen and civilian officials in the 1920s made a conscious effort to learn at least basic Cantonese.[7] While this was officially done through formal classes and day-to-day activities, some naval personnel favoured finding and supporting a local Chinese girlfriend, although how commonplace this was is difficult to tell. Certainly, there were occasional cases that became the talk of the town, particularly where a married officer's British wife was also present in Hong Kong.[8] Not all such liaisons were temporary or transactional, however, with some resulting in happy marriages. To the Hong Kong population all of this was normal life, even if they did not always approve of what it entailed. As a major port and trading hub, the city maintained a significant transitory population and so Hongkongers, whether of Han Chinese, British or other descent, were used to the regular rotation of new faces.

For most Royal Navy personnel on the China Station, Hong Kong was not their end destination, although it was a regular halt for those aboard ocean-going warships or the West River gunboats. Those men took the next step, further into the unknown, immersing themselves in a very different environment. One destination in particular stood out in the minds of many of those who visited it: Shanghai. In recent years the city has become one of the largest in the world, but the roots of that growth date back to the early twentieth century. Between 1900 and 1920 Shanghai underwent a vast transformation in size and stature. In those twenty years its population grew from approximately 350,000, comparable with Lisbon or Bristol at the time, to roughly 800,000, including over 23,000 foreigners.[9] While that was still relatively modest compared with the major global metropolises, Shanghai gained a reputation as the bustling hub of East Asia.

The loosely regulated British-led International Settlement and neighbouring French Concession, both at the heart of the city, oversaw a wave of economic growth and construction, adopting many of the latest elements of municipal planning. This was fuelled by an influx into the wider city of economic migrants and refugees from around China, along with many wealthy and enterprising Chinese businesspeople. As a result, Shanghai modernized at a rapid pace with the population embracing new technologies, such as the installation of an electric traffic light system before New York or London.[10] There was nowhere else quite like it in China and few rivals around the region as a whole. Royal Navy crews were thrown into the hubbub of Shanghai life – a world of theatres, racecourses, dance halls, brothels and a confusing mixture of nationalities, social classes and identities. Arriving at the Bund in 1920 would have been no less impressive than standing by those same buildings today and looking across the river at the skyscrapers of Pudong, representing another new era for Shanghai (Figures 1 and 2). At the time, however, Chinese observers tended to see 'that imposing place as a visible proof of the exploitation of China by the foreigner'.[11]

Resentment in Shanghai was not one dimensional or limited to race. Behind the well-lit facades of the International Settlement there were serious underlying tensions between the different segments of society. The elite Shanghailander community regarded itself as superior to all but a few outsiders, including the British policemen, teachers and other professionals who enabled their comfortable imperial outpost to function. In return, the lower-status British expatriates regarded the Shanghailanders as pompous, rich and disconnected with reality.[12] Both acted more 'British' than the British, yet their first loyalty was to the Settlement. Likewise, the entire city was reliant upon its links with

Figure 1 Shanghai Bund in 1928.
Source: Shanghai Bund, 1928, Naval History and Heritage Command (NHHC), NH81603.

the Chinese population, through business connections, as workers in factories or through the Shanghai Municipal Police, most of whom were local recruits, and yet racial prejudice was endemic.[13] A large proportion of British trade, for example, went through Chinese middlemen 'Yanghang' firms based in the major cities.[14] On a day-to-day social basis, even those well-educated and successful Chinese city elites who engaged in similar cultural pursuits were shunned by the Shanghailanders.[15]

The arriving seamen found themselves in an unusual position amid all that tension. With the International Settlement's safety largely reliant upon the background presence of the Royal Navy, the Shanghailanders were relatively welcoming of their guardians. The Royal Marines were particularly popular and received extra loud cheers during the Empire Day parade, as they were always the first servicemen to head ashore during periods of trouble.[16] Not all interactions were so positive though, with Commander Cedric Holland noting in his diary that while the men were friendly and entertaining, the Shanghailander women were rude, despite having 'nothing to be snobbish about … They are

Figure 2 HMS *Hawkins* at Shanghai in 1927.
Source: HMS *Hawkins* at Shanghai, 1927, NHHC, NH105067.

in fact a truly terrible lot.'[17] Likewise, the local Chinese population seemed to have been surprisingly welcoming of Royal Navy crewmen. Perhaps as outsiders who behaved in a different and less dismissive manner to the Shanghailanders, Britain's seamen were treated on their own merits. That said, one cannot help but question how positively they were regarded when marching through the Settlement with bayonets atop their rifles during times of trouble.

For most naval personnel their memories of Shanghai are perhaps best summarized by 'Robby' Roberts who described it as having one of the best nightlives of any city in the world. Petty Officer Douglas Poole attempted a more poetic account: 'The jazz bands clash and clang high – In Shanghai in Shanghai – and people dance – at every chance – until the night is gone.'[18] Roberts's one criticism was that he disapproved of the open prostitution that took place in many bars and hotels.[19] Indeed, one or two more religious crewmen took a strong dislike to 'wicked' Shanghai given the all-night partying and mingling between men and women.[20] Aside from hazards to their health associated with the heavy partying, there were a few more pronounced risks to the 'exciting' city. Crewmen were mugged and occasionally disappeared, presumed killed when they drifted onto quieter backstreets at night.[21] For most, however, Shanghai felt to be a 'fabulous' location for shore leave.[22]

After Shanghai the experiences of China Station crews depended to a large extent on which warships they were assigned to and therefore where they would patrol. The Station's cruisers were relatively large vessels with hundreds of men and boys aboard, all of which had been constructed during the latter years of the First World War. While hardly luxurious, those vessels had many of the latest modern conveniences, making life afloat a little more bearable. Crucial for a posting in East Asia, they had large fridges for storing fresh food in the hot conditions, but a wide range of new electrical appliances had a cumulative positive impact upon life aboard. The new 5,850-ton HMS *Diomede* that joined the China Station in 1922, for example, contained a greater length of electrical wiring than the 34,050-ton battleship HMS *Queen Elizabeth* launched only a fewer years earlier.[23] In addition to those comparatively comfortable conditions, the cruisers and sloops spent their time touring China's coastal treaty ports and on diplomatic visits to Japan, the American-ruled Philippines, Dutch East Indies, French Indo-China and beyond. These visits provided the opportunity to enjoy shore leave in exotic new locations, but the ceremonial events themselves were a source of pride and enjoyment if hard work for the crew. Awnings would be strung across the decks for hosting cocktail parties with local dignitaries and officials, with parades and ship bands adding a degree of pomp to the occasions.[24]

Not all such visits were so pleasant for the crews. One emergent role for the Royal Navy during this period was the rendering of humanitarian assistance during natural disasters. Having steamed at top speed carrying supplies and medical teams to Yokohama after the 1923 Great Kantō earthquake, for example, the crew of HMS *Hawkins* encountered horrific scenes, with dead bodies floating all around the harbour. Marine William Greenland recorded in his diary that most of the marines had seen service on the front during the war and so were accustomed to such horrors, but still felt ashamed that they were not able to do more to help.[25] In addition, Royal Navy crews also offered their assistance to city authorities as firefighters during major incidents.[26] These sorts of events were still relatively rare but added a new edge to life on the China Station.

For those aboard the China Station's smaller warships, particularly the gunboats patrolling the various waterways on which British merchant steamers passed, life was quite a different experience. The small West River *Heron*-class gunboats and slightly larger upper Yangtze gunboats were all under 150 tons, carried up to twenty-five crew and were normally only capable of chugging along at a sedate walking pace. While crews did their best to keep them shipshape and homely, they were rather uncomfortable vessels – right down to the tent-like 'heads' (latrines) perched atop the stern. Sometimes hundreds of miles from other British warships, deep into China where only small colonial communities existed at the local ports and starting the decade without radio communication, life was described as 'humdrum'.[27] That mundane existence was not without danger, however, involving occasional firefights with groups of brigands and through misunderstandings with Chinese troops, and also occasional groundings along an unpredictable and ever-changing river. Captain John Clegg, for example, noted that even two years was not long enough for commanders to gain a reliable knowledge of troublesome stretches.[28] Simply catching a rapid section at the wrong angle was sufficient to jolt a gunboat severely, in one case resulting in the destruction of half of HMS *Widgeon*'s crockery and glassware.[29]

The men who joined the gunboat force entered a colourful, natural environment steaming up and down stretches of river between the various inland treaty ports. With limited storage facilities aboard, fresh food was generally obtained along the route. Some officers used the relative freedom of their location to supplement their diet, often through pausing to go shooting, with duck a favourite choice.[30] In contrast to those serving on coastal routes, shore leave for gunboat crews offered much less in the way of entertainment, except when lucky enough to call at Shanghai or Hong Kong. Within the general briefing notes for China Station commanders, there were rough descriptions of the key attributes of a range of ports along the main waterways. For many locations, under the subheading 'entertainment' there was a simple 'none' recorded in bold.[31] As a result, when posted to or patrolling along the Yangtze, only Hankou and Nanjing really offered the prospect of much more than sport to help crews unwind.

Reactions from the local Chinese populations to the arrival of British gunboats varied to a considerable degree. When Royal Navy commanders arranged ceremonial port calls or feasts to coincide with local celebrations or anniversaries, they were given 'extremely hearty' welcomes.[32] The presence of a foreign warship in such circumstances appears to have been regarded as an honour rather than a threat or insult. At quieter times, British officers would dine with local dignitaries. Twenty-four-year-old Lieutenant Anthony Pugsley recounted how he and his commanding officer ended up playing Mahjong for money stakes against General Yang Sen in Wanxian. Pugsley enjoyed the game until it was brought to a polite halt when he stumbled upon a particularly strong set of tiles. Yang Sen's advisor apparently informed him later that Pugsley was about to win $500 – quite a large sum at the time, which might upset the general.[33] As clashes and the body count started to grow over the decade, such genial welcomes to British gunboats became rarer, with growing hostility at the unequal treaties that framed their presence on China's waterways.

The toughest conditions were reserved for the two submarine flotillas serving in the region, although somewhat counter-intuitively they also seem to have had the happiest crews. The often-undermanned *L*-Class submarines were cramped and prone to engine problems. In one case *L2* was forced to 'limp' into Singapore with only a few cylinders from its two diesel engines still running. With minimal supplies of fresh water and heads (toilets) that occasionally malfunctioned in spectacular style, life afloat was an unpleasant one. In addition, the submarines struggled in stormy conditions and often ran a gauntlet of unpredictable local shipping when entering harbour, and so accidents were not uncommon. Against those hardships, however, a remarkable degree of camaraderie was established among the boats operating around each flotilla depot ship, which offered somewhere for the crews to socialize and recover. While they tended to operate half-detached from the rest of the Station, submarines did receive occasional, slightly unusual honours. In mid-1925, for example, the commander-in-chief remained at Weihai during a changeover between surface warships, leading to the diminutive *L2* temporarily becoming the flagship for the fleet, much to the amusement of its crew.[34] In many ways that moment sums up what life on the China Station meant. While it was a single command drawing men from the same organization, life on the Station involved a diverse range of experiences and one where any of the many quite different warships present could suddenly become the central focus of events in the region.

Looking beyond the battle fleet

During the interwar period, the China Station was the Royal Navy's only fleet north-east of Singapore, with its crews patrolling Britain's most exposed outposts of the Empire. One of a global chain of naval commands (see Figure 3), the China Station played a vital role in enabling Britain to project power around East Asia and the western Pacific Rim, both as a tool for promoting British foreign policies and to counter any emergent state or sub-state threats. The main duties had therefore long involved regular flag-waving tours of the region, as a deterrent against the Russian Pacific Fleet (pre-1905), the German East Asia Squadron (pre-1914) and then the Imperial Japanese Navy (IJN; post-1921), supporting the defence of Britain's scattered imperial possessions and protecting British mercantile shipping against piracy.[35]

Prior to the Anglo-Japanese Alliance (1902) and First Sea Lord Sir John 'Jackie' Fisher's subsequent decision to concentrate the Royal Navy in home waters, Britain maintained a sizeable force around the Pacific Ocean to achieve those aims. It had not been a single entity, however, and was divided between the 'China', 'Australia' and 'Pacific' commands.[36] The China Station had always been the largest of the three, after its predecessor 'East Indies and China Station'

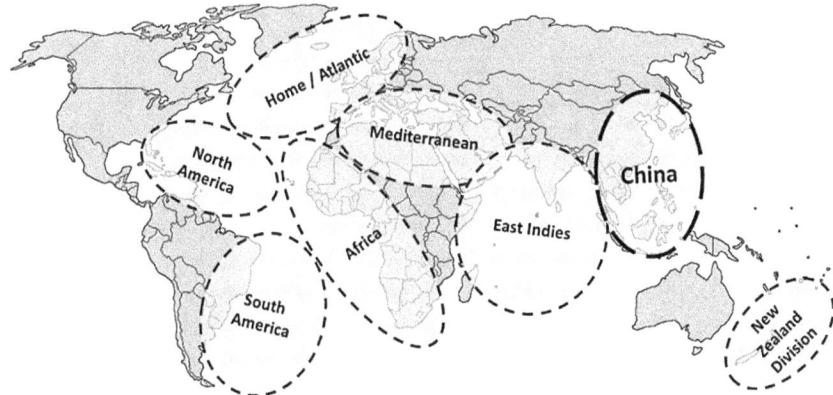

Figure 3 Royal Navy 'stations' during the 1920s (simplified).
Source: Produced by the author.

was split into two in 1865.³⁷ As a result of Fisher's reforms the Pacific Station was disbanded in 1905, with a decision made not to renew it in 1912. Likewise, the Australia Station was dissolved in 1913 with the creation of the Royal Australian Navy.³⁸ By the 1920s, therefore, the China Station formed the Royal Navy's only significant standing formation beyond Singapore, although during crises it could be supported by the fledgling Royal Australian Navy, the Royal New Zealand Navy division and the East Indies Station.

With its focus on the South China and Yellow Seas, the China Station was nominally based around three main naval bases: Hong Kong at its centre, Weihai in the north and Singapore in the south. Given the vast geographic expanse of the command and the numerous small coal-fuelled warships present in the region, the Royal Navy had also established a network of coaling stations around the Chinese coast and along the Yangtze River. Covering such a large area, command of the station was highly mobile, with the commander-in-chief (an Admiral or Vice-Admiral) spending most of his time at sea touring with the cruisers. Indeed, a requisitioned vessel, HMS *Alacrity*, was provided as an Admiral's yacht at the end of the First World War in order to improve the mobility of command around the station. *Alacrity* was then replaced in 1923 by a First World War minesweeper, HMS *Petersfield*, which had been converted especially for the role.³⁹ His deputy (a Rear-Admiral) was a little more settled and usually present aboard the gunboat HMS *Bee*, either patrolling the Yangtze or moored at Hankou (Hankow).⁴⁰ To ensure that there was always a reliable contact point, a Commodore was permanently stationed at Hong Kong, in charge of the naval dockyard and local naval forces. Likewise, numerous less-senior

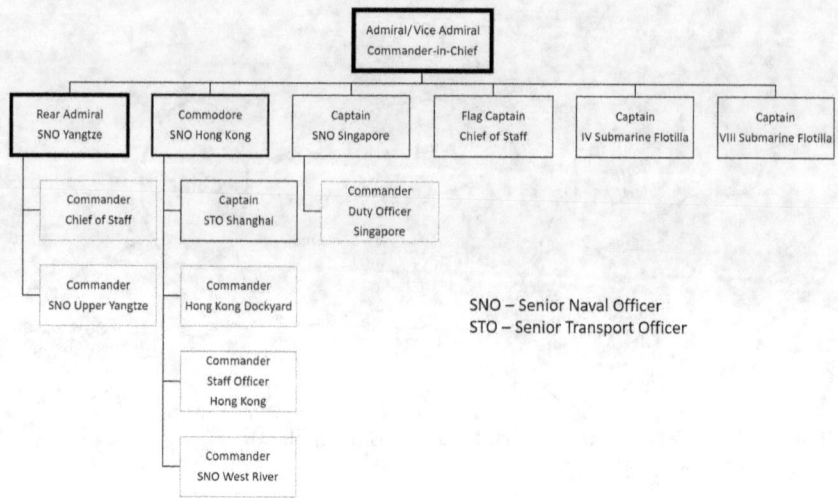

Figure 4 China Station command structure in the 1920s.
Source: Produced by the author.

officers were posted at other shore facilities around the region, particularly at Singapore and Shanghai, working in administrative and duty roles. Given their relative operational detachment, two Commanders were also given the designation 'Senior Naval Officer' for the upper Yangtze and West River areas, with responsibility for guiding their junior colleagues and providing immediate leadership during moments of crisis (Figure 4).

Built up during the second half of the nineteenth century, Britain's imperial presence in China epitomizes Ronald Robinson and John Gallagher's assessment of the British Empire's unstated strategy of 'trade with informal rule if possible; trade with rule when necessary'.[41] In essence, as long as Britain got what it wanted in terms of expanding its economic and strategic interests, there was no underlying desire for formal control, given the cost of maintaining armies against potential wars of independence. While critics have raised questions over the applicability of the theory when used over such a diverse entity at the late Victorian British Empire, it still works well to explain the Empire's long-term position in China.[42] Britain's stewardship of China's Salt Administration and Customs Service serves as a clear example of how much control Britain was able to wield over China in order to reap the economic benefits, despite China remaining an independent sovereign nation.[43] There have been questions about whether informal imperialism was a deliberate policy, but within the dynamics of Britain's relationship with China there was a long-term pragmatic acceptance of arm's-length mercantile trade via informal rule, so long as no other power tried to dominate the country.[44] Indeed, the British government's ability to secure trade and military concessions often on an informal footing limited official interest in territorial expansion, at least in comparison to elsewhere in the world.[45]

In 1911, the Xinhai Revolution brought about the collapse of the Qing Empire and presented a series of challenges for those powers with imperial interests in China. After the failure of the subsequent Provisional Government of the Republic of China and resulting collapse of the central government, a range of threats to British interests emerged. In particular, there was a significant increase in piracy and banditry. The warring also brought with it the growing possibility that violence would impact foreign residents directly, through warlord armies wrestling for control of the treaty port cities.[46] As trading centres those ports offered a significant potential source of income for the different factions, and many were located in strategically important locations. For much of the 1920s, the Foreign Office attempted to follow an official strategy of non-intervention in China, hoping for the emergence of a new central regime, which could be pressured into addressing Britain's concerns.[47] Nonetheless, given the uncertainty resulting from the fluid situation in China, the Royal Navy was tasked with defending against the perceived and actual threats against Britain's interests.[48]

Often when Great Britain took part in these expeditions, in China or elsewhere around the world, it was not the battle fleet that shaped the events. Instead, the Royal Navy's light cruisers, destroyers, sloops and gunboats conducted most of its interwar peacetime work, which were only reinforced by larger vessels when necessary.[49] Even then, most of the light cruisers would spend their time either held at a strategic port or on a flag-waving tour around their assigned region.[50] In the aftermath of the First World War, it was those more modest vessels that formed an increasingly important part of the Royal Navy. While only a gradual process, capital ships slowly declined in value with the development of new threats to their dominance, such as the submarine, higher quality torpedoes and effective military aircraft.[51]

The Royal Navy's role in Britain's interwar foreign policy

Great Britain's early interwar foreign policy can be broadly divided into three key priorities: to maintain its status as the relative superpower of the era, to keep its newly further enlarged empire secure and to ensure the smooth flow of global trade and finance.⁵² One of the key tools available to the policymakers in Whitehall in order to meet the demands of all three goals was the Royal Navy – in Greg Kennedy's words, 'Britain's most important diplomatic and military asset'.⁵³ The Royal Navy was vital to the first of those foreign policy goals: maintaining global power status. Since airpower was still in its infancy, the Navy's position as the world's largest and most powerful sea power force was therefore the ultimate guarantor of Great Britain's global position.⁵⁴

Core to maintaining the British Empire's overall global power status was the Royal Navy's battle fleet. There are numerous accounts of the battle fleet during the 1920s, ranging from technical assessments of the comparative capabilities of key vessels to those exploring the impact of newer military aircraft upon the relative strength of the main fleets.⁵⁵ While those are of great value in discussions of major power conflict in the 1930s, they are of limited value in direct regard to the 1920s. Designed and intended for decisive engagements against other naval powers, capital ships were of minimal use in dealing with the littoral and land-based confrontations that occurred in the earlier decade.⁵⁶ While larger vessels were prominent in the diplomatic wrangling over arms limitation treaties during the period, their practical military role was effectively limited to deterrent status.⁵⁷ Moreover, in line with the strategy first introduced by Lord Fisher to concentrate the battle fleet, few of the Royal Navy's major vessels were deployed outside of the North Atlantic or the Mediterranean in peacetime.⁵⁸ A notable exception was the global tour made by HMS *Hood* and the Special Service Squadron of 1923–4, which was intended to impress upon both allies and potential enemies alike the scale of Great Britain's naval power.⁵⁹ The only real threat to Britain's status was from the United States. Despite its rapid growth, however, the US Navy (USN) still fell short of the Royal Navy overall (although in some areas such as destroyers the USN was already dominant) and would not overtake it until the Second World War.⁶⁰

A growing rivalry with the United States was not the only potential disruptive force to the global naval power balance. The collapse of the Anglo-Japanese alliance, with its official expiration in 1923, contributed to growing concerns about the emergent threat to the British Empire's East Asian territories. Worsening Anglo-Japanese relations in the 1920s have been a topic of considerable historical debate. This has focused on the direct long-term threat of war posed by an imperialist Japan, particularly after the Manchurian Crisis in 1931 and the fortification of Singapore to counter that perceived threat.⁶¹ However, it was not until the 1930s that the threat from Japan became far more serious. The nominal power of the 1920s IJN relative to the Royal Navy and the USN should not be overstated. Nonetheless, the expansion of the IJN during the First World War and its immediate aftermath had altered the global balance of power.[62] In particular, the launching of the two *Nagato*-class battleships (1919 and 1920); the aircraft carriers *Hosho*, *Agagi* and *Kaga* (1919–20); the six *Sendai*, *Yubari* and *Furutaka*-class cruisers (1922); and thirty-four new submarines (1919–23) changed the Pacific naval equation to a significant extent.

The threat posed to the established world order by Japan's rise was highlighted by the effort put into the 1922 Washington Treaty by Britain and the United States to restrict the IJN, even if the limits were of little practical value.[63] Containing a range of restrictions on the number and size of various warships that each signatory was allowed to possess, in addition to a variety of additional clauses covering naval base enhancement among others, the treaty was intended to prevent a major arms race and curtail international rivalries. In the years following the Washington Conference, debates between the Admiralty and Cabinet show that despite caution about the threat posed by Japan to British colonies and the dominions of Australia and New Zealand, government ministers repeatedly dismissed it as a peripheral issue to the British Empire.[64] The British government felt safe in the belief that the IJN did not have the resources to achieve a decisive victory in East Asia, before the Royal Navy's battle fleet could reinforce the China Station.[65] This only started to change to a significant extent after General Tanaka Giichi's hawkish government was elected in Japan in 1927, with its expansionist attitude towards China.[66] There were concerns during the 1920s, however, within both the Admiralty and Foreign Office that Japan sought to lure Britain into a military response in China, as a means to facilitate a further expansion of Japan's commercial interests in the country.[67] While British officials were undoubtedly apprehensive about the direct long-term threat posed by Japan to the Empire as a whole, they were primarily wary of the indirect consequences of Japanese foreign policy in China.

The simultaneous growth in power of the United States and Japan, challenging Britain's global dominance, was not a significant strategic concern. In naval terms, Whitehall had already abandoned the 'two-power standard' in 1911, whereby the Royal Navy was expected to be larger than the next two navies. Over the following decade the Admiralty shifted towards a 'one-power standard', whereby Britain simply needed to maintain the world's single largest navy.[68] There are even questions about how sincerely the Admiralty treated the one-power standard, with suggestions in some documents that it was only seriously used during discussions with the Treasury and publicly in Parliament.[69] Over the course of the 1920s the USN's growing strength also started to be regarded more widely around Whitehall as a positive development, given that neither nation really saw the other as a likely aggressor.[70] As a result, the other two major naval powers were growing stronger, but neither seriously threatened the British Empire's global status. Indeed, when considering the Royal Navy's power in the 1920s against its potential enemies, that is, not including the United States, Britain was no less dominant in global naval power than it had been before the First World War.[71] Recent economic assessments have also highlighted that Britain maintained the highest level of military expenditure of any country in the world during the 1920s, with its naval budget at a comparable level to the 1890–1910 period.[72] Maintaining Great Britain's prominent position may therefore have been a feature of the top-level diplomatic wrangling at various disarmament and naval conferences. Nonetheless, the Royal Navy's day-to-day concerns during the 1920s focused upon the other two areas of imperial concern, maintaining the security of the Empire and protecting its arteries.[73]

Keeping the British Empire secure was no small challenge. One of the defining characteristics of the 1920s was the extent to which the Empire was overstretched in a variety of ways. Having obtained stewardship of various territories after the First World War, primarily in the Middle East, the British Empire had reached its peak size, covering twelve million square miles – roughly one-quarter of the global land mass.[74] As a result, there were countless potential threats worldwide, both internal and external, to the maintenance of the status quo.[75]

In addition to its horrific cost in blood, the First World War had also severely drained Britain's coffers. The burden of debt interest payments alone had skyrocketed from £16.7 million (9.6% of budget receipts) pre-war to £308.7 million (22.4%) during 1920–1.[76] Earlier historical accounts tended to emphasize the significance of the resulting swathing cutbacks to Britain's defence budget after the First World War, particularly through the 'Geddes Axe' – a planned reduction in public expenditure chaired by Sir Eric Geddes.[77] Over the years this has been tempered, however, with a better understanding that while there were significant cutbacks, they were designed to reduce the exceptionally high wartime levels; Britain maintained the largest defence budget in the world throughout the 1920s.[78] Nonetheless, cutbacks did occur and amid inflationary stresses the Royal Navy faced greater financial concerns than it had done in many years. Defending and maintaining order in the Empire was therefore as much a challenge for accountants as admirals and generals.[79] At its most basic the Royal Navy was being asked to do more, while simultaneously making cutbacks and finding what would now be called 'efficiency savings'.[80]

It was against that background that the Admiralty came under sustained pressure from the Foreign Office to boost its resources on China's waterways.[81] As a result, the Admiralty decided to finance the construction of four new gunboats and a further four motorboats purpose-built for use on the Yangtze from the 1925–6 estimate, when finances were increasingly tight for the Royal Navy.[82] While the total construction cost of £81,000 for these boats was hardly extraordinary in comparison to a capital ship, it represented a noteworthy level of expenditure on such a specific element for defending the British Empire's wider interests. It was also made at a point when the Admiralty had to justify even the £1,600 bill for new motorboats for Singapore in direct correspondence with the Chancellor of the Exchequer.[83]

The Foreign Office's unease about the Royal Navy's capabilities on the China Station ranged from the basic monetary concern about losing an export market worth over £12 million a year to the growing rivalry with former ally Japan.[84] There were also broader concerns about the impact British response to the situation in China would have upon the perception of the power of the British Empire among its colonial populations. Protests against the British presence in Shanghai were felt to be intrinsically linked to similar protests in Singapore, for example.[85] This was to directly impact the work of the Royal Navy, with the cruiser HMS *Dauntless* held at Singapore in early 1927, awaiting the arrival of the Shanghai Defence Force at its destination, in order to make a visible statement about British power in the region.[86] Within the Foreign Office discussion of the decision to retain *Dauntless* there is clear concern that protests in China could easily spread to Singapore and then Malaysia, and was therefore a significant threat to the safety and integrity of the British Empire as a whole.

These challenges provided a strong case for the Royal Navy to make structural, strategic and tactical changes, and where possible to adopt new technologies, although sometimes there was a reluctance among the Service's officers to do so. Many of the early and influential historical accounts of the Royal Navy during the period tended to outline how early interwar military thought was guided by what were felt to be the lessons of the preceding war.[87] Roskill, for example, stated that the only proactive naval planning in the 1920s was intended to solve the problems encountered in the First World War, such as the development of ASDIC to counter the submarine threat.[88] Later accounts have gone a little further to explore whether or not the Royal Navy learned any lessons from the First World War, but generally dismiss any developments from the 1920s.[89] This discussion has been strongly influenced by the background debate about the extent to which there was an institutional culture of anti-intellectualism within the interwar Navy.[90] Examining the Service's peacetime frontline work in China provides the other half of the picture to Moretz's recent work on the education of the Navy's officer corps, by looking at how some of those men behaved in practice.[91] As we shall see later in the book, many Royal Navy officers demonstrated a willingness and even eagerness to develop new ways of doing things to improve the efficiency and effectiveness of the China Station.

A background of interservice rivalry also needs to be taken into account when examining Britain's interwar armed services. Not all developments were necessarily as simple as they first may seem. The Admiralty had its battles not only with the Treasury and Cabinet over funding, and Foreign Office over strategy, but also with the other services.[92] In 1929, for example, a proposal was raised by the Royal Air Force (RAF) to the Cabinet for flying boats to replace four Royal Navy sloops in the Persian Gulf, taking on their anti-piracy and slave trafficking tasks.[93] The logic presented to cabinet was that flying boats would be cheaper to operate than sloops. Such schemes, however, came as part of a long-term campaign started by the first Marshal of the RAF, Hugh Trenchard, to secure a more prominent role for the fledgling RAF against the two long-established services.[94] Indeed, the displacement of conventional military capabilities with what was still novel air power began even before the First World War had ended. Air Vice-Marshal Sir Frederick Sykes argued clearly in 1918 that the RAF would provide 'a rapid and economical instrument' for securing the Asian and African frontiers of the British Empire.[95] Such frictions pushed the Royal Navy into finding ways to prove its value to the British Empire, while simultaneously finding ways to improve the cost-effectiveness of its work against the test posed by the RAF. As a result of all these factors, when the interwar China Station returned to peacetime duties in 1919 it was already under pressure to change from within the British defence establishment. Soon it would become apparent that a rapidly changing China and East Asia in general would add to those challenges.

Britain's China conundrum

The Xinhai Revolution was met with comparatively muted concern from Britain and other Western nations. The events in 1911 represented a major shift in China's domestic political situation, but initially they were less significant for global events. For those foreign powers with interests in the country the revolution appeared similar, at least superficially, to earlier large-scale rebellions, such as the

Taiping Rebellion and Boxer Uprising.[96] With efforts in the mid-1910s to form a new republican government in China and little hostility directed against foreign powers, the Xinhai Revolution appeared a minor concern when compared with the events seen just over a decade earlier. During the Boxer Uprising, popular discontent in Northern China between 1897 and 1899 became increasingly focused against foreigners living in the region. That tension exploded into open conflict when a British-led multinational military force attempted to reach their besieged diplomatic compounds in Beijing in June 1900, which was seen as an invasion by the local population.[97] Many thousands died during the various bursts of violence.[98] The subsequent humiliating terms imposed by the international coalition changed the path of Chinese politics. In contrast, the British establishment in 1911 agreed that as the revolution was not anti-foreign, the best course of action was to remain neutral and wait for order to be restored.[99]

The First World War soon absorbed Britain and the other major powers, but the situation worsened in China with the failure of the Provisional Government and subsequent schism between the two main Beiyang (northern) and Guomindang (southern) regimes in 1917. Nonetheless, prior to the mid-1920s the threat to British interests was relatively mild, mostly in the form of piracy and banditry, resulting from the lack of effective governance in many areas.[100] For the Royal Navy, this posed the challenge of trying to provide an effective policing presence over large areas where British shipping and communities were present. Not only did the China Station face global, top-down challenges in terms of cost-cutting and interservice rivalry, but it was also required to meet the regional problem posed by piracy. The growing number and severity of attacks on merchant shipping threatened the smooth flow of trade in the region, which was so important to the economy of the wider British Empire.[101] China accounted for roughly 3% of total goods exports from Great Britain in the mid-1920s, making it a modest but valuable external market for British manufacturers, although the links with the Empire as a whole were far greater. With those additional exports from Britain's colonies, the British Empire was China's largest trading partner, despite growing competition from Japan and the United States.[102] Prior to the First World War British businesses and banks had also invested heavily in and around the treaty ports, backing the construction of railways, for example. As the different factions and local warlords intermittently resorted to conflict, the violence potentially put the security of both their staff and their assets at risk.[103] Beyond the formal boundaries of the Empire, with only a small British Army presence in East Asia, the Royal Navy offered the primary source of direct protection.

As the years passed and the conflict continued to erupt in bursts, the Shanghai press in particular started to draw parallels between the Boxer Uprising and growing anti-foreign rhetoric, warning of potentially catastrophic violence.[104] The murder of foreign missionaries and their families in that earlier crisis and horrific accounts of how they were killed, often exaggerated, had been seared into the collective memories of the treaty ports' foreign populations. At first the fears of the British expatriate population were soothed by Royal Navy warship visits, but the situation became far worse after the May Thirtieth Incident in 1925. British-led policemen in Shanghai shot and killed twelve Chinese civilians, who had been protesting against the prior death of a Chinese factory worker.[105] As a result, Britain became the focus of anti-imperial sentiment in China, a process catalysed by the Shanghai Municipality Police's frequently heavy-handed approach to policing.[106] The situation worsened further in 1926, when the Guomindang launched its Northern Expedition towards the valuable treaty ports and strategic cities along the Yangtze.[107] Not only was there the risk of British persons and property suffering as collateral damage in the fighting, but the Guomindang was still linked to the Chinese Communist Party (CCP), whose rhetoric was profoundly anti-imperialist.[108] As a result, British officials believed that the threat was far more direct and so the China Station was tasked with a further challenge, to adjust its approach against the emergent and evolving threat of war.[109]

The link to the CCP meant that the China Station's localized challenge in dealing with China's civil wars fitted into the Royal Navy's and British Empire's general struggle against communism.[110] A string of real and fictional scandals at home and abroad fuelled a fear that the newly formed Soviet Union was attempting to undermine the British Empire from 'Dublin to Peking'.[111] The effectiveness of a naval response to a localized incident in Shanghai, for example, was therefore felt to have a much wider potential impact upon the security of the British Empire. In responding to the events of 1926–7 the Royal Navy was forced to adapt to deal with the unconventional threats posed by anti-imperial violence in the post-First World War era.

China was certainly not the only country where Britain's armed forces were tasked with protecting the extended interests of the Empire during the 1920s, with deployments to Arkhangelsk and Chanak earlier in the decade. Likewise, the emergence of Pan-Arab nationalism and Zionism posed significant threats to the stability of the not-so-carefully constructed Anglo-French-mandated Middle East. In some cases the resulting violence far exceeded that seen in similar incidents in China.[112] The uprisings in Iraq against the award of the British mandate over the country in 1920, for example, resulted in the deaths of 426 British and Indian servicemen and over 8,000 'insurgents'.[113] What occurred in Iraq was, to some extent, exceptional in its severity when considered in a wider context, and the British Empire generally attempted to follow a doctrine of minimum force.[114] However, while the use of such levels of lethal violence was relatively rare, threats of force were used and prepared more regularly. A large naval force was stationed at Malta in 1925, for example, when Mosul province was awarded by the League of Nations to the British mandate in Iraq.[115] As we shall see in the next chapter, events in 1920s China triggered the deployment of a significant military force, providing an excellent insight into how the Royal Navy changed over the decade and responded to threats to the British Empire.

What occurred in China was not shaped by grand strategy between major powers, or the residual impact of the First World War, but by domestic changes as some warlord groups attempted to build a new China and others acted simply for personal gain. It therefore tested the Royal Navy's ability to react to unforeseen circumstances, where it was difficult to form a proactive strategy given the lack of clearly defined opponents and allies, and obvious strategies that could be countered. As a reactionary scenario, it tested whether the Royal Navy had developed its capability for responding to and securing the British Empire against potential new threats thrown against it.

Notes

1 Unpublished memoirs of William Roberts, Undated, IWM, Documents 7214a.
2 Diary of Marine William Greenland aboard HMS *Hawkins*, 13 May 1923, Royal Marines Museum (RMM), 1978/48b.
3 George Wright-Nooth, *Prisoner of the Turnip Heads* (London: Leo Cooper, 1994), p. 30.
4 Interview with Private Ernest Whitney, 1992, IWM Interview Series, Catalogue Number 12499, 12 minutes.
5 Ting-yan Cheung and Pablo Sze-pang Tsoi, 'From an Imported Novelty to an Indigenized Practice: Hong Kong Cinema in the 1920s', in *Early Film Culture in Hong Kong, Taiwan, and Republican China: Kaleidoscopic Histories*, ed. Emilie Yueh-yu Yeh (Ann Arbor: University of Michigan Press, 2018), 71–90.
6 Interview with Private Ernest Whitney, 13 minutes.
7 John Darwin, 'Imperialism and the Victorians: The Dynamics of Territorial Expansion', *English Historical Review* 112/447 (1997), p. 632.

8 Wright-Nooth, *Prisoner of the Turnip Heads*, pp. 22–30.
9 Shanghai Municipal Gazette, 18 November 1920, Shanghai Municipal Archives (SMA), U1-1-985.
10 Interview with I. L. Wight, 1982, IWM Interview Series, Catalogue Number 6196, Reel 1, 19 minutes.
11 Diary of Arthur Ransome, March 1927, Brotherton Library, BC MS 20c Ransome/1/A/9/3/3.
12 Bickers, *Empire Made Me*, pp. 80–106.
13 Nicholas Clifford, 'A Revolution is not a Tea Party: The "Shanghai Mind(s)" Reconsidered', *Pacific History Review* 59/4 (1990), 504–16.
14 Jürgen Osterhammel, 'Imperialism in Transition: British Business and the Chinese Authorities, 1931–37', *China Quarterly* 98 (1984), 267.
15 Shu-Mei Shih, 'Gender, Race, and Semicolonialism: Liu Na'ou's Urban Shanghai Landscape', *Journal of Asian Studies* 55/4 (1996), 939–41.
16 Diary of Marine William Greenland, May 1923.
17 Diary of Commander Cedric Holland, 20 May 1928, National Maritime Museum (NMM), HND 2/4/1.
18 Journal of Chief Petty Officer Douglas Poole, 3 February 1925, Museum of the Royal Navy, 1994/253/1.
19 Unpublished memoirs of William Roberts, Undated, IWM, Documents 7214a.
20 Diary of Marine William Greenland, May 1923.
21 Diary of Commander Cedric Holland, 1928.
22 Interview with Frank Short, 2003, IWM Interview Series, Catalogue Number 25210, Reel 1, 8–18 minutes.
23 Cabinet Committee on Reduction of National Expenditure, January 1923, TNA, CAB 24/160/72, p. 10; Chesneau (ed.), *World's Fighting Ships*, pp. 7–10.
24 Interview with A. A. Heron, 1975, IWM Interview Series, Catalogue Number 681, Reel 11, 3–4 minutes.
25 Diary of Marine William Greenland, September 1923.
26 Shanghai Municipal Council Annual Report 1920, SMA, U1-1-933; Diary of Marine William Greenland, January 1926.
27 Anonymous British naval officer, 'An Incident in China', in *The Anatomy of Neptune*, ed. Brian Tunstall (London: Routledge, 1936), p. 362.
28 John H. K. Clegg, 'The Yangtze and the Situation in China', *Naval Review* 15/1 (1927), p. 205.
29 Record of Passages made by HMS *Widgeon*, 24 May 1918, NMM, JHS/5/1.
30 E. M. C. Barraclough, *I Was Sailing: An Old Sailor Remembers* (unpublished), Brotherton Library, p. 65; Record of Passages made by HMS *Widgeon*, January 1920, NMM, JHS/5/1.
31 China Station general briefing giving details of various cities, 1921, NMRN, 1979/240.

32 Quarterly report from Captain Brodie on HMS *Titania* to CinC China, 21 January 1924, TNA, ADM 116/2262.
33 Anthony Pugsley and Donald Macintyre, *Destroyer Man* (London: Weidenfeld and Nicolson, 1957), p. 14.
34 Barraclough, *I Was Sailing*, pp. 58–61.
35 W. C. Bridgeman, Admiralty memorandum to Cabinet about the Navy Estimates, 4 February 1925, The National Archives (henceforth TNA), CAB 24/171/68; Philips P. O'Brien, 'The Titan Refreshed: Imperial Overstretch and the British Navy before the First World War', *Past & Present* 172 (2001), 150; Bell, 'Singapore Strategy', p. 610.
36 O'Brien, 'The Titan Refreshed', pp. 149–56; Peter Padfield, *Rule Britannia: The Victorian and Edwardian Navy* (London: Routledge & Kegan Paul, 1981), pp. 209–22.
37 Scott Lindgren, 'A station in transition: The China Squadron, Cyprian Bridge and the first-class cruiser, 1901–1904', *International Journal of Maritime History* 27/3 (2015), 466.
38 Nicholas Lambert, 'Admiral Sir Francis Bridgeman-Bridgeman (1911–1912)', in *The First Sea Lords*, ed. Malcolm Murfett (Westport: Praeger, 1995), p. 68; Peter Overlack, 'The Force of Circumstance: Graf Spee's Options for the East Asian Cruiser Squadron in 1914', *Journal of Military History* 60/4 (1996), 661; Padfield, *Rule Britannia*, p. 222.
39 Admiral Arthur Leveson to Admiralty, 11 October 1923, TNA, ADM 1/8665/142.
40 See TNA, ADM 53/75691; Ship's log of HMS *Hawkins* 1923–4, TNA, ADM 53/78593. The Vice-Admiral switched regularly between flagship *Hawkins* and 'Admiral's yacht' HMS *Petersfield* to tour the other cruisers.
41 John Gallagher, and Ronald Robinson, 'The Imperialism of Free Trade', *Economic History Review* 6/1 (1953), 13. See also C. C. Eldridge, *Victorian Imperialism* (London: Hoddern and Stoughton, 1978), pp. 75–79; Ronald Robinson, John Gallagher, Alice Denny, *Africa and the Victorians: The Official Mind of Imperialism* (London: Macmillan, 1981), pp. 1–15 and 35.
42 E.g. Desmond Platt, 'The Imperialism of Free Trade: Some Reservations', *Economic History Review* 21/2 (1968), 296–306; Peter Cain and Antony Hopkins, *British Imperialism: 1688-2000* (Harlow: Longman, 2002); Osterhammel, 'China', p. 646.
43 Osterhammel, 'Imperialism in Transition', pp. 263–4.
44 Darwin, 'Imperialism and the Victorians', pp. 618–34; Bernard Porter, *The Lion's Share, A History of British Imperialism 1850 to the Present*, 5th edn (Harlow: Longman, 2012), p. 137.
45 David Cannadine, *History in Our Time* (Yale: Yale University Press, 1998), pp. 143–53.
46 James Sheridan, *China in Disintegration: The Republican Era in Chinese History 1912-1949* (New York: Free Press, 1975), p. 48.

47 Arthur Waldron, *From War to Nationalism: China's Turning Point, 1924–1925* (Cambridge: Cambridge University Press, 1995), pp. 161–2.
48 James Cable, *Gunboat Diplomacy: Political Applications of Limited Naval Force* (Basingstoke: Macmillan, 1981), pp. 17–38.
49 Memoranda on the Political and Military Situation in China, 1924–9, TNA, FO 228/2929; H. M. Trenchard, Memorandum on the Fuller Employment of Air Power in Imperial Defence, November 1929, TNA, CAB 24/207; Clayton, 'Deceptive Might', pp. 289–91.
50 E.g. Ship's log of HMS *Diomede* 1924–5, TNA, ADM 53/75887; ship's log of HMS *Carlisle* 1924–5, TNA, ADM 53/72682; ship's log of HMS *Despatch* 1924–5, TNA, ADM 53/75691; ship's log of HMS *Hawkins* 1923–4, TNA, ADM 53/78593.
51 Report of Sub-committee on Staffs of Admiralty Office, War Office and Air Ministry for the Cabinet Committee on Reduction of National Expenditure, January 1923, TNA, CAB 24/160/72; Karl Lautenschlager, 'The Submarine in Naval Warfare, 1901–2001', *International Security* 11/3 (1986), 123; Harford Montgomery-Hyde, *British Air Policy between the Wars 1918–1939* (London: Heineman, 1976), pp. 98–9.
52 Clayton, *The British Empire as a Superpower*, pp. 116–40; Butler, Moore and Thomas, *Crises of Empire*, pp. 18–19.
53 Kennedy, 'Britain's Policy-Making Elite', p. 624.
54 Bell, *The Royal Navy*, p. 7; Karl Lautenschlaeger, 'Technology and the Evolution of Naval Warfare', *International Security* 8/2 (1983), 27; Jon T. Sumida, '"The Best Laid Plans": The Development of British Battle-Fleet Tactics, 1919–42', *International History Review* 14/4 (1992), 682; Geoffrey Till, *Seapower: A Guide for the Twenty-First Century* (London: Routledge, 2013), p. 231.
55 John Jordan, *Warships After Washington: The Development of the Five Major Fleets 1922–1930* (Barnsley: Seaforth, 2011); Sumida, '"The Best Laid Plans"', pp. 681–91; Arthur Hezlet, *Aircraft and Sea Power* (London: Davies, 1970); Lautenschlaeger, 'Technology and the Evolution of Naval Warfare', pp. 3–51.
56 Joe Maiolo, 'Anglo-Soviet Naval Armaments Diplomacy before the Second World War', *English Historical Review* 123/501 (2008), 353–7; Moretz, *The Royal Navy*, p. 156.
57 Kitching, *Britain and the Problem of International Disarmament*, pp. 2–10.
58 Moretz, *The Royal Navy and the Capital Ship*, p. 259; Till, *Seapower*, p. 230.
59 Ralph Harrington, "'The Mighty Hood': Navy, Empire, War at Sea and the British National Imagination, 1920–60', *Journal of Contemporary History* 38/2 (2003), 177.
60 Chesneau, *All the World's Fighting Ships*.
61 E.g. Field, *Royal Navy Strategy in the Far East*, pp. 5–11; Neidpath, *The Singapore Naval Base*. Butler, 'The British Empire, 1918–1945', pp. 18–21.

62 Chesneau, *All the World's Fighting Ships*, pp. 167–217; Jordan, *Warships after Washington*.
63 Jordan, *Warships after Washington*, p. 98.
64 Admiralty reply to Cabinet about the Navy Estimates 1925–6, February 1925, TNA, ADM 116/2300.
65 W. S. Churchill, Memorandum by the Chancellor of the Exchequer about the Navy Estimates, 29 January 1925, TNA, CAB 24/171/39; M. P. A. Hankey, Note on Imperial Defence Preparations for Committee of Imperial Defence, 2 July 1928, TNA, CAB 24/196/32.
66 Memoranda from Foreign Office officials in China on British Policy towards contending factions, October 1927, TNA, FO 228/3507/46; Fung, *The Diplomacy of Imperial Retreat*, p. 158; Ian Nish, 'An Overview of Relations between China and Japan, 1895–1945', *China Quarterly* 124 (1990), 611–15.
67 Harumi Goto-Shibata, *Japan and Britain in Shanghai 1925–31* (London: Macmillan, 1995), pp. 22–8; Field, *Royal Navy Strategy*, p. 64.
68 Bell, *The Royal Navy*, p. 2.
69 W. S. Churchill, Memorandum by the Chancellor of the Exchequer about the Navy Estimates, 29 January 1925, TNA, CAB 24/171/39, p. 6; M. P. A. Hankey, Minutes from a meeting of the Committee for Imperial Defence to discuss the Navy Estimates, 8 November 1928, TNA, CAB 24/198/48. Attitudes in Whitehall to the one-power standard were relaxed in the 1920s because of the largely theoretical threat posed by the United States compared to the real threat posed by Germany before the First World War.
70 See Christopher Bell, 'Thinking the Unthinkable: British and American Naval Strategies for an Anglo-American War, 1918–1931', *International History Review* 19/4 (1997), 789–808, or Clifford, *Amphibious Warfare*, p. 198.
71 Bell, *The Royal Navy*, p. 2.
72 David Edgerton, *Warfare State: Britain 1920–1970* (Cambridge: Cambridge University Press, 2006), pp. 21–3.
73 Carolyn Kitching, *Britain and the Geneva Disarmament Conference* (Basingstoke: Palgrave Macmillan, 2003), pp. 11–15.
74 Ronald Hyam, 'The British Empire in the Edwardian Era', in *The Oxford History of the British Empire: Volume IV: The Twentieth Century*, ed. Judith M. Brown and William R. Louis (Oxford: Oxford University Press, 1999), p. 48.
75 Clayton, *The British Empire as a Superpower*, pp. 116–227.
76 Martin Daunton, 'How to Pay for the War: State, Society and Taxation in Britain, 1917–1924', *English Historical Review* 111/443 (1996), 883.
77 E.g. Michael Howard, *The Continental Commitment: The Dilemma of British Defence Policy in the Era of the Two World Wars* (London: Ashfield, 1989), pp. 84–89; Paul Kennedy, *The Realities Behind Diplomacy: Background Influences*

on British External Policy, 1865–1980 (London: Fontana, 1985), pp. 226–42; Roskill, *Naval Policy between the Wars*, p. 276.
78 Christopher Bell, *Churchill and Sea Power* (Oxford: Oxford University Press, 2013), pp. 88–105; John Ferris, 'Treasury Control, The Ten Year Rule and British Service Policies, 1919–1924', *Historical Journal* 30/4 (1987), 860–67; Jon T. Sumida, 'British Naval Procurement and Technological Change, 1919–1939', in *Technology and Naval Combat in the Twentieth Century and Beyond*, ed. Philip P. O'Brien (London: Routledge, 2001), pp. 129–34; Edgerton, *Warfare State*, pp. 16–36.
79 Derek Aldcroft, *From Versailles to Wall Street 1919–1929* (London: Allen Lane, 1977), pp. 100–104; Robin Higham, *Armed Forces in Peacetime* (London: Foulis, 1962).
80 Butler, Moore and Thomas, *Crises of Empire*, p. 19; Hastings Ismay, *The Memoirs of Lord Ismay* (London: Heineman, 1960), pp. 50–6.
81 W. C. Bridgeman, Appendix for the Navy Estimates for 1925–6, TNA, CAB 24/171/38.
82 2x 'Tern' and 2x 'Peterel' class river gunboats, launched 1927–8. These were followed by *Falcon, Sandpiper and Robin* 1931–4. Chesneau, *All the World's Fighting Ships*, p. 78.
83 Admiralty correspondence with the Chancellor of the Exchequer about the Navy Estimates, 1928, TNA, ADM 1/8724/68.
84 Goto-Shibata, *Japan and Britain in Shanghai*, p. 54.
85 Thomas, *Violence and Colonial Order*, pp. 76–8.
86 Foreign Office request to the Admiralty for the stationing of HMS *Dauntless* at Singapore, December 1926, TNA, FCO 141/16373.
87 Basil Liddell-Hart, *The Liddell Hart Memoirs: Volume 1* (London: Cassell, 1965).
88 Roskill, *Naval Policy between the Wars*, pp. 348–53. ASDIC: An early form of sonar device.
89 Marder, 'The Influence of History on Sea Power', pp. 414–28; Marder, *From the Dardanelles to Oran*, pp. 34–8; David MacGregor, 'The Use, Misuse, and Non-Use of History: The Royal Navy and the Operational Lessons of the First World War', *Journal of Military History* 56/4 (1992), 603–16.
90 Christopher Bell, 'The King's English and the Security of the Empire: Class, Social Mobility, and Democratization in the British Naval Officer Corps, 1918–1939', *Journal of British Studies* 48/3 (2009), 699; Mary Jones, 'Towards a Hierarchy of Management: The Victorian and Edwardian Navy 1860–1918', in *Naval Leadership and Management, 1650–1950*, ed. Helen Doe and Richard Harding (Woodbridge: Boydell & Brewer, 2012), p. 167; Marder, 'The Influence of History on Sea Power', p. 439.
91 Joseph Moretz, *Thinking Wisely, Planning Boldly: The Higher Education and Training of Royal Navy Officers, 1919–39* (Solihull: Helion, 2014).

92 Higham, *Armed Forces in Peacetime*. See also David R. Woodward, *Lloyd George and the Generals* (London: Associated University Press, 1983); Roskill, *Naval Policy between the Wars*, pp. 202–3; Clayton, *The British Empire as a Superpower*, p. 19.

93 H. M. Trenchard, Memorandum on the Fuller Employment of Air Power in Imperial Defence, November 1929, TNA, CAB 24/207.

94 Montgomery-Hyde, *British Air Policy between the Wars*, pp. 98–100.

95 Keith Jeffrey, *The British Army and the Crisis of Empire 1918–22* (Manchester: Manchester University Press, 1984), p. 67.

96 See Stephen Platt, *Autumn in the Heavenly Kingdom: China, the West, and the Epic Story of the Taiping Civil War* (London: Atlantic Books, 2012); Bickers, *The Scramble for China*.

97 Bickers, *The Scramble for China*, pp. 337–47.

98 Paul Cohen, 'The Boxer Uprising', in *China: Adapting the Past, Confronting the Future*, ed. Thomas Buoye, Kirk Denton, Bruce Dickson, Barry Naughton and Martin Whyte (Ann Arbor, MI: University of Michigan Press, 2002), pp. 62–74.

99 Kim Salkeld, 'Witness to the Revolution: Surgeon Lieutenant Bertram Bickford on the China Station 1910–12', *Journal of the Royal Asiatic Society Hong Kong Branch* 51 (2011), 133.

100 Report by Chiefs of Staff with attached correspondence, January 1929, TNA, CAB 24/202/24; Osterhammel, 'China', pp. 648–51; Sheridan, *China in Disintegration*, pp. 76–92.

101 A. W. Flux, 'British Export Trade' *Economic Journal* 36/144 (1926), 552–6; Fung, *The Diplomacy of Imperial Retreat*, pp. 50, 190–1.

102 Osterhammel, 'Imperialism in Transition', p. 261.

103 Osterhammel, 'China', pp. 654–7; Eric Teichman, *Affairs of China: A Survey of the Recent History and Present Circumstances of the Republic of China* (London: Methuen, 1938), p. 46.

104 Clifford, 'A Revolution Is Not a Tea Party', p. 513.

105 Bickers, *Empire Made Me*, pp. 164–7; Fung, *The Diplomacy of Imperial Retreat*, pp. 40–1.

106 Robert Kagan, 'From Revolutionary Iconoclasm to National Revolution: Ch'en Tu-hsiu and the Chinese Communist Movement', in *China in the 1920s: Nationalism and Revolution*, ed. F. G. Chan and Thomas Etzold (New York: F. Watts, 1976), p. 69; Martin Thomas, *Violence and Colonial Order – Police, Workers and Protest in the European Colonial Empires 1918–1940* (Cambridge: Cambridge University Press, 2012), pp. 76–8; Goto-Shibata, *Japan and Britain in Shanghai*, pp. 13–40.

107 Hans Van de Ven, *War and Nationalism in China 1925–1945* (London: Routledge, 2003), pp. 109–19.

108 Bruce Elleman, *Modern Chinese Warfare, 1795–1989* (London: Routledge, 2001), p. 168; Fung, *The Diplomacy of Imperial Retreat*, p. 115; Van de Ven, *War and Nationalism in China*, p. 117.
109 Michael Murdoch, 'Exploiting Anti-Imperialism: Popular Forces and Nation-State-Building during China's Northern Expedition, 1926–1927', *Modern China* 35/1 (2009), 69–73; Fung, *The Diplomacy of Imperial Retreat*, p. 33.
110 Fung, *The Diplomacy of Imperial Retreat*, p. 9.
111 Houshang Sabahi, *British Policy in Persia 1918–1925* (London: Cass, 1990), p. 63; Nigel West, *MASK: MI5's Penetration of the Communist Party of Great Britain* (London: Routledge, 2005), p. 11.
112 Clayton, *The British Empire as a Superpower*, pp. 116–40.
113 David Fieldhouse, *Western Imperialism in the Middle East 1914–1958* (Oxford: Oxford University Press, 2006), p. 87.
114 Mark Mazower, 'Violence and the State in the Twentieth Century', *American Historical Review* 107/4 (2002), 1175.
115 Peter Elliot, *The Cross and the Ensign: A Naval History of Malta 1798–1979* (London: Granada, 1982), pp. 100–101.

2

Between China and Japan, the China Station's strategic balance

An exploration of the Royal Navy's China Station and its main deployments during the 1920s should consider how those operational demands were balanced against wider strategic concerns. There are already many histories about the nature of Britain's interwar relationship with Japan and how the China Station was positioned to counter Japan's growing power in the region.[1] Few accounts, however, consider the naval and geopolitical implications of Britain's changing involvement in China and the interrelationship between the various power struggles occurring in East Asia at the time. In discussing Hong Kong's position within the Royal Navy's long-term planning, for example, even Christopher Bell's broader approach to the topic did not explore the extent to which maintaining that naval base had to do with neighbouring China.[2] This section will avoid delving too far into existing debates about the shift towards a Singapore-focused grand strategy, but will help explain why Britain maintained a modest force at a relatively exposed outpost. As we shall see, events involving second-tier powers, such as China, could and did have a significant influence upon the grand strategies of the major powers.

There are four broad areas that need exploring when considering China and the China Station's position within the 1920s East Asian naval power struggles. Firstly, the nature, disposition and operational employment of the China Station – what was it intended to achieve in relation to the two regional rivals? Secondly, Britain's changing strategy for maintaining bases in the region, which has been a feature of existing discussion, must be expanded to explore their role in relation to China, including the often-overlooked withdrawal from Weihai. Thirdly, the degree of cooperation and conflict that occurred between Britain, China, Japan and the other European powers with interests in the region. Lastly, we will consider what role America played as a rising influence over regional events and the extent to which Anglo-American naval interactions around

China influenced Britain's East Asian strategy. Together the four themes provide greater depth to our understanding of Britain's interwar plans for East Asia and how naval strategy was influenced by concerns about China as well as Japan. This will delineate between Britain's Far Eastern strategy and Anglo-Japanese relations, to treat events in the 1920s in context rather than with the hindrance of hindsight about what happened in 1941.

Britain's diplomatic relationship with Asia's two main powers, China and Japan, developed during the latter part of the nineteenth century along quite different lines. Whereas there remained a degree of official intransigence and sometimes outright hostility between Britain and China, events with Japan slowly moved towards the signing of the Anglo-Japanese Treaty in 1902. That alliance, however, was in reality little more than a marriage of convenience and gives a false impression about the strength of the bond between the two countries. Britain faced the conflicting aims of wanting to keep its East Asian interests secure, while simultaneously concentrating the Royal Navy's power in and around European waters to mitigate worsening ties with Germany.[3] In return, Japan sought a powerful ally to help strengthen its hand against Russia, particularly by removing the threat of third-party interference from France or Italy.[4]

Almost before the ink was dry, the global power balance was shifting to undermine the common perceived threats that lay at the heart of the alliance. Beginning with Japan's victory over Russia in 1905, the temporary incentives binding Japan and Britain together started to dissipate. The complete naval victory gained at Tsushima by the IJN eliminated what was previously the second-largest naval force in East Asia, after the Royal Navy, and with it cemented Japan's position as a serious regional power.[5] Germany's East Asian Cruiser Squadron would eventually fill the gulf left by Russia as a prominent third naval power in the region, but only really in 1914 during the march to war.[6] More immediately, the decisive victory at Tsushima triggered growing concern within the British establishment about Japan itself. That debate was stoked by the sudden realization that Japan had emerged as a major military power, but it was fuelled by a deep underlying racial distrust of the Japanese in general. As early as 1909, for example, reports of Japanese agents operating in the Xinjiang province of China provoked near-paranoia among British officials, concerned about a threat to the northern border of India.[7] While with hindsight it seems highly unlikely those agents, if indeed they actually were spies, might have been exploring invasion routes, the incident serves to highlight British suspicion about Japan's strategic plans. Britain did not expect the Anglo-Japanese alliance to be a permanent arrangement.[8]

The alliance survived into the First World War as situations still arose where it proved invaluable to both nations, particularly in China where their interests overlapped. Throughout the Wuchang Uprising, forming the first months of the Xinhai Revolution, the two navies cooperated to protect their interests in the treaty ports from riot damage. While that mutual assistance was not extended without reservations, it occurred against a backdrop where the various foreign powers in China were generally not on cordial terms. Compared with the alternative potential allies, continued Anglo-Japanese cooperation remained the preferred choice. In contrast, German officials were reportedly extremely antagonistic in their attitude towards other nations' navies, above all in their dealings with the IJN. That hostility led to a situation in 1911 that serves well to show how the Anglo-Japanese alliance remained relevant to both parties.

During times of trouble in such remote locations, even when cooperation between different navies was conducted reluctantly, it was generally accepted that rank would be mutually respected, and the highest-ranking officer present would lead the multinational response. When Vice Admiral Alfred Winsloe prepared to leave Hankou, which would involve his relinquishing command as the senior international naval officer present, the Japanese ambassador in London lobbied the British government to instruct Winsloe to remain in place. Had he departed as planned then the next in line to take command was a German officer, a possibility that the Japanese found intolerable. After due consideration, the Admiralty ordered Winsloe to remain at Hankou a little longer in acquiescence to the Japanese request.[9] That decision was aided by long-term Anglo-German rivalry on the Yangtze and British suspicions that German officers had hidden agendas, given reports at the time that they were training Chinese soldiers.[10] In such situations, both allies worked willingly together in China, although perhaps with a sense of resignation that it was due to a lack of viable alternatives rather than an ideal union.

The First World War ultimately steered the uncertain alliance on its course towards complete collapse, starting with the very first month of the conflict. Japan's government hesitated almost three weeks, after German troops entered Belgium triggering Britain's entry into the European conflict, before finally declaring war. That delay caused significant friction with the British government, because it was perceived as Japan failing to honour the spirit of the alliance.[11] In return, the British government formally notified Japan in 1914 that an agreement had been signed with the United States, making it unlikely that Britain would join a conflict between the two Pacific powers.[12] Nonetheless, the biggest influence upon Anglo-Japanese relations as a result of the war was an indirect one, heavily linked to China.

Expanding Japanese economic activity in China, particularly in the Yangtze valley, was already causing friction between the allies when war broke out in 1914.[13] The British Empire's dominance over trade with China had declined from a peak of 80 per cent in the 1870s to just under 50 per cent by 1913, but faced further fierce competition during the war years.[14] Likewise, Britain's share of foreign direct investment into China declined from 33 per cent in 1902 to 27.7 per cent in 1914.[15] With resources increasingly focused on the war effort, Japanese businesses were free to step into the resulting void, accelerating the pace of the existing trend. This was part of a much wider picture in which British dominance of global merchandise exports was generally waning, with its market share almost cut by half between 1870 and 1929. While the United States played the primary role in that decline, the displacement of British trade by Japanese businesses was particularly pronounced in China. Between 1872 and 1921, for example, Japan was the single largest source of foreign direct investment into Shanghai.[16]

In conjunction with that economic challenge, the war also increased the relative growth in Japan's hard power. In roughly twenty-five years, Japan had gone from having a navy barely worthy of note to creating a force capable of causing significant damage to the Royal Navy, and with it Britain's position in East Asia.[17] As a result, background suspicion started to solidify into official caution, with intelligence-sharing and joint planning with Japan cut to a minimum by the end of the war.[18] This was not purely a British attitude towards its Asian ally, with Japan also increasingly wary of its European counterpart and taking similar steps to limit its collaboration.[19]

What occurred during this period, however, was not just a one-way process of Britain becoming suspicious of their nominal ally. Britain's temporary wartime alliance with Japan's main regional rival, America, had highlighted the degree to which Anglo-American defence interests overlapped, and how well their forces could work together. Just as Japan had become a potential threat to Britain's interests, it looked increasingly likely that Britain would side with America in a Pacific conflict. Indeed, Japanese suspicions about the latter scenario were quite close to the truth. Even before its official expiration in 1921, the Admiralty had already issued orders stating that in the event of war between America and Japan, the China Station was to ignore the alliance and prepare to assist America.[20] There were factors at play in the final few years, particularly after David Beatty's appointment as First Sea Lord, that pushed the relationship between Britain and

Japan into rapid decline.[21] Japanese commentary on the Indian Independence Movement in 1919, for example, in response to Britain's heavy-handed policies on the subcontinent was interpreted as an effort to undermine the British Empire.[22] The collapse, however, had been long in coming and was not just a result of Beatty triggering a sudden reassessment within the Admiralty of the potential threat posed by Japan. Entering the 1920s, the Anglo-Japanese alliance was still in place, but the treaty was largely worthless and in practicality the two countries had long regarded each other with suspicion as potential threats.

Looking at East Asia in 1919, British officials would have seen a region dominated by recent wartime allies, but few of whom could be counted on as true friendly states. The marriage of convenience with Japan was approaching a potentially acrimonious divorce. America was returning to relative international isolation, while simultaneously challenging Britain economically, militarily and geopolitically worldwide. France, the Netherlands and Portugal were seen as comparatively supportive powers, although they were no longer in a position materially to assist Britain in East Asia. Russia had new Soviet leadership and presented an apparently existential threat to the British Empire. Britain's response to the heated environment in China, and the challenges posed by the leading Chinese factions, had to be weighed against that new geostrategic background.

The right warships in the right places?

In 1904 the commander-in-chief of the China Station, Admiral Cyprian Bridge, wrote to the Admiralty arguing for a radical change to the structure and operational deployment of his force. Within his argument he stated that the China Station was effectively split into two very different squadrons, one of gunboats and one true naval fleet. Bridge proposed retiring his gunboat force, given that he felt they were maintained for political purposes and had little military value.[23] The request was denied by the Admiralty, but it does serve to highlight one of the long-standing unusual features of the China Station – it was not really a single command. While the precise dispositions had changed since Bridge's time, particularly during the First World War interlude, entering the 1920s the situation was very similar to that in 1904.[24] The China Station was still split between ocean-going vessels intended for battle at sea against other major powers, such as America or Japan, and a brown-water force of smaller warships for littoral operations.

Possessing a mixture of vessel types was not unusual for a naval station, but the China Station's size and split between fleet and patrol vessels does make it stand out, as the challenges it faced exceeded those at most other locations. The Africa and East Indies stations, for example, had both cruisers to protect trade routes and smaller sloops for counter-piracy and other naval policing work. In practice, however, the handful of warships posted to most naval stations around the world were only sufficient to deter lone mid-sized raiders, should war break out.[25] In contrast, the China Station was the third-largest global deployment of Royal Navy warships, even if it was still relatively lightweight when compared with the fleets in home waters and the Mediterranean.

While the cruisers and submarines posted to China were nominally there to deter Japanese aggression, the force was still relatively small and exposed if truly intended to achieve that goal. The world's third-largest navy was based only a few days sailing away from Hong Kong. That position has previously been explained by exploring the expectation in Whitehall, prior to 1931, that Britain would potentially have had thirty to sixty days' warning in which to prepare for war with Japan.[26] Even three weeks would have provided sufficient time to despatch a task force from Malta, although war orders stated that the fleet would only initially sail as far as Singapore.[27] Built around an initial squadron of *Iron Duke*-class battleships, that relief force could potentially rendezvous with the China Station in the vicinity of Hong Kong within a week of leaving Singapore.[28] The full battle fleet was expected to be able to join from home waters in the following two weeks, providing an overwhelming naval force at Hong Kong within a maximum of fifty-four days of being ordered to sail by the Admiralty.[29] Once the fleet controlled the South China Sea, securing British imperial territories, the Royal Navy's cruisers would begin a campaign of attrition, which it was hoped would slowly force Japan to seek a settlement.[30] In the following six weeks, two infantry divisions would also arrive ready for deployment in and around Hong Kong, assuming it had survived any initial Japanese assault.[31]

Even in the early 1920s four to eight weeks was a significant lag, during which time the China Station would have been exposed to attack from Japan. Most explanations so far have focused on the submarines present at Hong Kong, suggesting that they could, or were at least expected to be able to, delay any Japanese advance across East Asia during the critical first two months of a conflict.[32] These fit with the plans for the station's cruisers and light vessels to harry the Japanese advance, while falling back upon Singapore.[33] Likewise, Joseph Moretz has discussed a theoretical study from 1921 looking at a Japanese assault on Hong Kong via landings in Mirs Bay, which suggested that the city might be able to hold out for a couple of months, although it was ultimately inconclusive over the final result.[34] With such a delay, the balance of global naval power was still in Britain's favour during the 1920s.[35] It has been proposed that the focus on enforcing global naval disarmament treaties was felt by Whitehall to keep a lid on Japanese naval development, to ensure a British naval task force to East Asia would be dominant for the foreseeable future.[36] These points do provide a solid basis for understanding Britain's grand strategy for dealing with Japan, but all assume either complacency or a cold detachment in the Admiralty's leaving its third-largest force, and associated ground forces, exposed to destruction before help could arrive. That risk was all the greater when considering that the Fifth Light Cruiser Squadron spent much of the year based not at Hong Kong, protected by shore batteries and submarines, but at undefended Weihai, some 400 miles closer to Japan.[37]

To better understand the decisions behind that vulnerable position, it is crucial to appreciate that the Admiralty was operating under the assumption that Japan would not declare war outright against Great Britain. As with America's 'Plan Red' envisioning a theoretical future war with the British Empire, the Royal Navy also had to plan for every eventuality.[38] Those scenarios included surprise attacks by Japan against Singapore, even if they were considered unlikely in the short term.[39] Believing such a direct attack was improbable was not unreasonable or unrealistic at the time, given that there were few British possessions in East Asia of sufficient potential strategic value to Japan, either economic or military, that would justify risking a major war. Instead, the Admiralty believed that the most likely cause of conflict would come either from Japan first clashing with America or through a Japanese campaign of expansion in China spiralling out of control.[40] While events in 1941 saw the former scenario ultimately come to fruition, during the 1920s it was the latter that presented the greatest risk to Britain and largely dictated the Royal Navy's strategy for the China Station.

The Admiralty's war orders issued in 1920 and updated in 1924 made clear that they did not expect or desire a war with Japan but acknowledged that a Japanese territorial drive in northern China appeared increasingly likely. Such a campaign might then trigger a wider conflict and draw in other major powers.[41] The belief that a campaign of imperial expansion was imminent stemmed back to Japan issuing the Twenty-One Demands to China in 1915.[42] That ultimatum sought Chinese acceptance of Japan's acquisition of the former German concessions in Shandong, along with further extraterritorial rights that would effectively turn China into a Japanese protectorate.[43] Coming without advance notice, taking the Foreign Office by surprise, and with serious implications for Britain's position in

China, the episode also played a part in the slow decline of the Anglo-Japanese alliance.[44] No longer distracted by its peripheral role in the First World War, Japan was free to focus on an underlying desire to acquire territory and build its own empire. It was not certain that the resulting imperial drive would aim west into China, with an alternative maritime policy considered, which would have primarily targeted the Dutch East Indies.[45] Ultimately, however, Japanese expansionism came to focus upon the Asian mainland.

During a series of Royal Navy War College lectures between 1924 and 1925, numerous presentations explored the risk of a war with Japan and the power balance in East Asia. Listing the four possible causes of such a war, for example, Lieutenant Commander Arthur Armitage placed events in China as the most likely to occur. Exploring that risk in detail, Lieutenant Commander Ivan Franks produced a full complementary lecture discussing how events in China could trigger just such a war with Japan.[46] In contrast, the three alternative scenarios that were seen as plausible were all ones in which Britain would have some influence over when and in what way it might become involved. The first of these was a Japanese invasion of the Dutch East Indies, which was seen as a potentially fast-moving event, where Britain would most likely choose militarily to support the Netherlands. As Japan would have attacked a neutral power, Britain would have had some leeway to delay a declaration of war, allowing time to ready the fleet and potentially form a multinational coalition. Likewise, the other two cases that were explored revolved around escalating diplomatic crises caused by Japanese attempts to push for immigration rights in British colonies or through interference in India. Both those proposals involved Britain instigating the conflict, primarily as a pre-emptive move to defend control over India.[47]

It is unclear whether Whitehall felt that Japanese imperial expansion in northern China alone was sufficient to provoke a diplomatic crisis that would lead to a war directly with Britain or whether it just opened the door to Britain later being drawn into a conflict. The latter seems more likely though, given that if Japan's territorial appetites were being satiated in the north, it might deflect them away from Britain's primary areas of interest in the Yangtze and south.[48] Japanese expansion in northern China might have distracted or applied pressure on the Soviet Union – also of benefit to British foreign policy. What is clear, however, is the way in which the Admiralty intended to respond in either event, in conjunction with the wider defence apparatus of the British Empire. The Royal Navy's war orders proposed that the China Station should instigate a managed retreat of military and civilian personnel, and assets from northern China and the Yangtze. Should that process occur in the face of a direct war with Japan then the submarine flotillas were expected to play a crucial role in warding off an attack on Hong Kong and harrying Japanese advances. Emphasis was placed on the China Station's warships following unusual patterns of behaviour, to avoid the British naval force being located and destroyed. Precise interpretation of that instruction was left to individual commanders if hostilities were considered probable. The key protective element to the plans, however, was that the managed retreat would occur when a situation had developed in China that could lead to a war with Japan, and therefore before Britain was a formal participant in the hostilities.[49]

With the naval antennae of the British Empire falling back on Hong Kong, the commander-in-chief, China was ordered to assume additional control of the East Indies Station, and the Admiralty strongly suggested he should then concentrate his two squadrons at Singapore. From that position guarding the Strait of Malacca, the combined group of six to eight cruisers was considered sufficient to hold off any provisional IJN forays into the Indian Ocean, intercept Japanese merchant vessels and wait while the battle fleet steamed to their relief. As the Rear Admiral formerly commanding the East Indies Station was instructed to assume control of the naval forces defending Singapore itself, the strengthened China force would have been free to return to Hong Kong, once reinforced by the battle fleet. Crucially, the 1920 orders and all those issued for the rest of the decade only loosely referred to a war involving Japan in China, one which might not initially include Britain as a combatant.[50] Those preparations for war might therefore occur while Britain was still at peace. In either event, the Admiralty did not believe that British possessions would be primary objectives in a Japanese campaign, allowing enough time for that managed retreat to occur.

Central to the Admiralty's planning was an assumption that no other naval power would ally itself with Japan, allowing the Royal Navy to concentrate its force against a single, weaker opponent. A 1923 revision to the war orders, for example, outlined that the three main possibilities where Japan might seek to form an alliance were Germany, the Soviet Union and China, none of which posed a significant direct threat to the Royal Navy at that point.[51] Moreover, given that the Admiralty saw a Japanese invasion of China as the most likely trigger of British involvement in an East Asian conflict, it was probable that Britain could form a working alliance with some of the Chinese warlords.

During his time as commander-in-chief of the China Station, Admiral Arthur Leveson emphasized to the Admiralty how important he felt it was that Britain should seek Chinese support. Leveson argued that Japan would find it difficult to seize Hong Kong quickly should Britain have either tacit or explicit support from China, presumably referring to the Guomindang given their control of Guangdong province.[52] Nor did Leveson's opinions come as the lone voice of a diligent but distant station commander. Rear Admiral Herbert Richmond as commander-in-chief of the neighbouring East Indies Station repeated the proposals in the following year.[53] Their ideas addressed one of the key concerns raised in the 1912 review of the plans to defend Hong Kong, which identified the greatest threat as one coming from a land-based attack from the direction of Guangzhou, a thrust that would render the harbour largely defenceless. The Committee for Imperial Defence had agreed with that earlier report and predicted that four thousand men could overcome the city from landwards, but China was the only power in the position to arrange such an attack at short notice.[54] An amphibious assault against the island of Hong Kong itself was at the mercy of Britain's submarines, shore batteries and potentially any military aircraft that might have been despatched to the colony. Preventing Japan, or any other major power, from moving troops through Guangdong province was therefore seen as pivotal in securing Hong Kong.

Two interesting points are raised by the tactical assumptions made by Leveson and Richmond for the potential defence of Hong Kong. Firstly, it is significant that the Foreign Office did not put greater effort into building a better relationship with the Chinese authorities in Guangzhou, given that the Royal Navy recognized the strategic value of doing so. Secondly, the neglect of land-facing defences at Singapore in the 1930s appears even more complacent, when the not so dissimilar planning for Hong Kong in the 1920s had emphasized the vulnerability of naval harbours to an indirect attack. The latter is a little tangential to this study and so should be left for future histories of Singapore, but the former is particularly pertinent.

It appears that discussion of potentially allying with China in the event of a war with Japan did not, at least officially, go beyond the Admiralty. The most plausible explanation is that for much of the 1920s it was China, and increasingly the Guomindang, that the Foreign Office and Admiralty saw as the greatest threat to Britain's position in Hong Kong. In June 1925, for example, the Committee of Imperial Defence considered that growing anti-imperial sentiment among Han Chinese populations presented a 'menacing' situation that threatened the security of both Hong Kong and Singapore.[55] Shared aspects of identity, culture and language meant that there was the potential for Guomindang anti-imperial rhetoric to spread unrest to two of Britain's key imperial outposts. In contrast, while there was growing concern about Japan's long-term ambitions, senior members of the Royal Navy repeatedly emphasized that they believed Britain's relationship with Japan to be satisfactory.[56] If the British authorities saw China as the greater threat for much of the 1920s, it does raise the question about the extent to which the China Station was actually deployed to counter that threat, and not the longer-term theoretical one from Japan.

China: Friend or foe?

Head-to-head, the Chinese navy of the 1920s was no match for the Royal Navy, even if operating as a single body, which was far from likely given that the allegiance of individual warships was often unclear and changed between warlords. Chinese naval power in 1920 was based around eight outdated cruisers, mostly built on-order for the Qing regime, some of which had already been downgraded to armoured transport vessels. The Qing had ordered a range of newer vessels prior to 1911 from Western powers, but those warships were sold on to third parties after the revolution, while still under construction.[57] The largest available in 1920 therefore, the *Hai Chi*, had been built in Newcastle-upon-Tyne twenty-two years earlier and was over a thousand tonnes lighter than the smallest British cruisers in use after the First World War.[58] To place China's naval power in perspective, the single *Kongo*-class battlecruiser spotted leading a Japanese squadron off Weihai and around the Yellow Sea in 1924 could deliver a broadside greater than the entire Chinese navy at the time.[59] A pitched battle with one of the major powers' navies would not have ended well for China. In turn, the Royal Navy had far more pressing concerns, both in East Asia and globally, than the limited threat posed by a head-on confrontation with China.

While incapable of fighting a decisive battle against a major power, the Chinese cruisers nonetheless posed a real threat to the Royal Navy's gunboats and sloops, with whom they had frequent contact, and to Britain's interests ashore. The Chinese Southern Navy, for example, attracted much attention in 1920 while based on the Pearl River, just a few hours journey from Hong Kong. The targeted intelligence reports gathered by the Royal Navy at that point suggest a degree of concern about the warships, particularly the political leanings of their crews after they refused to sail and join the Northern Navy.[60] That relatively small Chinese force was still sufficient to cause the Royal Navy a significant headache among the warren of waterways around Guangzhou, where the West River gunboats would be at risk of ambush. Those fears proved groundless in the end as over the following three years the Southern Navy's warships spent much of their time in port with their crews ashore.[61] After 1923 the Chinese factions made greater use of their naval resources, but by then the main warships had finally travelled up to join the North East Fleet, in and around the Yellow Sea, and so posed less of an imminent threat to British interests.

Divided up between the different Chinese factions there were also three small destroyers, ten heavy gunboats and at least twenty-three other fighting vessels of various types, which operated under different allegiances over the years.[62] As with the cruisers, these posed no real threat to the Royal Navy as a whole, but could overwhelm the China Station's often isolated gunboats. With an influx of modern artillery into China after the First World War, Britain's gunboats also reported a growing challenge of being fired upon from riverbanks and shorelines, with weapons increasingly capable of causing critical damage.[63] In combination, this meant that the Royal Navy's gunboat force faced the growing prospect of having its bluff called. Gunboats could be an effective tool for threatening to use force, but in isolation the same gunboats were a liability against organized opposition possessing relatively modern heavy weaponry both afloat and ashore. The Fifth Light Cruiser Squadron's presence in East Asia was therefore not solely intended to deter Japan and protect sea lanes but also provided supporting capacity to maintain British naval dominance over China. Without that squadron, both the China Station's gunboats and Britain's imperial interests in the region would have been left extremely vulnerable to the threat of attack. Questions would arise about whether the British Empire really remained the dominant global power.

The presence of large warships offered a deterrent reminder that the Royal Navy could take significant punitive action against anyone who attacked British interests. While this did mean that the cruiser squadron was exposed to a potential surprise attack, the Admiralty did not believe Japan would consider launching one in the short term. Nor was Britain really capable of developing an alternative strategy. In dealing with China the British government could, and in 1927 did, post additional infantry battalions as a show of strength, but without the mobility provided by the Navy those troops could only protect British interests at one or two major ports, such as Shanghai. The RAF could potentially provide a cheaper and agile deterrent, in a similar style to its previous employment in the Middle East, but again would still struggle to cover more than a few treaty ports.[64] A sustained RAF deployment east of Singapore also brought other problems. Given the limited range of interwar military aircraft, an aerial deterrent would require a number of official military airfields, which would have been taken by Japan and America as a breach of the Washington Treaty.[65] With Britain's grand strategy predicated on maintaining the limitations enclosed within that treaty, Whitehall was careful to avoid providing Britain's rivals with an excuse to abandon the agreement.[66] A naval solution was therefore the only one that could bridge the contrasting demands of providing effective strategies for countering the threats posed by both China and Japan.

There were few alternatives for the structure of the naval force itself. Until the planned upgrades to Singapore were completed, there were no docks east of Suez large enough for the Royal Navy's battlecruisers and only one capable of making basic repairs to some of its battleships.[67] It was not operationally feasible, therefore, for a stronger battle fleet to be sustained in East Asia, even if the Admiralty were willing or able to consider amending its grand strategy. To do so would also have involved heightened financial costs. Estimates in 1922 placed the premium of posting a battleship overseas, compared to a domestic base, at £11,000 per annum and that of a destroyer flotilla at £18,800 per annum.[68] Roughly two-thirds of the supplementary expense was attributed to greater use of fuel because warships posted overseas spent an average of ten additional days at sea. The remainder largely came from transporting and storing armament and ammunition supplies.[69] While only roughly a 10 per cent increase in direct expenditure, when combined with increased wear on the vessels themselves moving a single battleship would realistically match the cost of constructing a brand-new gunboat every year.[70]

Once Singapore's facilities were fully upgraded the Admiralty did plan for the China Station to merge with the East Indies Station and become a 'Future Peace Fleet', built around a core of three battlecruisers, eleven cruisers and two destroyer flotillas.[71] Strengthened to that degree, Britain's East Asian fleet would have been better suited to balance the opposing risks presented by China and Japan. The larger warships would be based safely beyond the range of a sudden strike from Japan at Singapore, at least in theory, while remaining close enough to quickly reach China's littoral regions. As events played out the balance of naval power swung further towards Japan before those facilities were complete. In 1923, however, the Royal Navy saw its solution as an acceptable, and crucially temporary, risk.

Surplus to requirements: The China Station ashore

Large docks for repairing capital ships, such as those being developed at Singapore, were not the only harbour requirements influencing the operational capabilities and strategic planning of the Royal Navy in East Asia. Equally, strategic planning over how to contain threats from Japan and China influenced the decisions made about the future of all naval bases in the region, and not just the major ones. While the China Station was focused around three main harbours at Hong Kong, Singapore and Weihai, the Royal Navy had built up a collection of facilities across a wide range of regional ports over the latter part of the nineteenth century. Shanghai, for example, hosted Royal Navy logistics facilities that were crucial for supporting the British naval deployment on the Yangtze, particularly in terms of fuel storage. Around 1890, there were further storage bases maintained by the Royal Navy at Xiamen, Fuzhou, Shantou, Zhenjiang and Jiujiang (see Figure 5).[72] The naval base at Weihai marked the final addition, with the first debate in the House of Commons over its acquisition occurring in March 1898. Initial proposals to construct a relatively substantial fortress at the harbour were quickly shelved due to budgetary constraints after the Boer War. An amended proposal was therefore tabled for the construction of a largely undefended forward operating base, which was adopted as official policy in February 1902.[73]

The geographic spread of naval storage facilities used in the early years of the twentieth century provided the host of small warships used by the China Station with the ability to maintain operations around much of China's coastline and its major waterways. It was this global chain of coaling stations that allowed

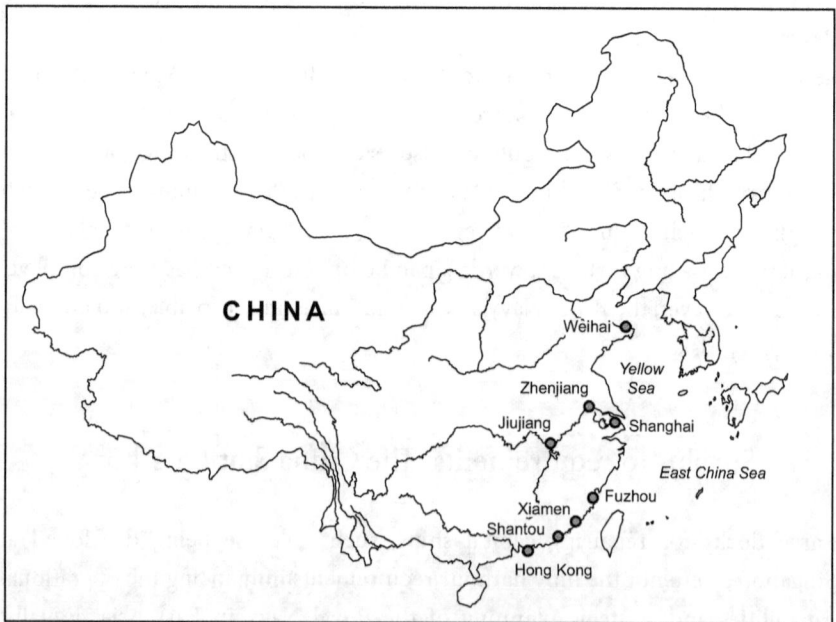

Figure 5 Official Royal Navy storage facilities 1900–14.

the Royal Navy to project power into a far wider range of areas than most other major powers, including the United States.[74] This was particularly important in China, given that gunboats were only capable of steaming for a maximum of roughly two weeks between re-coaling in harbour. Without the array of coaling posts, it would have been near impossible to patrol trade routes or apply coercive pressure effectively during times of crisis.[75] The shift to oil-fuelled boilers prior to and during the First World War meant that by the 1920s the Navy was removing many of its smaller coastal storage facilities. Coaling points continued to be maintained on the Yangtze, however, as many gunboats still relied upon coal to fuel their boilers. The declining residual demand for coaling meant that for the most part, the storage retained was generally supervised by the local concession councils, rather than the Navy itself. Most visibly, the Weihai naval base was left shrunken in stature as a single oil tanker was moored in the harbour, replacing most of the coal stores and additional shore-based staff.[76]

While the general debate over the move to using fuel oil in warships during the early twentieth century was a complicated one, there were a couple of key points in the context of the China Station. Fuel oil has up to twice the energy density of coal, enabling additional space to be made available within vessels, or alternatively it could extend their range, or a combination of the two.[77] The higher energy density also meant that the bulk transportation of fuel between storage points was a far more efficient process.[78] Despite testing different locally mined sources of Chinese coal, British officers had struggled to find a reliable supply of the higher quality steam coal required for ship's boilers. Welsh steam coal, for example, not only has an energy content over one-third higher than many regional sources but also produces far lower levels of ash, which reduced the requirement for boiler maintenance. Even blending different grades and using local coal for stoves only produced marginal savings, although the China Station did make greater use of medium-quality coal from Australia in this way.[79] The Navy therefore relied upon colliers continually shipping bulk quantities all the way from Wales and Australia to a range of coaling points around China.[80] In contrast, with oil having a higher energy density and sources far closer to the Far East than Wales, less merchant shipping capacity would be required to deliver the same fuel energy. With the same British dominance of the global oil tanker fleet as there was with colliers at the start of the interwar period, the resources were already in place for the switch.[81] As a result, in 1922 the Admiralty's Navy Stores department proposed deploying oil-fuelled warships overseas and coal-fuelled ones at home ports where possible given the potential cost savings.[82]

The simpler process of piping fuel oil between ships meant that fleet tankers could re-fuel warships on patrol in calmer conditions, something that was near impossible with bulk quantities of coal. A single fuel pump removed the slow task of having seamen man-handling tonnes of coal into ship's bunkers, which was particularly burdensome for smaller warships and their crews. Indeed, as the chorus to one Royal Navy seaman's song put it so eloquently: 'Coaling, coaling, coaling – Always bloody well coaling'.[83] Local labourers were sometimes used for the process, but this had become increasingly infrequent in the years before the First World War as cost-saving measures resulted in crews being seen as a 'free' alternative.[84] As a result of these factors the switch away from coal could and did have a transformative effect on the way smaller warships operated and the experiences of their crews.

By 1924, the China Station had six Royal Fleet Auxiliary (RFA) tankers ranging in size from transporting 680 to 4,000 tons of fuel, including the Navy's first 'oiler' RFA *Kharki*.[85] Rather than a gunboat departing from the section of river or coastline it was patrolling to take on coal at a port, one of the tankers would be despatched to refuel a number of warships in situ. Not only did this mean that ship-for-ship the China Station of the 1920s could be more productive, it also reduced the requirement for access to shore facilities. Provisions such as fresh food were less of a concern as they could normally be purchased at settlements along the coast and waterways, even during times of crisis, and so had a limited impact on the Royal Navy's storage requirements outside of major naval bases.[86] Ammunition had always been stored at a few guarded naval bases and was generally transported and passed on by other warships on the China Station. This resulted both from security concerns about ammunition presenting a tempting target for bandits and soldiers, and from the possibility of legal problems that might arise from merchant ships carrying military cargoes.[87]

Even in the context of Britain's relationship with China, the gradual disappearance of shore storage leased by the Royal Navy from the treaty ports did not attract any real attention. Over the long term, however, the shift had significant implications that influenced the development of the Navy's strategic planning. In particular, the value of Britain maintaining custody over Weihai declined as a result of the change in fuel. For a coal-fuelled Royal Navy to be capable of projecting power into the Yellow Sea, around northern China, and towards Japan, maintaining a naval base at Weihai was beyond question. By 1920, most battleships could reach those regions from Hong Kong, particularly if they re-coaled at Shanghai. The cruisers and smaller vessels required as part of a balanced battle fleet and to operate in the region on a day-to-day basis, however, would in some cases struggle to reach those distant expanses of water, let alone patrol them.

The shift to fuel oil meant that by the early 1920s the number of China Station vessels that might require coaling at Weihai had dropped to the dual-fuelled flagship HMS *Hawkins*, the four *Flower*-class sloops and any gunboats sent north to the Hai River during times of crisis. Coal storage at Weihai did still retain some wider strategic significance, as a few of the capital ships that might be despatched to East Asia during a crisis were still partially coal fuelled.[88] That residual value was set to disappear in the mid-1920s, with the planned retirement of the *King George V* class and the impending withdrawal of the *Iron Duke* class into reserve, the Royal Navy's last remaining coal-powered battleships.[89] Closer to home, *Hawkins* and two of the *Flower*-class sloops were also due for rotation back to home waters, to be replaced by newer fully oil-fuelled equivalents.

In a curious twist, the withdrawal of the *Iron Duke*-class battleships from the Mediterranean was in itself determined by events in East Asia. Prior to the upgrade of Singapore's oil storage facilities, the Admiralty was forced to retain coal-fuelled warships as part of any battle fleet responding to a war with Japan, to ensure sufficient fuel supplies were readily available.[90] Once those works were complete, only a sustained major conflict with Japan might force the Admiralty to deploy more coal-fuelled warships to the Far East. As a result, by the late 1920s just two of the China Station's sloops were expected to require coal at Weihai, and even then it would only be in minimal quantities.

The crisis that developed as a result of the Northern Expedition in 1926–7 did delay the Navy's planned switch to a largely oil-fuelled China Station, but by mid-1928 those rotations had been completed.[91] A brief exception to the expected requirements came during February 1929 when HMS *Magnolia* was temporarily held at Weihai, due to unrest at Yantai (Chefoo). With outside temperatures averaging −1°C, the stationary ship consumed roughly 50 tons of coal per week just in keeping men and machinery warm.[92] While that elevated usage did foster the briefest possible stay at the base before returning to warmer climates, the total consumption was still relatively modest compared with the quantities previously required to re-coal major warships like HMS *Hawkins*.

Without its prior role as a coaling point, Weihai's value to both the Royal Navy and the British Empire was no longer clear. During a 1924 strategic review, for example, it was noted that while a northern Chinese base might help in a war against Japan, possession of Hong Kong was the only location truly critical for enabling offensive operations.[93] As a naval base, Weihai's main role by the 1920s involved hosting the annual fleet manoeuvres during the summer months, when many of the China Station's ocean-going warships would congregate in the harbour. As similar training activity was regularly conducted at Mirs Bay, near Hong Kong, there were alternative locations available.[94]

The main reason Weihai remained the preferred option was because it enjoyed comfortably warm weather in the summer months, compared to hot and humid Hong Kong. As a result, the harbour was popular with the China Station's officers and crew as a relaxing, quieter alternative to Shanghai.[95] Indeed, the area around the base had already become a holiday destination for the British colonial population in China and hosted boarding schools for their children.[96] As superfluous naval buildings, including those previously used in conjunction with coaling warships, were demolished during the 1920s they were quickly replaced with private shops and residences.[97] Leading Seaman 'Robby' Roberts later recalled 'I always found it a pleasure to spend a few days there. It had a lovely swimming beach, several shops and its own church.'[98] Marine William Greenland likewise noted that the base contained a number of 'beautiful flower gardens' and nicely decorated buildings.[99] With a nine-hole golf course and bathing huts by Liugong Island's beaches, Weihai was starting to resemble a holiday camp by 1930, rather than a naval base.[100]

The declining strategic case for maintaining a British enclave in Northern China almost certainly played a role in the British establishment's growing willingness to return Weihai to Chinese control after the First World War. As early as 1919, for example, proposals were tabled and broadly supported by British officials for China to resume complete control of all mainland areas including the town of Weihai itself, but extending the lease covering Liugong Island including the naval base.[101] Protracted negotiations culminated without an agreement between Britain and China, however, with the fate of Liugong Island a red-line issue for both parties. The British government was also pressing for China to refund various expenses incurred in 'developing Weihaiwei', although it was unclear how the Beiyang government might pay, even if they agreed to the demand.[102] In contrast to those demands, complaints from the British business community in Weihai were largely dismissed or ignored by the Foreign Office. Consul A. P. Blunt, for example, acknowledged residents' concerns in 1923, but only provided vague assurances that compensation might be paid if serious personal financial losses could be shown to have been incurred as a direct result of the British government's action.[103]

While there were diplomatic imperatives behind Britain's return to the negotiating table in July 1928, the lack of Royal Navy opposition helped smooth the way to an agreement. In the final treaty, for example, the Navy conceded that in the event of either Britain or China becoming involved in a war, all Royal Navy and Fleet Auxiliary vessels would vacate Weihai in accordance with international accords. Effectively this downgraded the Royal Navy's rights from the extraterritoriality of an imperial outpost to that of a tenant, although one that retained the right to freely conduct live-firing training exercises both afloat and onshore.[104] That move was extremely symbolic against the backdrop of the wider struggle over British extraterritorial rights in the country. Moreover, the Navy's acquiescence was an acknowledgement that the naval base no longer played a part in the Royal Navy's plans for a potential conflict with Japan.

Without a role as a strategic fuelling point, leaving warships at Weihai amid wider hostilities in the region would have been a significant liability. After all, at that point the Admiralty believed war between China and Japan might produce scenarios where Britain was inexorably drawn into the hostilities. If the naval base had little value in such a war, then its immediate evacuation to try to avoid being drawn into the conflict was no real concession. This further supports existing assessments that those locations where Britain initially surrendered its extraterritorial rights in the late 1920s were relatively insignificant to the Empire.[105] Contrary to Edmund Fung's argument, however, Weihai did still possess strategic value in the years between 1905 (when the enclave should have been returned to China after Russia lost Port Arthur) and the early 1920s when coaling facilities were no longer a critical requirement for the Royal Navy.[106] The timing of the return was therefore not solely down to a change in imperial policy after the December Memorandum in 1927 but also due to the change in practical naval circumstances.

The Hong Kong question

In contrast to Weihai, the maintenance of Hong Kong's military facilities continued to serve a vital strategic purpose in Britain's plans for a potential war with Japan. While the debate raged about prioritizing units for the defence of Singapore, the importance of holding Hong Kong remained largely unchallenged within the Royal Navy, as the only location from which offensive operations could be launched. The then commander-in-chief, East Indies Station, Rear Admiral Richmond, summarized the position in a letter to the Admiralty in April 1925. Richmond stated that Japan's capture of Hong Kong would effectively secure their dominance of East Asia, and it would prove 'exhausting in the highest degree' for Britain to recapture the harbour.[107] Indeed, Richmond went further to argue that if the United States remained neutral then Britain's only hope for a favourable outcome involved preventing Japan from securing a shift in the balance of power in East Asia through the seizure of either Hong Kong or Singapore.[108] Singapore was vital to the defence of the Empire.[109] However, Hong Kong was the key that could unlock a potential victory. Richmond may have been a particularly vocal critic of naval policy in the period, but in terms of the Admiralty's war planning for Japan, his arguments were favourably received in Whitehall and influenced the official strategy.[110]

The strategic value to Hong Kong's location did not necessarily come from enabling a submarine and cruiser blockade of the Japanese mainland, although that element of the war plan would have been near impossible without the territory.[111] The Admiralty's economic assessment of Japanese import requirements centred on three core assumptions. Firstly, the British Empire controlled a number of key strategic raw materials that Japan required, particularly rubber, which could be limited and then cut off if relations broke down between the two powers. Secondly, in the event of hostilities Britain was unlikely to risk upsetting America by being heavy-handed with neutral shipping crossing the Pacific, but a partial eastern blockade might limit Japan's ability to source materials via the Americas. Lastly and crucially, the Yangtze basin provided significant quantities of raw materials vital for the Japanese economy. This included alternative sources for some of those resources that were otherwise imported from the British Empire.[112] If Britain's attrition strategy was to succeed, slowly pushing Japan towards either a rash and decisive naval engagement or the negotiating table, then the Yangtze would be pivotal.

The Yangtze River basin in the 1920s, as it still does today, provided vast quantities of rice, iron ore and other raw materials for the domestic Chinese and international markets. At the river's mouth, Zhejiang and Jiangsu provinces also contained roughly half of China's manufacturing capacity, with GDP per capita levels at the time behind only Japan and the island of Taiwan in Asia, and were growing at roughly 12 per cent per annum.[113] Much of that trade flowed through Shanghai, which processed roughly half of all China's foreign trade in the 1920s and was home to a similar proportion of China's modern factories.[114] Royal Navy estimates from 1930 suggest that the Central China region provided almost two-thirds of Japan's oilseed imports and roughly one-quarter of Japan's iron ore and manganese supply (required for steel and aluminium alloys). The interlinked loss of trade routes with southern China, by blockade from Hong Kong, would further compound the problem. Those two routes combined accounted for 45 per cent of Japanese manganese imports, which were crucial for strategic heavy industrial production, such as warships, tanks and aircraft.[115] While the Korean peninsula and Manchuria provided alternative sources of some resources, the abundance of capacity and ease of transportation along the Yangtze made the region an obvious target for a wartime economic blockade. Britain's strategic theory was that victory should be possible through blockading 'the raw materials obtained from China, (upon which) Japan depends for her ability to carry on the war'.[116]

The value of an economic blockade was disputed within the Royal Navy of the time. Rear Admiral Richmond, for example, argued that Japan could easily replicate enough trade routes to overcome a general British blockade. Richmond contended that the weak-link Pacific routes would prove impossible to cut unless America sided with Britain. There is certainly logic behind that assessment. The only resource whose loss could cripple Japan quickly in a war was oil, which the United States could and did provide.[117] A distant blockade might slowly damage Japanese efforts to build large new warships, but it would do a better job of making America rich, rather than winning the war for Britain. As Admiral of the Fleet David Beatty mused in 1925, the American approach in the First World War of sitting on the sidelines while 'plucking the Chestnuts from the fire' had proven fruitful for them.[118] It was therefore one that in all likelihood would be repeated if the opportunity arose. Richmond nonetheless made the case that the Royal Navy should adopt the very same blockade approach, but with a reversed focus. His argument was based upon the assumption that any aggressive Japanese actions to increase influence in China, which might lead to a war with Britain, would also result in a military clash with Chinese forces. The primary location where that might occur was the Yangtze basin. In such a war, Richmond proposed aggressive naval attacks against Japanese supply lines, allowing the gradual destruction of the Japanese army ashore. That strategy would also comply with international law on submarine warfare, a prerequisite to American goodwill, when compared with the vague allusions to submarine attacks on merchant shipping around Japan itself.[119]

Hong Kong is over 1,400 miles closer to the Yangtze River's mouth than Singapore, a distance that would have made a British blockade of either type considerably more effective. The Royal Navy's submarines would be able to spend longer on patrol, with supply and maintenance easier with the reduced distance, particularly before the *L*-class boats were replaced by the larger *O*-class with enhanced endurance from 1929. In addition, aggressive battlecruiser or cruiser raids, similar to those undertaken by the *Kaiserliche Marine* against Britain in the First World War, would be able to strike supply routes or exposed naval patrols before falling back to the relative safety of Hong Kong's guns.[120] The 1924 Royal Naval War College syllabus on Japan argued that a potential military blockade should focus on the trade routes with China, while all diplomatic efforts should focus on encouraging America to enforce a voluntary embargo.[121] That strategy was only likely to succeed if the Royal Navy still had its key forward operating base on the Chinese coast.

As a gateway to China, Hong Kong was expected to play another crucial role. Admiral Richmond argued in 1925 that with British support, potentially including a quickly deployed expeditionary force, China could be encouraged to push Japan economically and militarily out of its footholds on the mainland.[122] While Richmond's generalized statements suggest he did not fully appreciate the fractious state of Britain's relationship with the main Chinese factions in 1925, he was one of those who helped set the groundwork for later proposals. Richmond had taken Leveson's ideas and applied them in a broader sense to Britain's grand strategy for East Asia, which then tentatively fed into official policy going into the 1930s.

Existing discussion of Britain's grand strategy has highlighted the second part of that process, but it has not acknowledged the crucial role played by Admiral Leveson and the importance of the Yangtze basin. It is highly likely that Richmond's ideas were just a restated, if refined, version of those submitted the previous year. As neighbouring station commanders, the two Admirals would have corresponded on such issues, but they also had a long history of sharing ideas. Having first worked together in 1909, they had not always seen eye-to-eye, most notably during the months Richmond served as Leveson's deputy, when he was Director of the Operations Division in late 1914.[123] Richmond's brusque and arrogant manner clashed with the 'considerate' Leveson, who was a strict adherent to naval hierarchy and protocol. By the end of the First World War, however, an unlikely bond had developed, with the two regularly socializing and debating naval issues. Richmond's comments about his friend, who he liked 'immensely', are particularly prescient: 'He never writes down his opinions and in consequence never develops them.'[124] When Leveson's rudimentary suggestion was recorded as 'controversial' and then politely shelved by Director of Plans, Captain Dudley Pound, he would not appeal out of a belief in due process. Unafraid of confrontation and rocking the boat, Richmond took up the fight, redrafted the proposals and his determined lobbying the following year was more successful, for which he has been awarded the credit.[125] Feeding into the debate over the legend or myth of Richmond's stature as one of the great naval thinkers of his time, in this one example he was certainly a talented analyst but one who matured the fruits of Leveson's imagination.

Discussion about China's military capabilities throughout Britain's war planning for East Asia is rather sporadic and says much about the attitudes of many individuals within the British establishment at the time. Flippant dismissals of Chinese military capabilities did occur on purely racial grounds. As the Director of Naval Intelligence Gerald Dickens later proposed in 1935, the Royal Navy had been guilty of regarding Asian nations as 'picturesque rather than important', with officers disbelieving that a 'coloured' nation could ever match a Western one.[126] Those unprofessional earlier assessments notwithstanding, the wider geostrategic situation was a factor behind the intermittency of serious, objective top-level debate about China's military strength. China in the early twentieth century was certainly not a first-class world power, but it was nonetheless a large country that could wield significant military clout, or at least it could in theory. With the bulk of China's strength on land, however, the Royal Navy focused on the more likely threat from Japan. Likewise, the British Army had bigger concerns elsewhere, particularly the northern border of India and the threat posed by Soviet Russia through Afghanistan.[127] When combined with the lack of a clear central authority in China after 1911 and minimal territory formally or informally held by Britain in the country, it was unlikely that China would or could directly threaten more than the furthest outposts of the Empire.

The cooperation challenge

While China and Japan did pose geostrategic challenges for the British Empire after the First World War, particularly in balancing opposing requirements, the relationships were not always combative. Throughout the 1920s, both Asian nations also cooperated with the British authorities in the region, at times providing significant tangible assistance. Along with other powers with influence in East Asia, including America, France and Italy, the varying degrees of support expected from temporary and ad hoc international arrangements influenced both the structure and operational behaviour of the China Station. Over the course of the decade it was increasingly the ability to establish a multilateral approach to threats that had a defining influence on the outcome of many potentially pivotal moments in Britain's evolving relationship with China.

Working with China to help support British interests was a difficult proposition in the 1920s, particularly as some of the most pressing concerns saw the two countries on opposite sides of the table. Trying to build common ground over extraterritoriality rights even with individual local warlords, for example, was unlikely to yield any worthwhile results. Those rights had been secured through the imposition of the 'Unequal Treaties' on China in the decades after the First Opium War (1839–42) and were a cause of significant discontent by the 1920s. Moreover, the lack of a central figure with meaningful power over the country as a whole negated the possibility of solid agreements upon which Britain could build elements of an effective collaborative defensive strategy. Even working with individual factions was problematic. The strongest faction with which Britain regularly interacted, the Guomindang, spent the first half of the decade vociferously and ideologically opposed to Britain having formal or informal imperial influence over parts of China. In addition to those historic grievances, Britain had become one of the most unpopular foreign powers in the eyes of the Chinese population, particularly in the two years after the May Thirtieth Incident in 1925, during which British-led policemen shot dead roughly a dozen protestors in Shanghai.[128] In spite of all the diplomatic difficulties, however, there was some common ground upon which it was possible to build working relationships between individual Royal Navy officers and local Chinese officials.

Joint anti-piracy work was one such area where it was relatively easy to come to an understanding. While some of what Britain classed as piracy was in fact boycott picketing, which was often either tacitly or explicitly supported by the main factions, a significant portion involved small bands that attacked all merchant shipping, regardless of the flag flown. Operations where Royal Navy warships transported Chinese troops to investigate and clear reported pirate 'nests' occurred throughout the decade. The scale, scope and frequency of such raids, however, were insufficient to materially impact the Royal Navy's gunboat force in the region. Apart from short periods when one or two gunboats were held unused in reserve, the Royal Navy was unable to reduce the number of gunboats or significantly lower the intensity at which they operated. The efforts made may have had some localized effect on shipping safety, but their real wider value was diplomatic rather than strategic.

The deeper strategic collaboration proposed by Admirals Leveson and Richmond in 1924–5 appears to have struggled to gain any tangible support during discussions within the Admiralty or Whitehall.[129] This is probably a reflection of the diplomatic realities of Britain's relationship with China in the mid-1920s, which would have made it all but impossible to secure an agreement. Indeed, the Admiralty appears to have believed that there was a strong possibility that the reverse of the two Admirals' plan might take place, with Japan securing Chinese support for a war against Britain. Suspicions about Japan's efforts to seduce China with promises of returning Hong Kong certainly lingered on into the early 1930s.[130] It was only after

1927, when the fractious relationship between Britain and the Guomindang started to soften, that an agreement of any real significance could potentially have been brokered. With the communists purged from the Guomindang, Britain having made concessions to appease Chinese anti-imperial fervour and softer rhetoric used by both sides, meaningful negotiations were a possibility. The rise of General Tanaka Giichi's government in Japan that same year, advocating an aggressive foreign policy towards China, also meant that there was growing reason for the Guomindang to be interested in securing British goodwill.[131]

From being on the verge of war in 1927, Britain moved quickly to re-establish some modest means of collaborating with China, harking back to an approach used in the last years of the Qing dynasty. Between 1904 and the 1911 Xinhai Revolution, when the programme was effectively suspended, Britain trained forty-six Chinese naval officers at the war colleges in England.[132] That process was resumed in late 1929, when twenty cadets made the journey to spend part of the following year on a gunnery training course aboard HMS *Erebus*, based out of Devonport.[133] The sudden shift in policy is all the more remarkable given that cadets from the Guomindang's Whampoa Academy were suspected of organizing many of the picket boats that had severely hampered British trade in Guangzhou in 1925.[134]

In the early 1920s, Whampoa cadets either received training in Japan or based around Japanese principles, including a nationalistic interpretation of the Bushidō mentality.[135] Offering British military education therefore provided an opportunity to swing Chinese officers' attitudes back towards European ideas, as well as build a sense of camaraderie. Indeed, shortly after the resumption of training Chinese officers in Britain, the Royal Navy sent Captain Harold Baillie-Grohman to take a post as Head of Training with the Nanjing Government's Navy. That mission was in response to a request by Admiral Chen Shaokuan, the Minister of the Navy, for British assistance in developing a new Chinese navy.[136] Tellingly, the briefing given to Baillie-Grohman by Admiral Howard Kelly at Hong Kong emphasized that his primary goal was to build friendly relationships with the Chinese officers, rather than to focus too heavily on actually training them.[137]

It was around that same point, at the end of the decade, that the Royal Navy started actively working with the Guomindang against communist groups as well as pirate bands. HMS *Aphis* was involved in a series of events on the middle Yangtze between Dongting Lake and Jiujiang (Kiukiang), for example, from towing struggling transport vessels to bombarding communist troops in support of Guomindang ground forces.[138] So long as the Guomindang was perceived to represent a clear and present threat to Britain's interests, no accommodation could be reached. Once those short-term issues were resolved, however, China became a potential part in the grand strategy to secure Britain's interests in East Asia, against the spread of communism as well as Japan.

During the years preceding 1927, in which Britain became the focus of anti-imperial sentiment in China, it was Japan that provided the assistance necessary to mitigate some of the new or growing risks. In contrast to cooperation with China, which was reluctantly desired but impractical, collaboration with Japan was often seen as disagreeable but the pragmatic choice. On a day-to-day basis, it was not unusual for the two nations' navies to work together on anti-piracy duties or in coordinating additional mutual security measures for international concessions at treaty ports. In November 1923, for example, HMS *Cicala* was despatched quickly to assist a Japanese merchant steamer near Guangzhou that had grounded while trying to escape a pirate attack.[139] Similarly, a Japanese naval squadron proceeded to Xiamen in March 1924 during a period of anti-foreign unrest at the city. Admiral Leveson reported that he was grateful for the calming influence the force had upon the area, while the Royal Navy was focused upon events around Guangzhou and Hong Kong.[140]

Even in those early years, with the Anglo-Japanese alliance a recent memory, there were signs that the two navies did not necessarily see eye-to-eye. While visiting Yantai in September 1924 the captain of HMS *Bluebell* was forced, reluctantly, to place his ship in front of Japanese guns to act as an intermediary during a dispute. A Chinese merchant steamer had accidentally hit the bow of a Japanese submarine, causing minor damage.[141] Such incidents involving submarines were not uncommon in Chinese waters, including the sinking of HMS *Poseidon* in 1931 with the loss of twenty-one lives.[142] Lieutenant Charles Drage of *Bluebell* described how both the submarine and a nearby Japanese destroyer quickly aimed their main guns at the steamer and threatened to sink it, even though the vessel's deck was crowded with civilians. Drage noted that the passengers included a number of white women, which may have precipitated the stern demand by *Bluebell's* Commander Algernon Smithwick that the Japanese not use force. The steamer's Norwegian captain reportedly later complained that the Japanese had also attempted to arrest him, until a British motor launch inspected the damaged submarine and proposed a compensation fee.[143] While British service personnel were themselves guilty of heavy-handedness at times, the uncompromising reaction and threat to foreign civilians appears to have fuelled suspicions about the reliability of Japanese servicemen among *Bluebell's* crew. Such sentiment was absent in Drage's entries prior to the incident, but became a common feature in the following months.

Similarly, in a slightly more light-hearted case from July the following year, *Bluebell* was at Fuzhou with the USS *Sacramento* trying to establish whether reports of rioting in the city were true. When the IJN *Komahashi* arrived, both *Bluebell* and *Sacramento* attempted to contact the new arrival, but to no avail. Drage recalled with amusement that both the British and American warships went so far as to light up the *Komahashi* with their ships' searchlights, which still had no effect. While the incident was apparently taken in good humour and there may have been reasons why *Komahashi* failed to respond to being hailed, the British officers regarded the move as having been a deliberate snub.[144]

A normal encounter between British and Japanese servicemen in those earlier years, however, was perhaps one similar to a dinner hosted by Governor Reginald Stubbs at Hong Kong, honouring the visit of Vice Admiral Seizō Kobayashi (Saito) in November 1923. The same Charles Drage noted that while pleasant, the evening was not particularly enjoyable and did not lead to any lasting friendships. There was no outright hostility, nor was there much success in building a sense of camaraderie.[145] Such feeling was not exclusive to the officer class, with Chief Petty Officer Douglas Poole leaving an uncharacteristically unemotional description in his journal, after attending the same official events.[146]

Nonetheless, with significant military resources at their disposal and a growing willingness to employ them, Japan became a significant participant in talks about multinational deployments to meet some of the challenges encountered in 1920s China. As a result, it was not just relatively small, reactive scenarios where cooperation was considered. During a Committee for Imperial Defence meeting in June 1925, for example, the service heads agreed that Britain was reliant upon multinational forces, particularly involving Japan, to defend its interests adequately in Northern China.[147] While it would take Britain five weeks to move an infantry brigade from India to Tanggu (Taku), even if one was available for redeployment, Japan had the men ready and could transport them in a fraction of that time. Similarly, that same month Foreign Minister Baron Kijūrō Shidehara informed his ambassador in London that the IJN was to push for greater naval cooperation with the Royal Navy, particularly on the Yangtze River, because of the wider benefits for Japan.[148] Thanks to the Government Code and Cypher School intercepting and decrypting Japanese diplomatic messages, Whitehall was aware of that desire to work together in China, although it is unclear whether the intelligence was passed onto the China Station.

The rising crisis in late 1926 going into 1927 presented a situation where deep strategic cooperation could prove particularly beneficial to both Britain and

Japan, as the Guomindang's Northern Expedition seized control of city after city along the Yangtze. Even during the early stages, however, there were the first signs that what had been discussed in theory all the way to the highest levels was not so appealing to those decision makers in practicality.

Throughout the second half of 1926, the Admiralty was supported by the British government in repeatedly strengthening the naval forces available to the commander-in-chief of the China Station, irrespective of what other powers were doing. With the Shanghai Defence Force to follow from December 1926, Britain was committing significant quantities of men and materiel in an effort to shore up its imperial prestige. Moreover, diplomatic realities meant that the kind of multinational response previously envisaged would prove extremely difficult to bring to fruition. America and Japan as the other major imperial powers operating in China were both reluctant to stand too closely alongside Britain, which had become the main focus of the Guomindang's anti-imperial rhetoric and actions.[149] The surprise with which the other powers greeted Austen Chamberlain's new policy for China, announced with the December Memorandum, highlights the fact that during this phase Britain recognized its isolation and therefore followed a unilateral approach.

As the Northern Expedition neared the larger cities of the lower Yangtze, in which Britain along with the other major powers had invested more, military rather than diplomatic concerns took priority. Proposals to form a multinational force therefore resurfaced, particularly those involving Japan. By April 1927 these ideas were being debated widely around the China Station, as recorded by Midshipman Leonard Sheppard in his official journal, while aboard HMS *Despatch*. The main plan under consideration involved ten thousand British and Japanese troops forcibly occupying key sites along the Yangtze between Hankou and Shanghai. Sheppard summarized the 'severe facts against this plan' that he perceived from discussions among his fellow officers. Firstly, a sustained deployment of thousands of British troops, in areas where there was no existing military infrastructure for stationing land forces, would come at an enormous financial cost. The potential benefits were not expected to justify that hefty bill. Secondly, such a provocative act would undermine all the good work, as they saw it, that the Navy had done up to that point in remaining neutral during China's internal conflicts. Lastly, it was felt that pre-emptively occupying Chinese territory would play into the hands of Bolshevik propaganda, weakening rather than strengthening Britain's position. Sheppard concluded that a firm but defensive military approach would be more advisable, with a focus on propaganda and diplomatic efforts to push China towards 'sensible' governance.[150]

Curiously Sheppard made no mention of an issue highlighted by Foreign Office staff during this period, that of Japan's response to the Nanjing Incident. While IJN warships were present at Nanjing, they operated separately from the Anglo-American naval force and did not open fire upon the city. Given the location of the Japanese civilians in the city, the separate evacuation was fully understood by the Royal Navy. However, to avoid being caught by the Chinese backlash after the incident, Japan's diplomats worked hard to draw a distinction between the different foreign powers. This included distributing a letter to the Chinese press blaming Britain and America for what had occurred.[151] While not entirely inaccurate in its content, the spirit of that move was not in keeping with Britain's expectations that the major powers would act in concert. It may be that junior officers in the Royal Navy, like Sheppard, were not aware of all the diplomatic complexities of the situation. Alternatively, the letter may have been accepted as an illustration of how the IJN was increasingly operating by itself and was no longer seen as a team player among the major powers.[152]

Irrespective of diplomatic disputes with Japan, the British establishment continued to consider further proposals for a joint force to secure their mutual interests. Highlighting the influence of the Tanaka government's more aggressive foreign policy, there was a rapid increase in the scale of the schemes suggested by Japan after mid-1927. In October, for example, a plan was proposed for an Anglo-Japanese military occupation of all the major railways and ports in the lower Yangtze region. The argument made by Japan's envoys was that by controlling the main transport hubs, it would be possible to force a peaceful settlement upon the two main Chinese factions. The proposal was supported by the experience of the two Imperial Japanese Army regiments, totalling eight thousand men, which had been taking up positions along the Qingdao–Jinan railway since May, in the First Shandong Expedition.[153] That deployment ended in controversy and violence the following year, as the Northern Expedition continued its advance. When Guomindang forces reached the key strategic city of Jinan, occupied by five thousand Japanese troops, disagreements and clashes soon spiralled into outright conflict. By the end of the incident thousands of Chinese troops and civilians were dead, along with a few dozen Japanese. The horrific manner in which some of the killings took place led to accusations of barbarity and fuelled the surge in hostility between the two Asian powers.[154] However, in late 1927 when the proposals were made to British officials the Shandong deployment still appeared, at least superficially, to be a successful pseudo-peacekeeping effort.[155]

Some individuals within the Foreign Office were cautiously welcoming of the proposals, but they were summarily rejected by the British armed forces. The

War Office appears to have voiced the strongest opinions, arguing that it would be unwise to have independent battalions spread across the region, as they might find themselves isolated and cut-off from support. Moreover, the British military attaché to the Foreign Office argued that in order to control all the main transport points across the lower Yangtze, which would be necessary for the plan to prove effective, it would require between three and six additional infantry divisions.[156] Given that the Shanghai Defence Force only equated to roughly one division, the plan would require Britain to at least quadruple its core land forces in China. Even using skeletal divisional structures that would have equated to roughly forty thousand men. Finding sufficient manpower to achieve that during peacetime was nigh-on impossible, from both a political and practical standpoint.

The Royal Navy was also hesitant about committing to such a plan. Policing the Yangtze and protecting the various treaty ports was already stretching the China Station's resources, even with the reinforcements it had received. Indeed, the Admiralty had pushed the prime minister into ordering the return of 208 men from the 12th Royal Marine Battalion in July 1927, roughly one-fifth of the unit's manpower. A shortage of marines back in Britain was making it 'very difficult to provide officers and men for necessary duties'.[157] Ordering a British expeditionary force into Chinese sovereign territory to seize strategic locations was a sufficiently aggressive move that would likely provoke a Chinese military response. Should that happen, forts along the Yangtze were expected to start firing on British naval and civilian vessels. The Royal Navy would therefore have had to demolish a significant number of fortifications, as a pre-emptive measure, which in itself would prove a challenging task. Such a sweep would probably also have proven ineffective, given the ease with which artillery batteries could be quickly entrenched at locations overlooking the river. As a result, Sir Miles Lampson reported to Whitehall that while he found aspects of the Japanese proposal attractive, it was militarily impractical. The British government would neither deploy enough resources to enact the plan nor authorize the use of sufficient 'coercive force' for it to prove effective.[158]

Discussion of such grand plans in the late 1920s does not disguise that in practice there was a growing belief within the British military and diplomatic corps that relations with Japan had reached a tipping point, between cooperation and confrontation. Colonel F. S. G. Piggott, commanding the nascent military intelligence establishment in East Asia, reported on this issue in February 1928. He stated that while Britain was sharing roughly 80 per cent of the intelligence it obtained on the situation in China with their Japanese colleagues, the amount being shared in return was decreasing and perhaps only amounted to half. Piggott suggested that where Japan had a direct interest in securing British assistance, particularly involving naval issues, they were willing to share information and cooperate. When that was not the case, the opposite was felt to be true.[159] It is difficult to assess how accurate Piggott's statement was, but it nonetheless illustrates the breakdown in trust between the two powers in the late 1920s.

This situation was not helped by some Royal Navy officers' attitudes towards their Japanese counterparts and the difficulty of accommodating their very different naval culture. Upon arriving at Jiujiang in May 1927, for example, Commander Louis Hamilton of HMS *Wild Swan* messaged his international counterparts, introducing himself and taking command of defending the city's international concession, as the senior naval officer present. He recorded angrily in his diary that the Japanese commander apparently ignored the message, forcing Hamilton to despatch one of his officers to investigate and 'request' a meeting. When the two men met the following day, Hamilton accepted that language was a challenge. However, his account also indicates that there was a mutual dislike on racial grounds, which reinforced an underlying dislike that Hamilton held for Japan.[160] This is a particularly curious scenario, as Hamilton was a long-term loyal follower of the then commander-in-chief, Vice Admiral Reginald Tyrwhitt, who was moderately pro-Japan by interwar Royal Navy standards and whose interactions contrasted with those of his understudy.[161]

What stands out about the relationship between Britain and Japan in China, particularly in the impact it had upon military cooperation, is the relatively steady trend observable over the decade. While individual Royal Navy officers had different opinions and racial attitudes towards their Japanese counterparts, and willingness to work with them, at any one point in time the extent of assistance offered or requested by IJN commanders was broadly similar. This suggests the IJN overall tended to dictate what degree of collaboration occurred, a consequence of the comparatively rigid IJN command structure and the resulting uniformity of behaviour, in line with their orders from Tokyo.[162] In contrast, the Royal Navy's interactions with the warships of other major powers during times of crisis could prove unpredictable.

Europe's retreat and an emergent 'special relationship'

During the 1920s France, Italy, the Netherlands, Spain and Portugal all sent small flotillas of warships to China's waterways and coastline. While the Royal Navy regularly socialized with the crews of those warships, particularly the

Dutch, only the first two nations really had sufficient naval strength in the region to have any potential, tangible impact upon Britain's strategy for East Asia.[163] When in 1927 a multinational force was amassed to defend Shanghai, for example, the second-tier participants only accounted for roughly 1 per cent of all foreign military personnel ashore.[164] Afloat the situation was much the same, with France, Italy and the Netherlands all making token displays of force, with lone warships anchored on the Huangpu River at Shanghai (see Figure 6). The majority of international warships not from Britain or Japan that were sent to the city were moored out of sight downriver.[165] As a result, the second-tier navies focused on planning a safe evacuation of their own civilians from the city, while passively acquiescing in the defence plans formulated by the major participants. Similarly, in June 1929 during the ceremonial second funeral of Doctor Sun Yat-sen, at the newly constructed mausoleum for him at Nanjing, only Britain, France, Italy, Japan and the United States had warships available to attend as symbolic gestures of respect.[166] While they infrequently provided some assistance with particular naval tasks, the Dutch, Spanish and Portuguese warships in East Asia had little impact on events in and around 1920s China.

Neither France nor Italy deployed genuinely significant numbers of warships or troops to China during the 1920s, but they are worthy of discussion in the impact they had upon the course of events. Diplomatic ties between Britain, France and Italy may have been strained at times, but on a day-to-day basis far

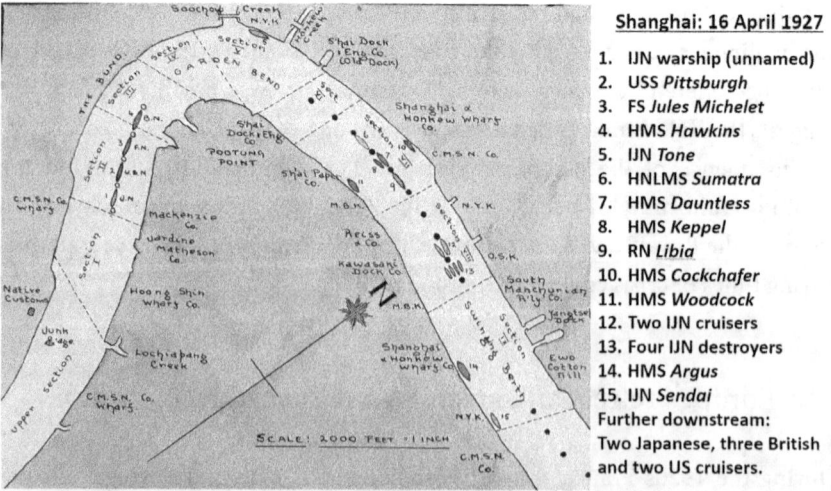

Figure 6 International warships anchored at Shanghai in April 1927.
Source: Map of Huangpu River, produced 23 April 1927, NMRN, 1991/101/67.

from home their navies tended to socialize regularly. The arrival of an Italian warship in particular often heralded much merrymaking.¹⁶⁷ Those bonds were reflected in their operational behaviour, with the three navies generally happy to cooperate. In dealing with the piracy threat around Daya Bay, for example, the French Navy agreed to adjust the routes taken by their warships as part of the Royal Navy's visible deterrent strategy. In addition, the French would join their British counterparts in conducting gunnery drills in the bay, in an effort to further enhance the impact of their passage upon the local pirate bands.¹⁶⁸ While appreciated by the British, such collaboration had negligible practical impact upon their plans for East Asia. A few additional vessels assisting intermittently was welcome, but only supplemented existing approaches. Moreover, it appears that none of those few French warships actively assisted their British counterparts during the period, including during moments when they were present on the fringes of key clashes. The *Doudart de la Grée*, for example, was recorded as having been at Wanxian throughout the disastrous events in 1926, passively observing the entire incident.¹⁶⁹ Even a British request for the French gunboat to move its moorings in order to ensure the French vessel's own safety was reportedly rejected. Likewise, at Hankou in May the following year, the local French commander chose not to coordinate his defensive plans with the joint Anglo-American preparations, although the two groups did discuss their respective approaches.¹⁷⁰

The 1927 crisis provided a rare exceptional case, when additional French military resources were sent to China. As the Northern Expedition neared Shanghai, both France and Italy adopted a policy that was broadly similar to Britain's in wanting to protect the extraterritorial status enjoyed by the International Settlement and French Concession in the city. When summarizing the positions taken by 'Friendly Powers', Major General John Duncan took comfort from having those two nations, along with Spain, as willing participants in his planned defensive line.¹⁷¹ Their stances meant that Britain had symbolic allies and would not stand alone if the worst were to happen. As a result, a section of the defensive line around Shanghai's International Settlement was nominally controlled by the Italian shore parties, although the district was actually guarded by Indian soldiers from the British Army's Twentieth Infantry Brigade.¹⁷² Likewise, on paper, the three thousand additional troops and eight cruisers from France also provided something tangible, more than just words of support.¹⁷³ In practice, however, those forces were focused solely on the French Concession and operated in a state of friendly isolation from the main Shanghai Defence Force, mirroring what was happening at Hankou.¹⁷⁴ Even during times of crisis, therefore, Britain's European allies provided little in the way of real, practical support that could assist with even temporary strategic deployments of its armed forces.

The first signs of definitive collaboration only occurred with the French Navy after the 1927 crisis and Japan's new, increasingly aggressive foreign policy.[175] The appointment of Admiral Stotz to France's East Asia fleet in late 1927 led to proposals being made at a local level that would genuinely assist with Britain's strategy for the region. Stotz and the senior officers sent with him all spoke English to a standard considerably above what was normal in the French Navy, and they had been reportedly chosen for the role based upon their comparatively anglophile views.[176] The stronger bond between Stotz's and Tyrwhitt's, then later Vice Admiral Arthur Waistell's, senior officers appears to have stimulated greater discussion of how France might be able to assist Britain, perhaps unofficially. While none of the proposals gained sufficient support for a formalized agreement, informal understandings do appear to have been reached.

If Britain had lost Hong Kong during the opening stages of a war with Japan, for example, there was a degree of willingness among France's East Asian authorities to overlook the Royal Navy using Cam Ranh Bay, on the coast of modern-day Vietnam. Roughly half-way between Singapore and Hong Kong, Cam Ranh could offer the Royal Navy warships an intermediate location to refuel and reorganize, ready for a fight off the Chinese coast. There was some disagreement over the bay's precise value among the British military officials who reported on the location, mainly over the lack of local supply sources, but overall there was general agreement that access to the bay would be strategically beneficial.[177] Ultimately, however, the absence of a signed treaty meant that the Royal Navy chose not to base their strategy on unreliable, regional good intentions. As a result, Admiral Kelly recommended in 1932 that official permission should be sought from the French government to use the bay as a staging point, although in such a format that France would be able to remain neutral.[178]

If the informal, localized agreements made between the China Station and its European allies were felt to be too tentative to rely upon, and Japan was increasingly seen as a potential foe, there was still one further actor in the region from whom Britain might draw support. As with the China Station and Japan's First Expeditionary Fleet, the USN Asiatic Fleet was tasked with projecting power across the Yellow, East China and South China seas, and along China's main rivers, but it also covered the Western Pacific. In particular, the Asiatic Fleet was required to protect America's pseudo-imperial position in the Philippines. With a considerable expanse of water to operate across, eighteen modern destroyers were based out of Cavite Navy Yard near Manila, in addition to a dozen submarines and an old cruiser.[179] A sub-command existed for inland work in China, titled the Yangtze Patrol, which started the decade with eight ancient mostly ex-Spanish gunboats that dated from before the Boxer Uprising.[180] Further strengthened by the presence of a battalion from the US Marine Corps, the Asiatic Fleet had sufficient resources potentially to influence Britain's strategic plans for the region.

Based upon their respective governments' policies throughout the decade, the USN's Asiatic Fleet and the China Station should have found it difficult to collaborate effectively. The United States was the only major power 'genuinely admired by the urban elites of Republican China', with a strong cultural presence in the country.[181] In conjunction with the relative comfort derived from that admiration, the US government tended to limit the interventions made by its armed forces. While Washington insisted on its businesses retaining access to the Chinese market, along similar lines to Britain, influential State Department officials such as John MacMurray urged restraint to avoid drawing the ire of China's warring factions. Those officials' arguments were aided by the reports submitted by America's Minister to China, Jacob Schurman. Schurman felt the main protagonists in China cared more about being respected as a modern power than they genuinely believed the communist rhetoric they sometimes espoused.[182] To some extent that hypothesis was proven correct in the case of the Guomindang, when the 1927 schism revealed the divisions between nationalists and those genuine communists. The heavy emphasis on restraint, to avoid stoking anti-American feelings among the Chinese population, was passed down along the chain of command, and sometimes featured heavily in local officials' deliberations.[183]

The contrasting approaches taken at the top level by Britain and America were at their most pronounced during times of crisis, particularly in the aftermath of the May Thirtieth Incident in 1925 and later when the Northern Expedition neared Shanghai in 1927. In both cases, Washington authorized landing seamen and marines as part of international efforts to protect their civilians and property in Shanghai, as well as other ports. There was considerable unease about the USN becoming caught up defending other nations' interests, particularly when it was not as a result of a conscious decision by American officials. In June 1925, for example, Rear Admiral Charles B. McVay Jr USN protested angrily to Rear Admiral David Anderson RN that some British civilian officials were deliberately trying to exploit America's relative neutrality. While he maintained a friendly relationship with Anderson, McVay subsequently reduced the size of the USN landing party in Shanghai.[184] Similarly, in 1927 the US government pursued a comparatively cautious policy towards the defence of its interests in Shanghai, instructing its military forces there to maintain civil order but not to engage in hostilities against Chinese troops.[185]

America's policy for China may have been heavily influenced by top-down decision making during the 1920s, but implementation is always reliant upon personnel on the scene. While the interwar USN was generally an extremely formal organization, with strict adherence to hierarchy and obeying orders, the Asiatic Fleet was not. In the Royal Navy, the China Station was the second most senior overseas command after the Mediterranean and so high-ranking roles aboard the major vessels were relatively prestigious, if not always popular. In contrast, the Asiatic Fleet was low down the list of US Fleets and was not seen as somewhere an officer could make a career. Indeed, for some ordinary crewmen the Asiatic Fleet presented the opportunity to 'hide' from various troubles that might catch up with them elsewhere.[186] By its very nature therefore, the Asiatic Fleet was somewhat maverick.

On a day-to-day basis, the Asiatic Fleet's destroyer and gunboat crews operated on the Chinese coast thousands of miles from home and frequently hundreds of miles or more from their nearest fellow USN warship. They would often be in close proximity, however, to Royal Navy warships that were equally isolated, that carried crews who spoke the same language and who had been comrades in arms just a few years beforehand. As a result the two navies' crews regularly socialized together and to a greater degree than either did with other foreign powers in China, with the possible exception of the Dutch.[187] Even in the major ports such as Shanghai where there were opportunities for other entertainment, the British organized Anglo-American boxing tournaments and USN warships invited their Royal Navy counterparts to watch the latest Hollywood films in makeshift mess-deck cinemas.[188] In October 1925 when HMS *Magnolia* was at Shantou, for example, the British crew spent most evenings attending informal cinema screenings held aboard the different USN vessels in the harbour.[189]

When at liberty ashore, Anglo-American rivalry did sometimes reveal itself, and not just among the enlisted men. In one case two officers became embroiled in an unofficial boxing match in the street, after an exchange of bravado in a bar, much to the entertainment of the enlisted seamen present. The British officer was apparently very popular with his crew, after having won the impromptu bout.[190] Arguments over girls were a relatively common cause of disagreements, along with British seamen resenting the fact that their American counterparts were better paid and flaunted it when ashore.[191] It was common, for example, for

US crews to privately hire Chinese labourers to perform their more burdensome tasks when in port.[192] While British seamen did also sometimes outsource tasks, their disposable incomes were stretched thin in comparison, in part due to higher mess bills when serving in East Asia.[193] Senior officers were generally relaxed about this fighting between their crews, particularly when compared with more serious developments with other nations. At least two clashes involving American personnel led to significant diplomatic incidents.[194] In 1919, for example, a disagreement between a few sailors in a Tianjin brothel escalated into a mass fight between roughly thirty-five US marines and one hundred Japanese servicemen. All sporting and social events between American and Japanese personnel in the city were subsequently banned to prevent further clashes. In a similar case in December 1925 four US cruisers arrived at Yantai after a long sea voyage. A quiet word appears to have been passed to Lieutenant Commander Reginald Ramsbotham who restricted shore leave for the crew of the only British warship in port. An unfortunate party of French sailors, however, set out into the town only to be badly beaten when outnumbered in a brawl with a large group of drunk American servicemen. Commonality of culture and language meant that it was easy for Anglo-American servicemen to insult each other and start fights, but also for cooler heads to calm those involved and prevent things from spiralling out of control.

Official, formal social events were different scenarios, and officers from both navies treated them extremely seriously. In one case, an American captain was forced to berate his crew after they deliberately ate all the food at a dinner they were hosting for a Royal Navy warship, including the meals intended for their guests. A second event was held shortly afterwards, during which everyone involved was ordered to be on their best behaviour.[195] While a little day-to-day friendly rivalry was tolerated, or even seen as beneficial, it could not be allowed to cause a loss of face when senior officers were present. There was undoubtedly a rivalry between the two navies, but strong bonds of friendship were formed.[196]

In practice, therefore, Asiatic Fleet crews tended to collaborate enthusiastically with their British counterparts, an attitude that extended up the full length of the two respective regional commands. Admiral Joseph Strauss USN reported in 1921, for example, an agreement with his British and Japanese counterparts to divide patrolling sections of the Yangtze between the three forces, with the Royal Navy even sometimes referring to it as 'our strength on the River'.[197] By 1924, Rear Admiral Anderson gave a speech to the Shanghai Branch of the China Association, during which he commented on the heavy collaboration with the USN and that Rear Admiral McVay was 'always most willing to co-operate'.[198]

In return, McVay stated around the same time that the two navies operated alongside each other almost as if they were the same force.[199] Often this came in the form of relatively simple acts. In the aftermath of the Wanxian Incident in 1926, for example, USS *Stewart* steamed upriver and then transported wounded British servicemen quickly back downriver for treatment, as the American vessel was considerably faster than the gunboats and steamships that were otherwise available.[200] Likewise, the commanders of HMS *Wivern* and USS *Paul Jones* were both praised for conducting a rapid and largely peaceful joint evacuation of seventy-five British and American civilians at Zhenjiang on 26 March 1927, rather than attempting two separate efforts.[201]

What that bond meant was that while officially American warships were only meant to protect their own civilians and interests, in practice they also extended their guardianship to British subjects and property, almost without question. In September 1926, for example, Commander Shaffer USN announced that his gunboat would protect the British community at Chongqing during unrest at the city, as the Royal Navy was busy responding to and dealing with the aftermath of the Wanxian Incident.[202] Moreover, the Royal Navy knew that Shaffer had been authorized to extend that protection by Admiral Clarence Williams, commanding the USN Asiatic Fleet.[203] As a result, such incidents meant that the commander-in-chief of the China Station could feel confident that British interests would be protected at more treaty ports than the Royal Navy could guarantee on its own.

Whereas Japanese warship captains rigidly adhered to the policies and approaches dictated by the IJN's high command, the Asiatic Fleet's officers operated in a relatively flexible system that enabled them to bend rules. With generally strong bonds of friendship, commonality of culture and fairly similar views about mutual Anglo-American priorities in East Asia, USN officers were more motivated to work with the Royal Navy. The events involving Shanghai in 1927 are highly illustrative of how an unofficial, regional approach was adopted by the Asiatic Fleet, which influenced how Britain responded to the crisis.

The seven USN warships and 1,200 marines stationed at Shanghai in early 1927 were officially under orders from Washington to protect only American lives and property.[204] In the event of the Guomindang attempting to seize the International Settlement violently, those forces were expected to conduct a managed evacuation of the city. Indeed, the choice by President Calvin Coolidge only to deploy ships and marines was part of a wider public display that America was looking to avoid enflaming the situation and being drawn into a conflict.[205] Whether deliberately or unintentionally, those orders were sufficiently vague to provide the American commanders on the scene with considerable room to act on their own discretion.

It has already been identified that Brigadier General Smedley Butler of the US Marine Corps sought to exploit loopholes in the orders issued by Washington to take a stronger stance in the defensive plans for Shanghai.[206] When the first Guomindang troops approached the city in late March, Admiral Williams USN and Butler argued about the marines exceeding their instructions by taking up positions in the defensive perimeter and not limiting their activities to internal policing.[207] While the marines maintained a public stance of neutrality, they were collaborating fairly heavily with the British behind the scenes. Indeed, on at least one occasion American marines were ordered back to quieter locations by Williams after that collaboration became too obvious. Butler went far beyond just words, however, in the extent to which he exceeded Washington's orders.

In the days after the Nanjing Incident, the General Staff of Britain's Shanghai Defence Force sought greater assurances about what assistance America might render. Under a heading of 'Very Secret' an unnamed British colonel confirmed that the US 'Commander' had agreed to commit his forces as part of a contingency plan for the International Settlement. As Admiral Williams was repeatedly arguing with Admiral Tyrwhitt at this point, it seems highly probable that the mystery commander was Butler.[208] In the event of a concerted attack by Guomindang forces, the US marines would prepare themselves along the border between the Settlement and the French Concession. This would be done under the guise of their existing patrols within the interior of the settlement.[209] Should the French lines look at risk of collapse, the marines would then march into the concession, evacuate all British and American civilians, and take up a defensive line along Avenue Joffre – now known as Huaihai Middle Road.[210] As a wide boulevard offering a broad field of fire, it was hoped that Avenue Joffre would be sufficiently defendable to secure the Southern flank of the International Settlement. US servicemen would then have been fully committed to the fight for Shanghai, well beyond America's official line of protecting its civilians in the city.

The secrecy and deliberate anonymity of the document highlight the sensitivity surrounding the unofficial collaboration undertaken by the US Navy and Marine Corps. Major General Duncan described the planned involvement of US marines in defending the French Concession, for example, as 'a purely unofficial understanding between General Butler and myself and a ruse on his part to over-ride his instructions'.[211] The American consul in Shanghai also threw his weight behind the secret agreement, adding to the impression of wider support among the local US representatives.[212] Those reassurances and actions, taken at a local level, were sufficient for the British high command to feel confident enough to plan for American marines to secure the southern boundary. As a result, within a week of that agreement with Butler, the 12th Royal Marine Battalion was moved from acting as a reserve force within the International Settlement to guarding British businesses in Pudong, on the other side of the Huangpu River.[213]

While Brigadier General Butler showed a particularly strong desire to work closely with his British counterparts in Shanghai, there are also plenty of suggestions that even the allegedly Anglophobe Admiral Williams was guilty of privately exceeding his orders, or at least bending them. According to Major General Duncan, Williams told him that in the event of Guomindang troops attacking Shanghai, he would 'take any action that I (i.e. Williams) considered necessary for the safety of Americans under the conditions then existing'.[214] That statement was interpreted by the British commander to mean that American forces would stay and fight, but could not be seen to place themselves in the front line.

A single comment from Williams could of course have been misconstrued by the British. There is evidence to suggest a deal was struck, however, committing both nations' armed forces to defend each other's interests at Shanghai. Williams had been faced with the challenge of defending St John's University campus, an American-run institution, situated over a mile beyond the boundaries of the International Settlement. William's orders included protecting the campus, but doing so would have left American marines isolated and in the path of the advancing Chinese forces, in breach of those same instructions. A subsequent agreement to extend the British-led defensive line to include the university was inherently linked to US marines assisting British forces if they came under attack and were at risk of being overrun (see Figure 7). It was only on this basis that Duncan agreed to uphold the agreement after his arrival in Shanghai, despite the fact that it exceeded his instructions from Whitehall.[215] Again, by itself the incident could simply have been a misunderstanding, but it adds to a pattern of incidents where Admiral Williams risked Washington's ire by going beyond the letter of his orders. At the very least it shows that the protection afforded to the American staff at the university by British forces was not wholly magnanimous.[216] Cooperation and deal-brokering between Anglo-American forces in Shanghai were far more widespread and detailed than has previously been acknowledged, with numerous officers from both nations conducting their own diplomacy.

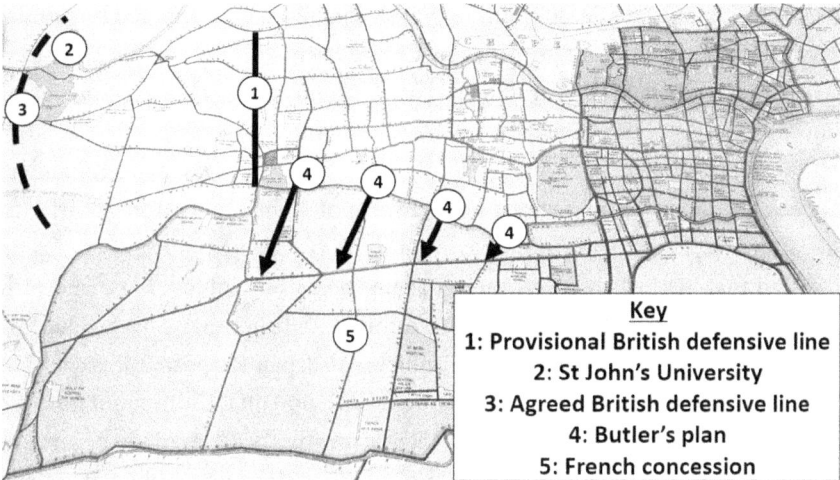

Figure 7 Foreign defensive lines for the Shanghai International Settlement 1927. *Source*: Map of Shanghai, 1919, TNA, MR 1/758.

While Britain and America's overall strategies for China may have differed in tone, there were enough practical overlaps for naval commanders to find common ground to work with. Against a background of heavy socializing, officers of the China Station and Asiatic Fleet saw each other as comrades in arms, right up to the most senior positions of command. For all the diplomatic posturing over the official stances taken over China, and top-level antagonism between the two navies, events on the scene were quite different.[217] While there was a general understanding between the foreign powers that their gunboats would assist each other, the Anglo-American bond came with an expectation of unfettered assistance. For Britain, the impact of that close relationship was similar to a force multiplier, enabling the China Station to achieve more comprehensive protective coverage across the treaty ports without an increase in its own vessels.

Summary

The military situation in East Asia during the 1920s was based around a dynamic series of relationships, which changed over the years and not always along a linear progression. As a result, it would be incorrect to focus too heavily on a narrative of declining relations between Japan and its Anglo-American rivals. Assistance was sought and rendered in both directions between Britain and

Japan throughout the decade, although it was increasingly tempered by mutual suspicion and conflicting priorities in China. Events on the mainland in East Asia, however, had far greater influence on the grand strategy between the major powers than just that of a playing field for the conflict of interests.

The plan proposed repeatedly by the Royal Navy's regional commanders to seek an understanding with China, or at least some of its leading warlords, to counter Japanese aggression may never have come to pass. Events in China dictated that the British government was unable, or less willing, to pursue such an informal alliance. Nonetheless, the Admiralty's belief that China would be on the same side as Britain in any conflict with Japan supported the decision to continue actively defending Hong Kong. With potential Chinese support the defence of the city was far from 'untenable' during the 1920s, even if it became so in later years.[218] As long as Britain held Hong Kong, it could cut the flow of raw materials and foodstuffs from Shanghai and the Yangtze in what was expected to prove a far more effective blockade strategy than targeting the Japanese mainland itself.

In contrast, the declining value of Weihai as a refuelling base to enable naval operations in North-East Asia and its exposed position to a potential Japanese attack played a role in the decision to return the territory to Chinese sovereignty. Indeed, growing concern about Japan in the last years of the decade played a part in fostering a willingness on the part of the Royal Navy and British authorities in general to work with the Guomindang. In both cases, however, geostrategic priorities were reliant upon changes in the local environment to enable those negotiations to take place.

While the narrative of Britain's declining interwar relationship with Japan broadly holds true, even if it was complicated by events in China, the situation with the other major powers was more confusing and does not fit so easily with top-level developments. Informal arrangements between individual warships in isolated areas all the way up to the regional Admirals often stood in contrast to official government policies. Decisions were regularly made to act in collaboration with international counterparts to help maintain Western dominance over East Asia, rather than purely in support of national interests. There were still some exceptions, notably Vice Admiral Tyrwhitt and Admiral Leveson who were less enthusiastic about working so closely with perceived rivals. Nonetheless, cooperation was widespread and generally acknowledged as part of life on the peacetime front line in China. Truly understanding the power dynamics at play in China during the 1920s requires an acknowledgement of that difference between what was said and agreed at the top level thousands of miles away and what happened on the scene.

Informal agreements made at a local level could have far-reaching repercussions. On a day-to-day basis it, in effect, increased the Royal Navy's protective and patrol coverage on the Yangtze and around the Chinese coast. Without that support, the Admiralty would have had to consider diverting resources from elsewhere or demand additional funding from the Treasury. With the Royal Navy's budget already under significant pressure after the First World War, neither of those were popular prospects.

The bonds of friendship and camaraderie formed between the officers and men of the China Station and Asiatic Fleet, during their service in and around China, also played an important role in further developing Britain's grand strategy for a war with Japan. Behind all the strategic debates and calculations was an almost unwavering belief of a minimum of tacit support from America in the event of such a conflict.[219] This fed into Britain's war plans, with either 'sympathetic' or 'benevolent' neutrality expected, as a minimum, from the US armed forces.[220] There remained an underlying assumption that a direct conflict with Japan was unlikely in the near future, but should the worst happen the Royal Navy felt that its blockade efforts would be supported by the United States. Likewise, it seems likely that Britain anticipated that the Asiatic Fleet would extend its protection to British civilians around China, given the plans for Royal Navy gunboats to fall back rapidly on Hong Kong, based upon their pattern of doing so during smaller crises.

Japan's growing power and its eventual shift towards an increasingly aggressive foreign policy after 1927 was a significant influencing factor in Royal Navy strategy. Up until that point, however, fears about Japan were not the only, or even the primary, influence on regional events. Instead instability in China was by far the greatest influence upon Britain's relationship with the other major powers in East Asia. At regular intervals, concerns about Japanese intentions were overridden by operational priorities in China. The Royal Navy's presence in East Asia during the 1920s, as its title suggested, was focused on events in China. It was that country and the events occurring within its borders that the Admiralty felt would decide the security of the British Empire. The Singapore strategy and a perceived direct threat from Japan only started to take centre stage at the very end of the decade, and even then, the decisions made relied upon assumptions about the future of China. Ultimately, events in China also provided Britain's Far Eastern fleet with most of its day-to-day work, and as we shall soon explore those challenges led to one of the largest-ever peacetime deployments of Royal Navy warships east of Suez.

Notes

1. E.g. John Ferris, 'The Last Decade of British Maritime Supremacy: 1919-1929', in *Far Flung Lines*, ed. Keith Neilson and Greg Kennedy (London: Cass, 1996); Bell, 'The "Singapore Strategy" and the Deterrence of Japan'; Field, *Royal Navy Strategy in the Far East*; Marder, 'The Influence of History on Sea Power'.
2. Bell, 'Our Most Exposed Outpost', pp. 61–88; Bell, 'How Are We Going to Make War?', pp. 123–41.
3. O'Brien, 'The Titan Refreshed', pp. 149–53.
4. Yoichi Hirama, 'The First World War and Japan: From the Anglo-Japanese Alliance to the Washington Treaty', *The Sea in History: The Modern World*, ed. N. A. M. Rodger (Woodbridge: Boydell & Brewer, 2017), p. 413.
5. Kwong Chi Man, Tsoi Yiu Lun, *Eastern Fortress: A Military History of Hong Kong 1840-1970* (Hong Kong: Hong Kong University Press, 2014), p. 36.
6. Overlack, 'The Force of Circumstance', p. 661.
7. Max Everest-Phillips, 'The Pre-War Fear of Japanese Espionage: Its Impact and Legacy', *Journal of Contemporary History* 42/2 (2007), 251.
8. Kwong Chi Man, 'Anglo-Japanese Alliance, the First World War, and the Defence of Hong Kong: The Emergence of the First Landward Defence Line in Hong Kong, 1898-1918', *Journal of the Royal Asiatic Society Hong Kong Branch* 54 (2014), 15.
9. Salkeld, 'Witness to the Revolution', pp. 120–35.
10. Kees van Dijk, *Pacific Strife: The Great Powers and their Political and Economic Rivalries in Asia and the Western Pacific 1870-1914* (Amsterdam: Amsterdam University Press, 2015), pp. 418–20.
11. Hirama, 'The First World War and Japan', p. 415.
12. Correlli Barnett, *The Collapse of British Power* (Gloucester: Sutton, 1984), p. 252.
13. Robert Gowen, 'Great Britain and the Twenty-One Demands of 1915: Cooperation versus Effacement', *Journal of Modern History* 43/1 (1971), 82.
14. Fung, *The Diplomacy of Imperial Retreat*, p. 5; Osterhammel, 'China', pp. 644–6.
15. Robert Bickers, *Britain in China: Community, Culture and Colonialism 1900-1949* (Manchester: Manchester University Press, 1999), p. 12.
16. Wolfgang Keller, Ben Li and Carol Shiue, 'Shanghai's Trade, China's Growth: Continuity, Recovery, and Change since the Opium Wars', *IMF Economic Review* 61/2 (2013), 347–52.
17. Bell, *The Royal Navy*, p. 63.
18. Man, 'Anglo-Japanese Alliance', p. 25.

19 Yoshio Aizawa, 'The Path towards an 'Anti-British Strategy by the Japanese Navy between the Wars', in *The History of Anglo-Japanese Relations, 1600–2000; Volume III: The Military Dimension*, ed. Ian Gow, Yoichi Hirama, John Chapman (Basingstoke: Palgrave Macmillan, 2003), p. 139.
20 War Standing Instructions for the Guidance of commander-in-chief Abroad and Senior Officers in Command of Foreign Stations, 12 January 1920, TNA, ADM 116/3124.
21 Ian Gow, 'The Royal Navy and Japan, 1921–1941', in *The History of Anglo-Japanese Relations, 1600–2000; Volume III: The Military Dimension*, ed. Ian Gow, Yoichi Hirama, John Chapman (Basingstoke: Palgrave Macmillan, 2003), p. 109.
22 Hirama, 'The First World War and Japan', p. 418.
23 Lindgren, 'A station in transition', pp. 467–73.
24 Navy List, December 1920, NLS, p. 714.
25 Navy List, December 1920, NLS, pp. 710–16.
26 Field, *Royal Navy Strategy in the Far East*, p. 11.
27 Admiralty to Atlantic Fleet commander, 4 January 1923, TNA, ADM 116/3124; War Memoranda for the Far East, November 1932, TNA, ADM 116/3118. There was a brief exception to this rule, between November 1932 and April 1933, when the Admiralty succumbed to lobbying from the China Station and ordered that the battle fleet should proceed straight to Hong Kong after refuelling at Singapore. The amendment was quickly rescinded after further discussion at the Admiralty.
28 E.g. Ship's log of HMS *Hermes* 1926, TNA, ADM 53/78830; Ship's log of HMS *Diomede* 1924–5, TNA, ADM 53/75887. Sailing with urgency at nineteen knots, *Hermes* managed the journey in three days in 1926. A battle fleet led by the slower moving Iron Dukes was expected to take a week in bad weather.
29 Memoranda by Admiral Charles Madden as Director of Planning, 3 February 1928, TNA, ADM 116/3126; War Memoranda for the Far East, November 1932, TNA, ADM 116/3118.
30 Ferris, 'The Last Decade of British Maritime Supremacy', p. 139.
31 Joint plans for events during a war with Japan, 25 October 1928, TNA, WO 106/91.
32 E.g. William R. Louis, *British Strategy in the Far East 1919–1939* (Oxford: Clarendon, 1971), p. 212; Man, 'Anglo-Japanese Alliance', p. 17.
33 Barry Hunt, *Sailor-Scholar: Admiral Sir Herbert Richmond, 1871–1946* (Waterloo: Wilfred Laurier University Press, 1982), p. 138.
34 Moretz, *Thinking Wisely*, p. 317.
35 Bell, 'Our Most Exposed Outpost', pp. 61–88; Louis, *British Strategy in the Far East*, p. 212.
36 Keith Neilson, 'Japan, Maritime Power and British Imperial Defence', *British Naval Strategy East of Suez, 1900–2000: Influences and Actions*, ed. Greg Kennedy (Abingdon: Frank Cass, 2005), p. 72.

37 Route charts for the Far East, 1933, TNA, ADM 116/3472.
38 Bell, 'Thinking the Unthinkable', p. 808.
39 Memoranda by Admiral Charles Madden as Director of Planning, 3 February 1928, TNA, ADM 116/3126.
40 War orders issued to Royal Navy station commanders, 12 January 1920, TNA, ADM 116/3124.
41 War orders issued to Royal Navy station commanders, 12 January 1920, TNA, ADM 116/3124; War orders issued to commander-in-chief Atlantic Fleet and Foreign Stations, August 1924, TNA, ADM 116/3125.
42 Osterhammel, 'China', p. 645.
43 Zhongping Chen, 'The May Fourth Movement and Provincial Warlords: A Re-examination' *Modern China* 27/2 (2011), 138.
44 Bell, *The Royal Navy*, p. 61.
45 Aizawa, 'The Path Towards', p. 140.
46 Lecture notes entitled 'China and the Policy of Japan', 1924, NMM, TRO, 401/17.
47 Part one of a lecture on 'Naval Strategy in the event of War with Japan', 1925, NMM, TRO 401/17.
48 Allan Millett, 'Assault from the sea: the development of amphibious warfare between the wars: the American, British and Japanese Experiences', in *Military Innovation in the Interwar Period*, ed. Williamson Murray and Allan Millett (Cambridge: Cambridge University Press, 1996), p. 56; Field, *Royal Navy Strategy in the Far East*, p. 87.
49 Standing instructions for commanders-in-chief during wartime issued by the Admiralty, 12 January 1920, TNA, ADM 116/3124; War orders issued by Vice Admiral Duff to the China Station, 21 February 1921, TNA, ADM 116/3133.
50 War orders issued to Royal Navy station commanders, 1920–4, TNA, ADM 116/3124.
51 War orders issued to Royal Navy station commanders, 4 January 1923, TNA, ADM 116/3124.
52 Admiral Leveson to Admiralty, 24 April 1924, TNA, ADM 116/3124.
53 Rear Admiral Richmond to Admiralty, 13 April 1925, TNA, ADM 116/3125.
54 Man & Lun, *Eastern Fortress*, pp. 57–69.
55 Report signed by Committee of Imperial Defence on Situation in China, June 1925, TNA, CAB 24/176/26.
56 Assorted correspondence about War Orders, 1920–5, TNA, ADM 116/3124.
57 Richard Wright, *China's Steam Navy* (London: Chatham, 2000), pp. 126–7.
58 Chesneau, *All the World's Fighting Ships*, p. 412.
59 Ship's log of HMS *Diomede*, 1 April 1924, TNA, ADM 53/75887.
60 Commodore Bowden-Smith to Admiral Duff, 1 January 1921, TNA, ADM 1/8593/133.
61 Wright, *China's Steam Navy*, p. 141.

62 Chesneau, *All the World's Fighting Ships*, p. 412.
63 E.g. Letter from Rear Admiral Cameron to Admiral Sinclair, 17 September 1926, TNA, ADM 116/2509; Chan, *Arming the Chinese*, p. 54.
64 David Killingray, '"A Swift Agent of Government": Air Power in British Colonial Africa, 1916–1939', *Journal of African History* 25 (1984), 429–44.
65 Jordan, *Warships after Washington*, Appendix 1: Washington Treaty 1922: Chapter 1: Article XIX.
66 Neilson, 'Japan, Maritime Power and British Imperial Defence', p. 72; Fung, *Diplomacy of Imperial Retreat*, p. 65.
67 Field, *Royal Navy Strategy in the Far East*, p. 61; Man & Lun, *Eastern Fortress*, p. 35.
68 Assorted correspondence between Admiralty planning and operations departments, 1922, TNA, ADM 116/3195.
69 Royal Navy Statistics Department memorandum on warship expenditure, 17 February 1922, TNA, ADM 116/3195.
70 Navy Estimates for 1925–6, 1925, TNA, ADM 116/2300.
71 Memoranda by Director of Planning Admiral Dudley Pound, 23 October 1923, TNA, ADM 116/3195.
72 Report on Coaling Stations maintained for Royal Navy vessels, c.1890, RNM, 1981/38/20.
73 Jianguo and Junyong, *Weihaiwei Under British Rule*, pp. 10–93.
74 Oreste Foppiani, 'The World Cruise of the US Navy in 1907–1909', *Il Politico* 71/1 (2006), 121.
75 Salkeld, 'Witness to the Revolution', p. 119.
76 Barraclough, *I Was Sailing*, p. 60.
77 Eric Dahl, 'Naval Innovation: From Coal to Oil', *Joint Force Quarterly* 2 (2000), 51.
78 Jon T. Sumida, 'British Naval Operational Logistics, 1914–1918', *Journal of Military History* 57/3 (1993), 461.
79 Papers of Sub-Lieutenant Douglas Claris, 1911–12, Imperial War Museum (IWM), Documents 10854; Steven Gray, *Steam Power and Sea Power: Coal, the Royal Navy and the British Empire, c.1870–1914* (London: Palgrave Macmillan, 2017), pp. 88, 263.
80 Salkeld, 'Witness to the Revolution', p. 119; Lambert, 'Strategic Command and Control', p. 381.
81 Martin Daunton, 'The Sea and the Economic Slump, 1919–1939', in *The Sea in History: The Modern World*, ed. N. A. M. Rodger (Woodbridge: Boydell & Brewer, 2017), p. 599.
82 Memo on fleet disposition from Navy Stores department to Admiralty, 3 March 1922, TNA, ADM 116/3195.
83 Cyril Tawney, *Grey Funnel Lines: Traditional Song & Verse of the Royal Navy 1900–1970* (London: Routledge, 1987), p. 20.

84 Gray, *Steam Power and Sea Power*, pp. 135–59.
85 Admiral Leveson to Admiralty, 14 March 1924, TNA, ADM 116/2262.
86 E.g. Intelligence report from HMS *Widgeon*, 15 October 1926, TNA, ADM 116/2509.
87 John Clegg, 'The Yangtze and the Situation in China', *Naval Review* 15/1 (1927), 207.
88 Summary of Admiralty Strategic View of the Fleet after Washington Treaty, 24 February 1922, TNA, ADM 116/3195.
89 Jordan, *Warships after Washington*, p. 63.
90 Memorandum on the distribution of the fleet by Director of Planning Dudley Pound, 22 March 1922, TNA, ADM 116/3195.
91 China Fleet Daily Summary, 15 July 1928, TNA, ADM 116/2624.
92 Report from HMS *Magnolia* to Admiral Stirling, 1 March 1929, TNA, ADM 116/2694; Foreign Office Handbook about Weihaiwei, July 1919, TNA, FO 373/4/6.
93 Appendix F to Admiralty War Orders, August 1924, TNA, ADM 116/3125.
94 E.g. Ship's log of HMS *Hermes* 1926, TNA, ADM 53/78830.
95 Interview with H. L. S. Fancourt, 1991, IWM Interview Series, Catalogue Number 12274, Reel 3, 16 minutes; Interview with H. C. Claxton, 1990, IWM Interview Series, Catalogue Number 11945, Reel 8, 9 minutes; Interview with A. Gaskin, 1986, IWM Interview Series, Catalogue Number 9344, Reel 6, 9 minutes.
96 Barraclough, *I Was Sailing*, pp. 4–60; Jianguo and Junyong, *Weihaiwei Under British Rule*, pp. 100–200.
97 Maps of Weihai, 1930, TNA, FO 93/23/36.
98 Unpublished memoirs of William Roberts, Undated, IWM, Documents 7214a.
99 Diary of Marine W. J. Greenland, 1 June 1926, Royal Marines Museum (RMM), 1978/48b; Photograph collection of Marine W. S. Phillips, 1923–5, RMM, 1998/24/C.
100 Diary of Paymaster Commander H. Miller, IWM, PP/MCR/16.
101 Jianguo and Junyong, *Weihaiwei Under British Rule*, pp. 286–90.
102 Sir Guy Francis Acheson to Sir Malcolm Ramsey, 13 February 1923, SOAS Special Collections, MS211354.
103 Correspondence between A. P. Blunt and E. E. Clark, 1923, SOAS Special Collections, CHAS/MCP/30.
104 Agreement for the Rendition of Weihaiwei, 13 February 1930, TNA, FO 93/23/36.
105 Osterhammel, 'Imperialism in Transition', p. 262.
106 Fung, *Diplomacy of Imperial Retreat*, p. 17.
107 Rear Admiral Richmond to Admiralty, 13 April 1925, TNA, ADM 116/3125.
108 'Part three' of Rear Admiral Richmond's memorandum to the Admiralty, 13 April 1925, NMM, RIC 5/1.
109 John Fisher, 'British Forward Defence in Asia during World War I', *Journal of Asian History* 37/1 (2003), 91–8.

110 Bell, 'How are we going to make war?', pp. 127–41.
111 Field, *Royal Navy Strategy in the Far East*, pp. 56–8.
112 Appendix X to War Memoranda Far East, August 1924, TNA, ADM 116/3125.
113 Debin Ma, 'Economic Growth in the Lower Yangzi Region of China in 1911–1937: A Quantitative and Historical Analysis', *Journal of Economic History* 68/2 (2008), 355–92.
114 Parks Coble, *The Shanghai Capitalists and the Nationalist Government 1927–1937* (Cambridge, MA: Harvard University Press, 1984), p. 17; Keller, Li, and Shiue, 'Shanghai's Trade, China's Growth', p. 345.
115 Appendix notebook to a lecture on the economic position of Japan, May 1930, NMM, PET/7.
116 Joint service plans for events during a war with Japan, 25 October 1928, TNA, WO 106/91.
117 Appendix notebook to a lecture on the economic position of Japan, May 1930, NMM, PET 7.
118 Memorandum sent by Admiral Beatty to Maurice Hankey, July 1925, NMM, BTY 8/8.
119 Memorandum by Rear Admiral Richmond to the Admiralty, 14 June 1924, NMM, RIC 5/1.
120 For the First World War, see Massie, *Castles of Steel*.
121 C. E. Fayle, Summary of conclusions made in the Royal Naval War College syllabus on Japan, 1924, NMM, TRO 401/17.
122 Rear Admiral Richmond to Admiralty, 13 April 1925, TNA, ADM 116/3125.
123 Nicholas Black, *The British Naval Staff in the First World War* (Woodbridge: Boydell & Brewer, 2009), pp. 248–50.
124 Arthur Marder, *Portrait of an Admiral* (London: Cape, 1952), pp. 92–108, 252, 290–3.
125 Letters and memoranda by Captain Dudley Pound regarding proposals by Admiral Leveson, June–July 1924, TNA, ADM 116/3124.
126 Lecture by Director of Naval Intelligence Captain G. C. Dickens at Greenwich War College entitled 'Japan and Sea Power', 15 May 1935, King's College London's Liddell Hart Centre for Military Archives (KCLMA), Catalogue ID 1114.
127 Clayton, 'Deceptive Might', p. 284.
128 Bickers, *Empire Made Me*, pp. 164–7; Fung, *Diplomacy of Imperial Retreat*, pp. 40–1; Osterhammel, 'China', pp. 649–50; Jay Taylor, *The Generalissimo: Chiang Kai-shek and the Struggle for Modern China* (Cambridge, MA: Harvard University Press, 2009), pp. 48–51.
129 Admiral Leveson to Admiralty, 24 April 1924, TNA, ADM 116/3124; Rear Admiral Richmond to Admiralty, 13 April 1925, TNA, ADM 116/3125.
130 Correspondence between Admiralty and Vice Admiral Waistell, January 1931, TNA, ADM 116/3118.

131 Thomas Havens, 'Japan's Enigmatic Election of 1928', *Modern Asian Studies* 11/4 (1977), 545–51; Nish, 'An Overview', pp. 612–15.
132 Appendix II to Captain Baillie-Grohman's report on the Naval Mission to Nanjing, 31 August 1932, TNA, ADM 1/8756/133.
133 Western Morning News, 11 December 1929, p. 4.
134 Vice Admiral Everett to Admiralty, 21 August 1925, TNA, FO 371/10947.
135 Elleman, *Modern Chinese Warfare*, p. 167.
136 Bruce Elleman, 'China turns to the sea, 1912–1990', in *The Sea in History: The Modern World*, ed. N. A. M. Rodger (Woodbridge: Boydell & Brewer, 2017), p. 320.
137 Report by Captain Baillie-Grohman on the Naval Mission to Nanjing, 31 August 1932, TNA, ADM 1/8756/133.
138 Private papers of J. W. Edwards, 1929–31, IWM, Documents 11614, Box 01/39/1.
139 Diary of Commander Charles Drage, 14 November 1923, IWM, PP/MCR/99, reel 2.
140 Admiral Leveson to Admiralty, 29 April 1924, TNA, ADM 116/2262.
141 Diary of Commander Drage, 7 September 1924.
142 *China Mail*, 10 June 1931, p. 1.
143 Diary of Commander Drage, 22 September 1924.
144 Diary of Commander Drage, 1 July 1925.
145 Diary of Commander Drage, 24 November 1923.
146 Journal of Chief Petty Officer Douglas Poole, 23 November 1923, Museum of the Royal Navy, 1994/253/1.
147 Minutes of Committee for Imperial Defence meeting, June 1925, TNA, CAB 24/174/26.
148 Foreign Minister Shidehara to Japan's embassy in London, 25 June 1925, TNA, HW 12/71.
149 Osterhammel, 'China', p. 651.
150 Journal of Midshipman L. C. S. Sheppard, 30 April 1927, RNM, 1991/101/67.
151 Memorandum on relations between Britain's legation to China and Japan's envoys, 1927, TNA, FO228/3507.
152 Rear Admiral Cameron to Vice Admiral Tyrwhitt, 1 May 1927, TNA, ADM 116/2510; Journal of Commander Hamilton, 12 May 1927, NMM, HTN 214.
153 Lampson's assessment of military proposals made by Japan, 31 October 1927, TNA, FO228/3507.
154 Taylor, *The Generalissimo*, pp. 79–82.
155 Nish, 'An Overview', p. 613.
156 Assorted correspondence related to Japan's military proposals, October 1927, TNA, FO228/3507.
157 Assorted correspondence between Adjutant General Hutchison RM, Lieutenant Colonel Carpenter RM, Vice Admiral Tyrwhitt, Major General Duncan, the

Admiralty and Prime Minister Baldwin, June and July 1927, TNA, ADM 1/8711/144.
158 Assorted documents outlining British military response to Japanese proposals for the occupation of the Lower Yangtze, TNA, FO228/3507.
159 Colonel F. S. G. Piggott to MI2, 21 February 1928, TNA, WO106/5258.
160 Journal of Commander Hamilton, 1927–8.
161 Personnel file for Louis Keppel Hamilton, 1 February 1919, TNA, ADM 196/145/22; Alfred Patterson, *Tyrwhitt of the Harwich Force* (London: Macdonald, 1973), p. 249.
162 Lecture on 'Japan and Sea Power' by the Director of Naval Intelligence, 15 May 1935, KCLMA, Catalogue ID 1114, Chapter two.
163 Hansard, 13 April 1927, vol. 205, cc. 342–3; de Winton, *Ships in Bottles*, p. 30; Barraclough, *I Was Sailing*, p. 60; Journal of Commander Hamilton; Interview with H. C. Claxton, 1990, IWM Interview Series, Catalogue Number 11945, Reel 8, 14–20 minutes.
164 William Braisted, *Diplomats in Blue: U.S. Naval Officers in China, 1922–1933* (Florida Scholarship Online, 2011), pp. 123–7.
165 Hansard, 23 March 1927, vol. 204, c. 401.
166 Vice Admiral Tyrwhitt to Admiralty, 14 June 1929, TNA, ADM 116/2694.
167 Martin Kitchen, *Europe between the Wars: A Political History* (London: Longman, 1988), pp. 53–64.
168 Documents supporting Cabinet discussion about piracy in China, June 1926, TNA, CAB 24/181/72.
169 Rear Admiral Cameron to Admiral Sinclair, 17 September 1926, TNA, ADM 116/2509.
170 Rear Admiral Cameron to Admiral Tyrwhitt, 1 May 1927, TNA, ADM 116/2510.
171 Major General Duncan to Earl Richard Onslow, the Undersecretary of State for War, 10 March 1927, TNA, WO 191/1.
172 Report by the General Staff of the Shanghai Defence Force, 1 April 1927, TNA, WO 191/2.
173 Hansard, 13 April 1927, vol. 205, cc. 342–3.
174 Major General Duncan to Earl Richard Onslow, the Undersecretary of State for War, 15 April 1927, TNA, WO 191/2.
175 Fung, *Diplomacy of Imperial Retreat*, p. 158.
176 Report by Consul General F. G. Gorton at Saigon, 30 January 1928, TNA, ADM 116/2624.
177 Military intelligence reports on Cam Ranh Bay, June–July 1925, TNA, WO 106/5452.
178 Vice Admiral Kelly to Admiralty, 19 January 1932, TNA, ADM 116/3118.
179 Braisted, *Diplomats in Blue*, p. 3.

180 Konstam, *Yangtze River Gunboats*, Appendix.
181 Osterhammel, 'China', pp. 644–5.
182 Braisted, *Diplomats in Blue*, pp. 8–16.
183 Diaries of Commander Drage, January 1924, IWM, PP/MCR/99.
184 Braisted, *Diplomats in Blue*, pp. 40–4.
185 General Duncan to Earl Richard Onslow, the Undersecretary of State for War, 10 March 1927, TNA, WO 191/1; Fung, *Diplomacy of Imperial Retreat*, pp. 146–51.
186 Thomas Hone and Trent Hone, *Battle Line: The United States Navy 1919–1939* (Annapolis: Naval Institute Press, 2006), pp. 158–62.
187 de Winton, *Ships in Bottles*, p. 30; Barraclough, *I Was Sailing*, p. 60; Journal of Commander Hamilton, 1927–8, NMM, HTN 214; Interview with H. C. Claxton, 1990, IWM Interview Series, Catalogue Number 11945, Reel 8, 14–20 minutes.
188 Midshipman P. W. Burnett's logbook, 1927; de Winton, *Ships in Bottles*, p. 30; Gloucester Citizen, Monday 16 January 1928.
189 Ship's log of HMS *Magnolia* December 1924–November 1925, TNA, ADM 53/80209.
190 Unpublished memoirs of Captain Ramsbotham, p. 88.
191 Interview with I. L. Wight, 1982, IWM Interview Series, Catalogue Number 6196, Reel 2, 9–11 minutes.
192 Hone and Hone, *Battle Line: The United States Navy*, p. 163.
193 Elinor Romans, 'The Internal Economy of the Royal Navy in the Twentieth Century', *Mariners Mirror* 94/1 (2008), 80.
194 Warren Tenney, '"Disturbance Not of Great Importance": The Tientsin Incident and U.S. – Japan Relations in China, 1919–1920', *Journal of American-East Asian Relations* 3/4 (1994), 325–44; Unpublished memoirs of Captain Ramsbotham, p. 86.
195 Interview with L. E. Brown, 1993, IWM Interview Series, Catalogue Number 13581, Reel 2, 7 minutes.
196 Unpublished memoirs of Captain Ramsbotham, p. 88; Interview with I. L. Wight, 1982, IWM Interview Series, Catalogue Number 6196, Reel 2, 9–11 minutes.
197 Braisted, *Diplomats in Blue*, p. 66.
198 Speech made by Rear Admiral Anderson, 11 August 1924, SOAS Special Collections, CHAS/MCP/30.
199 Braisted, *Diplomats in Blue*, p. 43.
200 'Report from an eyewitness', in *The Wanhsien Epic* (Hankow, 1926), NMRN, 1979/216, p. 21.
201 K. R. Buckley, 'The Third Destroyer Flotilla in China 1926–1928', *Naval Review* 18/1 (1930), 107.
202 Rear Admiral Cameron to Vice Admiral Alexander-Sinclair, 17 September 1926, TNA, ADM 116/2509.

203 Braisted, *Diplomats in Blue*, p. 103.
204 Hansard, 23 March 1927, vol. 204, c. 401.
205 Braisted, *Diplomats in Blue*, pp. 117–29.
206 Clifford, *Spoilt Children of Empire*, p. 230.
207 Braisted, *Diplomats in Blue*, p. 126.
208 Patterson, *Tyrwhitt of the Harwich Force*, p. 249; Braisted, *Diplomats in Blue*, pp. 126–39.
209 Clifford, *Spoilt Children of Empire*, p. 229.
210 Memorandum by a Colonel of the Shanghai Defence Force General Staff, 28 March 1927, TNA, WO 191/1. The author was probably Colonel Brownrigg, the staff officer commanding the force defending Shanghai.
211 Major General Duncan to Earl Richard Onslow, the Undersecretary of State for War, 15 April 1927, TNA, WO 191/2.
212 Memorandum by a Colonel of the Shanghai Defence Force General Staff, 28 March 1927, TNA, WO 191/1.
213 Entries in the 12th RMB War Diary, April 1927, TNA, ADM 1/8709/102.
214 Major General Duncan to Earl Richard Onslow, the Undersecretary of State for War, 10 March 1927, TNA, WO 191/1.
215 Major General Duncan to Earl Richard Onslow, the Undersecretary of State for War, 15 April 1927, TNA, WO 191/2; Clifford, *Spoilt Children of Empire*, pp. 229–30.
216 Clifford, *Spoilt Children of Empire*, pp. 202–4.
217 Roskill, *Naval Policy between the Wars*, pp. 210–15.
218 John Ferris, *The Evolution of British Strategic Policy 1919–1926* (Basingstoke: Macmillan, 1989), p. 186.
219 Neilson, 'Japan, Maritime Power and British Imperial Defence', p. 66.
220 War orders issued to Commander in Chief Atlantic Fleet and Foreign Stations, August 1924, TNA, ADM 116/3125; Vice Admiral W. Kelly to Admiralty, 19 January 1932, TNA, ADM 116/3118.

3

Adapting to a new China in a violent peace

The complicated web of international relationships spun across 1920s East Asia was caught in a whirlwind of developments. In eight short years between 1911 and 1919 the British Empire and China both underwent a series of significant transformative events. Britain was one of the many countries deeply affected by the First World War. In China, the Xinhai Revolution had triggered a wave of subsequent changes in the political environment. The influence those events had on Britain's relationship with China was delayed to some extent, given pressing domestic and other international concerns. Nonetheless, they started making their mark as the world returned to relative peace in 1919. Both the revolution in China and the First World War had a noteworthy impact upon Britain's approach to East Asia. This chapter will evaluate how that new environment changed the Royal Navy's priorities for the region and what role the Navy played in Britain's changing relationship with China during the 1920s. While the maps of Europe and the Middle East were substantially redrawn in this period and naturally attract much historical attention, the First World War had a much wider impact on world affairs.

The direct impact of the First World War on the China Station was both modest and temporary. After Admiral Graf Spee's cruiser squadron departed the region in 1914, on an eventful voyage culminating in its destruction at the Battle of the Falkland Islands, East Asia was left largely untouched by the naval war.[1] As a result, vessels and crews were redeployed west to the conflict zones, with many of the China Station's gunboats moored unmanned at Hong Kong and Shanghai. Shortly before the return to general peace in Europe, and the subsequent scuttling of the German Fleet at Scapa Flow, that process was slowly reversed. By October 1919, most of the China Station's peacetime complement had been restored, with the process completed in early 1920.[2] Just as with the elimination of Russia's Pacific Fleet during the Russo-Japanese War of 1904–5, the removal of Germany's East Asia Squadron only reordered the local balance of power.³ It did not fundamentally change the Royal Navy's desire to project power into the region, particularly on China's coast and waterways, where Britain's gunboats resumed their peacetime imperial duties.

Instead, the First World War had an indirect, but long-lasting, effect upon the China Station and the British Empire in East Asia. Financial cutbacks, greater political focus on domestic problems and changes in attitude towards both the Empire and the use of military violence all influenced the Royal Navy as a global entity. Moreover, China's previous impression of European order had been shattered. An understandable belief that 'all Europe had gone mad' weakened both imperial prestige and the argument that it was a civilizing force.⁴ Those relatively subtle, gradual changes to the China Station and Britain's imperial outposts stood in stark contrast to what had been happening in China during that period.

Entering the 1920s China was not a single unified country. While the Western world had been transfixed upon the growing diplomatic friction between the key European powers in the early 1910s, equally momentous events had taken place further east. In late 1911, the Qing regime finally succumbed to its long-term faults and weaknesses. A premature and relatively amateur attempt to provoke a revolution in Wuhan sparked a series of events that soon shattered the illusion of Qing control over China.⁵ The Qing authorities' failure to respond effectively to what was initially a localized crisis ultimately led to it developing into a nationwide movement – the Xinhai Revolution, which destroyed the Qing regime's frail domestic legitimacy.⁶ Subsequent attempts to form a Republic of China failed, due to the inability of a single leader to exercise sufficient economic, military or political power over the whole country. As a result, effective domestic power within China transferred to a collection of regional warlords.⁷ No single warlord or faction was able to build a monopoly of violence or an effective enough bureaucracy necessary to maintain control over more than its immediate region. As a result, the various warlords fought a series of civil wars, over the course of the following two decades. Estimates suggest a cumulative total of up to four hundred individual conflicts fought during the full warlord era.⁸

China of the 1920s may have been highly fragmented politically, but as a whole its geographic area remained broadly in line with the boundaries that existed for the Qing and those eventually inherited by Mao's Communist regime.⁹ China was still regarded as a single national entity at the time by many international observers as well as by the more powerful warlords, who in some cases aspired to become the new sole ruler of the country.¹⁰ Indeed, as concepts of nationalism gained wider understanding and acceptance among the ordinary population, there was a contradictory shift. More of China's four hundred million inhabitants believed in and came to see the nation as a single political entity, even if in practice the country had moved further away from that reality.

For the British diplomats and naval officers whose duties involved East Asia, contemporary reports show that there was a tendency to simplify the situation by focusing upon the two powerful northern (Beiyang) and southern (Guomindang) factions.[11] That simplification was not unique to British officials. Indeed, many of the weaker warlords would at times nominally ally themselves with one of the two leading factions.[12] There were specific circumstances when the British did consider the situation in greater detail. A 1927 RAF report, for example, on military aircraft in China examined seven main warlords' forces: the three northern clique leaders, two subdivisions of the Guomindang, the governor of Yunnan and the 'Dogmeat General'– Zhang Zongchang.[13] The latter reportedly received his nickname in reference to a gambling habit and not his culinary tastes.

Despite acknowledging those divisions, the same British officials only officially recognized and negotiated with the representatives of the supposedly ruling Chinese Republic. That government apparatus was normally controlled by the leaders of the northern faction occupying Beijing.[14] This complicated Britain's relationship with China, as perhaps unsurprisingly the northern leaders sometimes attempted to use international negotiations to their advantage in the domestic sparring. During negotiations between Chinese representatives and Britain's Foreign Office about famine relief, for example, the northern-led Chinese proposals would have seen the southern warlords shouldering the burden of debt repayments to international creditors.[15] Infighting within the cliques only further complicated the situation. There were four changes in president and twelve different premiers of the Beijing authorities alone, during the period 1916–24.[16]

To many a contemporary observer this collapse of central governance and the subsequent sustained period of violence, with no clear new leader or regime in sight, might have heralded the start of a more dangerous era for China. In reality, the assessment by the Foreign Office and Admiralty, as stated in the House of Lords by the Earl of Gosford, Archibald Acheson, in August 1925, was that little had changed. Acheson argued that under the Qing, day-to-day order had long been maintained by regional power brokers, and China's core power structure was built around 'the family, the village, and the province'.[17] This was perhaps a reasonable summary of the situation as there was considerable continuity of ruling elites between the Qing and warlord eras, with effective governance mainly taking place on a regional level.[18] Indeed, in nine of the fifteen regions to declare independence in 1911 it was the incumbent elites that led the events, to secure or enhance their existing power.[19] This continuity of local and regional Chinese officials, along with a willingness in the British authorities to cooperate with them, fed into a general maintenance of the status quo in and around the treaty ports immediately after the Xinhai Revolution.[20] It was not until the early 1920s that that modus vivendi started to break down, changing the relationship between the two countries.

Britain's stance towards China in the 1920s was not only based around the attitude that the Xinhai Revolution and subsequent warlord conflicts were part of a pattern of disorder and decentralized politics. British officials throughout the decade often considered China as being incapable of producing an effective national government, through a mixture of cultural, ideological and racial arguments. The head of the British legation in Beijing Sir Miles Lampson, for example, informed Whitehall that negotiations over debt repayments in 1928 were difficult as he felt that Chinese officials were 'quite inexperienced and politically incompetent'.[21] This was something of a feature in Lampson's memoranda as he felt the decisions made by the leaders of the factions were often reckless, with apparent lack of thought of the potential consequences. Lampson believed that this was not because those individuals did not understand what the consequences were. Instead he argued that it was because all too frequently they acted in their own self-interest, with no sense of responsibility for the wider consequences. This fed through to the Foreign Office and therefore Whitehall's understanding of each group's goals, such as during Lampson's assessment of the Guomindang's focus upon short-term goals in its relationship with Japan. He felt this was extremely dangerous because if it became 'a question of national honour with Japan – well God help the Chinese! And yet they are deliberately running that risk!'[22] While at that point in time those views were not too far from the truth, they further hardened existing imperial beliefs that China as a non-white nation was incapable of effective self-governance – without Western guidance.

Even with such dismissive views, Lampson and his Foreign Office colleagues were often at the softer end of the scale in their attitude towards Chinese officials and population. The 'Shanghailander' community of foreign settlers in the Shanghai International Settlement, predominantly of British origin, provided far less favourable reports. This included arguments that under Chinese rule foreigners would be at risk of being decapitated or worse, and there was the potential for a new Boxer Uprising.[23] Shanghailander's fearful and aggressive rhetoric resulted from the community's sense of racial superiority combined with an inability or unwillingness to understand the changes occurring in 1920s China.[24] The relatively rapid emergence of mass nationalism in the aftermath of the Xinhai Revolution did not fit with the established racial profile that British officials expected from Chinese people.[25] Jürgen Osterhammel describes it succinctly as the point when 'the Chinese had suddenly ceased being docile and deferential', at least in the way they were seen by the British.[26]

The Xinhai Revolution was a primary driver of that political and social transformation, but the First World War had also had a significant impact upon China's view of the world around it. Key to its relationship with the British Empire were Japan's Twenty-One Demands and the 1919 peace treaties. The announcement on 18 January 1915 by the Japanese foreign ministry demanding that China effectively become a Japanese protectorate had two significant impacts upon the region. Somewhat unsurprisingly it caused widespread outrage among the Chinese population, when details were made public. Coming with no forewarning, the initial move and later ultimatum also soured Britain's relationship with its Asian ally.[27] Distracted by the ongoing global conflict, the resulting surge in nationalist sentiment within China and how it might affect Britain's imperial interests was not immediately clear but was later revealed as a result of the 1919 peace settlements. The decision taken at Versailles to award Germany's former concessions in Shandong to Japan, rather than return them to Chinese sovereignty, sparked a wave of protests in what became known as the May Fourth Movement.[28] While that movement was not necessarily fervently anti-foreign, there was considerable anger over Britain's support of the move and failure to recognize China's contribution to the war effort.[29] A total of 140,000 Chinese labourers worked in Europe during the final year of the war, of whom 2,000 were buried in French graveyards.[30] Claims that British influence brought investment and development sounded hollow against that burning sense of injustice and betrayal.

The significant scale and pace of change occurring in China at the time also confused and confounded many British observers and went far beyond the influence of conflict and revolution. When Commander Cedric Holland returned to East Asia in 1928, for example, he noted with near shock how in just fifteen years the local women had undergone a complete transformation. Gone were the squeezed, bound feet and subservient attitudes. Instead the ladies were freely socializing and dining at previously male-only restaurants providing, as Holland noted with apparent pleasure, 'most intelligent' conversation.[31] Whatever Holland precisely meant is open for debate, but the rapid social change he highlighted is very clear from his account.

Against that backdrop, understanding in Whitehall of warlord China was formed around a picture of long-term weak leadership, inconsistent decisions and chaotic developments.[32] As a result, Britain's official stance was that peace and stability were unlikely to return to China in the foreseeable future, and so Britain should try to maintain a position of neutrality and non-intervention.[33] It has been suggested that this 'complacent' non-committal strategy resulted from Britain, along with many of the other major powers, not fully appreciating how significant the changes in China would be for their East Asian policies.[34] British politicians were also heavily concerned with domestic issues during the 1920s, and so events in Asia were therefore of a lower priority.[35] Bernard Porter goes so far as to argue that Stanley Baldwin, prime minister from 1924 to 1929, was uninterested in the Empire as his government 'had more important matters on their plates', particularly the 1926 General Strike.[36] In either case, the two causes were in many ways interlinked and resulted in a political focus upon domestic rather than East Asian imperial issues. A key exception to Britain's strategy of non-intervention, however, was that it should be maintained only as long as British interests were not directly threatened by the domestic sparring in China. There appears to have been a consensus of support for taking that approach and it formed a core tenet of Foreign Secretary Sir Austen Chamberlain's statements to the House of Commons towards the latter part of the decade.[37]

During the first half of the 1920s, China's main regional warlords honoured the agreements made by the Qing with Britain, such as the extraterritorial privileges held by the International Settlements, helping to avoid a British or multinational military response.[38] In addition, the regions in which Great Britain had most interest, particularly the treaty ports of Shanghai, Guangzhou (Canton), Nanjing and Tianjin (Tientsin), were less affected by actual fighting, prior to the start of the Northern Expedition. Nonetheless it was a new and different China that the Royal Navy encountered as it returned to East Asia. Distracted by domestic concerns and generally unaffected by the ongoing civil conflict, the British government assumed a non-committal neutral posture in China prior to 1925. In essence, Britain's politicians hoped that China would be reunified by a favourable regime, with whom it would be possible to work to protect and maintain the British Empire's interests.[39]

Britain's changing interests in China

The British Empire's primary interest in 1920s China remained largely unchanged from the Opium Wars, when the country was forcibly opened to Western trade, in the mid-nineteenth century. As a major trading nation, the British government sought to maintain and where possible expand the opportunities for trade in China whether proactively or following pressure from British companies. This trade was based around the cities along China's coast and major rivers, particularly a few key centres such as Shanghai and Guangzhou. Between the late nineteenth century and the 1920s, railways and modern roads had spread across China, but the web remained very thin, with the 5,237 miles of railway track only roughly equal to Britain's network in the 1850s.[40] As a result, China was still a littoral mercantile economy – its rivers, canals and coastline were the main arteries for trade.[41] British businesses dominated international trade with China prior to the First World War and were heavily engrained in that overall littoral economy. Long-term advantages in modern bulk transport shipping and trade finance, backed by the powerful Royal Navy, had allowed shipping firms such as Jardine Matheson and Co. to outmanoeuvre their rivals. British companies had also invested heavily in building local factories in key cities, much of which was constructed prior to the Xinhai Revolution.[42] That investment capital was largely concentrated in a few locations, with Shanghai alone accounting for roughly three-quarters of the £200 million in British investments in China in 1927. Events between 1919 and 1927 increased that concentration in Shanghai, but the city had long been a focal point for foreign investment. There were, however, numerous factories, mines and other business interests located in areas outside of the treaty ports.[43]

The level of British interest in China had been slowly changing in the early twentieth century, however, both on land and afloat. In particular, the First World War interrupted the pattern of global commerce and provided a boost to Japanese and American companies looking to export into China. Competition was therefore far higher going into the 1920s, although China remained a significant market for British manufacturers, accounting for over 3 per cent of total direct exports.[44] In return, the British Empire as a whole was by far China's largest trading partner, accounting for just under half of all Chinese international trade.[45] Business models were also changing rapidly, with greater focus on consumer goods branding and business networks, particularly working with local firms. This brought into question the long-term value of defending the network of smaller treaty ports and industrial centres such as Jiujiang.[46] Indeed, as anti-imperialist sentiment grew in China over the 1920s, some British firms supported a growing detachment from formal concessions. British American Tobacco, for example, decided that formal protection risked harming their business operations and damaging their image among Chinese consumers. Gunboats may open or keep open markets, but 'trade requires willing buyers and willing sellers'.[47] As a result, British businesses preferred maintaining a low profile, to try to avoid becoming the focus of protests and boycotts.[48]

Industrial and mercantile firms operating in China were not the only ones at stake from threats posed by the disorder in China. British financial institutions had significantly increased their exposure to the Chinese economy in the years before the First World War.[49] A high proportion of the railways in southern and eastern China, for example, were financed with long-term loans by British bondholders, such as the section of the Jinghu Railway between Shanghai and Nanjing, constructed in 1903.[50] However, Britain's exposure to these investments should not be overstated. In some cases, the capital raised actually came from continental European investors, with the British financiers merely acting as intermediaries. As a result, it was not always British money that was at stake when those assets were at risk. Nonetheless, that was often of little consequence in practice, as the Foreign Office was generally only aware that the paper trail went through London and did not know who owned the investments.[51]

As with global trade, the First World War had also interrupted global monetary flows and disrupted both Britain's financial influence over China and its nominal exposure to the market. The Beijing government alone took out almost CH$1 billion in foreign loans between 1916 and 1926, mostly with Japanese banks.[52] In addition, a considerable amount of borrowing had been undertaken by other warlords, with China's total external debts rising as high as CH$2.2 billion by 1925. As that debt and the interest payments required to service it soared, there was a growing risk that the loans would go into default. This was particularly true given the turmoil in the country, with the debtor governments, warlords and companies unable to generate significant, stable incomes. A mass default had the potential to cause a financial crisis in the City of London.

The British government was aware, however, that there was some flexibility in the degree of instability that could be tolerated before such a scenario might come to fruition. Loans issued by British financiers were generally secured against either tangible assets, such as railways or customs revenues.[53] The overriding concern for the British government was therefore to avoid a complete collapse of order in China that would result in both widespread loan defaults and loss of access to those securities. France was in a similar position, through a mixture of direct investment in the pre-war Chinese railway drive and indirect ownership of British-arranged loans.[54] As a result, French financiers owned roughly one-quarter of China's secured foreign debt.[55] This position was aided by British control of China's Customs Service, enabling considerable influence over ensuring that Chinese government repayments continued, a key source of debt servicing for British financiers.⁵⁶ Likewise, a contemporary assessment by the China Association indicates that most corporate loan agreements were still being honoured, with over one-quarter of all long-term British loans to Chinese railways, by value, having been repaid by the end of 1926.⁵⁷ Admittedly, there was considerable variety between different regions, with some railways effectively bankrupt due to levies imposed by local warlords.⁵⁸ However, the crucial point is that even with the regional conflicts, economic trouble and general instability in China after 1911, most loans managed by British entities were slowly being repaid.

In contrast to Britain and France, the Japanese government had guaranteed the largely unsecured ¥145 million 'Nishihara' loans issued to the Beiyang faction, leaving Japan liable for the cost should the loans enter into default.⁵⁹ This meant that the Japanese government was exposed directly to that risk, which in effect tied Japan rigidly into taking a far more active role in Chinese affairs, even if later governments had switched to a dovish foreign policy. Moreover, Japanese financiers in general had greater exposure to unsecured debt provided to Chinese warlords and businesses. The nature of the finance deal was particularly significant in this case, as it meant that Japan had no financial reason for restraint when in 1928 the Northern Expedition threatened the warlords and railways that the Japanese loans had financed.⁶⁰

Underneath all the monetary and business concerns was the human dimension. There were thousands of British civilians living and working in China, whose safety was a concern for the British authorities. Mirroring the location of business investment, the majority were resident in Shanghai's International Settlement (see Table 2), although there were smaller communities at many other treaty ports. Shanghai's British population had grown slowly in the 1910s, partly driven by children born to existing families. Those expatriates retained significant formal control over key institutions and the economic life of the city. As an illustration, roughly 2,750 of the 7,800 motor cars licensed in the city had British owners.⁶¹ Nonetheless, the overall influence of Britain's Shanghailander population was on the wane amid a rapidly changing city.⁶² Shanghai's other European populations were generally in decline after 1914. The German community almost disappeared during the First World War and the numbers of both Italians and Portuguese were steadily dropping going into the 1920s.⁶³ In contrast, the American presence had been progressively expanding, in conjunction with US business interests in the region. Likewise, a wave of Russian refugees fleeing the October Revolution added to the evolving face of the city and disrupted established racial norms.⁶⁴ Neither change was anywhere near as significant as Japan's, however, which over a

Table 2 Population of the Shanghai International Settlement 1915–20

	1915	1920	Change (%)
British	4,822	5,341	11
Japanese	7,169	10,215	42
American	1,307	2,264	73
Russian	361	1,266	251
German	1,155	280	−76
Total International Settlement	18,519	23,307	26
Chinese Shanghai	620,401	759,839	22

Note: Excluding the French concession.

Source: *Shanghai Municipal Gazette*, 18 November 1920, SMA, U1-1-985; Letter from the Canadian Trade Commissioner to the Shanghai Municipal Council, 20 August 1918, SMA, U1-2-551.

twenty-year period went from being a modest number of merchants to the largest foreign community in Shanghai by quite some margin. Britain still had a sizeable civilian population in China that it sought to protect, but other countries had a growing influence over local affairs.

As a result, Whitehall's key priority in protecting British interests in China after the First World War was the maintenance of some semblance of law and order. There was less concern over who it was that provided the desired localized stability. Over the course of the 1920s, but particularly after the launch of the Northern Expedition, Britain had the most day-to-day contact with the Guomindang, which British officials often referred to as the 'southern faction' due to its initial capital at Guangzhou. For much of the decade, however, an official policy of neutrality and a distrust of the Guomindang's links to the Soviet Union limited Britain's appetite to support any single 'faction'. The British government favoured a unified China but were content to wait and see who would emerge as the new leader, so long as there were no significant threats to Britain's interests.[65] Lord Curzon, as foreign secretary in 1924, even went so far as to criticize a memorandum from Lampson detailing events in the west and far south of China, because he felt that the power struggles in those regions had no direct impact upon the main areas of British interest. Beneath all those diplomatic considerations, Royal Navy commanders had to be more pragmatic in dealing with the challenges they faced in meeting that desire for stability.

The Royal Navy's growing piracy challenge

While the Xinhai Revolution and subsequent breakdown in centralized control over China had not significantly altered the situation for Britain in relation to its main interests in the country, there were nonetheless new challenges for Whitehall. One area in particular that posed a growing indirect threat was that of piracy. The Foreign Office copied the diplomatic strategy it had used with the Qing, by pressurizing the different warlords and factions to deal with the problem, including offering assistance. The Royal Navy occasionally provided logistical support to Guomindang forces, for example, when local officials were persuaded that it was also in their interests to deal with a troublesome pirate 'nest'.[66] This low-level cooperation, however, did not have a significant bearing on the overall relationship between Britain and the Guomindang, or other warlords. Indeed, one of the first things agreed by Hong Kong Governor Reginald Stubbs and Guomindang Foreign Minister Chén Yǒurén (Eugene Chen) when discussing the issue in 1924 was that such cooperation would be 'a strictly informal' arrangement.[67] Nor did it ultimately have a significant impact upon reducing the level of piracy in Chinese waters. With diplomatic efforts hampered and ineffective, the Admiralty was ordered to take responsibility for dealing with the threat posed to British shipping in the region. The changes that had occurred in China between 1911 and 1919, particularly during the period when global attention was transfixed on the First World War, had produced a new environment and set of challenges for the Royal Navy to deal with.

While piracy and wider banditry has featured regularly in accounts of the 1920s, there has been relatively little work done on what it actually entailed.[68] Those anti-piracy operations that went wrong in catastrophic style have seen considerable discussion, given the impact they had on anti-British sentiment in China. These included incidents on the boundary between piracy and diplomatic infringements on Britain's extraterritorial rights that involved local Chinese troops and resulted in major clashes. The Royal Navy's bombardment of Wanxian in September 1926, for example, during a botched rescue of two hijacked British merchant vessels has featured in most accounts of Britain's relationship with 1920s China.[69] The day-to-day reality was less dramatic.

With the widespread breakdown in law and order after the Xinhai Revolution and severe droughts negatively impacting the rural economies of large regions, groups of 'pirates' increasingly targeted merchant vessels on the Yangtze and Pearl Rivers as well as routes around China's coast.[70] The pirates were a mixture of organized criminal gangs, smaller groups of local brigands and in some cases simply communities of individuals driven to crime through economic necessity. This resulted in considerable variety in operating methods between the different groups, with some conducting largely amateur attacks, whereas other organized groups ran relatively sophisticated operations. Indeed, there is at least one account of pirates having paid informants in both the Guomindang's army units and aboard the Royal Navy vessels tasked with defeating them. Prior to a planned raid near Guangzhou in June 1925, General Leung had one of his subordinates arrested for passing on information to the pirate band. After a change of plans, the locally hired pilot of HMS *Robin* then warned the same group to prepare for the new alternative attack.[71] The length of the maritime trade and transport routes, with numerous bays and twists of river, made them difficult to police without a sizeable force of patrol boats. As an example of what was available, for most of the 1920s the Royal Navy had only ten gunboats covering the 1,500 miles of the Yangtze regularly used by British shipping, as well as all its tributaries and interconnected lakes.[72]

For British shipping companies, such as Jardines, the threat of piracy harming trade routes in China was not immediately a major concern given the size of their overall businesses. Losing a few insured cargoes to pirates would not significantly harm their profitability. However, repeated acts of piracy, increased costs from countermeasures and private guards or a shift in trade to better-protected merchant fleets could all harm their competitiveness over the long term. For the British Empire, it was not just the profitability of such major firms at stake. The regularity with which incidents occurred around Daya (Bias) Bay posed a growing threat to Hong Kong's position as a key trading hub, given it was only thirty-five nautical miles away. As with individual businesses, a few irregular incidents were an acceptable hazard, but a growing pattern of attacks was not. By the middle of 1924, no more than three or four days generally passed between reports of incidents involving piracy (or labelled as such) on the waterways and coast around Hong Kong.[73]

In dealing with the threat, the volume of trade itself posed a challenge. Given the levels of manpower available to the China Station, it was impossible to simply provide military or police guards for all British flagged vessels travelling along affected routes, although guards were used in some specific instances. Even during a particularly quiet month, for example, somewhere in the region of one hundred different merchant ships passed through Nanjing, of which a quarter were British-flagged vessels.[74] With a standard guard contingent of five seamen or marines per ship, roughly 120 personnel would have been required on a regular basis just for the Yangtze River.⁷⁵ During a busier phase in the summer of 1928, Rear Admiral Hugh Tweedie was forced to request additional manpower, with at least 150 men on guard duty along the Yangtze – equivalent to the crew of a large destroyer.⁷⁶

With 'run and hide' the long-established standard response by pirate groups when faced with professional fighters, such as the Royal Navy, it was rarely possible to tackle the problem on the water.⁷⁷ As a result, raids against what were considered pirate 'nests' were launched by the Royal Navy, but the sheer scale of the problem and British government concerns that raiding would stir up anti-British feeling limited the use of such operations.⁷⁸ Rear Admiral William Boyle later recalled that similar raids aimed at uncovering pirates living in normal villages were also unpopular with ordinary British seamen. Trying to unearth and punish criminals who were living amid innocent families was not what those seamen had signed up for, and conducting such operations on a regular basis would therefore negatively impact upon morale.⁷⁹ Indeed, British crewmen tended to find the normal punishment for piracy in China – public beheading – extremely distasteful and were sometimes given direct orders not to intervene when witnessing it being carried out.⁸⁰ Problems with existing tactics, the terrain and the ability of suspects to move inland and hide, along with the lack of a central government that could be held responsible meant that the Royal Navy had to develop new approaches to deal with piracy.⁸¹

To add to all these problems, one element of the piracy problem developing in the period was relatively unusual, providing a new challenge to the British authorities. There was a steady growth in the number of cases where passengers were hijacking vessels mid-journey, leading to their valuable cargoes being offloaded at prearranged locations.⁸² These incidents generally took the same format: small groups of hijackers would buy tickets to travel as passengers on vessels, with a selection of small arms concealed on their person or in their luggage. After reaching a quieter point on the journey the infiltrators would reveal their weapons and seize control of the vessel, in some cases using violence against the crew in the process. During one such incident in November 1920, for example, ten passengers aboard the Chinese steamer *Takhing* revealed hidden revolvers shortly after the vessel had left Hong Kong and seized control of the vessel. Three boats containing accomplices then joined the steamer, with the captain Cheung Fat forced to steer his ship in a failed attack on a second vessel, before taking it to Pakshawan Bay (Hebe Haven). The cargo of fourteen cases of sugar and a variety of ammunition crates was then offloaded before the pirates departed.⁸³ While that case resulted in a modest haul and no one was killed, some attacks yielded goods worth tens of thousands of dollars and others in multiple deaths.[84] In cases where no goods could be readily removed, hostages were occasionally taken for ransom. Mr J. Rasmussen of the Asiatic Petroleum Company experienced just such a fate in November 1921, although no details were made public of a ransom payment.[85] In a later example in 1928, bribes and ransoms made to secure the release of crewmembers from one merchant steamship added up to a total of $2,437 during a single journey, enough to pay for a couple of months' worth of fuel oil for the ship.[86]

Hijacking or 'internal piracy', as it was sometimes referred to, was not wholly new to the region and had first been recorded off the Chinese coast in 1890, when the SS *Namoa* was seized in an incident that caused a significant stir at Hong Kong. It had remained a relatively rare form of piracy under the Qing, however, as foreign pressure applied to local Chinese authorities often resulted in them taking a particularly hard line in punishing those individuals suspected of committing such attacks. Hijacking vessels only became a common tactic once that risk was largely removed following the Xinhai Revolution. Its popularity then soared during the First World War, through ongoing civil strife in China and a reduction in foreign gunboat patrols. By the time the China Station returned to normal duties towards the end of the decade, hijacking was well established as a regular form of piracy.[87]

As carrying passengers was an important source of income for shipowners, they were reluctant to risk driving them away by adopting stringent and intrusive security screening measures. Trials were conducted with 'protected bridges' to make it more difficult for pirates to seize control, but such efforts do not appear to have proven particularly successful. Metal grilles placed over important windows and hatches, for example, were criticized as both ineffective and against safety regulations.[88] Despite pressure from the Foreign Office, the Admiralty nominally considered hijacking to be a matter for the civil authorities in the ports of departure. Pertinently, the instructions issued to the commander-in-chief of the China Station defined piracy as involving 'predatory and violent acts', as opposed to general 'robbery upon the coast'.[89] In effect, this was an adaption of the traditional view that the Royal Navy dealt with piracy upon the high seas, with territorial waters policed by the local government.

The Royal Navy's desire to offload much of the piracy challenge on civil authorities quickly proved to be forlorn. Efforts made by city authorities were ineffectual, with pirates continuing to seize vessels even after inspections at British-administered ports. Indeed, the Shanghai Municipal Police (SMP) were already struggling to deal with the widespread smuggling of weaponry by passengers in general. Just thirty-five people were caught by the SMP over the course of 1923, for example, although they were found to be carrying 135 pistols and 10,000 rounds of ammunition between them. A key limitation was that the SMP only had authority to conduct searches when passengers came ashore. As a result, the *Shanghai Municipal Gazette* reported that weapons were quietly being offloaded to passing small local boats on the river, before ships docked and searches could take place.[90] Moreover, with punishments as light as five days in jail, the risks to individuals discovered carrying weapons were minimal, with some even released without charge.[91] While the police in other ports may have had greater success, preventing determined hijackers from successfully concealing the few handguns they might need for an attack was almost impossible. As a result, the Royal Navy was considered by many to be the only force capable of tackling the problem and so the China Station was left with its unwanted task.

Foreign Office correspondence about the piracy problem on the Yangtze River provides an interesting insight into just how reluctant the Royal Navy was about taking on the task of tackling the problem. Rear Admiral Crawford Maclachlan, as the senior naval officer on the Yangtze, was placed under considerable pressure by the British consuls in China, both those of junior rank in upper Yangtze treaty ports and those higher up the chain, such as Sir Ronald Macleay. Maclachlan politely rebuffed each argument to assign more resources towards piracy, or to request additional men, apparently tendering little or no explanation for his decision.[92] This caused Consul Lancelot Giles to apply pressure to individual gunboat officers. In one case, he successfully convinced Lieutenant Commander Colin Tucker of HMS *Woodlark* to provide armed guards for the SS *Changwo*.[93] Likewise Macleay lobbied Admiral Arthur Leveson, in vain, to assign additional men to Maclachlan's command, specifically for counter-piracy duties.[94]

The Admiralty did make requests to the Treasury for funding to replace a few of the aging China gunboats, notably the pre-Boxer Uprising *Woodcock* and *Woodlark*, to boost the resources available for anti-piracy work on the Yangtze in particular. Those older warships were due for replacement as they were 'in such a bad state that they are really useless for escort duty as they cannot keep pace even with the slowest river steamers'.[95] As a result, they were wholly unsuitable for anti-piracy patrols along their stretches of the upper Yangtze. In January 1925, four gunboats and five motorboats were included on the Navy's proposed new construction list for the following year.[96] Amid fierce battling in the British establishment over the financing of new warships during this period, however, the order for new gunboats was delayed and the motorboats rejected. It was only after the diplomatic situation in China changed and issues more pressing than piracy arose that the replacements were authorized and the first two, *Tern* and *Peterel*, were launched in 1927.[97] The earlier proposals therefore appear to have been included by the Admiralty more to assuage the Foreign Office, and as a secondary bargaining chip with the Treasury, than out of a genuine desire to improve their counter-piracy capabilities. Just as with two existing gunboats that remained idle at Malta, temporarily forgotten during discussions with the Foreign Office, the Admiralty was reluctant to divert resources to the task.[98]

The Royal Navy may have had plenty of previous experience in dealing with pirates that attacked from their own vessels, but there was little precedence for having to counter a threat such as hijacking.[99] This became a prominent feature during the Navy's official, and ultimately unsuccessful, argument that hijacking was an issue for the civil authorities.[100] As a result, not only did the newly reformed, peacetime China Station have to prepare itself quickly for dealing with a surge in piracy, it also had to develop an entirely new approach for doing so. On China's rivers, pirates could offload their loot quickly to shore or ferry it away along tributaries, long before the Navy's handful of slow-moving gunboats could reach the location. In some cases, a British gunboat arrived in time only to see pirate launches disappearing rapidly up shallow creeks, making pursuit even more challenging.[101] In such cases, the gunboat would usually just fire a few blank shells when passing the nearest village as a matter of prestige, to ensure 'that none of this valuable asset is lost'.[102] Likewise, the cruisers and sloops patrolling the coast were not designed or equipped for hostage situations. Unlike the present day, there were no helicopters or fast boats with which to transfer marines quickly to the affected vessels. Moreover, a Royal Navy response was almost wholly reliant upon their help being requested in the first place. This was rarely made in a timely manner, if at all, as pirates tended to occupy ships' wireless rooms before mayday signals could be issued. Indeed, Commander Malcom Maxwell-Scott noted in his capacity as senior naval officer on the West River in 1924 that most successful interventions occurred through his gunboats simply 'bumping' into the incidents.[103]

Britain was not the only nation involved in anti-piracy operations on China's waterways during the 1920s. Chinese gunboats were also despatched to tackle troublesome pirate groups, particularly those under Guomindang command based at Guangzhou. This included engaging armed vessels around the Pearl River Delta, as well as raiding pirate camps ashore. In some pre-planned operations, British assistance was sought and provided, with Royal Navy gunboats either actively helping to engage the gangs or passively mooring nearby as a background statement of force. Even with some form of official Chinese support, these operations were not devoid of diplomatic risks. One such raid highlights the complicated situations those junior British officers could find themselves in.

In the 1925 operation previously mentioned for having been compromised by pirate sympathizers, the British gunboats HMS *Cicala* and *Robin* were authorized to provide support after an official request for their help from General Leung. The twice replanned joint operation on 10 June led to the arrest of thirty individuals at the village of Songshi, of whom twenty-eight were suspected of being pirates and later tried as such. It had primarily been a Chinese effort in which the gunboats played a modest supporting role, helping to transport the Chinese troops and firing two high-explosive shells as a show of force.[104] After that success, a second raid was arranged against the village of Wangtong the following day. Lieutenant Commander Victor Alleyne was in overall command of the British forces aboard *Cicala*, but only the smaller *Robin* was able to navigate the shallow creek leading immediately up to the pirate group's fortified encampment.

Commanded by the 28-year-old Lieutenant Cyril Faure, *Robin* initially behaved in line with its orders, with its main gun and machine guns used to support the Chinese troops attacking the hill. When General Leung subsequently chose to go ashore from *Robin*, Faure provided him with a bodyguard of ten British seamen. Faure himself then went ashore and participated in a flanking charge by those sailors to help successfully break the pirate defensive line. Up until that point, *Robin's* comparatively light 6-pounder main gun had fired 144 shells, but to almost no effect against the solid earth banks built around the camp. Having been invited to participate by Leung, Faure's report of the incident suggests that he hoped that his bravery would be praised by senior figures.[105] Instead, he received a rebuke from the Foreign Office, with his superior officer Commodore Anselan Stirling reminding him that British service personnel were forbidden from landing on Chinese soil.[106] Praise from General Leung was sufficient to assuage Foreign Office concerns, and ultimately the Admiralty did issue a brief note of appreciation for both Alleyne and Faure's conduct, two months later.[107] It was a relatively minor infraction by an inexperienced officer, but one that had significant repercussions for both Faure himself and wider Anglo-Chinese relations. Faure responded extremely badly to the criticism directed at his actions and a month later played a pivotal role in the Shaji massacre, resulting in dozens of deaths, an incident that will be explored in greater detail later in the book.

While the collaboration between General Leung and British forces in 1925 was relatively successful in dealing with specific groups, such attempts had limited success overall. Joint efforts were often undermined by problems the Guomindang had in paying their naval staff. As a result, their gunboats often spent long periods sitting idle in port with the crews straying towards the temptation to join forces with the pirates themselves.[108] In one case on 19 June 1924, for example, some of the *Kwang Tsi*'s crew mutinied and rendezvoused with a pirate band, offloading the gunboats' machine guns and ammunition.[109] Looking around at a country facing civil conflict and famine, with little trust in local government to meet its obligations, such drastic actions may have seemed the only option for crewmen to support their families and themselves. On balance therefore, collaboration between the Royal Navy and local Chinese authorities generally had a negligible impact upon the level of piracy.

Alongside the sporadic work conducted with local Chinese forces, the Royal Navy also interacted with warships from numerous other naval powers operating in the region. The primary location where their work overlapped was on the Yangtze River, where ten Japanese, eight American and five French gunboats were regularly on patrol.[110] While river patrols do not appear to have been synchronized on a regular basis, the simple presence of additional warships proved beneficial. One foreign warship was just as dangerous as another to most pirate bands. During the 1910s there had been a significant increase in the number of gunboats from other foreign nations on the Yangtze. For example, the USN 'Yangtze Patrol', officially reformed as a separate command in 1921, acquired two brand new gunboats in 1914 capable of traversing the Yichang rapids and gorges to reach the upper stretches of the river.[111] Growing American naval influence was broadly beneficial in terms of British concerns about piracy on China's waterways. Cooperation with the American gunboats was commonplace, given a shared language and similar concerns about the safe flow of trade.[112] One British Acting-Consul, A. P. Blunt, went so far as to state that cooperation with the American naval forces was 'wholehearted' and 'went without question'.[113] There were differences in diplomatic approach to China, but day-to-day river policing was seen as mutually beneficial. Likewise, there is some evidence of official coordination of effort occurring with the French Navy. In 1926, for example, the Royal Navy and *Marine Nationale* agreed to both conduct gunnery drills regularly in Daya Bay, as a joint demonstration of force.[114]

Collaboration with the Imperial Japanese Navy was slightly more complicated, even when dealing with the threat of piracy. The gradual breakdown in Anglo-Japanese relations during and immediately after the First World War, leading ultimately to the non-renewal of the two nations' alliance in 1921, meant that interactions were not as cooperative as they once had been.[115] As the years went by, wider British geostrategic concerns about the possibility of a future war with Japan tended to surpass the possible anti-piracy benefits from formal cooperation with the second-largest naval force on China's waterways. In effect, growing support from the USN was counterbalanced by declining cooperation with the IJN. As a result, while international assistance was appreciated it did little to help Britain's conundrum over what to do with the surge in piracy, particularly in the vital waters around Hong Kong.

The piracy problem in China was made even more complicated by the emergence of anti-British strikes and boycotts after the May Thirtieth Incident in 1925. In theory, the boycott of British goods by the Chinese population in the aftermath of heavy-handed policing of a protest should have little to do with piracy. In practice, however, the two were interlinked in the minds of British officials and Royal Navy officers. Part of the reason for the blurred boundaries relates to incidents where boycott picketers detained, or attempted to detain, British shipping looking to dock in ports like Guangzhou. Hong Kong's Governor Cecil Clementi argued forcefully in a report to the Foreign Office in 1926, for example, that there should be no debate over the treatment of picketers as pirates. Clementi felt that they were 'brigands' who were also feared by the general Chinese population.[116] It did not help that some pirate groups were reported to consist of former soldiers from Guomindang forces, further obscuring the boundaries between the two.[117] As a result, local British officials and officers were either unwilling or unable to recognize, or perhaps simply unaware, that there was a distinction between pirates and picketers. When preparing for anti-piracy patrols, Royal Navy officers were almost certainly influenced in these attitudes by discussing events with British expatriates living in the region and reading the newspapers they produced.[118] Shanghailanders tended to see all displays of anti-British sentiment as threatening, with comparisons drawn to the violence of the Boxer Uprising.[119] With that in mind, it is possible to see how the maritime enforcement of the boycotts by Chinese picketers was seen as dangerous and tantamount to piracy, with those views then filtering through to naval officers on the China Station.

Of course, uncompromising attitudes labelling all protestors as pirates were not uniform. Many of the more internationally minded British businesses operating in China, including Jardines and the Hong Kong Shanghai Banking Corporation, lobbied the British government for a policy of appeasing the Chinese protestors.[120] This fits in with a general cultural divide in the International

Settlement: international businesses were a part of but not representative of the attitudes of the overall Shanghai settler community.[121] The degree of tension involved in the discussion of how to approach the boycotts was due to the relative impact on the businesses and communities involved as British exports to China plummeted. Edmund Fung gives the initial drop as being from £28.9 million in 1924 to £19.7 million in 1925, with Goto-Shibata providing a differently sourced figure of £12.1 million for 1925, leading to a further drop to just £7.5 million by 1927.[122] While the two figures are not directly comparable, they do provide an indication of the scale of impact the boycott was having.

For the servicemen aboard the warships assigned to counter the piracy threat, the discussion as to whether picketers were pirates was perhaps an academic one. They were dealing with fast-moving situations where potentially armed men were boarding ships and their precise motives were difficult to establish in the heat of the moment. Indeed, British servicemen who served in China later recounted the difficulty experienced in simply identifying who Chinese groups were, even when walking around Shanghai's streets. Both ordinary civilians and pirates often wore elements of army- or military-style clothing and could be seen carrying weapons. In return soldiers' uniforms were frequently in poor condition, sometimes supplemented by unofficial garments, and they carried a wide range of weaponry.[123]

The discussion about picketers did feed into what proactive steps might be taken and whether force could be used to prevent potential shipping seizures, rather than just respond to them.[124] Against the highly charged backdrop, the Royal Navy had to balance the potential for heavy-handedness, which would fuel support for anti-foreign groups and boycotts, with the belief that being a light touch would result in a drop in British prestige. For the naval officers involved, their training and experience in which indecisiveness was seen to risk life and ship was a poor preparation for the diplomacy this work required. Commander Roderick Miles of HMS *Hollyhock*, for instance, was lobbied by Consul Cecil Kirke to take a strong stance to an affront to British prestige in Shantou (Swatow) in 1926 when a Chinese ship ignored demands not to use a pontoon belonging to a British company.[125] Miles argued that any action he could take was legally dubious and could have made the situation worse, but Kirke vigorously protested about Miles's inaction to the Foreign Office and Admiralty. Ultimately the Admiralty supported Miles's caution, but this may have been an exception to the rule. While the Shantou incident was different to those involving piracy and hijacking, it displays some of the conflicting non-military priorities that had to be balanced by the officers making decisions in the field. In contrast, Admiral Sir

Edwyn Alexander-Sinclair, the commander-in-chief of the China Station (1925–6), proposed a direct military attack on Guangzhou in 1925 to break the boycott, which was ultimately rejected by Cabinet because Britain would clearly be seen as the aggressor.[126] Sinclair's suggestion may have been wholly unsuitable for the tense situation in China after the May Thirtieth Incident, but it was much more in line with the aggressive and assertive mindset expected of a 1920s Royal Navy officer than Miles's pragmatic approach.[127]

The involvement of British service personnel in dealing with strikes, protests and boycotts was not unique to China in this period. The Royal Navy deployed to a variety of locations worldwide including Mexico (1924) and Egypt (1926–7), as well as on mainland Britain during the General Strike (1926).[128] What proved so challenging in China, however, was the variety of situations where a small force of one or two gunboats found itself involved in an unplanned flashpoint at a remote location. Those boats were primarily tasked with countering piracy, but then found themselves facing protestors and boycott pickets. By the end of 1925 British gunboats were also involved in direct clashes with Chinese troops, particularly after the May Thirtieth Incident triggered an escalation in anti-British feeling. Between July and October 1925 alone, there were at least three incidents involving the exchange of gunfire – at Shamian (Shameen) Island and Jiangmen, both near Guangzhou, and on the Yangtze between Chongqing and Chengdu.[129] A reconciliation between Britain and the Guomindang going into early 1926 temporarily calmed the situation. Nonetheless, the events of 1925 highlighted the weakness of using a handful of gunboats to deal with unconventional threats, where there was no clear enemy to combat. Throughout these events, the China Station had not had to, or been allowed to, call upon the significant global resources of the wider Royal Navy for assistance. Within the following eighteen months, however, that would all change.

An exceptional deployment: The Shanghai task force

Most existing accounts of the Royal Navy's deployment to China in the 1920s refer to there having been a large naval force on the China Station, which peaked in 1926–7 as the Northern Expedition neared the lower Yangtze.[130] This has supported the argument that the extent of Britain's military presence in 1920s China highlights a feeling of weakness within the British establishment and therefore that the final surge was a last attempt at using gunboat diplomacy in China.[131] While not entirely inaccurate, our core understanding about the behaviour of the Royal Navy and the size of the force posted to China requires additional context.

Between early 1920 and mid-1926 the number of vessels on the China Station remained almost entirely unchanged, with a squadron of five cruisers, four sloops, twelve submarines, sixteen gunboats and various support craft.[132] The cruisers and submarines were there largely in a deterrent capacity against a possible threat from Japan, while the sloops and gunboats were used on the Chinese coast and rivers in the anti-piracy work that has already been discussed.[133] The cruisers also made brief 'flag-waving' port calls at the cities of the lower Yangtze, however, while travelling between the naval bases at Weihai and Hong Kong.[134] During that period, the only notable change in deployment came from the attachment of the aircraft carrier HMS *Hermes* in August 1925.[135] This was despite the calls from the Foreign Office to strengthen the anti-piracy gunboats patrols, which were summarily rejected by the Admiralty.[136] The argument used by the Admiralty – that there were no spare suitable vessels – is a little suspect, given that two gunboats were sat unused at Malta. That line was therefore probably just used as a pretext to avoid incurring the additional cost of recommissioning gunboats, for what the Admiralty considered to be a non-core assignment. Nonetheless, the China Station was the Royal Navy's third-largest global commitment, after the vessels assigned to 'home waters' and the Mediterranean Fleet based at Malta.[137]

The China Station's position as the Royal Navy's third-largest force was unchanged from the early 1880s, well before both the First World War and the Xinhai Revolution.[138] Indeed, after the disruption caused by wartime requirements, the Admiralty largely restored its forces in East Asia back to the region's previous complement. The only significant alteration that had occurred between 1913 and 1920, excluding the war years themselves, was the replacement of three small pre-war submarines with a dozen newer, larger variants, purpose-built to serve as a deterrent against Japan. Of the surface vessels intended for local defence, a flotilla of Victorian torpedo boat destroyers had been replaced by wartime gunboats, better suited to navigating the rapids on the middle Yangtze. Given their broadly similar size and armament, however, that change did not represent a noteworthy shift in the Station's strength.[139] Likewise, the new cruisers were all powerful combat vessels, but few of those qualitative improvements were of much value in peacetime. Indeed, a layperson at the time would have struggled to recognize the difference, beyond more obvious visible changes such as funnel layouts. China's civil wars after the Xinhai Revolution may have caused the Royal Navy some concern, but there was no notable increase in the strength of surface vessels posted to the China Station. The overall focus for the post-war Admiralty was on returning to some form of pre-war normality, to a partial 'Pax Britannica', although one increasingly reliant upon American goodwill.[140]

The comparison used between the China Station in 1913 and 1920 also treats two submarine depot ships attached after the war as full warships, based upon the way they were employed during peacetime, particularly for anti-piracy and imperial policing work. If those vessels are assessed using their on-paper, supporting-role classification, then the Station's surface warship tonnage was 10 per cent below its pre-war level in 1920. The latter approach is worth keeping in mind when evaluating the symbolic impact of the fleet, as submarine tenders were less visually imposing for reinforcing imperial prestige than fully armed warships. Both HMS *Titania* and HMS *Ambrose*, posted to the station until 1927–8, were originally designed as cargo ships, only to be hastily converted into depot ships in 1914.[141] They were functional rather than imposing, with only their white ensigns advertising that they were Royal Navy vessels and not merchant ships.

Taken over an even longer time frame, looking back to the Boxer Uprising, there was still a strong degree of continuity. The China Station remained largely unchanged throughout the ten years prior to 1913, after the armada sent in response to the Boxer Uprising had been recalled. Newer warships had replaced most of the original contingent from 1903, with a reduction in boiler room personnel and an increase in fighting attributes. HMS *Hawkins* as the flagship in 1920, for example, was faster and better equipped to respond quickly to crises than its predecessors *Minotaur* and *King Alfred*. The greater use of machinery, however, meant that *Hawkins* had fewer crewmen available to put ashore when assisting in the policing of Britain's imperial outposts. *King Alfred* had a crew of roughly 900 servicemen in 1910 and *Minotaur* 825 in 1914, whereas *Hawkins* set off for the China Station in 1919 with 732.[142] That was particularly important when managing large protests or riots in Shanghai, or other treaty ports, because manpower was far more valuable than having slightly larger calibre main guns.

Measuring the level of manpower precisely is a challenge, as replacement ships arriving on the Station were often short-handed and it could take months for them to reach full peacetime complement.[143] As a result, submarines and gunboats were occasionally left on skeleton crews in harbour, with their crews used to supplement those on other warships.[144] Nonetheless, after taking this into account the background number of service personnel permanently posted to East Asia remained relatively steady after the mid-1890s, at between 4,250 and 4,750 men, excluding the war years, until the 1930s.[145] On balance therefore,

Britain maintained a remarkably similar peacetime naval presence off the Chinese coast in late 1925 to the one present in 1903. This is particularly significant given the major changes in the Royal Navy's pattern of global deployments in the intervening years. Combined with the complete withdrawal of the neighbouring Pacific Fleet in 1912, the Royal Navy's effective presence and ability to project power in early 1920s East Asia was actually relatively modest compared with pre-war standards.[146]

The 1926–7 task force is therefore of far greater significance than previously acknowledged, as it marks an exceptional escalation in the deployment of naval force to China and East Asia in general. At its peak in April 1927, Vice Admiral Reginald Tyrwhitt had at his disposal thirteen cruisers, two aircraft carriers, twenty destroyers, four sloops, seventeen gunboats and twelve submarines, in addition to a large collection of support vessels and hired armed merchantmen.[147] The majority of the additional vessels were dispatched in the short period between September 1926 and February 1927, as the Guomindang's Northern Expedition neared the lower Yangtze.[148] In addition, a battalion of one thousand Royal Marines was formed and despatched from the UK in January and placed under Tyrwhitt's command upon its arrival at Shanghai. In total, the augmented force had roughly eight thousand extra personnel and a total displacement of roughly 200,000 tons. As an indicator of what that meant in practice, that was over two and a half times its normal level and greater than most nations' entire navies at the time, including those of the Soviet Union, Spain and the Netherlands.[149] The strengthened Royal Navy force in East Asia was over twice the strength of Japan's First Expeditionary Fleet and three times the US Navy's Asiatic Fleet, even after they had also been reinforced.[150] Along with the naval task group, the British Army assembled a Shanghai Defence Force, which peaked at seventeen thousand men, with a further two thousand to three thousand in Hong Kong. Likewise, the RAF made its first deployment of shore-based front line units to Asia, consisting of at least thirty combat aircraft split between Shanghai and Hong Kong.[151]

Taken in a global perspective the task force was a major deployment of the Royal Navy's resources at that point in time, involving roughly one-third of its cruisers in active service and over one-quarter of its fully crewed destroyers.[152] This was in addition to the China Station's normal contingent of roughly half of the Royal Navy's total sloops and gunboats in active service. As a result of what was happening in East Asia, the remaining smaller warships around the world were also forced to abandon their existing duties, with seventeen sloops covering for missing cruisers around the Mediterranean and East Indies.[153] Of the eighteen cruisers not sent to China, three were being used for 'instructional purposes' leading destroyer flotillas, four were undergoing repairs and two were obsolete pre-war variants.[154] Events in China were pushing the Royal Navy to the limit and left the Admiralty with minimal spare capacity in active service to react to any further adverse developments.

The scale of the British Army deployment has been highlighted before, given that it was larger than the eighteen thousand men sent to deal with the Boxer Uprising, but the naval task force was just as significant and symbolic.[155] The Admiralty had not deployed such a large portion of its total fleet to the east of the Suez Canal since that same crisis at the turn of the century.[156] As a result, Lieutenant Commander Joseph Kenworthy MP questioned the First Lord of the Admiralty, William Bridgeman, in the House of Commons about whether it would be advisable to bring some vessels out of reserve to strengthen those stations weakened by the commitment to China.[157] Kenworthy was a curious character who has been described as 'a man who was neither easy to work with nor necessarily very competent' in his naval career and 'a solitary figure with a penchant for tilting at naval windmills' as a politician.[158] Nonetheless, in this case he aired a valid concern about the strain the Royal Navy was being put under by events in China. A partial mobilization of Britain's naval reserves would have been an exceptional step in peacetime, particularly when not related to a threat posed by a major world power. Indeed, mobilizing the Royal Navy's reserves was not publicly discussed when Britain was on the verge of war with Turkey during the Chanak Crisis, although the Mediterranean Fleet normally had greater resources at its disposal.[159] Far from Chanak having produced a 'reaction against an active foreign policy in general', it had only changed the way the British government publicly referred to its actions.[160] In this spirit, Bridgeman's response to Kenworthy's enquiry was, unsurprisingly, an unequivocal statement that the major deployment to China was purely temporary.

Bridgeman's emphasis on the temporary nature of the strain upon the Royal Navy was borne out by events. In August 1927, instructions were sent to China for preparations to be made for the gradual withdrawal of British forces, although none that would impede the defence of Shanghai.[161] That came only three months after the full Shanghai Defence Force had arrived at the city.[162] By November the China Station was back to its normal complement of cruisers and one of the two aircraft carriers had returned to Britain for a refit. Half of the destroyers then followed shortly afterwards in May 1928.[163] Similarly, the Shanghai Defence Force had halved by June 1928, with ten of the fourteen additional battalions present in mid-1927 withdrawn by January 1929.[164] The period between late 1926 and mid-1927 therefore represents a clear, significant and sudden escalation in the commitment of force to China, even if it was only a temporary one. Had the deployment lasted longer, then further questions would almost certainly have been asked about whether the Royal Navy needed, at the very least, to mobilize sufficient reserves in order to bring its seven cruisers on reduced crews into active service.[165]

That sudden increase in British military force available in and around China resulted from a relatively rapid change in environment during the preceding eighteen months. After the May Thirtieth Incident in 1925 and over the course of 1926, there was a shift from unconventional threats, in the form of piracy, banditry, strikes and boycotts, to direct threats against Britain's core areas of interest in China, the treaty ports. In part, this resulted from rising levels of unrest and anti-British sentiment in cities along the Yangtze and particularly around Shanghai in late 1926 going into 1927. Existing tension in the city due to the SMP's heavy-handed policing of the city's Chinese residents, combined with poor rice harvests, built a background of growing hostility. The situation in Shanghai reached crisis point in early 1927 as the National Revolutionary Army of the Guomindang's Northern Expedition approached.[166] While the British Empire was not directly involved in China's civil wars, the conflict nonetheless triggered the deployment of sufficient force to dissuade armed groups from attacking foreign, particularly British, persons and property in key cities.

Prior to 1926, when conflict between warlords had neared areas of British concern, it had been on a scale modest enough for existing resources based at Hong Kong to deal with. Changes in the warlord controlling Beijing and the area around it, for example, had led to one of Britain's four army battalions permanently based in East Asia prior to 1927 being stationed at Tianjin.[167] Deploying those eight hundred troops was largely symbolic, although it did unlock new options for the orderly evacuation or temporary defence of Britain's diplomatic outpost in Beijing. Likewise within forty-eight hours of the May Thirtieth Incident, the cruisers *Diomede*, *Despatch* and *Carlisle* were all ordered to steam at high speed from Weihai to Shanghai as a temporary reinforcement for the Yangtze gunboats.[168] Over one thousand additional seamen and marines did have practical value, but the presence of three 'steel castles' was a powerful statement in itself. One need only stand beneath the glittering skyscrapers of present-day Pudong and look across at the historic Bund with a photograph of British warships at anchor during the period to appreciate just how imposing a statement of imperial grandeur such a move was. In both situations the challenge was felt to be too great for the ordinary patrols of smaller vessels to manage, but they did not require requests for additional resources from elsewhere in the Empire.

The Royal Navy was aided in defending the largest treaty ports during times of crisis by civilian defence groups, such as the Shanghai Volunteer Corps (SVC), which was first formed in 1854.[169] Those units came under the nominal authority of the ports they were tasked with protecting and whose international residents volunteered for service. In practice, however, they were controlled to a large extent by the British government. Provided with leadership from the British Army, the eight main volunteer forces in Chinese cities totalled over 1,700 men in 1925, although the SVC accounted for the overwhelming majority.[170] Roughly two-thirds of the volunteers were British or from the British Empire, but the SVC also had two dedicated American companies, one Portuguese, one Japanese, one Chinese and a small Italian unit.[171] Likewise, while most training and equipment came from the British Army, the American company in particular also received weaponry and assistance from the US government, primarily through the US Marine Corps.[172] Those militias had been formed with the intention of providing 'military protection on the cheap', to handle minor disturbances until the arrival of regular forces.[173] In doing so, volunteers generally operated within the boundaries of the treaty ports or the Shanghai International Settlement, but they were occasionally sent inland to guard factories or power stations.[174] Foreign civilians living in more remote locations, beyond the reach of those forces, were increasingly advised to move for their own safety, particularly after the May Thirtieth Incident.[175] The ongoing civil war in China continued in close proximity to the International Settlements, but foreign forces remained largely sideline observers.

Britain's global struggle against communism

The situation changed in 1926 as civil unrest and disorder in the treaty ports combined with peasant uprisings around the Yangtze basin and the approaching Northern Expedition. These factors were felt to be all the more critical because of a wave of anti-British rhetoric that Britain's officials believed was being propagated by China's communists and Soviet provocateurs, which surged after the May Thirtieth Incident.[176] Such views were particularly pronounced among the British expatriate communities in China, but applied across wide swathes of the British establishment.[177] Increasingly militant workers, demanding better deals from their foreign employers amid rampant inflation, fitted into that broader picture of a communist threat.[178] While the general population in the Yangtze basin were supportive of what they understood communism to mean, the larger uprisings were generally connected to specific issues and not driven by ideology or thoughts of revolution.[179] Nonetheless, it was the British establishment's fear of a spreading communist threat, whether imagined or real, that influenced their decisions at key moments.

What the British perceived as communist-inspired civil threats to their interests in China combined with the fear of direct military action by the Guomindang's armies. Prior to the breakdown between the Guomindang and the Chinese Communist Party in late 1926 through 1927 the Northern Expedition was still partly led by the communists.[180] While ultimately relatively short-lived, a Soviet-brokered deal in 1923 resulted in a United Front between the Guomindang and the Chinese Communist Party, with the two nominally working together as a single force in the following years. Indeed, many of the National Revolutionary armies leading the Northern Expedition were armed with weaponry either gifted or sold by the Soviet Union.[181] As a result, Britain felt that the Guomindang was 'dominated by extremists working under Soviet influence'.[182]

As the Northern Expedition approached the Yangtze's major trading hubs, particularly Hankou and Nanjing, concern grew about what would happen when the fighting reached those cities and whether anti-British rhetoric would translate into violence. After the British had been forced to evacuate and abandon their concessions on the middle and upper Yangtze, concern turned to panic as Guomindang forces neared Shanghai and its International Settlement. The SMP and SVC, and similar smaller civilian groups in other treaty ports, had provided an effective-enough defence for the foreign concessions when nearby fighting was between different warlords, such as during the 1924 Jiangsu–Zhejiang war.[183] That fighting had not been directed against foreign interests, and so the main risks came from potential collateral damage and lawlessness related to groups of disaffected defeated soldiers. In contrast, the threat posed by the National Revolutionary Army marching against those concessions, potentially linking up with agitators within the city, meant that the Royal Navy would be Britain's primary deterrent.[184]

A shift in the Royal Navy's strategy for the Yangtze region, which will be explored in greater detail in later chapters, played a role in the decision to send the vast task force in 1927. In particular, the catastrophic failure of the Wanxian expedition in September 1926 brought about a series of events that triggered a rapid reassessment of Britain's approach to inland treaty ports. The scale of the

Navy's response to the threat, however, was driven in part by the wider context of the communist influence in China fitting into what was seen as a global plot instigated by the Soviet Union against the British Empire. During a discussion of imperial defence issues in the *Naval Review*, for example, the clashes in China were directly associated with this wider battle against communism. It was considered 'common knowledge that Russia is the instigator of the hostile attitude of China towards the powers, especially the British Empire'.[185]

The British government's concern about communist involvement in the events in China in 1926–7 originated from the turmoil and bloodshed it had witnessed during the Soviet Revolution. At the height of its conventional power in the 1920s, having outlasted its main rivals in the First World War, the British Empire was comparatively relaxed about the threat of a major power conflict. The British government genuinely believed during the first half of the 1920s, for example, that Britain would not be involved in a major war for at least a decade – the infamous 'Ten Year Rule'.[186] The emergence of an ideology that could cause uprisings in its colonies and threatened to cause unrest at home therefore represented the most significant threat to the stability of the British Empire. In the eyes of its officials, communist-inspired uprisings heralded not only the prospect of weakened British power but also widespread death and destruction.

Communism was felt to be such a significant threat by Britain and the other remaining European colonial powers as to warrant the unprecedented regular exchange of information on potential communist agitators in Asia.[187] As a result, China came to be seen as the front line in a war against Soviet influence. That belief was based upon some hard evidence, and plenty of questionable reports, that Soviet agents were promoting an anti-imperial line in China, in an attempt to push out the Western powers from their lucrative and strategically valuable International Settlements.[188] Such sentiment appears to have increased over the early 1920s. Strikes by Chinese workers in Shanghai during 1921–2, for example, were primarily blamed upon economic conditions, particularly the rising cost of rice.[189] The following year, however, Captain Superintendent James McEuen of the SMP retrospectively blamed 'Bolshevik Propaganda' as having been solely responsible for stirring up trouble.[190] By 1925, Admiral of the Fleet David Beatty decisively announced to Cabinet Secretary Maurice Hankey that 'the present state of affairs in China is the result of Bolshevist exploitation of … anti-foreign feeling'.[191]

Events in China therefore added to the unrest in India and waning British influence over Persia, both of which the British establishment believed were being orchestrated by Soviet agents. For some of Britain's political elite there was a genuine fear that the Soviet Union was actively targeting the British Empire from 'Dublin to Peking', in an effort to undermine it.[192] The undersecretary of state for Foreign Affairs Ronald McNeill went so far as to state to the House of Commons in 1925 that he believed Russia was 'doing their worst, or their best, to injure us so far as they can'.[193]

The timing of the events on the Yangtze was particularly significant, given that it mirrored the growing hostility between Great Britain and the Soviet Union, which culminated in the Arcos Affair in May 1927.[194] The police raid on Arcos' offices in Moorgate, based upon information that the premises contained stolen War Office files, ultimately led to a temporary severance of diplomatic relations between the two countries.[195] The period between 1927 and 1929 was a low point in Anglo-Soviet relations, producing heightened feelings among the British political class.[196] Against the backdrop of those Anglo-Soviet clashes, the events in China were not just a concern for Great Britain in their impact upon trade but was a part of a global ideological battle against communism. The effectiveness of Britain's response to events in Shanghai and along the Yangtze was therefore felt to have a much wider potential impact upon the security of the British Empire as a whole. Sending a large task force to China did not just convey a statement to the Guomindang leadership about how serious Britain was in defending Shanghai. It was also a crude display of British imperial muscle in front of the global press as part of that wider propaganda war against the Soviet Union.

While the Guomindang's decision to purge its communist members in mid-1927 started to allay Britain's fears that it was part of a wider Soviet plot, the Guomindang still officially maintained an anti-imperial stance.[197] Even without the communists, most British officials were not particularly keen about the Guomindang, but recognized that they were more aligned with Western values and so regarded them as the lesser of two evils.[198] A memorandum from Foreign Office official Harold Porter to Whitehall in January 1928 stated that he saw the nationalist groups as being more cooperative and friendlier to deal with than other options in China, even if they were not ideal allies.[199] Likewise for the Guomindang, the shift to a friendlier attitude towards foreign powers in 1926–7 was the result of pragmatic reasoning that they needed some level of support from the great powers to secure arms deals and financing. It was in September 1926, for example, that the derogatory term 'ying fan' disappeared from Chiang Kai-shek's diary entries, in reference to the British, marking an apparent shift in attitude.[200] That subtle change was invisible to the wider world, but more tangible developments followed. The schism between nationalists and communists in 1927 was the most significant of those, removing the key barrier to the Guomindang and Britain being able to soften their rhetoric and shift towards a mutually beneficial relationship. Once that had occurred and the immediate battle against communism was seen as having been won, the Royal Navy could start withdrawing warships from their temporary attachment to the China Station.

This does not mean that the British government were entirely comfortable about the Guomindang, even without their prior communist links. As previously detailed, much of the 1927 task force dispersed around the Empire by mid-1928, but the China Station retained part of its enhanced strength on a permanent basis. A full destroyer flotilla and two additional gunboats remained until the new global conflict erupted in 1939, strengthening the Navy's capabilities in defending Britain's interests in East Asia.[201] The scale of the task force and subsequent enhanced China Station came at a cost, however, one that had a bearing on the long-term viability of the British Empire in East Asia.

The Royal Navy's previous strategy for China had generally been based around the use of force to provide short, sharp and often violent responses to potential threats, such as in the aftermath of the Boxer Uprising.[202] That emphasis on avoiding long-term sustained commitments of force became all the more important in the years leading up to the First World War, but particularly after it. Britain's politicians felt that the cost of policing the Empire was increasingly unsustainable, amid the apparent Soviet attempts to stir up hostility among colonial populations. Given the huge financial cost of the Great War, and Britain's acquisition of mandates over large tracts of the Middle East, there was a growing reluctance to be drawn into further expensive military commitments.[203]

Convoying measures introduced by the Royal Navy to counter piracy on the Yangtze were alone enough to raise questions about whether the cost was worth the results. By May 1928, for example, Rear Admiral Tweedie noted that the additional fuel consumed convoying British merchant vessels on the middle Yangtze had reached £12,000 per annum.[204] That growing background burden was nothing compared to the costs incurred as a result of the 1926 task force. To bring a single cruiser out of reserve to replace one of the eight sent to China, for example, would have cost the Navy almost £100,000 per annum just to pay the crew's wages, even before all the additional expenses associated with active service.[205] To put that figure in context, Hong Kong contributed £250,000 per year towards the Royal Navy's East Asian commitments, only a fraction of the outlay of supporting the existing squadron by the mid-1920s.[206] As a result, the economic burden of maintaining the enlarged force, if Britain was drawn into full conflict with China, would soon outweigh the value from a peripheral area of informal empire. With Treasury restrictions on the naval budget, the Admiralty were also aware that the burden of a sustained large commitment to China would require either the cancellation of new vessels or a significant increase in Hong Kong's financial contributions. It was not only the economic burden of military action, however, that played upon the minds of those in Whitehall when deciding upon how to handle the 1926 crisis in China. Britain's leaders had to consider domestic public opinion and changes in attitudes towards the use of military force and the protection of civilian lives, trends with origins back beyond the First World War.[207]

A changing role in protecting British civilians

The British government's response to the 1926 crisis was not made solely in order to intervene militarily on behalf of Britain's foreign or economic policy in the region. One of the Royal Navy's primary roles in its deployments to Chinese cities in the late 1920s was the safe evacuation of civilians during moments of crisis, both those from the British Empire and from other nations. Over the course of February 1929, for example, HMS *Magnolia* was stationed off Yantai at the start of the month only then to shuttle to Weihai and back twice, in response to the situation escalating and then calming in different locations around Shandong Province.[208] The log books from the earlier part of the decade, in contrast, show that even over the course of a number of years it was rare for those sloops to make so many visits to cities other than Shanghai and Hong Kong.[209] While *Magnolia* was shuttling between Weihai and Yantai, HMS *Foxglove* was also stationed at Yantai, in the belief that its guns and men would offer suitable short-term protection to the 495 international civilians while preparations were made for a potential evacuation.[210] Such tasks were a relatively new role for the Royal Navy in China, which came about from two changes in circumstances.

Prior to 1911, if a British civilian was not on official business in China, such as embassy staff, the British armed forces were unlikely to offer much direct protection outside of key locations. The safety of British civilians and officials was dependent upon the Foreign Office's encouraging the Qing authorities to protect foreigners, often through the threat or use of violent reprisals.[211] The murder of two British missionaries and their Chinese maid in 1902, for example, led to the Qing authorities arresting three hundred people, executing ten and more dying in jail, after coming under pressure from the Foreign Office.²¹² State-level intimidation, coercion and on-the-spot policing, using the background threat of violent retaliation by the Royal Navy, were central to how British gunboat diplomacy offered a degree of protection to those of its civilians who ventured beyond the boundaries of the Empire.²¹³ With the collapse of the Qing Empire and subsequent breakdown in central control in China after the Xinhai Revolution there was no government to be held responsible for the protection of British civilians, and so that strategy was no longer possible. As a result, while the stated priorities for the armed forces still emphasized the protection of property at Shanghai and other major trading ports, there was also a growing emphasis on proactively protecting civilians.

The switch to a proactive approach was not simply due to the new inability to reactively threaten a Chinese government capable of extending effective protection over foreign civilians – a second factor was at play. The British government felt increasingly duty-bound to use its resources to prevent the death or serious injury of its subjects around the world. General responsibility for safety outside the Empire did remain with the individual. This is illustrated by the Foreign Office instructions from early 1927 that all British civilians living upriver of Hankou should move immediately, as the Royal Navy was no longer going to maintain an active presence on the upper Yangtze.²¹⁴ The growing number of cases during the 1920s where civilians were evacuated from treaty ports ahead of potential trouble, however, indicates a steady and subtle underlying shift.

The growing number of foreigners living in China with their families, rather than as small groups of merchants and missionaries, was almost certainly a significant factor in that process. The presence of women and children, who were regarded as vulnerable and defenceless, catalysed the process leading towards the British government protecting its own expatriates.²¹⁵ This was not unique to events in China. In 1922, for example, the RAF conducted the world's first-ever airlift evacuation of civilians from Sulaymaniyah (Sulaimaniya) in present-day Iraq, in the face of growing unrest among the local population.²¹⁶ Back in China, merchant steamships were generally employed to transport such groups, but the overall process was managed by the Royal Navy. In the immediate aftermath of the May Thirtieth and Shamian Island incidents in 1925, for example, the Navy employed a P&O Steamship to move sixty women and children from Guangzhou to Hong Kong.²¹⁷

The task of potentially evacuating civilians from smaller coastal locations, as seen with *Magnolia* and *Foxglove* in northern China, was not the only way in which the new official attitude towards the protection of civilians was evident. For those occasions when events took a dangerous turn, and might result in the use of force, the British establishment had put in place a series of rules of engagement. In the orders for 'C' company 12th Royal Marine Battalion, for example, upon their deployment to the Nanjing International Settlement in August 1927, clear emphasis was placed on negotiating an agreement for the resumption of trade first. If that was not possible then the protection of property followed, but if all else failed then it was the protection of 'the lives of international persons'.[218] Throughout these orders there was a recurrent emphasis upon trying to avoid enflaming the situation by exercising restraint and avoiding casualties, for both local and foreign civilians. This is highlighted by the paragraph outlining the rules of engagement:

> The use of firearms is justifiable and may be resorted to when it appears that loss of life or serious damage to property or to protect the troops should they be in danger of being overwhelmed. <u>No more than the minimum amount of fire required to achieve this object is permissible nor can it be justified</u>.[219]

An explicit warning for the officers followed: they would be held personally accountable for any excessive violence committed by their men. The order was motivated by a desire to avoid escalating the situation through reports of British servicemen shooting unarmed civilians, rather than newfound unease with using violence against Chinese protestors. A later paragraph detailed, for example, that the use of rifle butts and bayonets was perfectly acceptable in dealing with groups of Chinese rioters, but only if they were felt to pose a risk. Over the preceding eighteen months the Royal Navy had been involved in a series of violent incidents where British servicemen had been involved in the deaths of Chinese civilians. Those in Whitehall were primarily worried about further tarnishing Britain's reputation, which might fuel anti-British protests and violence, both in China and across the region.

In the previous year, London had given clear guidance to the China Station that the Royal Navy would be given relatively free reign while operating around the coast and waterways of China, but British personnel should avoid setting foot on Chinese soil where possible.[220] That qualification came from a disagreement between Hong Kong Governor Clementi and London over the limited application of military force in China. In July 1926, for example, Clementi and his local military chiefs made the decision to send a company of troops from the East Surrey regiment, a naval aircraft and thirty policemen into Chinese territory to secure the release of Hong Kong police motorboat No.10

and its crew.²²¹ Cantonese boycott picketers had seized the motorboat after it grounded on the Chinese shore on the night of 20 July due to storms and flooding. Ultimately the incident passed peacefully when Mr Wood, a teacher taken on the expedition as a translator, persuaded the picketers to release the policemen, their boat and their weapons. Nonetheless, sending troops ashore had risked a significant escalation, with the very real possibility it could have ended in bloodshed.

As a result of the incident, an order was issued by the Admiralty to the China Station on 26 September that no British military personnel or aircraft were to be sent into or over Chinese territory without express permission from London.²²² Austen Chamberlain and Leo Amery stated that they were sympathetic to Clementi's arguments and were willing to provide a caveat giving the Royal Navy freedom of operation when afloat on Chinese waterways. However, neither of them wanted to further inflame the situation given the protests and boycott after the May Thirtieth Incident. The subsequent flurry of correspondence between London and the British officials in China over the 26 September order did not change Whitehall's new, more pragmatic stance towards China, which was announced in greater detail shortly afterwards with the December Memorandum.²²³ The main purpose of that memorandum was to shift Britain's relationship with China and negotiate some moderate concessions, but it also involved clarification about how the British government felt the Royal Navy should approach events in China.²²⁴

It would be tempting to assume that the August 1927 orders included greater emphasis upon avoiding casualties due to the violence involving British forces over the previous year. During earlier clashes in 1924 and 1925, however, there was a similar emphasis within the armed forces upon minimizing any potential violent encounters. In July 1925, for example, Lieutenant Anthony Pugsley from HMS *Widgeon* led a shore party of four naval ratings in a bayonet charge to disperse a crowd of protestors outside the international area of Chongqing. As a result of that action, a Chinese civilian was stabbed in the stomach.²²⁵ While Pugsley ensured the civilian was treated by the ship's medical officer and later released to a local hospital, and no one died as a result of the incident, Pugsley's name was notably absent from the official dispatches made to the Admiralty. This is despite a number of letters sent on behalf of British merchants from Chongqing praising his actions. From the Admiralty file, it appears that it was felt within the Navy that Pugsley should have shown greater restraint in using force. The protestors were clearly angry, but they had only thrown stones at the British servicemen and so did not present a clear threat to property or life.²²⁶ Indeed, Pugsley himself later made no mention of the incident in his autobiography, despite going into vivid detail about numerous other, sometimes trivial, developments during his first year on the upper Yangtze.²²⁷

What made the new orders issued in late 1926 different to those that had gone before was the effort made to clarify the precise details of the rules of engagement.²²⁸ A spate of Royal Navy bombardments in 1926 against targets large and small, building up to the one at Wanxian in September, contributed to renewed anti-British outbursts and highlighted the problems inherent with the existing set of vague rules, which had been set in 1920.²²⁹ Designed to cover a range of scenarios that might be encountered by the armed forces around the world, the emphasis in 1920 had been upon the judgement of the individual officer in command. While some officers exercised caution, others acted disproportionately, although the actions in both cases could still be well within the bounds of the guidance they had received. As a result, frequent new orders and guidelines were issued to the China station from October 1926 into early 1927, culminating in the comparatively comprehensive set of instructions issued by Cabinet in May 1927.²³⁰

This is not to say that those rules established in 1920 remained identical throughout the period up until 1926. Faults with the orders issued to the relatively inexperienced junior commanders of its China gunboats had been identified as early as 1920, leading to discussions about potential revisions. One major amendment that would have clarified when violence was considered acceptable was dropped, however, as there was concern that the new definition might allow officers to simply act as they saw fit.²³¹ The Admiralty's unwillingness to reduce the freedoms afforded to its regional commanders and Foreign Office objections about recognizing combatants in China as belligerents meant that such efforts to improve significantly the instructions issued to gunboat commanders failed.²³²

By itself clearer guidance from Whitehall would not have guaranteed the proportionate use of force. Even with the sudden impetus in late 1926 to improve the rules of engagement, each round of instructions from Cabinet contained major revisions, intended to overcome areas where previous versions had been vague. The final May 1927 orders, for example, included clauses intended to prevent a repeat of the Nanjing Incident, which had occurred only three weeks earlier.²³³ The events at Nanjing resulted in the deaths of up to two thousand Chinese civilians through the combined fire of HMS *Emerald*, USS *Noa* and USS *William B. Preston*.²³⁴ The incident arose after armies of the Guomindang's Northern Expedition entered Nanjing, pushing out the troops from the incumbent warlord and the city descended into disorder. The exact number of civilian casualties remains a subject of debate, which will be explored in more detail in later chapters, but high figures were widely circulated at the time in the Chinese press and in Soviet propaganda.[235] The incident marked another key moment in fuelling anti-foreign rhetoric among the Chinese population, highlighting how the major powers were struggling to adapt to the new dynamics in the country.[236] As a result, the May 1927 rules explicitly stated that all civilian casualties should be strongly avoided, a considerably sharper statement than in all prior guidance.[237] In relaying the rules, Vice Admiral Tyrwhitt added that if international civilians or military personnel were fired upon, the Navy should return fire with the minimum expenditure of ammunition and the vessels' main guns could only be used when the target was clearly visible.[238]

Throughout the early 1920s there was a slow progression towards emphasis in Whitehall that the minimum level of force possible should be used, primarily in the defence of individuals rather than property. The shift towards a preference for less lethal strategies stretched back to the First World War and the influence that conflict had upon wider British attitudes towards casualties as a result of military action. The rapid tightening of the rules of engagement in 1926 and 1927, catalysed in part by the December Memorandum, came from a long-term failure among the British establishment to act upon those well-established concerns. Despite efforts to frame the declaration in December 1926 as moralistic, it was instead driven by cold hard recognition of the new circumstances.[239] There was background concern about the deaths of innocent civilians, but until that point there had been insufficient interest in ensuring guidelines issued to gunboat commanders were up to the purpose. Moralistic or ethical concerns only went so far when dealing with threats to the British Empire from non-white populations, particularly those possibly in league with the Soviet Union. Moreover, what happened in December was only one step in a longer process that continued over much of 1927. Over the course of that year, the wider legal setting changed from one in which individual commanders were afforded considerable, perhaps excessive, personal freedom to conduct diplomacy to one with much tighter control from the metropole.

No matter how clear and strict a set of orders or instructions, the deployment of armed units into a threatening conflict zone almost invariably results in some form of violent clashes. That is particularly true when dealing with a heated environment, such as in 1920s China, where there was growing ideological opposition to the presence of foreign military forces. For example, when sent upriver to Chengdu with two merchant vessels in June 1925 to evacuate missionaries and foreign civilians, HMS *Teal* came under fire from Chinese soldiers on the riverbank and returned fire in response.[240] The Chinese troops erroneously believed the British ships were heading upriver for hostile purposes. The vessels were not heading towards an official treaty port, nor had they declared their intentions to the local Chinese general.

Misunderstandings such as this were particularly common in early 1927, when the Northern Expedition reached the Yangtze. In April 1927 alone eleven incidents were recorded of Royal Navy vessels on the river exchanging fire with organized units of Chinese soldiers.[241] In one such example, HMS *Magnolia* came under rifle fire from Guomindang-affiliated forces near Shanghai, in the early morning light, to which the British warship returned fire.[242] Within ten minutes both sides ceased firing, however, after the sloop was identified as a British vessel and not one belonging to a rival Chinese force. More cautious orders for the naval personnel may have been intended to reduce the number and severity of flashpoints, but over the decade many Chinese regions were active warzones, where mistakes of identity could occur with subsequent events escalating very quickly.

Some of the clashes involving the Royal Navy in China resulted from a subtler factor, the difficulty British officials had in coming to terms with the nascent sense of nationalism among the urban Chinese population. China's long-held *Tianxia* concept of the world, where the imperial court was of primary importance and 'barbarian' foreigners were peripheral concerns, was being replaced by one focused on becoming a respected and independent modern nation state.[243] As a result, the deployment of international troops into Nanjing as the new capital of nationalist China, for example, was much more of an affront to the local population in 1927 than it had been a decade before.[244] The British establishment, including the Admiralty and naval personnel, were all guilty of acting at times as they had been doing for many years previously, seemingly without realizing that in the new environment those actions were almost certain to provoke a widespread hostile reaction. While some such acts were intended to provoke a reaction, the potential for alternative, adverse reactions was not understood.

In December 1926, for example, Rear Admiral John Cameron inspected a parade of naval personnel on shore at Hankou, after weeks of Chinese protests against the foreign concessions in the city.[245] Cameron acted in line with long-established practice on the China Station, although with less fanfare than similar parades at Hankou eighteen months earlier, when HMS *Despatch*'s brass band went ashore to 'create an impression' among the Chinese protestors.[246] The Navy had long believed that parades were an effective display of force, to intimidate and subdue the local population.²⁴⁷ Whether such spectacles had that result or provoked greater bemusement at the spectacle is another question. Within days of Cameron's parade in 1926, however, the situation in Hankou escalated from *Magnolia* posting twenty men as part of the force to guard the concession to every man possible from all British warships in the port being sent ashore. The situation was sufficiently tense that seamen were ordered to sleep wearing full equipment, with half the crew always awake ashore. While it is difficult retrospectively to apply causality, the major protests that occurred so soon after the parade suggest it had the opposite effect to the one intended. Rather than intimidating the local population, the move fanned the flames of resentment. While new rules of engagement were intended to limit the possibility that the Navy might provoke protests through the use of violence, the very act of deploying servicemen into the city had come to be regarded as a hostile act.

As the British establishment struggled to understand those local factors, the approach taken towards imperial policing was already changing. Some of this dated back to the aftermath of the unilateral action taken by Britain in the Second Boer War.²⁴⁸ Both the international and domestic reaction to the tragic events in southern Africa left a strong scar on British foreign policy. The reputation of Britain's armed services had been damaged by the struggles against what was, at first, a largely amateur militia. The resulting heavy-handed use of new ideas and tactics, particularly concentration camps for Boer civilians, then meant that the British Empire was pilloried in the international press. Contemporary events in China, specifically the Anglo-French looting and burning of the Summer Palace in Beijing, had added to that wave of criticism.²⁴⁹ An early sign of this less assertive attitude was seen in 1907 when Russian troops entered northern Persia, which in the nineteenth century would most likely have provoked a firm response. Instead, Britain opened negotiations over creating spheres of influence within the country.²⁵⁰ There remained a desire to defend the Empire, but the Victorian confidence that Britain reigned supreme had been shaken.

The British Empire may have emerged from the First World War as a victor, but questions about how Britain approached substate threats around the world soon reappeared. Nowhere was this more apparent than the indiscriminate use of aerial bombing as a method of imperial policing in Somaliland in 1920 and then elsewhere around the Middle East. Those events highlighted the unpopularity of causing civilian casualties and often the counterproductivity of the tactic when trying to secure imperial stability.²⁵¹ There were some voices that spoke favourably about the use of repressive violence against civilian populations. Indeed, it proved particularly popular with the Colonial Office as a cheap method of imperial policing. Such attitudes tended to focus on the cost of maintaining the Empire, with military aircraft seen as the next step from the Maxim gun in enforcing Britain's will around the world. Using aerial bombing and strafing, for example, had helped reduce the British Army presence in Iraq from twenty-three to just two battalions, over a seven-year period. However, events in the Middle East tended to be an exception rather than the rule.[252] The approach may have proven popular among some quarters in Whitehall, but the wider reception was less forgiving. Disquiet about the morality and ethics of such tactics affected the RAF pilots themselves, with many becoming increasingly unhappy with being ordered to attack civilians. Some even resigned over what they saw as 'cowardly' acts.[253] As a result there was a growing unwillingness to use significant levels of force unilaterally, to push British diplomatic ends, except to defend existing territory against a direct external attack.

In relation to China by the 1920s, that slowly growing sense of caution contributed to Britain repeatedly attempting to secure an 'Allied' response, rather than act in isolation and risk facing international criticism. In dealing with piracy in Chinese waters, for example, Britain attempted to develop a united multinational response. That effort was undermined by the unwillingness of the United States to support any major action, which led to both Italy and France also abstaining, leaving only Japan willing to cooperate on major schemes, a country no longer considered to be a reliable ally.[254] While there was some mutual cooperation in practice, the absence of a unified front meant that the success of joint anti-piracy operations was heavily limited. Likewise, when British forces deployed to Shanghai in 1927, the Committee for Imperial Defence agreed that they would not object to Japan sending troops into the region around the city should it be considered necessary.[255] There were no doubt reservations about what exactly might occur if that were to happen. Given concerns about the risks and legality involved in sending British personnel outside of Shanghai's boundaries, however, an unofficial and therefore deniable arrangement with Japan could prove acceptable.[256] Not only would informal collaboration shelter the British Empire from domestic and international criticism, but it would also avoid paying the full cost involved.

The shifting attitude within the British establishment away from the callous Victorian attitude towards killing non-British civilians was only ever a slow and gradual process. Moreover, it was one driven more by a desire to avoid negative headlines than by a sudden change in heart over the morality, although that was a contributing factor. As a result, while there was a greater preference for multilateral approaches that avoided innocent deaths going into the 1920s, this did not stop British officials and officers from ordering violent actions to suppress and subjugate populations around the world, including China.

Summary

Upon its return to peacetime duties in East Asia in 1919, the Royal Navy was operating in a new era, one no longer defined by British Imperial dominance but one scarred by the First World War. Amid massive post-war cutbacks, the China Station was restored in large part back to the state it had been throughout most of the fifteen years before 1914. That continuity is quite surprising, given what had occurred over the 1910s. The world order had changed. The United States was increasingly influential, Germany and Austria defeated, France exhausted, Russia in a state of revolutionary flux and Japan taking an independent path in shaping developments across Asia. With it the entire global balance of naval power had shifted, away from Europe and towards the Pacific, and yet the Admiralty attempted to continue as if it was business as usual. The China Station had never just been about those major power struggles, and within its remit was the protection of British trade and interests in China. With the Xinhai Revolution having transformed the political situation in the country, and challenges such as piracy growing in complexity and scale, the Admiralty's stance is all the more remarkable. Compared with the tasks it faced, the Royal Navy's presence on the Chinese coast in the early 1920s was actually quite modest. The near futility of holding onto the furthest outposts of Empire was one that the China Station accepted only with great reluctance.

The immense task force deployed to China quite suddenly in late 1926 is perhaps one of the greatest crises to have beset Britain in the twentieth century, and it is remarkable that so little is known about it. Putting the Navy on the verge of a war footing, of mobilizing its reserves, showed just how seriously the Admiralty and British government were about defending key imperial locations. The December Memorandum of 1926 showed a new willingness of the British Government to return some secondary imperial assets, but core ports like Shanghai were non-negotiable.[257] In this regard, it is key to note that many of the additional warships were only deployed to China after the December Memorandum had been announced. The Shanghai naval task force was a globally significant event. As has been identified with other topics, the whims of early naval historians have had a huge influence upon what we have since remembered from the interwar period.[258]

With communist links to the Guomindang and its National Revolutionary Army, Britain's response was aimed at a far wider audience. While many of the warships were despatched slightly before Anglo-Soviet relations hit their nadir at the start of April 1927, with the Arcos Affair, events in China must be taken against that wider background. Sending a naval force vastly in excess of even that sent by the Imperial Japanese Navy, and of greater power than the entire Soviet Navy, was a global statement and a reminder of British power. The Shanghai Defence Force was formed primarily as a means of imperial enforcement, but the Royal Navy ensured that the British Empire was not defeated in what it considered to be a form of proxy war against the Soviet Union.

Amid an ever more challenging regional environment and changes in the rules of engagement, there was a growing strain upon the Royal Navy as it attempted to meet its operational requirements. In the Middle East Britain turned to aerial policing as a new and highly controversial means of cutting the cost of Empire. While a similar strategy was not attempted in China, the Admiralty also turned to new technology while attempting to prolong the life of Britain's imperial outposts in East Asia, as we shall now explore.

Notes

1. Overlack, 'The Force of Circumstance', pp. 661–2.
2. Navy List, October 1919 (1919), NLS, p. 562.
3. Peter Padfield, *Rule Britannia: The Victorian and Edwardian Navy* (London: Routledge & Kegan Paul, 1981), pp. 215–22; Bell, 'Our Most Exposed Outpost', p. 61.
4. Speech by China Association Chairman David Landale, 7 November 1923, SOAS Special Collections, CHAS/A/08.
5. Bickers, *Scramble for China*, pp. 362–5; Sheridan, *China in Disintegration*, pp. 20–48.
6. Xinhai Revolution also known as Wuhan/Wuchang Revolution, Revolution of 1911 and the Chinese Revolution.
7. Andrew Nathan, *Peking Politics 1918–1923* (London: University of California Press, 1976), pp. 190–200.
8. Sheridan, *China in Disintegration*, p. 88.
9. Osterhammel, 'China', p. 646.
10. Transcript of a debate in House of Lords about the situation in China, 5 August 1925, TNA, FO 371/10922. Fung, *The Diplomacy of Imperial Retreat*, p. 48.
11. E.g. Memoranda on the Political and Military Situation in China, 1924–9, TNA, FO 228/2929. Foreign Office correspondence about the situation in China and China's

relationship with the League of Nations, 1927-8, TNA, FO 228/3882. War Diaries of 12th RMB on service in China, 1927, TNA, ADM 1/8709/102.
12 Nathan, *Peking Politics*, pp. 150-2.
13 RAF intelligence report on the Chinese air forces, 1927, TNA, AIR 5/865.
14 V. Wellesley, Memorandum for Cabinet detailing Britain's policy towards China, 23 November 1926, TNA, CAB 24/182/24.
15 Memorandum from Lampson to Foreign Office regarding the situation in China, October 1927, TNA, FO 228/3882.
16 Fung, *Diplomacy of Imperial Retreat*, p. 22.
17 Transcript of speech by Earl of Gosford, 5 August 1925, TNA, FO 371/10922.
18 Wen-Hui Tsai, *Patterns of Political Elite Mobility in Modern China 1912-1949* (Hong Kong: Chinese Material Centre, 1983), pp. 238-44.
19 Sheridan, *China in Disintegration*, pp. 37-46.
20 Transcript of speech by Earl of Gosford, 5 August 1925, TNA, FO 371/10922; Osterhammel, 'China', pp. 648-50.
21 Telegram from Lampson to Foreign Office regarding situation in China, January 1928, TNA, FO 228/3882. In the draft copy Lampson was even stronger in his criticism of the Chinese officials, but the language was toned down in the official cable to London.
22 Memorandum from Lampson to Hubbard, January 1929, TNA, FO 228/2929.
23 Bickers, *Empire Made Me*, p. 174.
24 Shu-Mei Shih, 'Gender, Race, and Semicolonialism', pp. 939-41; Phoebe Chow, *British Opinion and Policy towards China, 1922-1927* (unpublished PhD thesis, LSE, 2011), pp. 50-4; Clifford, 'A Revolution Is Not a Tea Party', p. 514.
25 Daniel O. Spence, *Colonial Naval Culture and British Imperialism 1922-67* (Manchester: Manchester University Press, 2015), pp. 155-81; Lipkin, *Useless to the State*, pp. 1-9.
26 Osterhammel, 'China', p. 651.
27 Chen, 'May Fourth Movement', pp. 137-8; Osterhammel, 'China', pp. 645-6; Gowen, 'Great Britain and the Twenty-One Demands', pp. 87-9.
28 Chen, 'May Fourth Movement', p. 142.
29 Osterhammel, 'China', pp. 649-50.
30 Johnathan Clements, '23 August 1914: Japan declares war on Germany', in *June 28th: Sarajevo 1914 - Versailles 1919: The War and Peace That Made the Modern World*, ed. Alan Sharp (London: Haus, 2014), p. 241.
31 Diary of Commander Cedric Holland, 1928.
32 Robert Bickers, 'Shanghailanders: The Formation and Identity of the British Settler Community in Shanghai 1843-1937', *Past and Present* 159 (1998), 204-10.
33 Transcript of debate in House of Lords, 5 August 1925, TNA, FO 371/10922.
34 Waldron, *From War to Nationalism*, pp. 161-2.

35 Akira Iriye, *The Origins of the Second World War in Asia and the Pacific* (Harlow: Longman, 1987), p. 19.
36 Bernard Porter, *The Absent Minded Imperialists* (Oxford: Oxford University Press, 2004), pp. 257–72.
37 Memoranda and speeches from Chamberlain, 1927–8, TNA, FO 228/3882.
38 Osterhammel, 'China', p. 648.
39 Fung, *Diplomacy of Imperial Retreat*, pp. 6–9; Waldron, *From War to Nationalism*, pp. 161–2.
40 Julian Fenby, *The Penguin History of Modern China: The Fall and Rise of a Great Power 1850 to the Present* (London: Penguin, 2013), p. 151.
41 Darwin, 'Imperialism and the Victorians', p. 634.
42 Osterhammel, 'China', pp. 654–6.
43 Fung, *Diplomacy of Imperial Retreat*, p. 4; Osterhammel, 'Imperialism in Transition', pp. 266–8.
44 Flux, 'British Export Trade', p. 552; Harumi Goto-Shibata, *Japan and Britain in Shanghai 1925–31* (London: Macmillan, 1995), pp. 13–45.
45 Fung, *Diplomacy of Imperial Retreat*, p. 5.
46 China Station: list of incidents and important questions 1925–32, TNA, ADM 1/8756/137; Fung, *Diplomacy of Imperial Retreat*, p. 114; Osterhammel, 'China', p. 653.
47 Philip Pugh, *The Cost of Seapower* (London: Conway, 1986), p. 67.
48 Osterhammel, 'Imperialism in Transition', pp. 267–75.
49 Darwin, 'Imperialism and the Victorians', p. 633.
50 Hansard, 23 May 1927, vol. 206, cc. 1639–41; Chen Qianping, 'Foreign Investment in Modern China: An Analysis with a Focus on British Interests', in *Britain and China, 1840–1970: Empire, Finance and War*, ed. Robert Bickers and Jonathan Howlett (Abingdon: Routledge, 2016), p. 153.
51 Ian Phimister, 'Foreign Devils, Finance and Informal Empire: Britain and China c. 1900–1912', *Modern Asian Studies* 40/3 (2006), 737–59.
52 Hsi-Sheng Ch'I, *Warlord Politics in China 1916–1928* (Stanford: Stanford University Press, 1976), pp. 157–8.
53 Fung, *Diplomacy of Imperial Retreat*, p. 95.
54 Phimister, 'Foreign Devils', p. 739.
55 Osterhammel, 'China', p. 644.
56 Fung, *Diplomacy of Imperial Retreat*, p. 23.
57 Annual Report by the China Association, 1927, SOAS Special Collections, CHAS/A/08.
58 Speech made by S. H. Strawn – Chairman of the International Commission on Extraterritorial Jurisdiction in China, 7 December 1926, SOAS Special Collections, CHAS/A/08; Donald Sutton, *Provincial Militarism and the Chinese Republic* (Ann Arbor, MI: University of Michigan Press, 1980), p. 281.

59 Fung, *Diplomacy of Imperial Retreat*, p. 95.
60 Madeleine Chi, 'Bureaucratic Capitalists in Operation: Ts'ao Ju-lin and His New Communications Clique, 1916-1919', *Journal of Asian Studies* 34/3 (1975), 680-2.
61 Diary of Arthur Ransome, March 1927, Brotherton Library, BC MS 20c Ransome/1/A/9/3/3.
62 Bickers, 'Shanghailanders', pp. 171-8.
63 *Shanghai Municipal Gazette*, 18 November 1920, SMA, U1-1-985; *Shanghai Municipal Gazette*, 7 August 1924, SMA, U1-1-989.
64 Jeffrey N. Wasserstrom, *Global Shanghai, 1850-2010: A History in Fragments* (London: Taylor & Francis, 2008), pp. 71-2.
65 Waldron, *From War to Nationalism*, pp. 161-2.
66 Minutes of meeting of Committee for Overseas Defence discussing piracy in China, June 1926, TNA, CAB 24/181/72; Memorandum from Sir Miles Lampson to the Foreign Office regarding the history of Britain's efforts in piracy suppression on the Chinese coast, 21 September 1927, CAB 24/202/24.
67 Memorandum from Sir Miles Lampson to the Foreign Office regarding the history of Britain's efforts in piracy suppression on the Chinese coast, 21 September 1927, TNA CAB 24/202/24, p. 13.
68 E.g. Bernard Cole, *Gunboats and Marines: The United States Navy in China, 1925-1928* (Newark: University of Delaware Press, 1983), p. 91; Braisted, *Diplomats in Blue*, p. 75; Clayton, *The British Empire as a Superpower*, pp. 193-7; Osterhammel, 'China', pp. 648-50.
69 E.g. Cable, *Gunboat Diplomacy*, p. 38; Fung, *Diplomacy of Imperial Retreat*, p. 132; Murdoch, 'Exploiting Anti-Imperialism', p. 75; Osterhammel, 'China', p. 652.
70 Minutes of meeting of Committee for Overseas Defence discussing piracy in China, June 1926, TNA, CAB 24/181/72.
71 Report by Lieutenant C. M. Faure, 10 June 1925, TNA, ADM 1/8683/140.
72 Questions in the House of Commons on the situation on the Yangtze, November 1925, TNA, FO 371/10922.
73 Royal Navy Intelligence Report on Piracy in China, 3 December 1924, TNA, FO 371/10252.
74 Shipping report for Nanjing, June 1927, TNA, ADM 116/2510.
75 Briefing on Piracy in China for the Committee of Imperial Defence, January 1929, TNA, CAB 24/202/24.
76 Hugh Tweedie, *The Story of a Naval Life* (London: Rich & Cowan, 1939), p. 250.
77 Max Boot, 'Pirates, Then and Now: How Piracy Was Defeated in the Past and Can Be Again', *Foreign Affairs* 88/4 (2009), 100-2.
78 Cabinet discussion of Piracy in Bias Bay, 25 November 1926, TNA, CAB 2/4/218.
79 William Boyle, *Admiral of the Fleet the Earl of Cork and Orrery, My Naval Life: 1886-1941* (London: Hutchinson, 1942), pp. 145-6.

80 Interview with A. Gaskin, 1986, IWM Interview Series, Catalogue Number 9344, Reel 6, 11 minutes.
81 Osterhammel, 'China', pp. 648–50.
82 Minutes of meeting of Committee for Overseas Defence discussing piracy in China, June 1926, TNA, CAB 24/181/72; Assorted memoranda on piracy in Chinese waters, 1929, TNA, CAB 24/202/24; Anonymous, 'China, Its Past and Present Situation, April 1928', *Naval Review* 16/3 (1928), p. 464.
83 *China Mail*, 4 November 1920, p. 4.
84 E.g. the two attacks recorded in the *Hong Kong Telegraph*, 28 October 1925, p. 1.
85 *Hong Kong Daily Press*, 28 November 1921, p. 3.
86 Colin A. G. Hutchison, 'Notes from a Yangtze Diary – November 1927 to February 1929', *Naval Review* 17/3 (1929), p. 543; Rear Admiral Tweedie to Admiral Tyrwhitt, 28 May 1928, TNA, ADM 116/2624.
87 R. R. Beauchamp, 'Piracy in the South China Sea II', *Naval Review* 14/1 (1926), 35–9.
88 Summary by Chairman L. N. Leefe in the Annual Report of the China Association, 30 September 1925, SOAS Special Collections, CHAS/A/08; Anonymous, 'China, Its Past and Present Situation April 1928', *Naval Review* 16/3 (1928), 465.
89 Instructions issued to the commander-in-chief – China Station, 1 February 1921, TNA, ADM 1/8727/146.
90 *The Municipal Gazette*, 24 July 1924, SMA, U1-1-989.
91 Shanghai Municipal Council Annual Report 1923, SMA, U1-1-936.
92 Report by Consul A. Archer, 23 September 1923, TNA, FO 371/9193/88.
93 Report by Consul L. Giles, 23 September 1923, TNA, FO 371/9193/88.
94 Report by Sir R. Macleay, 1 October 1923, TNA, FO 371/9193/88.
95 Report by Consul L. Giles, 23 September 1923, TNA, FO 371/9193/88.
96 Memorandum by the First Lord of the Admiralty on the Navy Estimates, 4 February 1925, TNA, CAB 24/171/68.
97 Chesneau, *All the World's Fighting Ships*, p. 78.
98 Cabinet Meeting Minutes, 15 December 1926, TNA, CAB 23/53/35.
99 R. R. Beauchamp, 'Piracy in the South China Seas', *Naval Review* 13/4 (1925), 628.
100 Memorandum from Sir Miles Lampson to the Foreign Office regarding the history of Britain's efforts in piracy suppression on the Chinese coast, 21 September 1927, TNA CAB 24/202/24.
101 Unsigned memo on piracy in China, 3 September 1924, TNA, FO 371/10252.
102 Diary of Paymaster Commander Hugh Miller, January 1920, IWM, PP/MCR/16.
103 Commander Maxwell-Scott to Commodore David Anderson, 3 October 1924, TNA, ADM 116/2262.
104 Report by Lieutenant C. M. Faure, 10 June 1925, TNA, ADM 1/8683/140.

105 Report by Lieutenant C. M. Faure, 12 June 1925, TNA, ADM 1/8683/140.
106 Commodore A. J. B. Stirling to Lieutenant C. M. Faure, 19 June 1925, TNA, ADM 1/8683/140.
107 Commander M. Maxwell-Scott to Commodore A. J. B. Stirling, 16 June 1925, TNA ADM 1/8683/140; Admiralty to Vice Admiral Edwyn Alexander-Sinclair, 31 August 1925, TNA ADM 1/8683/140.
108 Wright, *China's Steam Navy*, p. 141.
109 Royal Navy Intelligence Report on Piracy in China, 3 December 1924, TNA, FO 371/10252.
110 Osterhammel, 'China', p. 647.
111 Braisted, *Diplomats in Blue*, pp. 65–6.
112 Memorandum on the views of the former US ambassador to China, 1925, TNA, CAB 24/174/18; Field, *Royal Navy Strategy in the Far East*, p. 5.
113 Memorandum from A. P. Blunt to Foreign Office, 1925, TNA, ADM 1/8707/219.
114 Memoranda in appendix to meeting of Committee for Overseas Defence discussing piracy in China, June 1926, TNA, CAB 24/181/72.
115 Everest-Phillips, 'The Pre-War Fear of Japanese Espionage', p. 251; Gowen, 'Great Britain and the Twenty-One Demands', p. 82.
116 TNA, ADM 116/2527: China – Protection of British Life and Property (1926).
117 *China Mail*, 4 November 1920, p. 4.
118 Journal of Lieutenant William Andrewes, 1925–6, IWM, DS/MISC/12.
119 Clifford, 'A Revolution Is Not a Tea Party', pp. 513–14.
120 Letter from the British business community in Shanghai to Foreign Office, August 1925, TNA, FO 371/10947.
121 Bickers, 'Shanghailanders', pp. 171–2.
122 Fung, *Diplomacy of Imperial Retreat*, p. 50; Goto-Shibata, *Japan and Britain in Shanghai*, p. 54.
123 Interview with Private Ernest Whitney, 1992, IWM Interview Series, Catalogue Number 12499, 23–24 minutes; Interview with Lieutenant Ian Wight, 1982, IWM Interview Series, Catalogue Number 6196, Reel 1, 20 minutes; Interview with Lance Corporal Sidney Johnson, 1983, IWM Interview Series, Catalogue Number 6719, Reel 2, 1–2 minutes.
124 Assorted correspondence and memoranda regarding protection of British life and property in China, 1926–7, TNA, ADM 116/2527.
125 Memoranda from Military Branch discussing legal aspects of Commander Miles's actions at Swatow, October 1926, TNA, ADM 116/2527.
126 Fung, *Diplomacy of Imperial Retreat*, p. 63.
127 Field, *Royal Navy Strategy in the Far East*, p. 16.
128 Clayton, *The British Empire as a Superpower*, pp. 116–227; Moretz, *The Royal Navy and the Capital Ship*, p. 158; Porter, *Absent Minded Imperialists*, pp. 269–81.

129 Memoranda by the outgoing Rear Admiral David Anderson – Senior Naval Officer Yangtze, 12 October 1925, TNA, 1/8707/219.
130 Clayton, *The British Empire as Superpower*, pp. 206–9.
131 Osterhammel, 'China', pp. 647–8.
132 Hansard, 13 April 1927, vol. 205, cc. 342–3; Navy List, December 1920 (1921), NLS, p. 714; Angus Konstam, *Yangtze River Gunboats 1900–49* (Oxford: Osprey, 2011), Appendix.
133 Bell, 'Our Most Exposed Outpost', pp. 61–88.
134 Ship's log of HMS *Diomede* 1924–5, TNA, ADM 53/75887; Ship's log of HMS *Diomede* 1923–4, TNA, ADM 53/75886; Ship's log of HMS *Diomede* 1922–3, TNA, ADM 53/75885; Ship's log of HMS *Carlisle* 1924–5, TNA, ADM 53/72682; Ship's log of HMS *Despatch* 1924–5, TNA, ADM 53/75691; Ship's log of HMS *Hawkins* 1923–4, TNA, ADM 53/78593; Ship's log of HMS *Durban* 1922–3, TNA, ADM 53/76428.
135 Ship's log of HMS *Hermes* 1925–6, TNA, ADM 53/78829.
136 Correspondence between the Foreign Office and Admiralty, August 1925, TNA, FO 371/10922.
137 Technically the vessels based around the UK were split into various separate commands, but broadly speaking they all had a similar role – to dominate the waters around the British Isles and Northern Atlantic.
138 NLS, Navy List (March 1913), p. 270; Navy List (June 1884), p. 189; Padfield, *Rule Britannia*, pp. 209–22; O'Brien, 'The Titan Refreshed', pp. 149–51.
139 NLS, Navy List (March 1913), p. 270; NLS, Navy List (May 1920), p. 510.
140 Paul Kennedy, *The Rise and Fall of British Naval Mastery* (London: Macmillan, 1983), p. 279.
141 *Jane's Fighting Ships of World War I*, Reproduction (London: Studio, 2001), p. 90.
142 Ship's log of HMS *Hawkins*, 1919–20, TNA, ADM 53/43950; Ship's log of HMS *Minotaur*, 1914–15, TNA, ADM 53/49545; *Jane's Fighting Ships of World War I*, p. 33.
143 Diary of Commander Cedric Holland, September 1928.
144 Barraclough, *I Was Sailing*, p. 58.
145 Copies of the Navy list, NMM.
146 Lambert, 'Admiral Sir Francis Bridgeman-Bridgeman', p. 68; Padfield, *Rule Britannia*, pp. 209–22.
147 Hansard, 13 April 1927, vol. 205, cc. 342–3. Vice Admiral Reginald Tyrwhitt, commander-in-chief of the China Station between 1926 and 1929.
148 Hansard, 1 December 1926, vol. 200, cc. 1168–71; Hansard, 24 February 1927, vol. 202, cc. 1943–4.
149 Chesneau, *All the World's Fighting Ships*.
150 Hansard, 13 April 1927, vol. 205, cc. 342–3; *Annual Reports of the Navy Department*, 15 November 1927, University of Michigan (via Hathi Trust Digital Library, last accessed 8 January 2018), p. 6.

151 Telegram from the Admiralty to Vice Admiral Tyrwhitt, 26 January 1927, TNA, ADM 1/8711/144; Keith Stevens, "Duncan Force' – the Shanghai Defence Force in 1927, & the Career of Captain Ronald Spear', *Journal of the Royal Asiatic Society Hong Kong Branch* 48 (2008), 157.
152 Hansard, 2 March 1927, vol. 203, cc. 358–9; Correspondence between Admiralty and Chancellor of the Exchequer regarding Navy Estimate, 1928, TNA, ADM 1/8724/68.
153 Admiralty correspondence with the Chancellor of the Exchequer, 1928, TNA, ADM 1/8724/68.
154 Journal of Midshipman L. C. S. Sheppard, 30 April 1927, National Museum of the Royal Navy (NMRN), 1991/101/67; Navy List, April 1927, NMRN.
155 Clifford, *Spoilt Children of Empire*, p. 188.
156 Navy List, 1901/2, NMM; Kathleen Harland, *The Royal Navy in Hong Kong* (Hong Kong: Royal Navy, 1985), p. 169.
157 Hansard, 2 March 1927, vol. 203, cc. 358–9.
158 Black, *The British Naval Staff*, p. 34; Moretz, *Thinking Wisely, Planning Boldly*, p. 94.
159 Cabinet discussions about the Chanak Crisis, 23 September 1922, TNA, CAB 23/31/3.
160 Kenneth Morgan, 'England, Britain and the Audit of War: The Prothero Lecture', *Transactions of the Royal Historical Society* 7 (1997), 139.
161 War Office to General Officer Commanding North China, 26 August 1927, TNA, WO 106/86.
162 Chronology of Shanghai Defence Force Deployment, 30 April 1930, TNA, WO 106/83.
163 Hansard, 16 November 1927, vol. 210, cc. 1007–8; Hansard, 12 March 1930, vol. 236, cc. 1299–300; K. R. Buckley, 'The Third Destroyer Flotilla in China 1926-1928', *Naval Review* 18/1 (1930), pp. 97–116.
164 Hansard, 27 June 1928, vol. 219, cc. 508–9; Hansard, 4 February 1929, vol. 224, c. 1414.
165 Hansard, 2 March 1927, vol. 203, cc. 358–9.
166 Van de Ven, *War and Nationalism in China*, pp. 109–19.
167 Minutes from a meeting of the Committee for Imperial Defence, 8 November 1928, TNA, CAB 24/198.
168 Ship's log of HMS *Diomede* 1924–5, TNA, ADM 53/75887; Ship's log of HMS *Carlisle* 1924–5, TNA, ADM 53/72682.
169 Jackson, 'Expansion and defence', pp. 189–201; Bickers, *Scramble for China*, p. 127.
170 Appendix to a report on the situation in China for Committee of Imperial Defence, 30 June 1925, TNA, CAB 24/174/26.
171 Shanghai Municipal Council Annual Report 1926, SMA, U1-1-939.

172 Shanghai Municipal Council Annual Report 1929, SMA, U1-1-942.
173 Bickers, *Britain in China*, p. 14.
174 Letter from Frank Turner to his mother, 10 May 1922, Brotherton Library, LIDDLE/WW1/CH/04.
175 Letter from Palairet to multiple recipients regarding rights of British civilians in China, 29 July 1925, TNA, ADM 1/8707/219.
176 Anne Foster, 'Secret Police Cooperation and the Roots of Anti-Communism in Interwar Southeast Asia', *Journal of American-East Asian Relations* 4/4 (1995), 334–5.
177 Osterhammel, 'China', p. 651.
178 Murdoch, 'Exploiting Anti-Imperialism', pp. 65–95; Van de Ven, *War and Nationalism*, pp. 113–17.
179 Chang Liu, 'Making Revolution in Jiangnan: Communists and the Yangzi Delta Countryside, 1927–1945', *Modern China* 29/1 (2003), 6–7.
180 Clarence Wilbur, *The Nationalist Revolution in China: 1923–1928* (Cambridge: Cambridge University Press, 1984), pp. 100–44.
181 Elleman, *Modern Chinese Warfare*, pp. 167–8; Wilbur, *Nationalist Revolution in China*, pp. 40–4.
182 Edmund S. K. Fung, 'The Sino-British Rapprochement, 1927–1931', *Modern Asian Studies* 17/1 (1983), 81.
183 Jackson, 'Expansion and defence', pp. 189–91.
184 Stevens, 'Duncan Force', p. 159.
185 Anonymous, 'Imperial Defence', *Naval Review* 14/1 (1926), p. 95.
186 Bond, *British Military Policy*, pp. 38–97.
187 Foster, 'Secret Police Cooperation', p. 335.
188 Fung, *Diplomacy of Imperial Retreat*, p. 9.
189 Shanghai Municipal Council Annual Report 1921, SMA, U1-1-934; Shanghai Municipal Council Annual Report 1922, SMA, U1-1-935.
190 Shanghai Municipal Council Annual Report 1923, SMA, U1-1-936.
191 Memorandum sent from Admiral Beatty to Maurice Hankey, July 1925, NMM, BTY 8/8.
192 Minutes of Cabinet meeting discussing the effect of Soviet activity on British trade, 25 February 1926, TNA, CAB 2/4/210.
193 Debate in the House of Commons on China and Russia, 7 August 1925, TNA, FO 371/10957.
194 Arcos: All Russian Co-Operative Society, part of the Russian trade delegation. Minutes of Cabinet meeting discussing the effect of Soviet activity on British trade, 25 February 1926, TNA, CAB 2/4/210; Sabahi, *British Policy in Persia*, p. 63.
195 Memoranda by MI5 on Soviet Intelligence Organization, 1922–9, TNA, KV 3/17; West, *MASK*, p. 11.

196 William Edwards, *British Foreign Policy 1815–1933* (London: Methuen, 1934), pp. 195–6.
197 Osterhammel, 'China', pp. 651–2; Wilbur, *The Nationalist Revolution in China*, pp. 100–144.
198 Fung, *Diplomacy of Imperial Retreat*, p. 9; Wilbur, *The Nationalist Revolution in China*, pp. 100–44.
199 Memorandum from Porter to Foreign Office regarding situation in China, January 1928, TNA, FO 228/3882.
200 Sherman X. Lai, 'Nationalistic enthusiasm versus imperialist sophistication: Britain from Chiang Kai-shek's perspective', in *Britain and China, 1840–1970: Empire, Finance and War*, ed. Robert Bickers and Jonathan J. Howlett (Abingdon: Routledge, 2016), p. 206.
201 Hansard, 12 March 1930, vol. 236, cc. 1299–300.
202 Bickers, *The Scramble for China*, pp. 346–52.
203 Bell, *The Royal Navy*, pp. 14–15; O'Brien, 'The Titan Refreshed', p. 149; Porter, *Absent Minded Imperialists*, pp. 267–81.
204 Rear Admiral Tweedie to Admiral Tyrwhitt, 28 May 1928, TNA, ADM 116/2624.
205 Navy Estimates 1925–6 and assorted Cabinet notes (1925), TNA, CAB 116/2300.
206 Navy Estimates 1925–6 and assorted Cabinet notes (1925), TNA, CAB 116/2300.
207 Alexander Kanya-Forstner, 'The War, Imperialism, and Decolonization', in *The Great War and the Twentieth Century*, ed. Jay Winter, Geoffrey Parker and Mary Habeck (New Haven, CT: Yale University Press, 2000), p. 246; William Kirby, 'The Internationalization of China: Foreign Relations at Home and Abroad in the Republican Era', *China Quarterly* 150 (1997), 442; Kier, *Imagining War*, p. 109.
208 Memoranda by Admiral Tweedie regarding military situation in China, February 1929, TNA, FO 228/2929.
209 E.g. ship's log of HMS *Magnolia* 1924–5, TNA, ADM 53/80209.
210 Does not include Japanese civilians as Japan's armed forces were involved in the hostilities at Yantai.
211 Osterhammel, 'China', p. 648.
212 Peter Zarrow, *China in War and Revolution 1895–1949* (London: Routledge, 2005), p. 159.
213 Robert Bickers, 'Ordering Shanghai: Policing a Treaty Port, 1854–1900', in *Maritime Empires: British Imperial Maritime Trade in the Nineteenth Century*, ed. David Killingray, Margarette Lincoln and Nigel Rigby (Woodbridge: Boydell, 2004), pp. 174–94.
214 Draft report by the Chiefs of Staff on 'The Situation in China', 29 March 1927, TNA, CAB 24/186/9.
215 Reports by Acting-Consul Archer, July 1925, TNA, ADM 1/8707/219.
216 Montgomery-Hyde, *British Air Policy between the Wars*, p. 121.

217 E.g. *Journal of Lieutenant William Andrewes*, 3 July 1925, IWM, DS/MISC/12.
218 War Diaries of 12th RMB on service in China, 1927, TNA, ADM 1/8709/102.
219 War Diaries of 12th RMB on service in China, 1927, TNA, ADM 1/8709/102. The second sentence was underlined in the original document to emphasize the desired level of restraint.
220 Cabinet discussion about piracy in Bias Bay, 25 November 1926, TNA CAB 2/4/218.
221 Memoranda from Clementi to Foreign Office regarding the protection of British life and property, July 1926, TNA, ADM 116/2527.
222 Orders from War Office to General Officer Commanding Hong Kong, 27 September 1926, TNA, ADM 116/2527.
223 Fung, *Diplomacy of Imperial Retreat*, p. 101.
224 Correspondence between Admiralty and Cabinet, December 1926, TNA, ADM 116/2527; Fung, *Diplomacy of Imperial Retreat*, p. 101; Osterhammel, 'China', pp. 651–2.
225 Reports from Acting-Consul Archer, July 1925, TNA, ADM 1/8707/219.
226 Memoranda regarding actions of Royal Navy officers in China, 1925, TNA, ADM 1/8707/219.
227 Pugsley and Macintyre, *Destroyer Man*, pp. 10–19.
228 Memoranda regarding protection of British life and property in China, 1926–7, TNA, ADM 116/2527.
229 Osterhammel, 'Imperialism in Transition', p. 278.
230 Orders from Admiralty to Admiral Tyrwhitt, 17 May 1927, TNA, ADM 116/2527.
231 Memorandum on the rules of engagement in China, December 1926, TNA, ADM 116/2527.
232 Memorandum by the Military Branch on the legal interpretation of various international treaties, December 1926, TNA, ADM 116/2527.
233 Orders from Admiralty to Admiral Tyrwhitt, 17 May 1927, TNA, ADM 116/2527.
234 Other vessels from the multinational task force were involved in the firing over the course of events, but the three vessels listed conducted most of the action.
235 E.g. Goto-Shibata, *Japan and Britain in Shanghai*, p. 50; Wilbur, *The Nationalist Revolution in China*, p. 95; Stevens, 'Duncan Force', pp. 159–60.
236 Murdoch, 'Exploiting Anti-Imperialism', p. 88.
237 Admiralty orders to Admiral Tyrwhitt, 17 May 1927, TNA ADM 116/2527.
238 Admiral Tyrwhitt's orders to China Station, 18 May 1927, TNA ADM 116/2527.
239 Fung, *Diplomacy of Imperial Retreat*, pp. 101–4.
240 Memoranda by Palairet regarding incident involving HMS *Teal*, July 1925, TNA, ADM 1/8707/219.
241 Hansard, 4 May 1927, vol. 205, cc. 1596–7.
242 Ship's log of HMS *Magnolia* 1926–7, TNA, ADM 53/80211.

243 Xu Guogi, 'China and Empire', in *Empires at War: 1911-1923*, ed. Robert Gerwarth and Erez Manela (Oxford Scholarship Online, 2014), pp. 216-18.
244 Lipkin, *Useless to the State*, pp. 9-10.
245 Ship's log of HMS *Magnolia* 1926-7, TNA, ADM 53/80211.
246 W. T. Allen (ed.), *With HMS Despatch to China 1925-1927* (Shanghai: Willow Pattern Press, 1927), p. 14.
247 Jeremy E. Taylor, 'The Bund: Littoral Space of Empire in the Treaty Ports of East Asia', *Social History* 27/2 (2002), 137.
248 O'Brien, *The Titan Refreshed*, p. 149.
249 Bickers, *The Scramble for China*, pp. 149-50.
250 Sabahi, *British Policy in Persia*, p. 33.
251 Victor Kiernan, *Colonial Empires and Armies 1815-1960* (Stroud: Sutton, 1998), p. 196; Porter, *Absent Minded Imperialists*, p. 281.
252 Clayton, *The British Empire as Superpower*, pp. 212-27; Clayton, 'Deceptive Might', p. 290.
253 Porter, *Absent Minded Imperialists*, p. 281.
254 Assorted memoranda on piracy in Chinese waters, 1929, TNA, CAB 24/202/24.
255 Committee for Imperial Defence report on the situation in China, 29 March 1927, TNA, CAB 24/186/9.
256 Teichman, *Affairs of China*, p. 159.
257 Osterhammel, 'China', p. 653.
258 Moretz, *Thinking Wisely, Planning Boldly*, pp. 69-70.

4

Technological development and imperial policing

> *One of the principal purposes of naval warfare is to establish a maritime superiority so decisive that military force can be brought into play in the form of descents upon the enemy's coasts.*[1]

Between 1812 and the 1890s Britain's global naval supremacy enabled regular, if piecemeal, additions of territory to the British Empire. The amphibious landings and gunboat diplomacy used to build and defend the Empire relied upon Britain having the capability to quickly and safely shift its modest military resources between regions by sea.[2] During the First Opium War, for example, Britain's ability to ship its military forces between Guangzhou and Tianjin was a key factor in neutralizing the Qing armies' numerical superiority. Without an established railway or paved road network in China, the only quick and effective means of transporting troops and equipment was by water.[3] Britain's superior mobility was only possible because the Royal Navy, along with ships from the East India Company, achieved complete naval superiority in China's littoral regions.[4] The outdated coastal vessels available to the Qing could not compete with Britain's warships – some of the most advanced in the world at the time. For the remainder of the nineteenth century, that ongoing disparity in capabilities helped the Royal Navy keep the China Station's running costs below the perceived rewards derived from Britain's informal empire in East Asia. Technology played an integral role in shaping the Royal Navy's, and therefore the British Empire's, relationship with China.

By the 1920s, further enlarging the British Empire was no longer a priority in Whitehall. The Victorian strategy of using amphibious operations as part of a policy of gunboat diplomacy, however, remained key to maintaining the existing imperial system. Relatively few warships and men could secure large areas, so long as it was possible to concentrate rapidly a force of sufficient strength at key locations during times of crisis. Financial restrictions after the First World War required the military and naval cost of empire to be kept to a minimum. Excluding the hefty burden of First World War pensions, roughly 30 per cent of naval expenditure by the early 1920s went towards paying ships' crews, with provisions and clothing accounting for a further 10 per cent.[5] In contrast, total pay and victualling costs had only come to 25 per cent of the pre-war 1914 budget. This was despite the Navy having undergone an overall reduction in service personnel by roughly a third, from 146,000 to just under 100,000. A key factor in that shift had been the significant increases in naval pay during the war, to better match those available in the British Army and partially compensate for wartime inflation.[6] As a result, the Royal Navy's operating costs (excluding pensions) increased from £46 million in 1913/14 to £55 million in 1922/23, while the overall naval vote was almost back down to the same nominal level as before the war.[7] There were attempts to save money by reducing the number of civilians employed by the Royal Navy, but it was recognized that this would only yield marginal gains.[8] If the imperial system was to remain financially viable it was ever more crucial to minimize the number of service personnel required to police and defend the British Empire.

The China Station had been fortunate that its manpower had remained broadly unaffected by the cutbacks, from its pre-war complement.[9] That left roughly 4,400 servicemen afloat on the Station, with hundreds more working in the shore facilities at Singapore, Hong Kong and Weihai. Precise numbers fluctuated as warships were not always fully manned in peacetime and some of the smaller gunboats were placed in reserve with skeleton crews for short periods. Against the background of overall cuts, however, maintaining the force on the Chinese coast cost the Admiralty, on balance, a greater proportion of the Navy's budget than it had done before the cuts. Efforts were made throughout the 1920s to raise locally financed Royal Navy Reserve units around the world to ease the burden of regional defence duties. This included the China Station, although it was not until 1933 that a reserve force was formed at Hong Kong.[10] Locally hired Chinese crewmen were also employed as cooks, stewards and for loading coal or other supplies, as a cheaper way of counteracting chronic understaffing, particularly on the lightly manned upper Yangtze gunboats. However, while many of those seamen built strong bonds of friendship and loyalty with their foreign shipmates, during times of crisis they stayed ashore, fearing that their families would be threatened if they were seen to be helping the British.[11] Against this background, adopting new technology offered qualitative improvements to the Royal Navy's capabilities, potentially easing the demand for manpower – limiting the cost of Britain's 'imperial gendarmerie'. The use of new 'mechanical devices' for that purpose was even explicitly recommended at Cabinet level in 1919.[12]

Advanced technology was expected to enhance far more than just the Royal Navy's capacity to engage potential opponents, particularly in a peacetime imperial environment. The benefits sought can be separated into three broad areas: maintaining prestige, understanding events and responding to crises. For the first of these, new equipment was often used to reinforce global perceptions of Britain's power. Imperial prestige had long served an important role in convincing both foreign governments and overseas populations that the British Empire could be a dangerous opponent or a valuable ally. In essence, the use of technology exemplified the 'stick and carrot' metaphor. The 'stick' – an underlying threat that the British Empire could wield unparalleled force – was used as a deterrent to try and avoid costly deployments of manpower. In contrast, the 'carrot' was the possibility that Britain might share some of its technology and expertise with those considered to be friends. In the early 1920s, for example, Britain provided both France and Greece with technical assistance to aid their efforts in naval aviation, as recent and potentially future allies.[13] The carrot also tended to come with an unwritten understanding, particularly where the technology gulf was significant, that the recipient would put British armaments manufacturers at the front of the queue for contracts.[14]

In the second case, the British Empire's ability to understand global events relied upon the timely collation of information and its subsequent dissemination to the relevant offices of government. For East Asia in the interwar period, and China in particular, the Foreign Office and Royal Navy formed the two key branches of Britain's intelligence gathering and official communications apparatus. The speed at which that information could be gathered and passed on affected both the nature and uniformity of Britain's policies and responses to crises. This could be in relation to either extremely localized events, such as piracy in Daya Bay, or the overall relationship between Britain and China. Using new technology could increase the coverage of those events around East Asia, without significant increases in manpower and therefore cost.

Finally, Britain's responses to both ongoing threats and extraordinary crises, such as the one seen in 1927, were influenced by the resources at the Royal Navy's disposal. Evolutions in fighting equipment, particularly the adoption of 'quick-fire' and automatic guns in the 1880s and 1890s, had previously altered how Britain dealt with substate violence as the Empire expanded.[15] The first generation of British quick-fire naval guns, for example, could deliver roughly ten times as many shells per minute as those they replaced.[16] Such weaponry had been instrumental in enabling Britain to subjugate large populations using only modest military forces. The First World War produced another similar step-shift in capability, catalysing the development of new platforms for bringing the Navy's manpower and weaponry into, or evacuating personnel out of, a conflict zone. Using naval aircraft or larger, faster ships, for example, provided the potential to transform the way in which the Royal Navy could respond to adverse scenarios. This did not necessarily involve acts of violence but had the potential to influence how evacuations of civilians were conducted. As the area that saw the most regular and active operational employment by the Royal Navy during the 1920s, China became a peacetime testing ground for those evolving new technologies.[17]

Maintaining imperial prestige

Exploiting the latest technologies in order to intimidate and impress around the world formed an integral part of the British Empire's strategy to emphasize its superiority. In particular, flag-waving tours by British warships were not just an opportunity for socializing with other nation's dignitaries and obtaining information. Those port visits were intended to emphasize the power of the Royal Navy and the wider British Empire, with displays of Britain's newest technologies often deliberately included in the carefully choreographed pomp and ceremony.[18] The Special Service Squadron's 1923–4 'Empire Cruise', for example, was led by the pride of the British fleet and largest warship in the world at the time – HMS *Hood*. During port calls, *Hood*'s powerful searchlights were frequently used to illuminate distant objects, given the reportedly striking effect they had upon local dignitaries.[19] The visually dramatic party trick also came with the unsubtle message that anywhere the ship could illuminate, it could also bombard, by day or night.[20]

In effect this approach of applying technology imitated the way sport had previously been used as a subtle element of Britain's gunboat diplomacy. Rugby and cricket matches were invariably staged by British gunboats during port calls in the nineteenth century to emphasize British mariners' physical prowess. Even cricket matches were apparently understood by foreign officials to carry the message that it was better to accept cricket balls than cannon balls.[21] The changing focus from physical to technical superiority had come as a result of the mechanization of violence in the late nineteenth century. While the

Special Service Squadron only briefly met with the China Station at Singapore, technology was still used on a day-to-day basis to reinforce British imperial prestige in East Asia.

Immediately prior to the First World War simple displays of moderately advanced vessels were generally considered sufficient to emphasize Britain's power. The number of ports visited was normally seen as the critical measure, rather than the scale of the impression made at each location. The officer commanding Britain's gunboats stationed on the upper Yangtze in 1907, Lieutenant Commander George Todd, argued in just such a way when requesting additional gunboats for his force:

> This would enable the Flag to be shown at many places it has, as yet, not been seen and would doubtless tend to increase the respect of the Chinese for us as a Nation, and impress upon them the preponderating nature of our interest both political and commercial in this part of China.[22]

When that same year one junior officer experimented with using displays of fireworks to amplify the impact caused by his gunboat arriving at Chinese cities, it was politely suggested to him by his senior colleagues that such behaviour was unbefitting of a Royal Navy warship. The White Ensign alone was felt to be enough to earn the respect of local populations. Indeed, a rumour was circulating around the China Station at the time that one group of pirates had immediately jumped overboard, into the night, after they were calmly informed by a Chinese crewmember that they had mistakenly boarded a British gunboat. The British crew were said to have slept soundly below deck, shielded by an invisible imperial aura.[23] Such stories, whether true or not, reinforced a belief among the British that the Chinese population were in absolute awe of the Royal Navy.

Relying on simple numerical displays of strength faced numerous problems by the 1920s. The Fisher reforms and the subsequent destruction of Germany's East Asia Squadron had led to a slightly smaller surface force being based on the China Station in 1920 than that in 1907.[24] While better suited to policing and patrol duties, many of the warships posted to China post-war were also less prestigious vessels. The 10,000-ton armoured cruisers *Monmouth* and *Hampshire* were replaced by 4,000-ton light cruisers. Four slow and lightly armed sloops and additional gunboats supplanted a destroyer flotilla. The latter change even led to unsuccessful calls in the Commons by Lieutenant Commander Joseph Kenworthy MP for a destroyer flotilla to be returned to China. Kenworthy's argument was that 'sloops cannot show the flag with dignity in peace nor with effect in war'.²⁵ While the pre-war destroyers were quite small by later standards, displacing less than 1,000 tons, they were warships designed for operating at sea with the battle fleet and reflected that in their appearance. In contrast, few people who have seen HMS *President* moored on the Thames, the lone survivor from the *Flower*-class sloop family, have realized that it was once a warship, since its deck guns were removed.²⁶ The *Flower*-class had been hastily constructed in wartime as minesweepers and later to escort convoys, and so they looked and performed like small merchantmen rather than world-class warships.

Among the various strategic reasons for the switch, the Admiralty was partially driven by two relatively simple practical considerations. The mainstay *W*- and *V*-class destroyers were notoriously uncomfortable for their crews and lacked refrigerators, whereas on the *Flower*-class sloops food had to be carried on the open deck between the kitchen and mess.²⁷ It is perhaps unsurprising therefore that with the return to peace, the former were stationed in Europe and the latter in warmer climates. Overall, most of the new vessels posted to the China Station after the First World War were suited to specific military tasks; only a few had the right attributes to make a powerful impression on those who saw them.

In contrast Britain's main rivals in the region were increasing and strengthening their regional fleets. Japan started the decade with an order for five modern gunboats, which by late 1923 doubled its permanent China river force.²⁸ With the expansion and modernization of the IJN's main fleet during the First World War, many pre-war destroyers were deployed on patrol duties around China, although on paper they were based in Japan.²⁹ Those destroyers were obsolete for fleet duties and had been rerated as second or third class, with most due for scrapping, but they made adequate gunboat substitutes to increase the visibility of Japan's growing maritime power. Likewise, while HMS *Hood* and its compatriots did not venture beyond Singapore, the IJN sent touring squadrons around East Asia, including battlecruisers twice the size of the China Station's flagship HMS *Hawkins*.³⁰ Japan was engaging in a show of naval theatrics just as Victorian Britain had so often done before, and could do so with far greater ease given the comparatively short distance from its main naval yards.

Even more crucially than the IJN's rising sun, the USN's Asiatic Fleet received eighteen brand new destroyers between 1918 and 1922, which had a sufficiently shallow draught to navigate as far upriver as Hankou.³¹ Those destroyers were larger, faster and more heavily armed than any of the smaller warships Britain or Japan had stationed off the Chinese coast. That increase also resulted in the Asiatic Fleet receiving a full Admiral on a permanent attachment from

September 1919, senior to Vice Admiral Alexander Duff who commanded the China Station at the time. Previously the Royal Navy's regional commander had always been senior to his USN counterpart. The balance was only restored in July 1921 when Duff was promoted to full Admiral, with his replacement the following year also newly appointed as a full Admiral – Arthur Leveson. Royal Navy officers were a little dismissive of the disparity, as the American 'Admiral' often only possessed a temporary rank. Admirals Edwin Anderson, Clarence Williams and Mark Bristol all reverted to being Rear Admirals upon leaving the Asiatic Fleet.[32] Nonetheless, the Chinese civilian officials they encountered were unlikely to be aware of that subtle distinction.

The USN was also making frequent requests in Washington for modern gunboats to strengthen its Yangtze Patrol, in order to raise America's profile and influence in China. After much lobbying, an order for six new mid-sized vessels was finally approved in 1924.[33] Delays in securing funding and then during construction at Shanghai, however, meant that the first of those new American gunboats was not launched until 1927. The one area where the USN Asiatic Fleet did not experience an upgrade was its flagship with the pre-war cruiser USS *Huron* (launched 1904) replaced in December 1926 by the equally outdated USS *Pittsburgh* (launched 1903). In contrast, the British flagship was first HMS *Hawkins* (launched 1917) and then HMS *Kent* (launched 1926), both of which were on their inaugural commissioned voyages. As the China Station was formed around the Fifth Light Cruiser Squadron, it remained the most powerful naval force based in the immediate locality. The growing strength of both America and Japan's deployments on the Chinese coast, however, meant that Britain's margin of superiority was slim and increasingly difficult to demonstrate to civilian observers.

Along with the shifting balance of international power in Chinese waters, Britain's gunboat force was affected by changes within China itself. After the collapse of the Qing rule, the fighting between rival warlords resulted in a rapid modernization in the land-based military equipment used in China. This was part of a long-term trend, as European and American technological supremacy in that area had been waning since the 1870s and 1880s, relative to China, but that process accelerated in the years after the Xinhai Revolution.[34] By May 1924, for example, even a relatively small band of three hundred bandits operating near Guangzhou was recorded as being armed with four field guns and thirty Thompson sub-machine guns.[35] The 'Tommy Gun' had only become available for sale in 1921 and was a far superior squad-level weapon than the heavy Lewis machine guns and bolt-action Lee–Enfield rifles carried by British service personnel at that time.³⁶ Where the Royal Navy could keep their distance, particularly while sailing along the lower Yangtze, the greater range and accuracy of the British weaponry was an advantage. Along narrower waterways or ashore that was not the case. While the average Chinese soldier or bandit was still likely to be less well armed than the British seamen and marines they might encounter, that advantage could no longer be taken for granted.

Steel plating, splinter mattresses and sandbags were often employed as relatively effective supplementary countermeasures against small-arms fire, with the river itself aiding defence by keeping snipers at a distance from the warships.³⁷ Caught by surprise and unprepared, HMS *Robin* reported in October 1920 that only minor damage was sustained and no injuries suffered when it was suddenly machine-gunned in the Pearl River delta.³⁸ The distance from shore alone had helped avoid a more serious incident for the slow-moving gunboat. Likewise, the better-prepared HMS *Gnat* counted over one hundred rifle rounds fired at it near Chongqing in March 1926, of which seventeen hit the vessel, but only three risked causing injury.³⁹ While relatively low risk, the experience could be unnerving for crews. Petty Officer Herbert Page wrote how 'bullets rattled like hail on the superstructure' when HMS *Mantis* came under fire from the riverbank in April 1927.⁴⁰ Not everyone was lucky, however, with Henry Onion severely wounded by a stray bullet while working at HMS *Widgeon*'s forge on 22 May 1926.⁴¹ The risk also applied to other nations, with one French sailor killed and another wounded when the gunboat *Alerte* suddenly came under fire in October 1926.⁴²

Moreover, those countermeasures could do little against heavy weapons, and a well-aimed artillery shell fired at relatively close range would cause significant harm.⁴³ On 29 May 1924, for example, HMS *Tarantula* came across two merchant vessels near Guangzhou that had been badly damaged by artillery shells fired from shore, with numerous casualties reported on both vessels.⁴⁴ With next to no armour plating on most of the Royal Navy's gunboats, they were little better suited to facing such an attack than those civilian steamers. Indeed, the smaller gunboats like HMS *Robin* at just 85 tons and 108 foot long would be at risk of suffering critical damage and numerous casualties if hit by an accurate artillery shell.⁴⁵ HMS *Bee* had a lucky escape from such a scenario on 8 September 1926, when fired upon by two field guns, leading to one shell inflicting substantial, but largely superficial, damage to its steel hull (see Figure 8).⁴⁶ Britain's gunboats still held an advantage given their firepower, but they were no longer able to cruise the river almost immune from harm, as they had done in prior decades. Even

Figure 8 Damage to HMS *Bee* 8 September 1926.
Source: Photograph album of Major Frederick Burden RMLI, 8 September 1926, RMM, 1992/112/1.

then, in the Victorian era it was not unusual for a few gunboats to carry the same weight of firepower as a small army, but by the 1920s that was no longer the case.[47]

Fortunately for Britain, the Royal Navy's perceived power protected it from serious, organized attacks for most of the decade. Between 1923 and 1925, for example, the quarterly reports sent to the Admiralty from the China Station often noted that no shots had been fired near or at British warships. This was despite regular reports of other vessels using the Yangtze and Pearl Rivers having been hit by both small arms and artillery.[48] In one incident in early 1923 the Chinese cruiser *Chao Ho*, after threatening to bombard 'enemy forces' in Shantou, was dissuaded from doing so by the arrival of the smaller HMS *Magnolia*.[49] The British warship may have posed a limited direct threat by itself, but a fight with the Royal Navy was almost certain to lead to the later destruction of the *Chao Ho*. In another curious incident, a Chinese cruiser hit just below the bridge by artillery fire near Nanjing placed itself behind the smaller HMS

Mantis for protection. The outgunned and vulnerable *Mantis* trained its two 6" guns on the cruiser and quietly steamed on as the shore batteries fell silent. The following day, the two ships exchanged pleasantries and the Chinese captain showed the British crew the considerable internal damage that had occurred, although fortunately without loss of life.[50]

It was not until 2 May 1927, therefore, that heavy weapons were first used against Royal Navy vessels, when the destroyer HMS *Wanderer* came under rifle and artillery fire from Guomindang troops near Jiangyin.[51] *Wanderer*'s subsequent, immediate heavy counter-bombardment was intended to remind the Chinese troops of the Royal Navy's superior firepower. Lieutenant Commander Louis Hamilton nonetheless felt that his ship had been lucky to escape with only one wounded sailor, with some shells only narrowly missing the ship's superstructure. As China's soldiers and bandits were increasingly capable of and willing to challenge British warships in this way, the invisible protection provided by the Royal Navy's waning prestige was of even greater importance.

The rapid modernization in East Asia's weapons pool after the First World War was not purely a hindrance to the Royal Navy. In 1921, for example, the SVC was loaned a range of surplus wartime weaponry by the British Government, including four 4.5" howitzers, nine hundred rifles and twenty-four machine guns.[52] Likewise, the American and Italian governments made similar, if much smaller, donations towards the SVC companies manned by their citizens.[53] The following year Shanghai's Municipal Council purchased a further four hundred brand new rifles, fourteen Vickers medium machine guns, along with revolvers, steel helmets and grenades. The Council also funded the construction of ten locally designed armoured cars over the decade, with seven in service by early 1925.[54] Prior to these purchases the SVC had generally relied on obsolete British Army weaponry donated as it was phased out of use, with infrequent small supplementary purchases funded by the SMC.[55] The Corps of 1918 had therefore been armed with a motley collection of weapons, some of which dated back to well before the Boxer Uprising, and with most in a poor state of repair.[56] Alongside an enthusiastic but largely amateur approach, the pre-1919 SVC was little more than a very basic part-time militia.

The mass influx of up-to-date, if slightly worn, equipment therefore provided a step change in capability. In addition, the attachment of experienced British Army Warrant Officers and many volunteers who had served during the war contributed to a growing professionalism within the Corps. As concern grew about the situation in China, so did the strength of the SVC as foreign residents were encouraged to play a role in the defence of the International Settlement. Between 1920 and 1927, for example, the number of volunteers increased by 40 per cent from 1,345 to 1,887 (see Figure 9). With better equipment being procured and experienced wartime officers replacing those previously appointed as social favours by the Commandant, morale improved significantly.[57] As a result, attendance increased from an 'active' participation rate of 73 per cent in 1920 to 86 per cent the following year, peaking at 88 per cent in 1924.[58] By 1927, favourable comparisons were even being drawn between the SVC and Territorial Army battalions back in Britain.[59] The SVC's Light Horse Company, drawn from the city's wealthier residents, proved to be the exception and retained their nickname as the 'Tight Horse' due to their drinking prowess.[60] Overall, however, the SVC was increasingly capable of dealing with all but the most extreme crises that might affect Shanghai from 1920 onwards, largely relieving the Navy of one task drawing on its manpower.

While there were such practical benefits, overall the flow of modern weaponry into China was steadily eroding the perceived strength and novelty value of the Royal Navy's river force. As a result, the British Empire was left with two options if it was to preserve its powerful image in the region. The first option was to strengthen the China Station. With the Treasury looking to cut rather than increase the Admiralty's funding that choice would have required

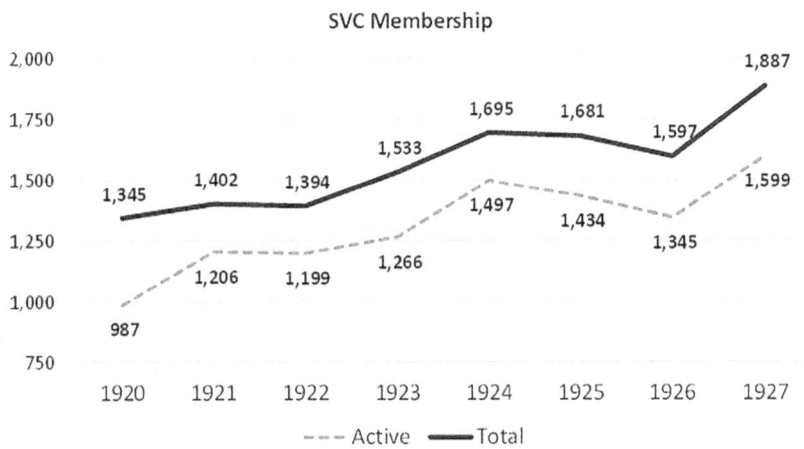

Figure 9 Shanghai Volunteer Corps membership 1920–7.
Source: Shanghai Municipal Council Annual Reports 1920–7, SMA, U1-1-933 to U1-1-940.

redeploying resources from elsewhere. Such shifts in vessels would either result in the abandonment of another post or greater force dispersal, which would go against the core element of Britain's post-Fisher naval grand strategy. Neither was acceptable to the Admiralty. Alternatively, the Royal Navy could make a qualitative improvement to its China force.

Hermes the trickster

Commissioned in 1924, *Hermes* was the world's first purpose-built aircraft carrier, and with a complement of relatively new aircraft (Fairey IIID and Fairey Flycatcher), for a very brief period it represented the cutting edge in the rapidly evolving field of naval aviation.[61] The posting of *Hermes* to Asia in August 1925 was therefore highly symbolic, having only recently completed its sea trials in the Atlantic and the Mediterranean. Shortly after arriving in the region, on 1 November 1925, three of *Hermes*'s aircraft took pride of place as a ceremonial escort for the ship delivering Hong Kong's new governor, Cecil Clementi.[62] The parade was an attempt to impress both the city's population and the warships from China, France, Japan and the United States that were docked in the harbour. The spectacle's impact was undermined, however, when one of the aircraft was caught in turbulence and crashed into the harbour. As a result, the local English-language newspaper, the *China Mail*, reported the accident as front-page news, relegating coverage of Governor Clementi's welcome to page seven.[63] Nonetheless, the intention had been to exploit the aircraft carrier's novelty in order to advertise British power in the region.

Hermes's first tour on the China Station was characterized by daily exercise and training flights over and around Hong Kong, up the Pearl River to Guangzhou, or across to Macau. During those six months there were only two recorded instances where the ship was used in an active military role. Even those were far from dramatic. In the first, an armed guard was simply sent by motor launch to inspect a Chinese steamer.[64] In the second, two aircraft were despatched in vain to find a Dutch cargo vessel, which was suspected of transporting weapons to the Guomindang in contravention of an international arms embargo.[65] The little real drama from the first visit came from formation flying displays, watched by crowds of onlookers, some of which were reported by the local press.[66] Articles in the same newspapers a few weeks later suggest that the novelty soon wore off, especially as the regular early morning practice flights over the city were less appreciated by the locals.[67] In contrast, after returning to the China Station in late 1926 *Hermes* was involved in monthly anti-piracy operations in Daya Bay, spending far less time in Hong Kong harbour.⁶⁸ Even then *Hermes*'s role was as much symbolic as military; during an anti-piracy raid on villages in Daya Bay in March 1927, for example, aircraft were flown overhead in part 'to add to the impression of power'.⁶⁹

The sedate nature of *Hermes*'s first visit to Hong Kong in late 1925 was aided by the military aircraft present in China not yet posing a significant threat to Britain's interests. Only the strongest factions had been able to finance the purchase of aircraft in any quantity, and even then most descended rapidly into a poor state of repair, due to a lack of fully trained mechanics.⁷⁰ In July 1925, for example, Consul General Jamieson reported to Michael Palairet that most of the Guomindang's aircraft were not in a sufficient state of repair to even reach Hong Kong from Guangzhou, a distance of just over one hundred miles.⁷¹ While the direct threat was limited, the contrasting absence of British airpower in East Asia was increasingly felt to be undermining Britain's powerful image. This was particularly true of the British colonial communities in the region, with the *China Mail* strongly advocating the need for military aircraft, arguing that they were vital in the competition between major powers for prestige in East Asia.⁷² Up until this point the only real display of British military aviation in East Asia had involved the outdated seaplane tender HMS *Pegasus* visiting Hong Kong in November 1924, as part of a global tour taking aerial photographs of strategically important harbours.⁷³

Hermes's deployment came at a point when military aviation in China was developing rapidly. Immediately after the First World War Britain had largely dominated the flow of aircraft into China. Sales of some of Britain's roughly ten thousand surplus wartime aircraft were made as part of a wider effort to recoup at least part of the estimated £1 billion of military equipment no longer required in peacetime.⁷⁴ Dominating the global surplus military aircraft market enabled the British government to influence the number and quality of aircraft sold to many second-tier powers. To some extent this had ensured that most aircraft in China in 1920 were already outdated compared with those used by the major powers' air forces. That situation did not last long. After signing the multinational treaty embargoing armament sales to China in mid-1919, Britain lost its tentative power of influence. While British arms manufacturers found ways to break the embargo, the French arms industry in particular exploited the absence of support in Whitehall for aircraft sales to China. Such was the shift to France that by 1923 one of Zhang Zuolin's trusted commanders, Colonel Wei, had been sent to establish an office in Paris purely for ordering new military equipment.⁷⁵ As a result, by early 1924 Britain had little influence over the flow of what were often brand new military aircraft being sold to China's warlords.

Concern about the prestige risk presented by growing interest in aerial power in China was exacerbated in mid-1925 when the Soviet Union sent five of its latest aircraft on a diplomatic tour from Moscow to Guangzhou. While technical faults forced two of the five to abandon the tour, the three that completed the journey were reportedly a big hit with Guomindang officials and the local population. Indeed, Hong Kong's two main English language newspapers, the *China Mail* and *Hong Kong Telegraph*, both featured articles in the following weeks arguing that the tour had been a victory for Soviet prestige and influence in the region.⁷⁶ This was not the first time another power had completed such a tour. The previous year a flight of four US Army Air Service aircraft visited Shanghai, Hong Kong and Guangzhou as part of their world record, world tour.⁷⁷ The Americans were received warmly at Hong Kong and set a stark contrast to the single RAF seaplane that was competing against them for the record. The British competitor arrived three weeks overdue and later crashed off the Japanese coast.⁷⁸ While that was considered bad luck, beaten by an admired friend, there were considerably stronger feelings about the Bolshevik foe having pulled off a propaganda coup in such a sensitive location for Britain. Along with the anti-British boycott, launched after the May Thirtieth Incident, these events around Hong Kong were combining to make the British Empire look weak. As a result, Cabinet were convinced that an effective way to remind the Guomindang and the people of Guangzhou of Britain's power would be to use military aircraft.⁷⁹

The role of military aircraft in China was not based around their combat effectiveness but rather the psychological impact of their use. *Hermes*'s normal contingent of fifteen Fairey IIID and Fairey Flycatchers only provided a theoretical maximum cumulative bombload of 1,200 lb (544 kg) per sortie, which was relatively trifling compared to the ordinary naval firepower available on China's main waterways. During the Nanjing Incident in 1927, for example, HMS *Emerald* alone fired roughly 600 kg of ordnance within the first minute.⁸⁰ Likewise, a few weeks later HMS *Wanderer* discharged almost 2,000 kg of shells at a group of Chinese soldiers near Jiangjiu, during a relatively short engagement.⁸¹ With ranges of between fifteen and twenty kilometres, the main naval guns could adequately cover the majority of territory immediately surrounding the treaty ports, although with questionable accuracy.

Aircraft did provide the new possibility of punitive raids far inland, but there are no records that such a mission was actively considered. In the event of accidents or aircraft being downed by enemy fire, RAF pilots would have been left far from help or rescue, particularly given the rules against ground forces being sent into Chinese territory. In authorizing the deployment, the Cabinet instead intended *Hermes* to operate in a colonial policing role similar to the RAF's activities in the Middle East, trying to use the fear generated by the novelty of military aircraft to intimidate and emphasize British superiority.[82] Their presence would also have the contrasting effect on the British colonial community in China, by reassuring them that Britain would do what was considered necessary to protect them.

It is unlikely that using military aircraft was a particularly effective means of impressing the Chinese audience or even had the potential to achieve the desired results in boosting British prestige. During the early years of military aviation in China, between 1917 and 1923, aircrafts did reportedly instil fear and respect among civilians and troops alike. By the time *Hermes* arrived in the region, however, aircrafts had become a common feature in the skylines over eastern China. Most warlords and factions possessed their own embryotic air forces and regularly employed them in dropping leaflets, reconnoitring enemy positions and bombing targets. The arrival of British aircraft therefore only added to a general normalization of the Chinese population to the presence of military aircraft. Not only that, but after the initial employment of aircraft the morale impact of bombing and strafing attacks tended to decline rapidly, a fact evident from the experience of air policing elsewhere in the Empire.[83]

While ostensibly *Hermes*'s tour was intended to boost British prestige in China, the Admiralty had an additional, nominally secret motive. During the tour, Fleet Air Arm and RAF personnel carried by *Hermes* spent a significant amount of time ashore while in Hong Kong, establishing military facilities at Kai Tak (Kai Teck) airstrip, Kowloon.[84] Founded only the previous year, Kai Tak was a quiet airstrip on newly reclaimed land in Kowloon Bay, suitable for both land-based aircraft and seaplanes.[85] The initially basic facilities established there were gradually expanded, with Kai Tak later becoming an official RAF airfield, although it also remained Hong Kong's main international airport right through until its closure in 1998.[86] Under the terms of the Washington Treaty, Britain had agreed to maintain the 'status quo' in regard to its military facilities at Hong Kong, theoretically but not explicitly banning the creation of a military airfield.[87] The clause was one that the Admiralty had been very reluctant about, regarding it as a dangerous concession, but one they had agreed to in order to secure the overall treaty.[88] Britain had not been willing to sacrifice existing naval bases during negotiations, but suspending upgrades to Hong Kong and Weihai were considered acceptable losses to secure Japan's agreement not to seek a harbour south of Taiwan (Formosa).[89] At the time of *Hermes*'s tour in 1925 the British government still wanted to avoid being seen to break the treaty, as it would have provided Japan and the United States with cause to revoke it, potentially threatening Britain's global defence strategy.[90]

Adapting the facilities at Kowloon's civilian airstrip under the guise that it was a 'temporary landing ground' for *Hermes*'s aircraft may not have been within the spirit of the Washington Treaty, but in Britain's view it was not a clear violation.[91] In 1923, the Admiralty advised its senior commanders that storing military aircraft supplies at Hong Kong would not contravene the Washington Treaty, so long as the equipment was transported by an aircraft carrier.[92] As carrier landings were still extremely hazardous, both on deck and using floats, it was not an outrageous argument that land-based facilities would be installed on a temporary basis for pilot safety. Roughly one in four carrier landings in the early 1920s resulted in damage to the aircraft, with one in twelve leading to the aircraft being written off.[93] Certainly during his time as Executive Officer aboard HMS *Hermes* during 1926, Commander Reginald Ramsbotham remembered aircraft regularly being written off from rough landings, although most aircrew escaped with minor injuries.[94] Such attrition rates were unsustainable and difficult to justify in peacetime. While an airstrip was safer for the pilots it also removed the need for the Fairey IIIDs to use floats and allowed them to carry more fuel, both of which increased the aircraft's potential range.[95]

Despite the safety argument, the discussion around the 1923 War Orders provided by the Admiralty suggests that the decision to establish ground-based facilities was actually primarily intended to strengthen Hong Kong against a potential Japanese attack. A military airfield also had additional value in strengthening Britain's position in relation to China. Should war with either of the two Asian powers have appeared likely, RAF squadrons could be quickly despatched to Hong Kong with the required front line stores, facilities and equipment ready for their arrival. Upon departure from Malta, *Hermes* had picked up sixteen spare aircraft and as many RAF supplies as the ship could carry, which were unloaded soon after arrival in Hong Kong.[96] When *Hermes* later went to make its departure from the China Station, its commander Captain Cecil Talbot recorded: 'We have left a few aircraft, and most of the RAF personnel, at Hong Kong.'[97] As a result, a study in early 1928 stated that in the event of war, Kai Tak was sufficiently prepared as a semi-military airfield that it could support three squadrons (*c.*50–70 aircraft) at short notice.[98] As the aircraft already available in the region aboard HMS *Hermes* provided Britain with sufficient air power to deter attacks from the Guomindang, the scale of the preparations further suggests that Kai Tak's development was quietly directed against the perceived threat from Japan.

By 1927, Britain stretched the terms of the Washington Treaty further by permanently stationing one flight of six fighter aircraft at Hong Kong's airfield. As the aircraft were transported to China by an aircraft carrier and on detachment from the Fleet Air Arm, they were publicly presented as a temporary defensive measure related to events in China.[99] This was officially discussed and authorized by the Chiefs of Staff, who were recorded as stating: 'We have never admitted that the use of (Kai Tak) is prohibited in so far as operations against the Chinese are concerned, by the Washington Agreement.'[100] A further disclaimer was made that the military aircraft sent to Shanghai were also not seen as restricted by the treaty, under Britain's interpretation, given that the city was neither official British territory nor a military base.

The first RAF flight appointed to the Far East then took yet another step in bending the terms of the Washington Treaty. While permanently based at Singapore, the four Supermarine Southampton flying boats also spent time working out of Hong Kong. As the flying boats did not require the use of Kai Tak's runway, they enabled the continued pretence that the airfield was only a civilian enterprise. It was only finally in January 1930 that the RAF officially put in place a command structure recognizing the existence of a Far East Command, including a presence in Hong Kong.[101] Curiously, after a decade of trying to avoid breaking the Washington Treaty, the creation of the Far East Command occurred three weeks before the opening of the London Naval Conference and six years before the expiration of the original agreement. It seems likely that by that point Britain was sufficiently confident that restrictions on base enhancements in the region would be rescinded. Signed in April, amid a range of negotiated compromises, the Admiralty got their way and the limitations on air power at Hong Kong were lifted.[102]

Throughout the process of developing Kai Tak as a military airfield at Hong Kong, the Admiralty does not appear to have formally consulted Cabinet. As an operational matter, which the Admiralty argued did not breach Britain's international treaty commitments, there was no requirement to seek political approval. In the June 1925 correspondence with Cabinet about *Hermes*'s deployment, the Navy referred to using an improvised landing ground at Happy Valley racecourse in Hong Kong to land its Fairey Flycatcher fighters, with no mention of Kai Tak.[103] When *Hermes* departed Portsmouth on 17 June, however, it was already loaded with additional aircraft equipment to be delivered to Kai Tak.[104] The omission is therefore highly suggestive that the Admiralty used the situation in China to quietly facilitate the controversial development.

This is supported by the Royal Air Force Marshal Hugh Trenchard when he proposed exactly the same plan during a Cabinet discussion in November 1926, after *Hermes* had already returned from delivering its first load of aircraft equipment to Hong Kong. Trenchard apparently had no knowledge of what had already happened at Kai Tak and was advised by Foreign Secretary Sir Austen Chamberlain that such a move would put the Washington Treaty at risk.[105] Likewise, at the end of *Hermes*'s first deployment, the Colonial Office lobbied the Navy to remove the equipment from Kai Tak, when it became clear it would be left behind when the warship was due to depart China. Talbot's diary indicates that an initial response from an unnamed individual at the Admiralty agreed with the Colonial Office that the Washington Treaty was at risk, but all opposition was dropped quite suddenly after senior command became involved.[106] Alternatively, it is plausible that successive British governments avoided officially recognizing the plans to help maintain the pretence that the Navy was only temporarily using what was otherwise a civilian airfield. In either case, the choice of *Hermes* to conduct the subterfuge, named after the trickster god of Greek mythology, seems particularly appropriate.

Such hidden motives raise the question whether the Royal Navy by the 1920s really believed that displays of naval technology were effective at boosting British imperial prestige. Certainly, image appears to have been an important factor under consideration. During Seaman Albert Heron's time aboard HMS *Carlisle* from 1919 to 1921, for example, 'much, much more attention' was paid to the cruiser's appearance than was normal on other stations, in order to make a strong impression when visiting Chinese ports.[107] A similar account from Seaman Thomas Wallace, stationed in China aboard HMS *Vengeance* between 1907 and 1908, indicates that this was a long-term trait of the China Station.[108] Indeed, warships on the China Station were painted white, in contrast to the standard grey used worldwide by the Royal Navy. That distinctive colour scheme ensured among other things that the vessels stood out from their peers, which is clear from contemporary photographs.[109] The disappearance by the 1920s of outright statements in official naval communications emphasizing the need for flag waving, however, would suggest that imperial prestige carried less weight after the First World War than it had done previously. Indeed, even in debate at the House of Commons there were only infrequent references to flying the flag in China in the early 1920s, such as Gershom Stewart MP suggesting it would help at the smaller concessions to 'reassure those of our people there'.[110] Was *Hermes*'s deployment to China in 1925 therefore actually more to do with preparing the facilities at Kai Tak rather than impressing the Chinese population?

The lack of even a brief visit to Shanghai or Guangzhou by the carrier on its first tour, obvious choices if the intention was to spread word of British aerial prowess in China, supports the idea that *Hermes*'s deployment was not primarily to boost imperial prestige. Likewise, during its time in Hong Kong only four official receptions for foreign naval officers were held, two from the USN and two from the French Navy.[111] *Hermes*'s captain was not going to great lengths to show off his new ship, particularly when compared with its time in the Mediterranean en route to China. The vague statement made to the House of Commons by Bridgeman is not particularly convincing either, referring to *Hermes* being sent for 'training and exercising the Fleet Air Arm' and possibly assisting in defending British interests in China.[112] Training could easily be done in the Mediterranean at a lower cost than making the trip to Hong Kong, and the quiet stationing of *Hermes* in Hong Kong harbour for almost the entire tour did little to support the second stated aim. Hong Kong was rocked during that period by major strikes after the May Thirtieth Incident, but the city had survived previous strikes and the main anti-British protests, and resulting violence, occurred at Shanghai and Guangzhou.[113] Investigating the impact of the local climate on flying conditions or testing the suitability of landing sites might have supported a deployment to China, but neither factor was mentioned in the correspondence. While strengthening imperial prestige therefore provided the opportunity for *Hermes*'s first deployment, the primary motive behind the Admiralty's decision was the establishment of military airfield facilities at Hong Kong.

With the Royal Navy's standing in East Asia under pressure from the growing power of both its international rivals and by China itself, in addition to the Admiralty's diminishing interest in overtly displaying its power, the China Station was in a precarious situation. For most of the 1920s, however, even if the Royal Navy's image of strength was waning, the service was still regarded with wariness and respect by China's leaders and population. No warlord or faction officially challenged Britain militarily during the 1920s, although during the 1927 crisis there was some willingness by the Guomindang to allow minor clashes between its troops and British warships, even if only through passive acquiescence. For the most part, the Royal Navy's experience was similar to that seen during the Nanjing Incident when HMS *Emerald*'s officers all reported that neither southern nor northern troops deliberately fired at the ship.[114] The only casualty aboard *Emerald*, Able Seaman John Knox, was hit in the head by a stray bullet when fighting first erupted between the rival Chinese troops, and before Captain England ordered his men down from exposed positions. It is therefore difficult to attribute the growing number of incidents where naval vessels were fired upon by Chinese troops to a shift in respect afforded to the Royal Navy or diminishing fears of potential retribution, particularly as the USN was exposed to the same trend.[115] The increase in violence was instead a result of the growing sense of nationalism in China and – crucially – the greater availability of modern weaponry.

This is supported by the ground-level interactions involving British servicemen in China. Seaman Arthur Gaskin remembered that during the troubles at Hankou in January 1927, Chinese protestors generally preferred toying with British personnel by trying to knock their steel helmets off using bamboo poles.[116] His opinion was that while Chinese protestors were boisterous and occasionally mischievous, they did not look to start fights with groups of foreign servicemen. Gaskin did note that lone foreigners were at greater risk of beatings during tense protests, recounting how a Royal Marine patrol rescued a badly injured German doctor who had tried pushing through the crowd. The local American newspaper, the *Hankow Herald*, also provides a slightly more dramatic account of the bamboo pole swinging antics, stating that two seamen were deliberately knocked unconscious during the course of events.[117] However, the weight of first-hand accounts tend to agree with Gaskin's core views on interactions with Chinese civilians. Both Lieutenant Ian Wight and Private Ernest Whitney, for example, felt that the Chinese were generally friendly with or at least respectful of British servicemen, when they were posted to Shanghai and Guangzhou, respectively, in 1927.[118]

Overall, while new technology was used at times in an attempt to reinforce British prestige in East Asia, those efforts had become a secondary aim targeted at reassuring the British colonial population in the region. The Admiralty placed much less value on waving the flag, in line with the general post-Fisher shift in strategy away from gunboat diplomacy. Crucially, however, any decline in the Royal Navy's perceived power in China did not significantly alter the events on the ground. Chinese troops and bandits were increasingly capable of engaging foreign forces, but even the worst clashes did not show any serious intent to challenge Britain militarily. The Royal Navy's use of technology was overwhelmingly focused upon the practical requirements of defending the British Empire, rather than reinforcing how it was seen by the Chinese.

Understanding China

Communications technology played a key role in influencing how the British Empire was organized and controlled, particularly in relation to the Royal Navy. As late as the mid-nineteenth century the reliance on ship-borne mail as the main long-distance means of conveying information and ideas resulted in significant discretionary power being placed with local officials and commanders.[119] For Britain's outposts in East Asia that situation only started to change after the first telegraph cable was laid to Hong Kong in June 1871, transforming London's ability to understand what was going on in the region.[120] In the following two decades the British government started to exploit this comparatively rapid form of communication as a means of actively influencing events as they happened.[121] Sending messages around the world with those early cables took hours and often required resending as a result of being garbled by poor-quality transmission, but that was still a huge leap forward from postal communication.[122] For the most part, however, the interpretation of events and subsequent formation and implementation of policy stayed with the China Station's commander-in-chief, in conjunction with his Foreign Office counterparts in Hong Kong and Beijing. Likewise, communication at the base of the Navy's command chain remained reliant on intermittent letters between ship and shore. It could therefore take weeks for orders to be distributed to all China Station vessels, or longer when the commander-in-chief was out on tour with his squadron. This could lead to policy being further diluted, as decision-making authority passed by default to officers lower down the scale.

Correspondence between Vice Admiral Arthur Moore, commanding the China Station in 1907, and the Admiralty provides a peacetime example of how communication prior to the First World War affected policy. On 28 July 1906 Lieutenant Commander George Todd, commanding the gunboats on the upper Yangtze, decided to hold a banquet at Leshan (Kiating) to promote better relations with the local Chinese officials. Using his own money, Todd spent thirteen dollars and two cents on 'wines and liqueres' (*sic*), five dollars and sixty-two cents on food and fifty cents on cigarettes.[123] While not an exceptional amount, equivalent to a few days' pay, if such banquets were held regularly the cost would soon add up for such junior officers. It was not until 12 January 1907 that Vice Admiral Moore, commander-in-chief of the China Station, received and was subsequently able to forward the report and associated expense request for the feast to the Admiralty.[124] A further two months lapsed before the Admiralty's answer was dispatched in March, stating that such banquets were not official Navy policy and so the cost would have to be met by the officers involved.[125] Moore responded with a passionate letter in April arguing that promoting warm relations with Chinese officials could provide Britain with 'a great deal of advantage'. In addition, Moore made particular reference to growing competition from other nations for trade in China while justifying the expense.[126] Perhaps feeling that he had overstepped his authority, Moore retracted his letter a week later with a statement that the order had been distributed to his officers that no official banquets or gifts were to be exchanged with Chinese officials.[127]

If there was a comparable further delay in Moore's order reaching the upper Yangtze, it had taken the Navy almost a year to clarify what authority junior officers had in exercising soft power in China. By that point, Todd had already been notified of his next command and his imminent departure from the Yangtze. The process could have been expedited during a crisis, by using dedicated despatch vessels, for example, but this example illustrates how Whitehall only had a distant and delayed ability to influence events on the ground.

Slow communications could have far greater consequences than matters of soft diplomacy, with junior officers sometimes facing the burden of decisions that could significantly impact upon Britain's relationship with China. This was true of the Navy worldwide, but was particularly pronounced in a command like the China Station where smaller warships often operated in comparatively remote locations.[128] In early 1907, for example, when a British steamer was seized by the Guangzhou authorities in relation to the death of a Chinese passenger, a young Lieutenant Commander in charge of the West River gunboats ordered 27-year-old Lieutenant Gerald Dickens to take his destroyer HMS *Hart* and recover the vessel.[129] His orders were to negotiate a peaceful release with the Chinese government officials, but if necessary to use force. Looking back on the events, Dickens later wrote in his memoirs that he felt it was amazing that such responsibility was left to junior officers who were not required, or indeed able, to get authorization from the Commodore at Hong Kong, but that the situation was quite normal before wireless sets became commonly available. In this case, Dickens convinced the Chinese officials that it would be better for everyone if the gunboats detaining the steamer were withdrawn, but the peaceful outcome relied heavily upon the amicable relationship between him and his Chinese counterpart.

Had the Chinese authorities refused Dickens's proposal, a small flotilla of British destroyers was being prepared nearby to engage the three Chinese gunboats and 'cut out' the steamer, much in the style of what was attempted during the 1926 Wanxian Incident. A potential battle between the two nations' warships, and the diplomatic crisis that it would have produced, was only avoided through a negotiation conducted on the British side by an officer with just one year's experience in sole command. Effective wireless equipment therefore offered the opportunity to accelerate the flow of information and orders along the chain of command, putting many decisions of similar importance in the hands of senior officers.

Wireless sets were first introduced by the Royal Navy around 1900, but it was not until shortly before the First World War that new advances really made them into effective tools.[130] Those sets available in 1904, for example, were capable of transmitting merely fifty miles in daytime, which was of limited value across the expanses of the China Station.[131] Even as wireless technology improved, the limited funding available to purchase sets and difficulties in finding sufficient space to house the equipment on smaller vessels meant that it was only during the First World War that most naval vessels had radios installed.[132] As an outlying outpost that was not integral to the Royal Navy's grand strategy, the China Station was a low priority for receiving those sets that were available. Indeed, in 1913 both Vice Admiral Martyn Jerram and Captain Frederick Powlett had bemoaned in letters to the Admiralty how the Royal Navy's effectiveness on the Chinese coast was hampered by delays in issuing wireless sets.[133] The planned issuing of wireless sets, however, which the two officers were attempting to expedite, was subsequently cancelled due to the outbreak of war in Europe. Wireless sets therefore only appeared on China Station warships in any numbers when relatively new, wartime-built vessels were sent out to East Asia in 1919. Crucially, most river gunboats still had to wait for older sets to be cascaded down to them, a process completed in 1924.[134]

One early incident in China where the value of wireless sets can be clearly seen was during warlord fighting around Beijing in late 1923. The telegraph lines out of Beijing were severed during the violence, removing the normal means of communication with the outside world used by the various international consulates within the city. As a result, the wireless link between the British consulate and a Royal Navy warship at Tianjin became the sole quick and effective means Britain had for communicating with the legation. While the situation in Beijing was felt to be sufficiently calm not to require a Royal Navy taskforce to be based at Tianjin, it was still tense enough to require a rapid means of requesting help should the situation take a turn for the worse. After hearing of the Great Kantō earthquake in Japan and the devastation it had caused, Admiral Leveson sent as many vessels to assist as possible, with three warships and two support vessels despatched immediately, all laden with supplies and medical personnel.¹³⁵ Leveson also wanted the sloop HMS *Foxglove* to join the humanitarian mission, but it was delayed while waiting for HMS *Bluebell* to take over its duties maintaining a link in the radio chain to the diplomatic mission in Beijing. Without the newly installed radio sets on the China Station's sloops, Leveson would have had no choice but to hold one of his valuable cruisers off the northern Chinese coast, reducing his force's ability to provide humanitarian assistance in Japan. Radio enabled the China Station to monitor events around China, without having to post forces sufficient to deal with possible, but not necessarily probable, adverse scenarios.

Sometimes the influence wireless had on the China Station's force disposition was less obvious. Prior to the First World War, for example, one light cruiser and two sloops were normally based on the Yangtze in order to afford rapid support to the resident gunboats.¹³⁶ When tracing through the ship's logs for the China Station's cruisers in the early 1920s, it is evident that visits to the Yangtze had become relatively rare, consisting of infrequent stops at Shanghai, Nanjing and occasionally Hankou. The cruisers spent most of their time docked or training at Hong Kong or Weihai, or making diplomatic tours of the wider region, as can be seen with the example of HMS *Carlisle* (see Figure 10). At times of crisis,

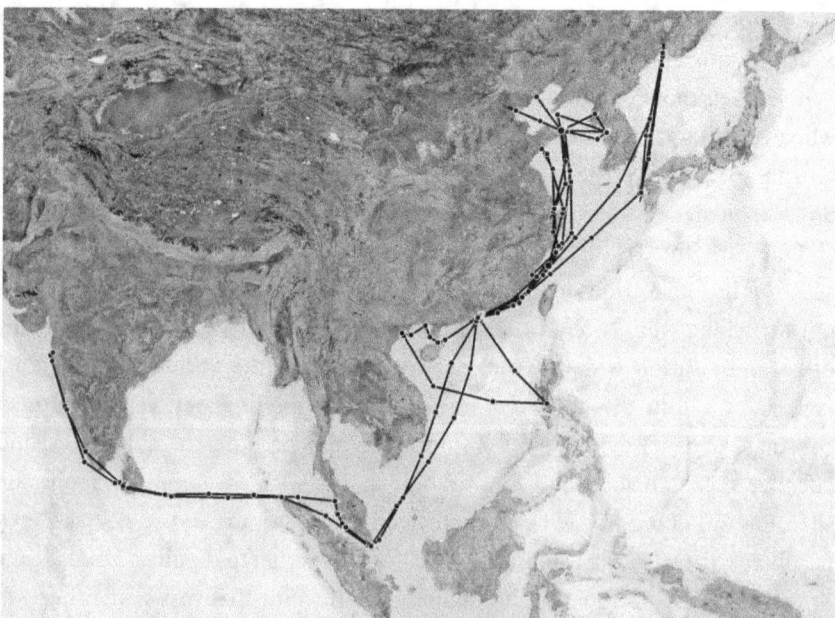

Figure 10 Movements of HMS *Carlisle* 1920–3.
Source: Courtesy of Journey Plotter and Naval-History.net, https://www.journeyplotter.nl/index.html, last accessed 31 October 2019.

however, the cruisers could still be summoned by radio. During an attack by Wu Peifu's troops near Qinhuangdao in late October 1924, for example, the cruisers HMS *Despatch* and HMS *Durban* along with the sloop HMS *Foxglove* were assembled from around the region with additional marines from HMS *Hawkins* and HMS *Diomede*. The force was issued with orders to land at the city if required to maintain order.[137] As it became clear that the fighting would not affect the city, the naval force was soon reduced and normality was resumed by 17 December, with the cruisers docked back at their berths in Hong Kong and Weihai.[138]

As conflicts came and went around China during the decade, the Royal Navy's wireless links became increasingly important for the wider British establishment. The Foreign Office's Consul at Chongqing, R. S. Pratt, reported in January 1927 that he was almost wholly reliant upon the news stream from the Navy's gunboats on the upper Yangtze.[139] Later that year most articles published by Hong Kong newspaper about inland China bore the label 'British Naval Wireless'.[140] With the telegraph network frequently disrupted through changes in frontier, the normal alternative was to wait for mail and newspaper deliveries by ship. Postal services could take weeks to travel that far upriver and bundles were occasionally lost.[141] Reliability of ground communication was not just a practical issue. Even when the cables were operational, cases were seen at Hankou where press telegrams had been altered either before or during transmission.[142] Instead the Navy's wireless transmissions kept the vessels, and the ports they were posted to, updated with the latest news. During January 1927, for example, Midshipman Philip Burnett recorded day-by-day the forces being despatched to China, while stationed aboard HMS *Emerald* at Nanjing.[143] Burnett was even able to note the exact units being assembled in Britain within days of those units receiving their orders, such as the 12th Royal Marine Battalion. The enthusiasm with which Burnett recorded the news provides some indication of the morale boost provided from hearing so quickly that reinforcements were on their way.

The greater flow of naval messages around the Station did not always have a positive impact upon the recipients. While at Weihai, Lieutenant William Andrewes serving as torpedo officer aboard HMS *Ambrose* noted a growing sense of unease and concern in June 1925 after the May Thirtieth Incident, as the ship received messages about clashes around China. This came to a climax on 24 June after overhearing reports from Guangzhou about the shootings on Shamian Island the preceding day. Andrewes wrote that he was very unsettled by reports of foreign women and children being hastily evacuated from Guangzhou and so spent his free time that evening at Weihai's club reading newspaper reports about the situation in China. Perhaps a statement about the questionable accuracy of the *North China Herald* in particular, Andrewes returned to his quarters that evening feeling no more certain or comfortable about what was behind the events.[144]

The desire to gain insights into both what was happening around China and the causes behind those events was even greater on an institutional level than the personal curiosities of Lieutenant Andrewes, Midshipman Burnett or their colleagues. The Navy had long made use of human intelligence to achieve those aims, but the arrival of radios provided the first opportunity to exploit signals intelligence. Adopting a policy of actively intercepting foreign warships' transmissions provided a new external source of information. While primarily intended to improve Britain's knowledge of other countries' naval codes and radio techniques, particularly Japan's, the messages also included valuable news and indications of the policy plans of other powers.[145] Instructions from an American Admiral to the warships of the Asiatic Fleet, in the aftermath of two USN destroyers being hit by artillery fire on the Yangtze, for example, were intercepted and then circulated by the Royal Navy ships at Hong Kong on 26 April 1927. The result was that when HMS *Wanderer* sailed upriver a few days later, it was fully prepared for a fight, allowing it to respond immediately when similarly fired upon by Guomindang troops near Jiangyin.[146]

Gathering secret intelligence from wireless signals extended an existing policy of intercepting and decrypting telegrams. British ownership of the main long-distance telegraph cables had long provided secret insights into other nations' plans.[147] Nor was it just naval communications that the Royal Navy targeted, as diplomatic communications were generally poorly encrypted in the early interwar period. As a result, they became a popular target for intelligence services the world over, including Britain's.[148] In contrast to telegraph intercepts, however, wireless intercepts came with a reliability problem, as some transmissions were only partially intercepted or were difficult to decipher. This appears to have been a regular issue with Chinese communications, given British naval telegraphers' inexperience in dealing with Chinese codes and transmission techniques. In one such example, two-thirds of a message from Guomindang officials in Nanjing to the Yunnan Provisional government detailing the movements of the 38th Army was either missed or unreadable.[149] The delays involved in sending complicated signals back to the Government Code and Cypher School, and deciphered copies back to the China Station, also reduced the operational or tactical value of time-sensitive intelligence.[150] Despite those limitations, radio intercepts did provide a valuable new supply of snippets of information to better inform decisions made by the Royal Navy.

While success in intercepting Chinese messages was decidedly mixed, Britain had less trouble with Japanese transmissions. In part this was due to the weakness of Japanese diplomatic encryption, linked with a habit of repeating messages to all its consuls in China and many overseas embassies. For example, in the aftermath of the May Thirtieth Incident in 1925 the Japanese foreign minister sent instructions to all his consuls in China updating them on Japan's official stance towards relations with Britain. While the original transmissions were missed by the Royal Navy, the British authorities were able to intercept and decrypt the message when it was forwarded to the Japanese ambassador in London. As a result, the British government was aware that the Japanese government believed its own citizens in China were trying to stoke anti-British sentiment, but did not approve of that behaviour.[151] Such reports added weight to the pre-1927 assessment that the Japanese government would not seek a war with Britain, but there was a growing risk the two powers could be driven to war due to Japan's aggressive commercial expansion in China.[152] This was not helped by a relatively rapid shift in Royal Navy officers' attitudes towards Japan and the Japanese in the mid-1920s, from patronizing and dismissive, based on a background of racial prejudice, to outright distrustful.[153]

Wireless equipment also sometimes resulted in unexpected developments, which included the creation of a new role for the *L*-class submarine flotilla. In the years after their first deployment to China in 1920, those submarines had generally been employed on regular training exercises. Their primary purpose as a deterrent targeted towards Japan came with few peacetime responsibilities. The Royal Navy generally avoided leaving the submarines in China's mercantile ports, as the boats themselves had too few crew to provide effective shore parties, except when deployed en masse as a flotilla. Submarines were also extremely vulnerable to being sunk through collisions with merchant vessels. One unfortunate submarine suffered that fate in June 1931, when HMS *Poseidon* was accidentally rammed and sunk by the Chinese merchant ship SS *Yuta* off Weihai.[154] The occasional exceptions to that mundane, if dangerous, routine usually resulted from the vessel's possession of a wireless set.

The radio sets aboard the *L*-class submarines had a range of up to 1,000 miles, although in practice reliability was poor when used over such long distances.[155] That enabled a submarine stationed at Qinhuangdao for much of 1924, for example, to act as a link in a wireless chain used for monitoring unrest in the region, in a similar fashion to the previously mentioned case involving

HMS *Foxglove*.[156] With twelve submarines available on the station, one could be regularly spared for relay duties without having a noticeable impact on the flotilla's day-to-day operations. The Royal Navy's efforts to maintain order at the various treaty ports in 1927, however, provided an additional new opportunity for meaningful peacetime employment of the submarines. The months of crisis placed high demands on the China Station's surface vessels, with the force spread thinly around China's many ports that contained British civilians. As a result, the warships were largely unavailable for sustained anti-piracy operations. With piracy still plaguing areas such as Daya Bay, the Navy remained under significant pressure to deal with the threat to British shipping. The Admiralty's defence for its approach towards Daya Bay, in particular, was the argument that at least three vessels would be required to patrol that expanse of water alone and such a deployment was unlikely to prove effective enough to justify the cost.[157]

On 28 October 1927 Commodore John Pearson, the Senior Naval Officer at Hong Kong, outlined a new plan to solve the problem, although the core proposal was most likely drawn up by Commander Allan Poland of the submarine tender HMS *Ambrose*.[158] Citing ad hoc deployments dating back to 1923, Pearson instigated permanent submarine patrols around Daya Bay at night searching for suspect vessels. If a ship failed to respond to hailing and the firing of a blank shell, the submarine could radio for assistance, while remaining at a safe distance to avoid being rammed and sunk. Should the ship attempt to flee, the submarine was to use its deck gun to target the engine room and prevent an escape. Surface vessels would therefore remain on watch at Hong Kong and Guangzhou, for example, but when requested could attempt to seize pirated vessels only a few hours sailing away. The submarine commanders also felt that such a role would provide valuable training and experience for their crews, given the similarities between the work and wartime commerce raiding.[159]

While the strategy was generally sound, things did not always go so smoothly in practice, as Lieutenant Frederick Halahan with submarine *L4* discovered on 20 October 1927. After challenging the SS *Irene*, the pirates controlling the vessel decided to take pot-shots at the submarine with their small arms. Halahan promptly returned fire with the submarine's 4" deck gun, which not only killed most of the pirates but also set fire to the *Irene*. While the *Irene*'s 234 crew and passengers were freed, the ship and most of its cargo ultimately sank.[160] Submarines were not ideally suited to stopping pirated vessels peacefully, but they nonetheless supplemented the China Station's other means of reconnaissance and intelligence gathering. Wireless technology therefore enabled the Navy to become more efficient in covering the expansive waters around China's coastline.

Numerous, cheap to maintain, small, lightly crewed vessels and aircraft equipped with radios could act as the Navy's eyes and ears, not just in wartime but also during peace.[161] The handful of larger vessels available would then be free to respond only when they were really needed.

Improvements in how fast news travelled between naval posts could and did help improve the accuracy of knowledge the Navy possessed about events in China. However, there was no organized system for gathering and assessing intelligence reports, and then disseminating guidance around the China Station. Whereas the Foreign Office compiled a single document containing summaries of the intelligence updates sent in by its consuls on a range of pertinent diplomatic topics, submitted on a quarterly basis, the Admiralty only received intermittent reports subject to individual officers' judgement.[162] The Foreign Office quarterly reports do not appear to have been shared with the Admiralty on an official basis, although informal exchanges of information between officials working in China seem probable. Technology had advanced, but the process used to report developments and keep ship's officers informed remained largely unchanged from the age of sail.[163] That absence of a coordinated understanding of the situation in China was sorely exposed by the escalating events of late 1926.

While there was a Secret Intelligence Service (SIS) presence in China, its regional officers were forbidden from sharing their reports with even senior British officials in East Asia.[164] As a result, SIS was blamed by the armed forces for the lack of forewarning about how tense the situation had become in China during 1926, leading to an order from Cabinet in January 1927 forcing greater disclosure. With SIS's Asian operations later described as the 'Cinderella Branch' of the Service – largely forgotten and starved of resources – it is unlikely that SIS had much information to disclose in any event.[165] Britain's failure to foresee the crisis of 1927 cannot be solely attributed to SIS's failings and was a result of the wider, disorganized nature of Britain's military intelligence gathering apparatus in East Asia. Indeed, several contemporary decisions indicate that the armed forces were starting to recognize that there were significant deficiencies in their own organizations.

In early 1927, there was a tense exchange of messages between the War Office and Major General John Duncan, commanding the Shanghai Defence Force. The orders and demands from Whitehall show a profound nervousness that Britain did not know the strength or intentions of the different Chinese armies.[166] As a result, on 23 April the War Office issued orders for the creation of a temporary Shanghai Intelligence Bureau, to gather information in support of the Shanghai Defence Force.[167] A further order was issued the following month that the new Bureau should become a permanent establishment, gathering military intelligence from Northern China to Malaya in coordination with the existing military attachés in Beijing and Tokyo.[168] In the subsequent months both the Admiralty and Air Ministry followed suit in making their own changes. For the Royal Navy, this involved clearly assigning an officer aboard every China Station vessel to intelligence duties, required to report regularly to regional staff officers based at Shanghai, Hong Kong and Singapore, who would in turn pass on vital information to a senior officer on the commander-in-chief's staff.[169] It was only through the combination of both structural and technological changes that the Royal Navy improved the consistency and accuracy of understanding what was occurring in China, across the China Station and along the command chain.

By 1930, the China Station was regularly using signals intelligence, rapidly passing news from ship to ship over long distances and had in place an organized structure to exploit that wealth of information to try to form a single, unified approach to dealing with China. While individual ship's commanders retained considerable leeway to act on their own initiative, this represented a significant shift towards a centralized command system. Counter-intuitively, however, the changes strengthened rather than weakened the position of the commander-in-chief. While Whitehall could issue tighter instructions and orders to guide developments, implementation of policy remained at the Admiral's discretion, which he was able to enforce over his officers with greater control. For all the changes, though, ultimately the strength of the system was still dictated by officers' behaviour, influenced by their training, personalities and experience. Those individual decisions were to play significant roles in some of the pivotal crisis moments during the decade.

Responding to crises

More efficient news gathering and transmitting capabilities had led to changes in how the Royal Navy's vessels were distributed across the China Station, which in turn influenced how the Navy responded to threats around the region. New technology also had a deeper impact in changing the way in which the Royal Navy went about its work. In dealing with piracy, for example, wireless technology not only allowed the substitution of submarines for surface vessels on patrol duties but also provided options for a very different underlying approach to the problem.

Before radios became readily available in East Asia, the Royal Navy was generally unable to respond to acts of piracy until well after the event. As a result, valuable goods were frequently stolen and sometimes the entire ship's cargo was lost. The only proactive steps the Navy could take involved maintaining a deterrent, in the form of naval patrols or stationing armed guards on vulnerable merchant steamers. Both options required significant amounts of manpower, which came at a cost. Indeed, with only fifty-three crew aboard each fully manned *Insect*-class gunboat and as few as twenty-five on others, the Navy did not have enough spare men to provide regular armed guards along river routes.[170] Even the Navy's preferred option of making the police in the main ports inspect passengers' luggage was manpower intensive and proved largely ineffective. In 1929, for example, the Shanghai Municipal Police checked for weapons the passengers of ninety-two ships set to depart the Bund, at the request of their captains, but only found one group of suspected pirates from all those efforts.[171] With many hundreds of ships passing through the main ports every month, inspections were disruptive, expensive and produced very limited results.

The ability of merchant vessels to radio for assistance in the event of emergency provided the possibility for naval vessels to catch pirates in the act, while still able to perform other day-to-day duties. Even if the attacked merchant vessel did not possess a radio, passing ships or patrolling warships could request assistance on the victim's behalf and then coordinate a search for the perpetrators. In essence, merchant vessels became additional eyes and ears for the Navy, in return for the protection the Royal Navy provided.

At 05.25 on 16 November 1926 the sloop HMS *Bluebell* radioed Hong Kong reporting that it had spotted a ship on fire in Daya Bay.[172] After reaching and boarding the affected ship, the Butterfield and Swire's steamer SS *Sunning*, *Bluebell* confirmed by radio at 09.18 that the vessel had been attacked by pirates. Within seven minutes the flagship HMS *Hawkins* ordered HMS *Hermes* to send out aircraft to search for the pirates, as well as passengers who were believed to have been taken hostage in the ship's lifeboats. As a result, two aircraft were underway just over half an hour after confirmation was received. The cruisers *Despatch* and *Vindictive* were ordered to sail for the bay as soon as possible. *Hawkins* also radioed other merchant vessels in the area both as a warning and to request their assistance in searching for the lifeboats. Through their combined efforts, by 15.32 a Norwegian merchant vessel and one of the *Hermes*'s aircraft had separately radioed in that they had located the missing lifeboats.

That night Admiral Edwyn Alexander-Sinclair radioed further, very precise, orders to Captain Ronald Howard of HMS *Vindictive* on exactly what action

Howard was allowed to take regarding reports that two female passengers had been taken hostage ashore.[173] Sinclair made it clear that landing parties could only be sent ashore if the reports were first confirmed, with advance warning provided to the local Chinese authorities. Indeed, Sinclair ordered *Vindictive* to use its three spotting aircraft to conduct the primary search for the missing women ashore, as it should avoid any accidental clashes with Chinese troops. In either event firing was explicitly forbidden, unless British servicemen first came under fire. Fortunately, it was established by the following noon that all but one of the *Sunning*'s passengers and crew were safe, with the exception believed to have drowned trying to escape the attack. Eighteen pirates were arrested during the recovery operation and some of the looted goods were recovered. The case highlights how radio equipment allowed a quick response to a piracy attack, along with the better coordination of the responding ships to secure a comparatively peaceful and diplomatic incident-free resolution.

The China Station commander's ability to guide events from a distance was only of real significance given a similar improvement in his ability rapidly to despatch reinforcements to those areas where he felt the situation to be critical. *Hermes*'s deployment was extremely valuable in that sense, because the high-speed and large capacity of aircraft carriers made them ideal for rapidly moving troops and supplies in response to crises.[174] Apart from the handful of cruisers, most warships posted to the China Station were only capable of transporting one or two dozen servicemen in addition to their small crews. The sloop HMS *Bluebell*, for example, was only felt safe to carry thirty-four marines for a short journey between Hong Kong and Guangzhou, in addition to its normal crew of seventy-seven.[175] Under normal circumstances, warships smaller than a cruiser were not regularly posted a marine detachment of their own. This was a problem during a crisis as Royal Marines or British Army troops were preferable for shore work, compared with ordinary seamen, given their training and equipment. The 'small' carrier *Hermes*, in contrast, could accommodate hundreds of additional service personnel and their equipment, if required. For the anti-piracy raid at Daya Bay on 31 August 1927, for example, *Hermes* and the cruiser *Danae* transported almost all of the 476 servicemen landed, with only the destroyer *Sirdar* and sloop *Foxglove* assisting.[176] There was also a 'substantial' reserve force held back aboard the vessels, in case the landing force got into trouble, making a sizeable total force transported by the four vessels. Indeed, based upon a 1938 assessment by the Navy, *Hermes* alone was capable of transporting the entire force while remaining fully functional as an aircraft carrier.[177]

Civilian steamers were generally used to transport personnel between distant ports, such as when the Shanghai Defence Force was deployed from the UK in early 1927.[178] With many weeks required for those long-distance journeys the slower, but more efficient, pace of commercial vessels was not considered to be a major disadvantage. The steamships also normally afforded greater comfort for the transported servicemen, particularly the officers who enjoyed the luxury of first-class booths.[179] The Atlantic Transport Line steamship *Minnesota*, for example, was used to transport the 12th Royal Marine Battalion to Shanghai, but only had a maximum speed of fourteen knots.[180] The Admiralty considered using the larger carrier, HMS *Furious*, which was capable of transporting the marines from Portsmouth to Shanghai an estimated twelve days sooner than *Minnesota*.[181] *Furious* was equipped with new oil-fuelled boilers and could sustain twenty-five knots over long distances if required, with fewer maintenance concerns compared with older coal-fuelled warships.[182] Illustrating Admiralty policy, *Minnesota* was selected as carriers were only the first choice when time was considered critical and so the higher expense in fuel and wear could be justified, and comfort was not a consideration.[183] One of the most impressive examples was in 1929 when HMS *Courageous* transported a full infantry battalion of 734 servicemen over a thousand nautical miles from Malta to Haifa in just forty-eight hours, averaging twenty-one knots.[184] For movement around China's coastline, *Hermes* therefore gave the Royal Navy a rapid 'heavy-lift' capability, which would have been entirely impossible just two decades earlier.

After transporting a force and once the shore parties had alighted into small boats to head ashore, *Hermes* was also capable of returning to its primary role as an aircraft carrier. During the 31 August 1927 raid, *Hermes* provided aerial cover for much of the mission. The value of an aerial overflight was highlighted during the short period when aircraft temporarily based at Kai Tak took over from *Hermes*. At 11.45 am, shortly after arriving on the scene, the aircraft's observers spotted a column of Chinese troops approaching the shore party. The regular updates subsequently provided through messages dropped directly to the shore party and radioed to *Danae* enabled Captain Lachlan MacKinnon to move his force away from the approaching Chinese troops and avoid a potential clash.[185] Despite two hundred Chinese troops coming within a hundred metres of the landing force at one point, Captain MacKinnon later reported that he only knew about their presence due to the aerial reports.[186] Photographs taken from the aircraft illustrate this point, with rows of houses and trees clearly restricting the ground observers' field of vision.[187]

Possessing an aerial scouting force was even more valuable to the Royal Navy by the 1920s, given the greater availability of modern weaponry in China. It was increasingly probable that Britain's shore parties might encounter armed groups of soldiers or bandits, who could bring to bear a comparable or superior level of firepower. As a result, naval officers were increasingly concerned about the possibility of suffering casualties during landing operations. At a senior level, there was also concern about what impact sustained firefights with Chinese troops would have on Britain's relationship with China. If a shore party came under heavy fire it would almost certainly call on naval fire support to provide a covering bombardment, to facilitate their evacuation, as happened during the Nanjing Incident. Firing large-calibre naval guns brought with it the almost certain likelihood of Chinese fatalities. If those killed were from the groups firing upon British servicemen then the incident, while hardly positive, could be defended under the contemporary understanding of rules of engagement. The situation was not that simple though, as most naval guns in use by Britain's gunboats, sloops and destroyers were not designed for shore bombardments. With targets often centred in locations inhabited by civilians or in close proximity to civilian areas, accuracy was a paramount concern.

Naval gunfire at Wanxian and Nanjing

Two of the most dramatic single moments involving the Royal Navy in China during the 1920s involved naval gunfire, both of which highlight the issues of accuracy. The casualties caused by shore bombardments during the botched 'cutting-out' expedition to Wanxian in 1926 and then by naval gunfire support at Nanjing in 1927 played a significant role in fanning the flames of anti-imperial fervour in China. Simple technical considerations played an important, but previously unreported role in the tragic outcomes.

The 6" 'quick-fire' guns on most of the British gunboats, twelve-pounder guns on the *Acacia*-class sloops and the different variations of main guns on Britain's cruisers were all naval guns. They were designed for hitting other vessels on a relatively flat trajectory, over a medium range, which would also be at sea level. When firing at ground targets at short range, often behind the riverine levees bordering China's rivers, shells were prone to overshoot the target due to the very precise angle required on such a shallow trajectory. A change in elevation of just one degree for a 6" gun, for example, would lead to the shell landing a further one thousand yards away.[188] The cruisers had basic systems to calculate accurate gun-laying angles at sea, but aiming was still largely reliant on manual estimation.[189] On the gunboats, accuracy was entirely down to the abilities of the gun commander and his crew, and their state of mind during the action. Many gunnery officers only had limited experience and training in shore bombarding, making precise shooting at ground targets very unlikely.[190] This was a factor in the cause of civilian casualties both at Nanjing and Wanxian, where over the course of events naval guns were fired at combatants located on a hillock and city wall, respectively. None of the following points are intended to deny or distract from the fact that British warships did fire upon the two cities and in doing so caused many innocent civilian casualties. The aim is to provide an objective assessment of factors that influenced the outcome and tender potential explanations for the discrepancies surrounding the numbers of those killed.

At Wanxian in August 1926, Royal Navy boarding parties aboard the armed merchant vessel *Kiawo* triggered a firefight with Chinese troops, while attempting to 'cut out' two British merchant steamers being detained by the city authorities. Named after the process of severing a stationary vessel's anchor or mooring lines, 'cutting-out' expeditions were common in former centuries but were rare occurrences by the twentieth century. In this case, when *Kiawo* came under fire, the supporting gunboat HMS *Widgeon* engaged Chinese troops on and near the city wall. Approximately twenty minutes into the fight HMS *Cockchafer* joined the fray and began firing at the military headquarters of General Yang Sen, sited on a hill within the city.[191] At Nanjing in March 1927, a bombardment was made in response to a request for fire support from a shore party of twelve American marines. The group had been cornered on 'Socony' Hill by rioting Chinese troops, while attempting to evacuate ninety mostly American civilians.[192] Bordered on its western edge by the city wall, Socony Hill is a relatively small and steep-sided hillock near the north-western corner of the old Nanjing city walls, approximately thirty metres above the river level at its peak. The cruiser HMS *Emerald* and destroyers USS *William B Preston* and USS *Noa* replied to the request with a few heavy opening salvoes of shrapnel shells, followed by a slow series of high-explosive shells as the shore party was withdrawn.[193] The American destroyers also opened fire at shore targets with machine guns.[194]

In both Wanxian and Nanjing, trying to hit precise targets on shore using the warships' main guns meant that the angle required had to be accurate to within a few minutes, rather than degrees. With such fine margins of error, gunnery officers were reluctant to risk firing short and potentially hitting their colleagues, and so guns were often aimed high.[195] Cases involving overshooting during shore bombardments were not unique to events in China. It had been a significant concern during the Gallipoli campaign in 1915, occurred during contemporary training exercises and was later seen during amphibious operations of the Second World War.[196]

Manual inaccuracy was a significant factor at Wanxian, particularly after the British gunboats came under fire. Rear Admiral Hugh Tweedie later attributed at least some of the civilian casualties to *Widgeon*'s gun crews being unable accurately to hit the Chinese troops and field guns positioned in front of and on top of the high city wall. Tweedie indicated that a significant amount of ammunition was fired over the top into populated areas beyond.[197] An anonymous eyewitness reported that *Widgeon* fired a few hundred two-pound (0.9 kg) high-explosive 'pom-pom' shells.[198] While there are grounds to doubt the accuracy of other sections within the account, that particular detail tallies with clues in other descriptions. This includes a report by Consul A. P. Blunt from October 1926, by which point he had been able to explore the city, detailing that large quantities of smaller calibre shells had hit buildings on the slope immediately behind the wall. In Blunt's opinion most of the damage caused there had been a result of secondary fires, although he made no mention of how many deaths were related to that damage.[199] Along with these lighter shells, an unquantified amount of machine-gun fire was also directed at the city wall, with bullets flying over the target just as deadly to bystanders as shells.

What Tweedie did not mention was the lack of shielding or temporary protection around *Cockchafer*'s 6" main gun. The absence of even basic defensive preparations led to the warship's captain Lieutenant Commander Leon Acheson and many of the gun crew being wounded during the incident. With the men left dangerously exposed and suffering casualties, aboard a moving vessel, *Cockchafer*'s attempted bombardment of Yang Sen's headquarters was not particularly accurate, with shells landing in the densely populated surrounding area.[200] Again this is supported by Blunt's account, which noted that most of the damage caused by the British bombardment had been up on the hill – *Cockchafer*'s target area.[201] While it is more difficult to corroborate the anonymous witness' figure for *Cockchafer*, they suggested that between twenty-four and thirty-six of the larger shells were fired into the city.[202] It is unclear why Acheson was unable or unwilling to prepare his vessel during the days while he was waiting for *Kiawo* and *Widgeon* to arrive in support. Acheson's motivation for attempting to shell the headquarters of the general with whom he had only recently had a ferocious argument is a little easier to deduce. The limitations of the weapons used did therefore play a role in the damage done to Wanxian, but a wider range of factors contributed to the scale of the destruction.

In contrast to Wanxian, reports from naval personnel and British, American and French civilian observers all agreed that the naval gunfire at Nanjing was generally well-aimed.[203] Monsignor Roger Caplain, of the *Postes Chinoises*, began his observation after the first salvo:

> The shot was admirably set upon the hill, where the residences of the Standard Oil Company … were located, about 300 metres south-south-west of our residence. I later learned that the shrapnel shot had been executed by Lieutenant O'Connor of HMS *Emerald* and as a (former) artilleryman, I would like to congratulate him.[204]

The British gun crews aboard the stationary *Emerald* were in comparative safety and conducted most of the firing at a steady and relatively slow pace of one round per minute.[205] Contemporary photographs support reports from the time that the hill and immediate vicinity was sparsely populated wasteland, limiting the likelihood of collateral damage from accurately directed fire.[206] Nonetheless, given the precise accuracy required to hit the apex of Socony Hill, it is probable that at least a few shells overshot the target. As thirty-six of the seventy-six shells fired by *Emerald* at Nanjing were shrapnel, with timed fuses that detonated before they could significantly overshoot the target, the precise number of shells detonating in areas well beyond the target was very low.[207] Based upon the information available, the bombardment at Nanjing appears to have been conducted as accurately as possible, within the restrictions of using largely manually aimed, high-velocity naval guns. Those technical limitations, however, meant that a small number of British shells almost certainly did miss their intended target, potentially by some distance.

Accusations made at the time and since that the Royal Navy deliberately bombarded civilian areas as a punitive measure are therefore partially true.[208] In both cases the decision to fire was made with the knowledge that any bombardment, with the naval guns available, was going to be at least moderately inaccurate and so shells would hit unintended, possibly populated, districts. Captain England's own testimony about the Nanjing Incident is telling in this regard, when he stated that three hours before the actual request was made, he had already decided that in the event of Socony Hill being rushed, he would order the bombardment of the area directly behind the hill in support.[209] While that target involved an unpopulated mixture of woodland and open waste ground, England would have known the limitations of his main guns, given the challenging trajectory required.[210] As a result, he would have also known the likelihood of missing that area and therefore the potential for civilian deaths, whether or not he intended them. Indeed, with both the British and American consulate buildings located near Socony Hill, England will also have been aware of the potential for 'friendly-fire' casualties.

A similar account for Wanxian is provided by Lieutenant Anthony Pugsley, who was aboard *Widgeon*, in which he later argued that the gunboats had only deliberately targeted military objectives. The reliability of Pugsley's account is open to question, however, as it does contain some rather obvious attempts to deflect blame, resulting from an apparent sense of guilt.[211] It is true that inaccurate gunnery contributed to the high civilian death count at Wanxian, something acknowledged by the Navy at the time.[212] Given the scale of damage caused though, it is also fair to say that accuracy was not the primary, or even a significant, factor that led to civilian areas of the city being bombarded. The events at the two cities were therefore slightly different. England's fervent desire to attack the city punitively on 25 March strongly suggests that he was entirely comfortable with Chinese civilian casualties. Nonetheless, regardless of those feelings, when he actually gave the order to fire on 24 March, he focused on an area of open ground. *Widgeon*'s firing at Chinese troops on the city walls may fall in a similar category, but *Cockchafer*'s bombardment of Yang Sen's Headquarters was of dubious military value and very probably intended for purely punitive purposes.

Even with the likelihood that some British shells were overshot at Nanjing, a small detail in Captain England's official report raises questions about the resulting number of casualties. When outlining the targeting of *Emerald*'s earlier salvoes, England noted that they were aimed at the area of open ground slightly to the rear-left of Socony Hill, from the ship's perspective (see Figure 11). This was the direction from which the Chinese individuals participating in the events were approaching the house. Given that *Emerald* was moored by the Butterfield and Swire's hulk at Hsiakwan, the resulting line of fire made it far less likely that overshot shells would land in densely populated areas of the city.[213]

In the northern half of Nanjing the two main populated areas were around the river shoreline outside the city walls, and a strip running from the Fung (Chung) Gate past the British and US consulates, to the small Sanpailou railway station. Neither of these districts was within *Emerald*'s field of fire. Instead the area directly beyond *Emerald*'s target was largely open, apart from Nanjing's fledgling agricultural college (now Nanjing University of Finance and Economics), a small

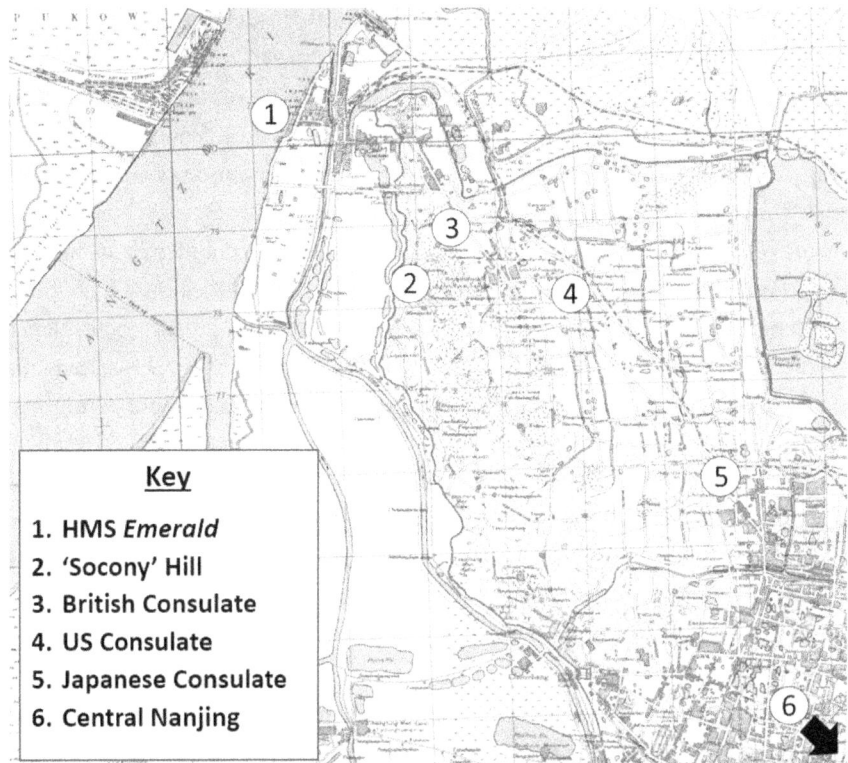

Figure 11 Map of Socony Hill and the surrounding area in 1927.
Source: 1927 British War Office Map of Nanjing, republished by the US Army 1945, Perry-Castañeda Library Map Collection, [Nanjing] Nanking 1945.

temple and a few bungalows among the wooded hillocks that formed the city's European residential quarter. This was not specific to the western section of the city, with large areas within the old walls formed of little more than sparsely populated wasteland in this period.[214] To have reached a densely populated city district, the shells would have had to overshoot by roughly three miles, a total of five miles from *Emerald*.[215] That was quite a distance given the increase in trajectory required, even when allowing for the difficulty in aiming at a hilltop. On flat ground, for example, that would have involved a change in gun elevation from 2.5 degrees to 13.5 degrees. It is therefore extremely unlikely that any overshot shells, from *Emerald*, hit a densely populated area of the city.

Assessing potential civilian casualties purely through using maps of the area only provides a very rough indicator and one that should not be used alone. Eyewitness testimonies provide supporting evidence to help us understand what was happening in northern Nanjing on the day. Consul General Giles states in his account that most Chinese civilians that he saw in the northern part of the city were located around the Fung and Jiang gates – well away from the target area. While he mentions numerous soldiers and a police officer near the British consulate, his account outlines that no shells landed in the immediate vicinity.[216] Roger Caplain was in the same area and also made no mention of shells landing in his immediate vicinity.[217] Likewise, Lieutenant Oliver-Bellasis who was in Socony House stated that 'The shells burst either in open country or against the walls and hills', although he acknowledged seeing one Chinese house hit.[218] Such written accounts have previously been open to question, given the allegiance of the individuals concerned. However, it appears likely that such statements contained a strong degree of truth, even if their subsequent assertions of minimal civilian casualties are more dubious.

The unpopulated nature of the target area and its hinterland does not appear to have formed part of Captain England's calculations. Indeed, he only mentioned the precise area the shelling was aimed at in passing, as part of the paperwork accounting for the expenditure of ammunition. His decision was not made, therefore, to avoid killing or wounding innocent bystanders. Nonetheless, that decision significantly reduced the number of shells fired by *Emerald* that could plausibly have landed in areas containing significant numbers of civilians, which would have been required for the thousands of casualties listed in some accounts.

With friendly forces under fire in both cases and the warships' commanders therefore bound to provide covering fire, accusations of punitive bombardments appear academic in terms of the actual incidents. The weaponry available was, unfortunately, incapable of providing sufficiently accurate fire support for civilian casualties to have been realistically avoided. This was particularly true of Nanjing, although it was a lesser contributory factor at Wanxian. Midshipman Burnett noted that the Royal Navy landing party he was with, helping evacuate those trapped on Socony Hill, were themselves almost hit by one shrapnel shell burst fired approximately hundred metres short of the target.[219] The group quickly fired two 'Very light' green flares as a warning for the warship to adjust its aim. It is also worth noting that even if there was an entirely accurate bombardment of the target area, it would still have resulted in civilian casualties, as some civilians were reported to have been present with the Chinese troops and looters on Socony Hill.[220]

The American bombardment will have involved many of the same issues and the first-hand reports suggest it was no less accurate than the British shelling. However, the two US destroyers also machine-gunned targets ashore, which adds a further complication. Consul General Giles's account of where crowds had formed indicates that if such machine-gun fire had been directed around the hulks at Hsiakwan, the foreshore abreast the warships, then numerous civilians would have been in the line of fire.[221] This may have been subsumed into Chinese accounts of casualties from the foreign bombardment of the city.

Not all the civilian casualties that occurred due to shelling that day were necessarily a result of Anglo-American actions. Gunboats operating under Guomindang authority bombarded various locations on 24 March, during fighting between troops from the different factions.[222] Reports of Northern Expeditionary shelling are supported by photographs of Pukow, located on the opposite bank of the Yangtze to the area targeted by *Emerald*, which show fierce fires on both 24 and 25 March. The *North China Herald* quoted eyewitness accounts of artillery belonging to southern forces on Shizishan 'Lion' hill, near the Fung Gate, opening fire across the river at Pukow.[223] Burnett and England's accounts, however, state that those guns only arrived into position on the 26th, indicating that the *Herald*'s sources were mistaken.[224] Fleeing northern troops also set fires and destroyed buildings during their retreat, so some of the damage likely resulted from that scorched earth activity.[225] What is particularly pertinent is that no account suggests that any foreign warship fired upon Pukow and so any shelling there was entirely the result of fighting between Chinese forces.

Together, all these various factors explain why there are such widely differing numbers quoted for how many civilians perished at Nanjing, ranging from as low as three, up to two thousand.[226] It is entirely plausible that the contemporary British assessment of fifteen was based purely upon those civilians killed on Socony Hill, whereas higher figures include casualties from Anglo-American shelling, firing by Guomindang forces and general violence in the city. Focusing upon the gunfire itself in detail, using a broad selection of alternative sources and not just general descriptions of the incidents, it is possible to say with reasonable confidence that the number of civilian casualties caused by British shelling at Nanjing was towards the lower end of the scale. In contrast, the inaccurate gunfire at Wanxian strongly suggests that official British estimates of only two hundred troops and eighty civilians killed were extremely conservative.[227] However, technical factors were not the only contributory factor in those deaths at Wanxian. Lieutenant Commander Leon Acheson's decision to direct *Cockchafer*'s fire directly into populated areas, based upon a threat by Rear Admiral Cameron, and Acheson's failure to prepare any form of protective shielding for his gun crews were both significant to the end result. As will be further explored later on, Acheson was not solely responsible for what happened at Wanxian in 1926, but he did play a pivotal role in the deadly outcome.

To some extent the precise numbers of those killed in both cases were tragic but minor details in the bigger picture. It was the very act of bombarding the cities that enflamed passionate anti-imperial responses. Reports of mass casualties only added fuel to the fire.[228] Nonetheless, whatever the exact figures attributable to the Royal Navy in those two cases, some of the problem of overshooting into civilian areas was avoidable with a relatively simple change in equipment. Arriving in the aftermath of the Wanxian Incident, the new senior naval officer on the Yangtze – Rear Admiral Tweedie – reported to the Admiralty that the gunboats' high-velocity naval guns should be replaced with howitzers as soon as possible.[229] Delays meant that it was not until HMS *Falcon* and HMS *Sandpiper* were launched in 1932 and 1933, respectively, replacing two older gunboats, that 3.7" howitzers finally appeared on the China Station.[230] With a high arc of fire and low muzzle velocity, howitzers were better suited to landing shells in a tighter spread at short range, reducing the risk of collateral damage and improving the chance of hitting the intended target. This would have significantly lowered the precision required from the gunnery officers in aiming their guns, while still being able to put shells into the right area. In doing so, the use of howitzers would have reduced the likelihood and magnitude of civilian casualties. The Shanghai Volunteer Corps had already had its field guns replaced with howitzers, in 1921, for that very reason.[231] Likewise, China's own warlord navies had long understood this issue, and most Chinese river gunboats launched after 1912 were equipped with howitzers.[232] It is unlikely that the presence of howitzers aboard the Royal Navy's gunboats would have significantly altered the general course of events at either Wanxian or Nanjing. The use of naval guns was a factor, however, in causing additional and avoidable civilian casualties.

Both events came against a backdrop where civilian deaths caused by British commanded personnel, whether civilian or military, were increasingly the cause of strikes or boycotts of British goods. The better use of technology, such as howitzers in place of naval guns or aircraft in place of shore parties, could reduce the possibility of creating significant headline incidents that would affect Britain's overall position in China. With growing nationalist sentiment in China, such incidents were no longer isolated to just the area they occurred in and could spark regional or nationwide reactions. This applied even to relatively small events, outside of major cities, which did not involve civilian casualties. For example, Commander Hamilton's use of HMS *Wanderer*'s main guns against Guomindang troops near Jiangyin, in May 1927, prompted protests and warnings directly from Chiang Kai Shek to Admiral Reginald Tyrwhitt.[233] Previously warships on the Yangtze would normally only respond with small arms or medium-calibre weapons to gunfire from the riverbanks. *Wanderer* expended seventy-eight 4.7″ shells during the short engagement, which even Hamilton later conceded was excessive. Reports that the Chinese had fired first with a field gun appear to have provided enough balance to the argument for the Guomindang not to publicize the incident. Two weeks after the incident, however, Tyrwhitt told Hamilton in private that he wanted no further such incidents while he was working with the Foreign Office to decide a new policy towards the Guomindang.

Controlling the violence

While the technical specifications of *Emerald*'s guns played a negative role in the violence at Nanjing, another technology had a more positive impact: the availability of radio equipment. The Anglo-American naval force present at the city was able to contact their respective commanders at Shanghai and receive a response within hours. The cautious joint reply by Admiral Williams USN, Vice Admiral Tyrwhitt RN and Rear Admiral Jirō Araki IJN was instrumental in Rear Admiral Henry Hough USN and Captain England's decisions to negotiate with Guomindang representatives on the second day. As with the earlier *Sunning* incident, the senior commanders were able to provide guidance during the crisis, rather than just issuing new advice after the event. It was during that second phase, after the events at Socony Hill, when England began advocating, ardently, his own plan of immediately returning to using force by punitively bombarding the city.[234]

At this point, it is worth briefly mentioning Japan's involvement in the course of events. The Japanese naval force at Nanjing had adopted a cautious approach from the outset, as Japan's consulate was situated deep within the old city. As a result, there was no realistic possibility of Japanese landing parties securing a safe evacuation if they used force. The consulate was also located well beyond the effective range of the IJN destroyers' main guns, and so fire support could only be provided through a request to HMS *Emerald*, with an inevitable loss of face.[235] In contrast, the Anglo-American community was largely based in the northern part of Nanjing, nearest the Yangtze and the main railway station on the line to Shanghai. That section of the city was readily accessible to small boats using the Qinhuai River and city moat. While it is now hidden behind high-rise buildings, the city wall by Socony Hill was visible from the warships on the Yangtze. Admiral Araki's involvement in the joint reply was therefore for diplomatic rather than practical purposes.

Given that the British establishment largely accepted the subsequent justification of the initial Nanjing bombardment as a defensive measure, it is curious that Tyrwhitt later claimed in private correspondence that he came close to replacing HMS *Emerald*'s commander during the radio exchange.[236] Tyrwhitt stated that he felt Captain England was far too eager to resume bombarding Nanjing, which Tyrwhitt believed could lead to outright war in China, although it is difficult independently to confirm or counter Tyrwhitt's claims.[237] Certainly a second bombardment would have been difficult to justify as defensive, coming after most British civilians and servicemen had been evacuated from the city. Tyrwhitt's official report only explicitly criticized *Emerald*'s Royal Marine Captain Heathcote for having failed in his duty. Heathcote had left unarmed marines at the consulate on their own devices, with no organized plan for their defence, evacuation or how he would return to them if required. Moreover, he was not present at the consulate during the events that followed.[238] The Nanjing Incident did lead to a form of punishment for Captain England though, who was removed from commanding HMS *Emerald* one month later and placed in a semi-administrative role.[239] In the intervening weeks, the Admiralty had received and relayed a flurry of messages in support of England and his actions.[240] Moreover, it was known that Captain England still suffered from injuries sustained during the First World War, which may have contributed to his terse exchanges with Tyrwhitt.[241] Nonetheless, what was tantamount to a demotion stands out against a backdrop of international praise for his actions. It is entirely plausible, therefore, that Tyrwhitt did consider ordering the replacement of Captain England by radio from Shanghai. Just a decade earlier it would have been impossible for Tyrwhitt to have even considered such an extreme measure when not actually on the scene at Nanjing.

New technology made it possible for the commander-in-chief to use at different occasions aircraft and radio messages as part of efforts to avoid or subdue potential diplomatic incidents. If those attempts proved ineffective, he could rapidly assemble a force to provide a powerful localized deterrent. While this helped improve the effectiveness of the Royal Navy's counter-piracy work, ultimately when crises occurred there was little the available technology could do to limit the damage done by using high-velocity naval guns against targets in urban environments. Against the backdrop of the Northern Expedition and anti-British sentiment in China, 1926–7, it was not technology that decided events. In practice, it was the willingness of the officers involved to use violence, their understanding of what gunboat diplomacy involved and often their mistakes that dictated the course of events. This was all regardless of whether or not those officers' actions were in line with the commander-in-chief's or indeed Whitehall's wishes.

Summary

By the 1920s the Royal Navy's use of new technology in 'waving the flag', as a means of boosting imperial prestige, had waned on the China Station. Efforts to uphold the image of the Navy still regularly influenced officers' behaviour, but below the surface residual references to 'waving the flag' were generally intended for British metropolitan and particularly British colonial audiences. Technology was primarily employed by the Admiralty where it served a practical purpose for the policing and defence of the British Empire. Intangible aims such as imperial prestige were secondary concerns. In that way, technological change altered significantly the way in which the Royal Navy approached the challenges it faced, in its dealings with warlord China, even if progress towards fully exploiting new technologies was neither smooth nor systematic. By 1930 many new pieces of equipment were being used to great effect in improving Britain's understanding of what was happening and how the China Station responded to adverse situations.

The most significant changes were the improvements in efficiency across the China Station, which were heavily linked to the Navy's evolving command structure. By the mid-1920s the commander-in-chief could draw on up-to-date reports, in some cases only minutes old, to issue timely orders to either proactively or reactively influence the course of events. Increasing centralization of command fundamentally changed the way that the Navy operated in the region. Foremost, it allowed the force to become more flexible in its approach. Rather than warships being posted to predefined areas and then acting independently, their actions could be coordinated. Forces could be dispersed to cover the widest area possible in suppressing piracy or concentrated at times on a crisis point. Moreover, senior officers were able to order changes with increasing rapidity as more warships received increasingly powerful wireless sets. Apart from the upper Yangtze, this meant that isolated smaller warships could, at least theoretically, be reinforced quickly by the Station's larger warships or ad hoc forces when required.

Knowing that hundreds of naval personnel, backed by large-calibre guns, were potentially only a radio message away was vital in maintaining Britain's position as China's armies and bandit gangs obtained modern weaponry. Indeed the withdrawal of gunboats from the upper Yangtze was not just because of the collapse in trade for British merchants operating deep inland during 1926.[242] The small upper Yangtze gunboats could not be reinforced in emergency, given the shallow gorges between Chongqing and Hankou, and they were no longer powerful enough to operate alone.[243] Elsewhere around the command, the greater flexibility afforded by wireless communication prolonged the Royal Navy's operations along most key stretches of China's waterways. Without that improvement, the Royal Navy would almost certainly have had to withdraw protection from many more treaty ports, years before Austen Chamberlain's diplomatic announcement in December 1926.

Greater centralization of command also slowly reduced the heavy burden placed upon the junior officers commanding the gunboats and sloops, which were involved in most interactions with the Chinese population and officials. By 1927, for example, the Commodore commanding the Pearl River Delta gunboats was able to take remote command of his whole force when responding to piracy incidents, with minute-by-minute updates from individual ships.[244] However, successful centralization and coordination was sometimes limited by individual behaviour. As we shall soon explore, some officers were unenthusiastic about relinquishing their historic freedom of command and others willingly exploited the unclear post-wireless command structure to pursue individual strategies.[245] Possessing the technical ability to communicate a centralized strategy in meeting challenges in China was not enough in itself to encourage greater adherence to that plan by individual officers. The training, career experiences and attitudes of the service personnel on the China Station were more significant than technology in defining the course of events at key moments throughout the decade.

Notes

1 Charles Callwell, *Military Operations and Maritime Preponderance: Their Relation and Interdependence* (London: Blackwood, 1905), p. 63.
2 John Ferris, 'The Greatest Power on Earth: Great Britain in the 1920s', *International History Review* 13/4 (1991), 732–4.
3 Edward May, *Principles and Problems of Imperial Defence* (London: Sonnenschein, 1903), p. 130.

4   Lovell, *The Opium War*, pp. 111–15.
5   Report on the reduction of naval expenditure by the subcommittee of staffs from the Admiralty, Air Ministry and War Office, 20 January 1923, TNA, CAB 24/160/72, pp. 4–12.
6   Correspondence between Admiralty and Cabinet about the Navy Estimates 1925–6, 1925, TNA, ADM 116/2300.
7   Report on the reduction of naval expenditure, TNA, CAB 24/160/72, p. 5; Ferris, 'Treasury Control', 880.
8   Cabinet Committee on Reduction of National Expenditure, January 1923, TNA, CAB 24/160/72; Navy Estimates for 1920–1, 1920, TNA, T 1/12533/16620.
9   Navy List, March 1913, NLS, p. 270; Navy List, December 1920, NLS, p. 714.
10 Spence, *Colonial Naval Culture*, pp. 18–21.
11 Rear-Admiral Cameron to Admiral Sinclair, 26 July 1926, TNA, ADM 116/2509.
12 Ferris, 'Treasury Control', p. 871.
13 Geoffrey Till, *Air Power and the Royal Navy 1914–1945* (London: Jane, 1979), p. 63.
14 See Donald Stoker, *Britain, France and the Naval Arms Trade in the Baltic 1919–1939: Grand Strategy and Failure* (London: Routledge, 2012), pp. 65–101.
15 Anthony Chan, *Arming the Chinese* (Vancouver: University of British Columbia Press, 1982), pp. 47–8.
16 J. Campbell, 'Naval Armaments and Armour', in *Steam, Steel, and Shellfire*, ed. Robert Gardiner and Andrew Lambert (London: Conway Maritime, 1992), pp. 161–4.
17 Moretz, *The Royal Navy and the Capital Ship*, p. 258.
18 Elliot, *The Cross and the Ensign*, p. 102.
19 Jon Wise, *The Role of the Royal Navy in South America, 1920–1970* (London: Bloomsbury, 2014), pp. 20–1.
20 Harrington, 'The Mighty Hood', pp. 179–80.
21 Daniel O. Spence, *A History of the Royal Navy: Empire and Imperialism* (London: Tauris, 2015), p. 98.
22 Letter from Lieutenant Commander G. J. Todd to Vice Admiral Moore, 17 July 1907, TNA, ADM 125/127.
23 Unpublished autobiography of G. C. Dickens, undated, KCLMA, Catalogue ID 1114, Chapter two.
24 Navy List, December 1920 (1921), NLS, p. 714; O'Brien, 'The Titan Refreshed', p. 150; Padfield, *Rule Britannia*, p. 222.
25 Hansard, 18 March 1920, vol. 126, cc. 2513–14. Kenworthy further stated that the submarine flotilla attached to the China Station was strategically useful but had no value for waving the flag.
26 HMS *President* (formerly *Saxifrage*) was a decoy ship, but its appearance was not substantially different from the rest of the *Flower*-class family. It is now in Chatham awaiting repair but spent decades on the Thames.

27. David Brown, *Nelson to Vanguard: Warship Design and Development 1923–1945* (London: Chatham, 2006), pp. 86 and 134.
28. Chesneau, *All the World's Fighting Ships*, p. 177.
29. E.g. Ship's log of HMS *Bluebell* 1920, TNA, ADM 53/35681; Ship's log of HMS *Magnolia* 1924–5, TNA, ADM 53/80209.
30. E.g. Ship's log of HMS *Diomede* 1924–5, TNA, ADM 53/75887.
31. Braisted, *Diplomats in Blue*, p. 3. The number of destroyers in the Asiatic Fleet varied during the 1920s, but generally averaged around 18.
32. Diary of Commander Cedric Holland, 1928.
33. Braisted, *Diplomats in Blue*, pp. 70–1.
34. Benjamin Elman, 'Naval Warfare and the Refraction of China's Self-Strengthening Reforms into Scientific and Technological Failure, 1865–1895', *Modern Asian Studies* 38/2 (2004), 317; Hamish Ion, 'The China Squadron and the Boxer Uprising', in *British Naval Strategy East of Suez, 1900–2000: Influences and Actions*, ed. Greg Kennedy (Abingdon: Frank Cass, 2005), pp. 48–56.
35. Memorandum by Commander Maxwell-Scott, 2 December 1924, TNA, ADM 116/2262.
36. George Forty, *British Army Handbook 1939–1945* (London: Dreadnought Books, 2000), pp. 140–80.
37. F. S. W. de Winton, *Ships in Bottles* (unpublished), KCLMA, Catalogue ID 1113, p. 29.
38. Commodore Bowden-Smith to Vice Admiral Duff, 1 January 1921, TNA, ADM 1/8593/133.
39. HMS *Gnat* to Rear-Admiral Yangtze, 1 March 1926, TNA, ADM 116/2510.
40. Diary of Herbert Page, 14 April 1927, IWM, 17545.
41. *China Mail*, 14 June 1926.
42. *Hong Kong Daily Press*, 15 October 1926, p. 7.
43. E.g. Midshipman's log of P. W. Burnett, 1927, KCLMA, Catalogue ID 2243; Ship's log of HMS *Magnolia* 1926–7, TNA, ADM 53/80211.
44. Commodore Grace to Admiral Leveson, 10 June 1924, TNA, ADM 116/2262.
45. Konstam, *Yangtze River Gunboats*, Appendix.
46. Photograph album of Major Frederick Burden RMLI, 8 September 1926, RMM, 1992/112/1; Report by Rear Admiral Cameron to Admiral Tyrwhitt, 17 September 1926, TNA, ADM 116/2509.
47. Till, *Seapower*, p. 276.
48. E.g. Admiral Leveson to Admiralty, 11 October 1923, TNA, ADM 1/8665/142.
49. Admiral Leveson to Admiralty, 17 March 1923, TNA, ADM 1/8665/142.
50. Diary of Herbert Page, 17 April 1927, IWM, 17545.
51. Journal of Commander Hamilton, 1927–8, NMM, HTN 214.
52. Shanghai Municipal Council Annual Report 1920, SMA, U1-1-933; Shanghai Municipal Council Annual Report 1921, SMA, U1-1-934; Shanghai Municipal Council Annual Report 1922, SMA, U1-1-935.

53 *Shanghai Municipal Gazette*, 8 April 1920, SMA, U1-1-985; Shanghai Municipal Council Annual Report 1920, SMA, U1-1-933.
54 Shanghai Municipal Council Annual Report 1925, SMA, U1-1-938.
55 Major General Anderson to the Shanghai Municipal Council, 29 May 1913, SMA, U1-2-445.
56 Major MacKenzie to the Shanghai Municipal Council, 18 April 1902, SMA, U1-2-725; Shanghai Municipal Council Annual Report 1921, SMA, U1-1-934.
57 Report of the Volunteers Corps Commission in the *Shanghai Municipal Gazette*, 1 April 1920, SMA, U1-1-985.
58 Shanghai Municipal Council Annual Report 1920, SMA, U1-1-933; Shanghai Municipal Council Annual Report 1927, SMA, U1-1-940.
59 Letter from J. Duncan to the Shanghai Municipal Council, 18 March 1927, SMA, U1-1-992.
60 Interview with I. L. Wight, 1982, IWM Interview Series, Catalogue Number 6196, 12 minutes.
61 David Hobbs, *Aircraft Carriers of the Royal and Commonwealth Navies* (London: Greenhill, 1996), p. 103; Hezlet, *Aircraft and Sea Power*, p. 114.
62 Ship's log of HMS *Hermes* 1925-6, TNA, ADM 53/78829.
63 *China Mail*, 2 November 1925.
64 Ship's log of HMS *Hermes* 1925-6, TNA, ADM 53/78829.
65 Diary of Captain C. Talbot, 11 October 1925, IWM, Documents.20134.
66 *Hong Kong Telegraph*, 28 October 1925.
67 Newspaper cuttings in the diary of Lieutenant William Andrewes, 1926, IWM, DS/MISC/12.
68 Ship's log of HMS *Hermes* 1926-7, TNA, ADM 53/78830.
69 Clayton, *The British Empire as a Superpower*, p. 193.
70 Chan, *Arming the Chinese*, pp. 117-21.
71 Jamieson to Palairet, 14 July 1925, TNA, FO 371/10947.
72 E.g. *China Mail*, 21 August 1925, p. 1; *China Mail*, 2 November 1925, p. 1.
73 Monthly reports from Admiral Leveson to Admiralty, 1924, TNA, ADM 116/2262; G. L. D. Alderson, *History of RAF Kai Tak* (Hong Kong: Royal Air Force, 1972), pp. 11-12; Cliff Dunnaway, *Wings Over Hong Kong: An Aviation History 1891-1998* (Hong Kong: Pacific Century, 1999), pp. 12-65.
74 Chan, *Arming the Chinese*, p. 118; Higham, *Armed Forces in Peacetime*, p. 19.
75 Chan, *Arming the Chinese*, pp. 57, 83.
76 *China Mail*, 21 August 1925; *Hong Kong Telegraph*, 8 September 1925.
77 Commodore H. E. Grace to Admiral Leveson, 10 June 1924, TNA, ADM 116/2262.
78 Dunnaway, *Wings over Hong Kong*, pp. 62-5.
79 Committee of Imperial Defence summary of situation in China for Cabinet, June 1925, TNA, CAB 24/174/26.

80 Midshipman P. W. Burnett's logbook.
81 Journal of Commander Hamilton, 1927–8, NMM, HTN 214.
82 Priya Satia, 'The Defense of Inhumanity: Air Control and the British Idea of Arabia', *American Historical Review* 111/1 (2006), 16–51; Killingray, 'A Swift Agent of Government', pp. 429–44.
83 Killingray, 'A Swift Agent of Government', p. 437.
84 Ship's log of HMS *Hermes* 1925–6, TNA, ADM 53/78829.
85 Alderson, *History of RAF Kai Tak*, p. 13.
86 Ray Sturtivant, *British Naval Aviation: The Fleet Air Arm, 1917–1990* (Annapolis: Naval Institute Press, 1990), p. 14.
87 Jordan, *Warships after Washington*, Appendix 1: Washington Treaty 1922: Chapter 1: Article XIX.
88 Philips P. O'Brien, *British and American Naval Power: Politics and Policy 1900–1936* (Westport: Praeger, 1998), p. 173.
89 Tadashi Kuramatsu, 'Britain, Japan and Inter-War Naval Limitation, 1921–1936', in *The History of Anglo-Japanese Relations, 1600–2000; Volume III: The Military Dimension*, ed. Ian Gow, Yoichi Hirama, John Chapman (Basingstoke: Palgrave Macmillan, 2003), 127–38.
90 Fung, *Diplomacy of Imperial Retreat*, p. 65.
91 Diary of Captain C. Talbot, June 1924 to April 1926.
92 Appendix C, 'War Standing Instructions for the Guidance of Commander-in-Chief Abroad and Senior Officers in Command of Foreign Stations', January 1923, TNA, ADM 116/3124.
93 Hezlet, *Aircraft and Sea Power*, p. 113.
94 Unpublished memoirs of Captain Ramsbotham (1968), IWM.
95 Memoranda discussing the operation of aircraft from aircraft carriers, 1925–6, TNA, AIR 5/387.
96 Diary of Captain C. Talbot, July–August 1925.
97 Diary of Captain C. Talbot, 14 October 1925.
98 Admiral Tyrwhitt to Admiralty, 11 January 1928, TNA, ADM 116/3126.
99 RAF Intelligence Report on China, 1927, TNA, AIR 5/865.
100 Chiefs of Staff report on the defence of Shameen, 18 January 1927, TNA, CAB 24/184/16.
101 Alderson, *History of RAF Kai Tak*, pp. 14–15.
102 Jordan, *Warships after Washington*, Appendix 2: London Treaty 1930; O'Brien, 'The Washington Treaty Era', pp. 504–6.
103 Committee of Imperial Defence summary of situation in China for Cabinet, June 1925, TNA, CAB 24/174/26.
104 Ship's log of HMS *Hermes* 1925–6, TNA, ADM 53/78829.
105 Cabinet discussion on piracy in Bias Bay, 15 November 1925, TNA, CAB 2/4/218.

106 Diary of Captain C. Talbot, June 1924 to April 1926.
107 Interview with A. A. Heron, 1975, IWM Interview Series, Catalogue Number 681, Reel 11, 3–4 minutes.
108 Interview with T. Wallace, 1976, IWM Interview Series, Catalogue Number 731, Reel 4, 9 minutes.
109 E.g. Photograph album of M.S. Spalding (RN), 1927, Brotherton Library, LIDDLE/WW1/RNMN/272; Photograph collection of C. E. Winslow (USN), 1927, NHHC, NH105067.
110 Hansard, 2 July 1923, vol. 166 c.19.
111 Ship's log of HMS *Hermes* 1925–6, TNA, ADM 53/78829.
112 *China Mail*, 7 August 1925.
113 Fung, *Diplomacy of Imperial Retreat*, pp. 38–53; Osterhammel, 'China', p. 650.
114 Letter from Captain England to Admiral Tyrwhitt, 29 March 1927, 'Papers relating to the Nanking Incident of March 24 and 25 1927' (London, 1927); Midshipman P. W. Burnett's logbook.
115 Braisted, *Diplomats in Blue*, p. 107.
116 Interview with A. Gaskin, 1986, IWM Interview Series, Catalogue Number 9344, Reel 6, 1–7 minutes.
117 Undated extract from the *Hankow Herald* included in report by Rear Admiral Tillard, 1927, TNA, ADM 116/2510.
118 Interview with E. C. Whitney, 1992, IWM Interview Series, Catalogue Number 12499, 21–28 minutes.
119 Anthony Wells, 'Naval Intelligence and decision making in an era of technical change', in *Technical Change and British Naval Policy 1860–1939*, ed. Bryan Ranft (London: Hodder and Stoughton, 1977), p. 123.
120 *New York Times*, 25 July 1871.
121 Lambert, 'Strategic Command and Control', p. 363.
122 Glen O'Hara, "The Sea is Swinging into View': Modern British Maritime History in a Globalised World', *English Historical Review* 125/510 (2009), 1114.
123 Memorandum and expense form submitted by Lieutenant Commander G. J. Todd 28 July 1906, TNA, ADM 125/127.
124 Report from Vice Admiral Moore to Admiralty, 12 January 1907, TNA, ADM, 125/127.
125 Memorandum from Admiralty to Vice Admiral Moore, 7 March 1907, TNA, ADM 125/127.
126 Letter from Vice Admiral Moore to Admiralty, 18 April 1907, TNA, ADM 125/127.
127 Memorandum from Moore to Admiralty, 25 April 1907, TNA 125/127.
128 Jones, 'Towards a Hierarchy of Management', p. 160.
129 Unpublished autobiography of G. C. Dickens, undated, KCLMA, Catalogue ID 1114, Chapter two.

130 Norman Friedman, 'Electronics and Navies', in *The Eclipse of the Big Gun*, ed. Robert Gardiner (London: Conway Maritime, 1992), p. 192.
131 John Chapman, 'Britain, Japan and the "Higher Realms of Intelligence", 1900–1918', in *The history of Anglo-Japanese relations, 1600–2000; Volume III: The Military Dimension*, ed. Ian Gow, Yoichi Hirama, and John Chapman (Basingstoke: Palgrave Macmillan, 2003), p. 77.
132 Lambert, 'Strategic Command and Control', p. 373.
133 Correspondence between Jerram, Powlett and the Admiralty, 1913, TNA, ADM 1/8376/109.
134 Commodore Stirling to Admiral Leveson, 10 April 1924, TNA, 116/2262; Speech by Rear Admiral Anderson to the Shanghai Branch of the China Association, 11 August 1924, SOAS Special Collections, CHAS/MCP/30.
135 Report from Admiral Leveson to Admiralty, 11 October 1923, TNA, 1/8665/142.
136 Memorandum from Vice Admiral Jerram to Admiralty, 23 September 1913, TNA, ADM 1/8376/109.
137 Report from Admiral Leveson to Admiralty, 10 November 1924, TNA, ADM 116/2262.
138 Report from Admiral Edwyn Alexander-Sinclair to Admiralty, 17 December 1924, TNA, ADM 116/2262.
139 R. S. Pratt to Admiral Leveson, 18 January 1927, TNA, ADM 116/2510.
140 E.g. *China Mail*, September 1927.
141 Letters from Commander Berryman to his mother, August and September 1926, IWM, Documents 1445.
142 Rear Admiral Anderson to Admiralty, 14 January 1927, TNA, ADM 1/8712/154.
143 Midshipman Burnett's logbook; War Diary of the 12th Royal Marine Battalion, 1927, TNA, ADM 1/8709/102.
144 Journal of Lieutenant William Andrewes, 1925–6, IWM, DS/MISC/12.
145 Interview with H. C. Claxton, 1990, IWM Interview Series, Catalogue Number 11945, Reel 7, 26 minutes.
146 Journal of Commander Hamilton, 1927–8, NMM, HTN 214.
147 Headrick and Griset, 'Submarine Telegraph Cables', p. 545.
148 Christopher Andrew, 'The British Secret Service and Anglo-Soviet Relations in the 1920s Part I: From the Trade Negotiations to the Zinoviev Letter', *Historical Journal* 20/3 (1977), 682–3.
149 Intercepted transmission between Nanjing and Chairman Hu of Yunnan Provincial Government, 31 July 1927, TNA, HW 12/98.
150 Chapman, 'Britain, Japan and the "Higher Realms of Intelligence"', p. 157.
151 Japanese Foreign Minister Tokyo to various embassies and consulates, 17 June 1925, TNA, HW 12/71.
152 Admiral Leveson to Admiralty, 24 April 1924, TNA, ADM 116/3124.

153 Lecture by Director of Naval Intelligence Captain G. C. Dickens at Greenwich War College entitled 'Japan and Sea Power', 15 May 1935, KCLMA, Catalogue ID 1114.
154 *China Mail*, 10 June 1931, p. 1.
155 Report from Captain Brodie to commander-in-chief China, 21 January 1924, TNA, ADM 116/2262.
156 Report from HMS *Titania* to commander-in-chief China, 20 October 1924, TNA, ADM 116/2262.
157 Minutes of Committee for Overseas Defence meeting about piracy in China, June 1926, TNA, CAB 24/181/72.
158 Orders compiled by Commodore John Pearson, 28 October 1927 and Operational orders by Commander Allan Poland, 18 October 1927, both in TNA, ADM 116/2502.
159 Captain Charles Brodie to Admiralty, 21 January 1924, TNA, ADM 116/2262.
160 Unpublished autobiography of Commander Brian Dean RN, IWM, Documents 7792, pp. 77–8; Telegram from Hong Kong administration to secretary of state for the Colonies, 21 October 1927, TNA, ADM 116/2502.
161 Thomas Hone, Norman Friedman and Mark Mandeles, *American and British Aircraft Carrier Development 1919–1941* (Annapolis: Naval Institute Press, 1999), p. 108.
162 E.g. Foreign Office Quarterly Intelligence Report, 3 August 1924, TNA, FO 371/6635; Royal Navy Intelligence Report on Piracy in China, 3 December 1924, TNA, FO 371/10252.
163 Wells, 'Naval Intelligence and Decision Making', p. 123.
164 Memorandum by Lieutenant Colonel Hanson, February 1928, TNA, WO 106/5258. The Secret Intelligence Service is commonly referred to as MI6.
165 Richard Aldrich, 'Britain's Secret Intelligence Service in Asia during the Second World War', *Modern Asian Studies* 32/1 (1998), 181.
166 Orders from War Office to Major General Duncan, 22 February 1927, TNA, WO 106/5258.
167 Memorandum by Colonel Wagstaff, 23 April 1927, TNA, WO 106/5258.
168 Instructions from Major General Charles to Colonel Blaker, 24 May 1927, TNA, WO 106/5258.
169 Naval intelligence organization chart, 1928, TNA, WO 106/5258.
170 Konstam, *Yangtze River Gunboats*, Appendix.
171 Shanghai Municipal Council Annual Report 1929, SMA, U1-1-942.
172 Report from Admiral Sinclair to Admiralty, 24 November 1926, TNA, ADM 116/2502.
173 Orders from Admiral Sinclair to *Vindictive*, 16 November 1926, TNA, ADM 116/2502.
174 Clayton, *The British Empire as a Superpower*, p. 80.

175 Diary entry of Commander C. H. Drage, 15 December 1923, IWM, PP/MCR/99, Volume 4 (1923–6).
176 Captain of *Hermes* to Commodore Hong Kong, 4 September 1927, TNA, ADM 116/2502.
177 Manual of Combined Operations, 1938, TNA, WO 287/43.
178 War Diaries of 12th Royal Marine Battalion on service in China, 1927, TNA, ADM 1/8709/102.
179 Interview with I. L. Wight, 1982, IWM Interview Series, Catalogue Number 6196, 5 minutes.
180 Jonathan Kinghorn, *The Atlantic Transport Line, 1881–1931* (Jefferson, NC: McFarland, 2012), pp. 178–242.
181 Memorandum on the despatch of naval reinforcements to Shanghai, 14 January 1927, TNA, ADM 1/8711/144.
182 Jordan, *Warships after Washington*, p. 155.
183 Memoranda discussing the importance of aircraft carriers to the Royal Navy, 1921, TNA, AIR 5/167.
184 Clayton, *The British Empire as a Superpower*, p. 142.
185 Reports by Lieutenant J. Findlay and Lieutenant R. Armour, September 1927, TNA, ADM 116/2502. Aircraft were meant to radio *Hermes* and the shore party, but due to technical difficulties were only able to raise *Danae*, hence the primitive but effective technique of dropping written messages to the shore party.
186 Report by Captain MacKinnon, 1 September 1927, TNA, ADM 116/2502.
187 Assorted aerial photographs, September 1927, TNA, ADM 116/2502.
188 *Instructions for Mounting, Using, and Caring for 6-inch Rapid-fire Gun* (Washington, 1917), p. 19. The manual refers to an older variant than that on HMS *Emerald* at Nanjing, but the range table is similar enough for indicative purposes.
189 Jon T. Sumida, *In Defence of Naval Supremacy: Finance, Technology, and British Naval Policy, 1889–1914* (London: Routledge, 1993), pp. 315–16.
190 de Winton, *Ships in Bottles*, p. 28.
191 Pugsley and Macintyre, *Destroyer Man*, p. 18; Eyewitness report reprinted from the Central China Post, 17 September 1926, in *The Wanhsien Epic* (Hankow, 1926), NMRN, 1979/216, p. 66.
192 Braisted, *Diplomats in Blue*, p. 134.
193 As seen in the photographs of HMS *Emerald* firing on Nanjing, 1927, IWM, Q 83188 & Q 83189.
194 Hone and Hone, *Battle Line*, p. 166.
195 Gunnery training log – 'Fall of shot and analyses chart' and associated notes, 17 July 1922, KCLMA, Catalogue ID 1238.
196 Gunnery training log – 'Fall of shot and analyses chart' and associated notes, 17 July 1922, KCLMA, Catalogue ID 1238; Peter Liddle, *Men of Gallipoli: The*

Dardanelles and Gallipoli Experience (London: Allen Lane, 1976), p. 43; Roskill, *Naval Policy between the Wars*, p. 191.
197 Tweedie, *The Story of a Naval Life*, p. 241.
198 'Report from an eyewitness', in *The Wanhsien Epic* (Hankow, 1926), NMRN, 1979/216, p. 16.
199 Consul A. P. Blunt to Sir Ronald Macleay, 15 October 1926, TNA, ADM 116/2509.
200 Pugsley and Macintyre, *Destroyer Man*, pp. 18–19.
201 Consul A. P. Blunt to Sir Ronald Macleay, 15 October 1926, TNA, ADM 116/2509.
202 'Report from an eyewitness', in *The Wanhsien Epic* (Hankow, 1926), NMRN, 1979/216, p. 17.
203 First-hand accounts and letters of commendation by British and American participants of the incident, April 1927, TNA, ADM 1/8711/149.
204 Report by R. Caplain (trans. M. Heaslip), 28 March 1927, TNA, ADM 1/8711/149.
205 Midshipman P. W. Burnett's logbook.
206 Photographs of Socony Hill taken by Midshipman Burnett, 24 March 1927, KCLMA, Catalogue ID 2243; Photograph of Socony House, April 1927, TNA, ADM 1/8711/149; Wilbur, *The Nationalist Revolution in China*, p. 91.
207 Report from Captain England to Admiral Tyrwhitt, 29 March 1927, TNA, ADM 1/8711/149.
208 E.g. Goto-Shibata, *Japan and Britain in Shanghai*, p. 50; Osterhammel, 'China', pp. 652–3; Wilbur, *Nationalist Revolution in China*, p. 92.
209 Copy of letter from Captain England to Admiral Tyrwhitt, 'Papers relating to the Nanjing Incident of March 24 and 25 1927', *China* 4 (HMSO, 1927).
210 Photographs of Socony Hill taken by Midshipman Burnett, 24 March 1927, KCLMA, Catalogue ID 2243; Photograph of Socony House, April 1927, TNA, ADM 1/8711/149.
211 Pugsley and Macintyre, *Destroyer Man*, pp. 18–19.
212 Rear Admiral Cameron to Admiral Tyrwhitt, 17 September 1926, TNA, ADM 116/2509.
213 'Short Account of the Voyages and Deeds of HMS Emerald October 1925 to June 1928', IWM, p. 50; Report from Captain England to Admiral Tyrwhitt, 29 March 1927, TNA, ADM 1/8711/149; Midshipman Burnett's logbook.
214 China Station General Briefing giving details of Nanjing, 1921, NMRN, 1979/240.
215 Japanese Government Railways Map, *Guide to China with Land and Sea Routes between the American and European Continents* (2nd edn) (Tokyo: Japanese Government Railways, 1924).
216 Report of personal experiences of Consul General Giles, 9 April 1927, 'Papers relating to the Nanjing Incident of March 24 and 25 1927', *China* 4 (HMSO, 1927).
217 Report by R. Caplain (trans. M. Heaslip), 28 March 1927, TNA, ADM 1/8711/149.
218 Report by Lieutenant R. Oliver-Bellasis, 1 April 1927, TNA, ADM 1/8711/149.

219 Midshipman Burnett's logbook.
220 Hone and Hone, *Battle Line*, p. 166.
221 Report of personal experiences of Consul General Giles, 9 April 1927, 'Papers relating to the Nanjing Incident of March 24 and 25 1927', *China* 4 (HMSO, 1927).
222 Cole, *Gunboats and Marines*, p. 116.
223 *North China Herald*, 30 April 1927, p. 2.
224 Midshipman Burnett's logbook; Report from Captain England to Admiral Tyrwhitt, 29 March 1927, TNA, ADM 1/8711/149.
225 E.g. Photographs of Pukow, March 1927, IWM, Q 83169 & Q 83184; Report from Rear Admiral Cameron to Admiral Tyrwhitt, 1 May 1927, TNA, ADM 116/2510; Midshipman Burnett's logbook.
226 Clifford, *Spoilt Children of Empire*, p. 223; Goto-Shibata, *Japan and Britain in Shanghai*, p. 50; Wilbur, *The Nationalist Revolution in China*, p. 92.
227 See Clayton, *The British Empire as a Superpower*, p. 200; Osterhammel, 'China', p. 652.
228 Clifford, *Spoilt Children of Empire*, pp. 179–224.
229 Tweedie, *The Story of a Naval Life*, pp. 241–2.
230 Konstam, *Yangtze River Gunboats*, Appendix.
231 Shanghai Municipal Council Annual Report 1921, SMA, U1-1-934.
232 Wright, *China's Steam Navy*, p. 131.
233 Journal of Commander Hamilton, 1927–8, NMM, HTN 214.
234 Braisted, *Diplomats in Blue*, pp. 137–8.
235 Ibid., p. 139.
236 Louis, *British Strategy in the Far East*, p. 133.
237 Patterson, *Tyrwhitt of the Harwich Force*, p. 253.
238 Vice Admiral Tyrwhitt to Admiralty, 22 April 1927, TNA, ADM 1/8711/149.
239 Ship's log of HMS *Emerald*, 27 April 1927, TNA, ADM 53/76701.
240 Assorted correspondence between American officials, the Foreign Office, the Admiralty and Admiral Tyrwhitt, April 1927, TNA, ADM 1/8711/149.
241 Reports on Hugh England by Admiral William Fisher, March 1934, TNA, ADM 196/91/135.
242 Intelligence report from Senior Naval Officer Upper Yangtze, 15 April 1926, TNA, ADM 116/2510; Letter from Consul Pratt to Sir Miles Lampson, 14 March 1927, TNA, ADM 116/2510.
243 Only the two Widgeon-class river gunboats had a sufficiently low draught to navigate the rapids and shallow waters of the upper Yangtze.
244 Record of Royal Navy wireless transmissions on West River, 2 September 1927, TNA, ADM 116/2502.
245 Journal of Commander Hamilton, 1927–8, NMM, HTN 214.

5

Changing attitudes, ideas and approaches

Technology was an important factor influencing the way events evolved on the China Station during the 1920s, but the decisions made on the scene often defined the outcomes. Despite being a uniform force in theory, with men from very similar backgrounds and life experiences, the Royal Navy's officers could make markedly different decisions and they were given significant freedom to be able to do so. Key crisis moments saw considerable variety in the way the commanders and crews of individual ships reacted to flashpoints. Royal Navy officers in the early twentieth century may have come from the same mould, but they were still individuals who possessed their own unique set of ideas and attitudes.[1] These differences extended along the full line of naval command into senior command, with Captain Francis De Winton recording shortly after the 1927 Nanjing Incident that 'Admiral Boyle wished to do some bombarding … and I believe the CinC had to restrain him.'[2] This chapter will explore both the mindsets of the naval personnel involved in some of those key moments and the extent to which differences in attitudes were a factor in the outcomes. The variety of approaches taken by Royal Navy officers to achieve their goals were incredibly important and changed significantly over the course of the decade. Many were willing and able to adapt quickly, developing and using alternative ways to fulfil their role defending Britain's interests across the region in the new interwar environment.

The different mentalities displayed by Royal Navy officers affected not only the outcome of individual events but also the formation and implementation of the Navy's broader strategies and as a result Britain's foreign policy. While improvements in communications technology enabled greater centralization of command structure, the Admiralty still allowed its commanders considerable freedom to act on their own initiative. As a result, officers on the China Station were allowed to, and often did, deviate from their Admiralty script, based upon their own views of how Britain should deal with the challenges faced in the region.

Ego and strong personalities sometimes sparked disagreements between officers over the best course of action to pursue. Likewise, nervousness and tension caused by the strain of the seriousness of the events unfolding undoubtedly also played a part in fuelling disagreements, but there were far deeper issues at play. A web of personal allegiance within the command structure shaped the behaviour of individual officers and vessels. For most of the decade the China Station maintained a relatively stable collection of vessels and commanders. This provided senior officers with many months or even years to develop a reasonably homogenous understanding of how to respond to developments among their subordinates. In 1927, however, there was a sudden influx of warships from all around the world, with new vessels attached on an ad hoc basis to the China Station's various sub-commands. As a result, a range of the Navy's different regional identities were drawn into the ensuing crisis in East Asia.

'Gunboat diplomacy' is often used to describe the Royal Navy's main strategy in China prior to the December Memorandum in 1926, when Foreign Secretary Austen Chamberlain announced a new policy for China. While the exact definition of gunboat diplomacy continues to feature in theoretical discussions, there is general agreement about many of its features as a strategy. At core it is 'the demonstration, threat, or use of limited naval force for political objectives', heavily linked to shows of force, but including the possibility of violence in an effort to coerce an opponent.[3] James Cable's four categories are often used as a broader definition, covering the range of approaches from 'expressive' behaviour conveying intangible, emotional messages to 'definitive' actions intended at achieving a fait accompli.[4] In practice the tactics involved ranged from peacetime pageantry involving marching, music and dinners to the violent destruction of strategic fortifications by naval guns or shore parties. This did not and still does not necessarily require the involvement of actual gunboats, although during the nineteenth and early twentieth centuries the strategy generally relied upon littoral warships of one sort or another. A few key characteristics are common to all scenarios: the threat or use of force should be limited, the action should be aimed at coercing the adversary to submit and it generally involves the opponent having to accept the long-term consequences of that submission.

While there has been considerable discussion of what gunboat diplomacy entailed at a strategic level, there has been little consideration of what ordinary naval officers interpreted it to mean in practice and in theatre. As it was those operational officers who implemented the strategy, their attitudes were central to how gunboat diplomacy affected Britain's relationship with China on a day-to-day basis. A top-level definition is of great value in understanding what Whitehall and the Admiralty intended Britain's strategy in China to be. Discovering what ground-level officers believed the strategy to involve, however, is vital in explaining how events panned out in reality. As we shall see, defining what individual warship commanders saw gunboat diplomacy to mean demonstrates how the approach went out of general use on the China Station before the change in diplomatic approach in December 1926. Rather than a top-down shift in strategy, from gunboat diplomacy enforcing extraterritorial privileges to a more balanced relationship between Britain and China, developments on the periphery of Empire were well in advance of Austen Chamberlain's announcement. Moreover, failures to effectively control individual officers and to prepare a wave of new arrivals for service on China's rivers from mid-1926 meant that events on the scene did not always conform to either the local or official strategies.

The existence or not of anti-intellectualist attitudes and behaviour among the early-twentieth-century Royal Navy officer class is something that has been a feature of discussion ever since the period itself.[5] Anti-intellectualism can be defined as a formative culture focusing on intangible personal attributes and social factors, at the expense of formal training and expertise in job-specific tasks. Indeed, anti-intellectualism is associated with the creation of a nepotistic system wherein those individuals whose abilities are purely meritocratic are discriminated against. That could take relatively subtle indirect forms, such as the promotion of officers who kept their vessels particularly 'shipshape', that is, clean and practised in general drill, over those who were better at the core technical requirements involved in sailing and fighting.[6] It is important to note that there is a difference between anti-intellectualism and a negative attitude towards advanced technology, as the two are not synonymous. A common attitude within the Royal Navy of focusing upon the 'Nelson Spirit' over formal training and education, with daring gentlemen inspired by a cult of Nelsonian heroism, did not preclude those same officers valuing the use of new technology and equipment.[7] Admiral Hugh Tweedie is a particularly good example of this, having expressed a strong belief that spirit was more important than technical knowledge for senior command, while also being a proponent for using the latest equipment.[8] How officers were trained to go about their roles and what equipment they used while doing their work were two separate if closely related issues. This section will discuss the former factor: the aptitudes and prior preparation of the officers deployed on the China Station, along with their attitudes towards new ideas of how they should go about their work.

Late-Victorian gunboat diplomacy in East Asia

Between the end of the Napoleonic wars and the Carnarvon Commission in 1887, a core facet of the Royal Navy's global strategy was the use of gunboats in enforcing Britain's will. With near-complete naval supremacy at sea after Trafalgar, the Navy was free to focus on projecting its power into littoral regions of the world, a key factor in the expansion of both the formal and informal elements of the British Empire. Trade agreements, port access and diplomatic approaches could all be influenced by the timely arrival of the White Ensign, and with it the regular implicit threat and occasional actual use of violence. Small steam-powered warships, particularly those broadly classed as gunboats, were pivotal in enabling that strategy by extending the Navy's reach far inland along navigable waterways. With those same waterways acting as the main arteries of transport and commerce across much of the world, Britain's ability to exert a degree of control over them was a significant strategic advantage.

The Carnarvon Commission heralded the end of that Victorian approach, when it reported that the maritime arteries of the British Empire were increasingly exposed to new threats due to changes in the strategic environment.[9] Rather than focusing on ports, harbours and convoys, the Royal Navy felt it needed to defend the new electric telegraph networks and utilize the rapid communication available to deploy fast cruisers in search of reported commerce raiders. In effect, rather than trying to maintain a passive background global deterrent, the Navy wished to switch to an approach of rapid, concentrated reactive force. As a result of that shift in strategic focus, along with the first signs of an emergent naval arms race, the number of gunboats and sloops maintained by the Royal Navy started to be reduced. That process accelerated during the 1890s with the development of 'destroyers' as a new class of warship intended for the Royal Navy's patrol and other day-to-day duties. While early destroyers were normally no larger than the gunboats they effectively replaced, they were fast and seaworthy enough to operate with the fleet.[10] One of the few exceptions to the rule of gunboat decline was the China Station, however, which retained both its gunboat force and the increasingly outdated approach of gunboat diplomacy.

The China Station's unique position in retaining a sizeable gunboat force came from a mixture of geostrategic circumstances and naval practicality. For coastal areas, destroyers could conduct many of the peacetime tasks previously done by gunboats, while also capable of operating with the fleet in wartime. That process of displacement occurred on the China Station, as it did elsewhere, with a flotilla of destroyers tasked with coastal patrols in the late 1890s.[11] In contrast, riverine environments had slightly different requirements. Vessels needed propulsion equipment suited to overcoming river-rapids along with high levels of manoeuvrability, which gunboats possessed, rather than the combination of speed and sea-worthiness inherent in destroyer designs. Early destroyers could and did travel along the lower sections of major rivers but venturing along smaller tributaries or far upriver was ill-advised. Indeed, even for purpose-built gunboats the Yangtze gorges were extremely challenging and featured many near-misses, ships sunk and the occasional stranding upon a rock (Figure 12).[12] Within the formal British Empire, particularly along the Nile in Egypt and Sudan, the gradual introduction of armoured cars and automatic weaponry also meant there were alternative options for deploying significant firepower. As the only significant series of inland waterways globally in which the Royal Navy still sought to project power on a regular basis by the turn of the century, China's rivers continued to house British gunboats in peacetime.

For the most part, gunboat diplomacy in East Asia during the late nineteenth and early twentieth centuries involved little more than 'waving the flag', a basic form of naval theatre, in other words, warships making regular patrols around the littoral regions of China and visiting the various treaty and open ports. At its most basic, it was believed that displaying the Union Flag and White Ensign atop a comparatively modern warship in a wide range of ports would increase

Figure 12 Merchant vessels and the upper Yangtze rapids in 1928.
Source: Photograph of vessels that did not make the rapids below Kun Lin Tan, 1928, US Naval History and Heritage Command, NH 95402.

the prominence of and respect for the British Empire. When China experienced periods of unrest, the implicit threat of force provided by the presence of a British gunboat was also generally sufficient to instil a wariness in the Chinese population and ensure British interests were left alone. When protests against foreign interference in China did occasionally result in violence, lethal military force was often readily employed.[13] The magnitude of violence during the Boxer Uprising, however, stands out as exceptional for the China Station between its formal separation as an independent command in 1865 and the start of the First World War. The events of 1900–1 therefore do not represent the ongoing day-to-day reality of gunboat diplomacy. Captain Gerald Dickens noted that during his first spell in China during 1903–5, for example: 'The people were friendly (although no doubt they had inward reservations about foreign devils generally) and such local bandits as existed kept out of our way.'[14]

When straying from their usual patrol grounds, or visiting a new port, officers occasionally dined at banquets with local Chinese officials to extend courtesies and build working relationships.[15] Otherwise, for the men employed in operating the gunboat patrols, life generally constituted long, uncomfortable days afloat aboard the cramped gunboats, in between weeks ashore boxing and playing games of cricket, football, golf, rugby and tennis. Indeed, sport was a defining feature of the China Station's brand of gunboat diplomacy. In part this was to emphasize the physical prowess of Britain's service personnel, but it was also simply conducted to pass the time in remote ports.[16] Of course, playing sport was not unique to the Royal Navy, with their American counterparts also keen sportsmen, but the British made it a public display of competitive fighting spirit to a much greater degree than other nations.

Sport was a subtler means of expressing power than many other options, such as parades or marching bands, which was useful during tense moments. In the aftermath of the May Thirtieth Incident at Shanghai, for example, on 5 June 1925 roughly two hundred Royal Marines were landed ashore in the International Settlement in response to protests. The following day, the Royal Navy held a series of impromptu football matches between ship's crews in the city.[17] Likewise, in March 1927 HMS *Cockchafer*'s commander deliberately sent his men ashore to play sports at Yichang, only a few days after his gunboat had been at action stations prepared for violence in the city.[18] In both cases, the servicemen were quietly reinforcing Britain's extraterritorial rights, but not in such a brazen way that might provoke a resurgence in hostility. This was not just done in response to demonstrations directed against the British. In June 1920, for example, Captain Arthur Walker of HMS *Colombo* landed the ship's company to march around

Hankou the day after general protests in the city. The reason he gave to his crew was that it would make a statement of British power and 'boost the morale of the (British) public'.[19] For the most part, however, sport was normally used just as a means of keeping crews fit, entertained and busy in a constructive way. Even with regular sporting events, crews still got into trouble by drinking, fighting and following other pursuits in port, so that the Navy surgeons were kept busy.[20]

The quiet reality of gunboat diplomacy led many in the Royal Navy to question the value of continuing the strategy. Admiral Cyprian Bridge, the commander-in-chief of the China Station between 1901 and 1904, dismissed the gunboat half of his force as being 'political and not naval' and even requested permission to retire the vessels.[21] Bridge argued that the response to the Boxer Uprising had shown to the Chinese that Britain was not to be challenged, and any future crisis could just as well be met by larger vessels from Hong Kong. Admiral Dudley Pound later noted that service on smaller vessels in East Asia was also increasingly unpopular with married men, who struggled to persuade their wives to move temporarily to Hong Kong, let alone the smaller ports.[22] This appears to have resulted from a combination of higher moving costs and poor expectations of the sanitary and social conditions in most treaty ports. Edward Barraclough recorded that during his time as a Lieutenant Commander on the China Station it was common for servicemen to go for two or three years without seeing their wives. Indeed, he was lucky that his wife decided to stay in Hong Kong, but they still went eleven months at one point without meeting. Even the major ocean-going warships only spent a few months of the year at Hong Kong, with Yangtze gunboat crews having to suffice with shorter periods at Shanghai. While officers had some influence over where they were sent, a shortage of fully paid deployments meant few took the risk of questioning an appointment.[23] Barraclough did also note, however, that some officers enjoyed the freedom and behaved very badly as husbands during their East Asian commissions, although he believed only a few marriages collapsed as a result.[24]

As a result of those factors, staffing the gunboat patrols generally fell upon young, junior officers, providing them with an opportunity to gain experience in command.[25] Despite that selling point, junior officers with better connections often sought out postings aboard the major warships on the station or even at the shore facilities, which gave them more frequent opportunities to catch the attention of their superiors. This could even extend to civilian roles, such as filling in as a temporary private secretary to Hong Kong's governor, if the officer had sufficient influence.[26] While gunboat commanders were afforded unusually high levels of independence for junior officers in the 1920s Navy, being posted to lead just twenty-four men aboard HMS *Woodlark* or *Woodcock* on the upper Yangtze in particular was not interpreted as a positive career development. In multiple letters to his mother, Commander Paul Berryman complained about being posted to command Britain's presence on the upper river, stating in one, 'I am not looking forward to my 2 years out here at all.'[27] Indeed, tracing the careers of those officers who commanded Yangtze gunboats during the 1920s reveals that very few achieved promotion to captain major warships or secured senior roles within the Admiralty later in their careers. A similar situation existed before 1914, although some officers who commanded the early destroyers on the lower Yangtze and around the Pearl River Delta did reach senior command, notably Roger Keyes and Gerald Dickens.[28] With many junior officers having gained practical command experience during the First World War, it may be that the experience available serving on China's rivers in the 1920s was less valuable for career development than it had been in previous years.[29]

Of course, with so many officers passing through the command there were exceptions. Antony Pugsley later referred to his time as a Lieutenant aboard the small gunboat HMS *Widgeon* as 'a vivid and enthralling experience' and an early step in his successful career in the Navy, later retiring as a Rear Admiral.[30] Moreover, with the Royal Navy heavily overstaffed in the aftermath of the First World War, a posting of any sort was better than being left in reserve.[31] Gunboat service might not have been many officers' preferred choice, but it still gave them a chance of developing a career in the Navy. Of the three officers commanding *Widgeon* during Pugsley's time aboard, however, two quit the Service shortly after their China tour, with the third injured during the Wanxian Incident and forced to retire.

Late-Victorian gunboat commanders appear to have understood their role, in implementing gunboat diplomacy, as needing to display diligently the dignity demanded of a Royal Navy officer and therefore a gentleman. They were expected to be firm with local Chinese officials, but had confidence that aggression was not generally required, nor desirable, in obtaining a resolution in Britain's favour.[32] Causing skirmishes over minor disputes was seen as beneath the dignity of an officer belonging to the world's most powerful navy. Captain Dickens recounted that in negotiating the release of an impounded British steamer in 1907, he knew that significant reinforcements were on the way and that his Chinese counterpart was also interested in finding a relatively quick and peaceful resolution.[33] Dickens believed that had he been direct and aggressive, demanding the steamer's immediate release, then the Chinese official would have felt pressured to respond with a similar tone. Dickens's thought process was framed by an unfettered belief in the supremacy of the Royal Navy and that if he chose to fight, then there would be only one victor. In the end his measured tone met with success. Even during a heated protest at Hankou in January 1911, with underlying anti-foreign sentiment erupting to the surface, the initial attempt by the British commander was to try to calm the situation and withdraw his sailors to the riverside. After some of the seamen were knocked down by protestors, however, there was no hesitation in opening fire to reassert control, killing thirty to forty Chinese civilians in the process.[34] Employing lethal force was not a concern in itself, but a Royal Navy officer was not expected to require using violence against what was regarded by the Service as a markedly inferior opponent.

The mindset focused upon maintaining a dignified approach extended well beyond just the use of violence. Indeed, one enthusiastic gunboat commander who took to firing off rockets and fireworks to impress the local population in a friendly, almost celebratory manner was quietly scolded by his colleagues for acting in a manner unbecoming of the Royal Navy.[35] Late-Victorian gunboat diplomacy at its most basic was the maintenance of an underlying threat of violence, but with officers normally behaving as diplomats, seeking to avoid actually using force. In any event, the day-to-day reality for Royal Navy servicemen was a monotonous one. The China Station's gunboat flotilla was not somewhere a junior officer could secure advancement, but if a flashpoint was mishandled it would certainly impede their careers. That situation and relationship was maintained until the start of the First World War, when the demand for experienced naval personnel led to the temporary suspension of most gunboat operations in China. During the war gunboats reappeared in service around the Mediterranean and Mesopotamia. Most of the new *Insect*-class vessels, constructed for those duties, were then sent to China with the return to peace in Europe and formed the backbone of the Yangtze force.[36]

A failed attempt at returning to pre-war ways

In contrast to the decades before the First World War, the 1920s China Station was increasingly a hotbed of action for the Royal Navy. Nowhere else during the period was there such an active deployment as along China's coastline and rivers. While day-to-day life on the Station retained its pre-war simplicity, with much time still spent repainting the gunboats and playing sport, there was a new unpredictable air of danger.[37] The breakdown in order resulting from the Xinhai

Revolution, an influx of modern weaponry and the growth in nationalist, anti-imperialist ideologies all removed the relative safety that Royal Navy warships had previously enjoyed. The first signs of this were apparent between the breakdown in order in 1911 and 1914, but the Navy had been increasingly distracted at that point by the European march to war.[38] For a generation of officers who had experienced the first major naval engagements since Nelson during the First World War, 1920s China presented the possibility of a little more action. There were occasional crises in the Middle East and elsewhere around the Empire, but no other region presented such a likelihood of being able to make a name for themselves as the China Station.[39] Service aboard remote China gunboats might not have been a sought-after posting, but a rare chance of independent command did appeal to some officers.[40] If an officer was likely to be placed in charge of a small warship, a location where they had a few opportunities for action was better than being sidelined on even quieter assignments elsewhere.

Entering the 1920s there was a greater risk that gunboats might become involved in firefights when navigating China's waterways, either with bandits or through cases of mistaken identity with warlord forces. For the first few years of the decade, however, violent incidents involving Royal Navy warships remained relatively rare. The pirates and bandits operating on or by the waterways were generally sensible enough not to start a fight with a well-armed warship.[41] In return, the instructions issued by the Admiralty to the commander-in-chief of the China Station emphasized that pre-war spirit of aloofness. The Admiral was told to impress upon his officers that they should be respectful of the Chinese population, as causing offence by heavy-handedness was expected to weaken China's respect for the British Empire, rather than enhance it.[42] The potential threat nonetheless required the Royal Navy to divert more time and resources to policing the waterways, responding to acts of piracy and deterring warlord armies from fighting in the treaty ports.

The accounts by Royal Navy personnel on service in China gradually changed in tone as a result of conducting more frequent, higher-risk tasks. Whereas those who served before the Xinhai Revolution referred to gunboat duty as having been a generally quiet assignment, those in the early 1920s indicate some degree of excitement from the disruptions to an otherwise sedate deployment. The then Lieutenant Commander Reginald Ramsbotham later recalled that China was a lively location, as 'we were always shooting off to a place where the Consuls wanted a bit of pressure put on'.[43] Pressure did not always equate to violence, with HMS *Bluebell* using a night-time display of its searchlights, Very lights, and a rocket to allude to its power during one such trip to Wenzhou in June

1924.⁴⁴ So busy were the Yangtze gunboats that in 1923 Admiral Arthur Leveson felt it necessary to take men off the cruiser *Carlisle* and supply ship *Titania* to recommission the gunboat *Cricket*, which was being held in reserve at Shanghai.⁴⁵

Growing pressure on the gunboats to tackle the piracy problem also saw the first retrenchment in the China Station's presence in China during this early period, although mainly around the Pearl River basin. Upon resuming full peacetime operations in late 1918 into early 1919, British gunboats returned to making journeys to a wide range of ports around Guangdong and even far into Guangxi province. Within eighteen months, however, their deployment shifted to concentrate upon a much smaller number of waterways, primarily the West River downstream of Wuzhou, around Guangzhou. This was not meant to be a permanent change. However, given Britain's weakening position in China and its volatile relationship with the Guomindang, the ruling force in Guangdong, the Royal Navy rarely ventured back upriver after 1922. This shift can be seen particularly clearly in the movements of HMS *Moorhen*, which visited cities far inland at Baituzhen, Chongzuo, Liuzhou and Napozhen between January 1919 and June 1921.⁴⁶ In contrast, after July 1921 *Moorhen*'s activities were largely restricted to the area around Guangzhou. It only made one solitary journey beyond Wuzhou, to Nanning, in the following two and a half years (see Figure 13).⁴⁷ This trend was particularly pronounced in *Moorhen*'s case but can be seen with the other Royal Navy gunboats assigned to patrol the Pearl River basin.

For ordinary seamen the tasks associated with the Navy's counter-piracy policing work seem to have proven quite enjoyable. HMS *Carlisle*'s regular night patrols of Daya Bay provided some low-risk action, with the warship stalking suspect Chinese junks in the dark, then boarding and searching them when they could not get away. In one case the crew was entertained when they discovered some known gangsters hiding in coffins, with *Carlisle* radioing the Hong Kong police to take charge of the suspects.⁴⁸ Guard duty aboard merchant steamers also provided freedom from normal duties and the opportunity to socialize with the passengers.

Anti-piracy work, however, was less popular with the officers, with many treating it with the same distain that Admiral Bridge had regarded the responsibilities of his gunboat force almost twenty years earlier. Admiral Leveson complained in 1924, for example, that there was little his gunboats could do to prevent acts of piracy and he felt pressure should be placed on searching passengers in harbour instead.⁴⁹ Instead, many officers felt that the Royal Navy should be focusing on seeking out and destroying pirate 'nests' and vessels, with

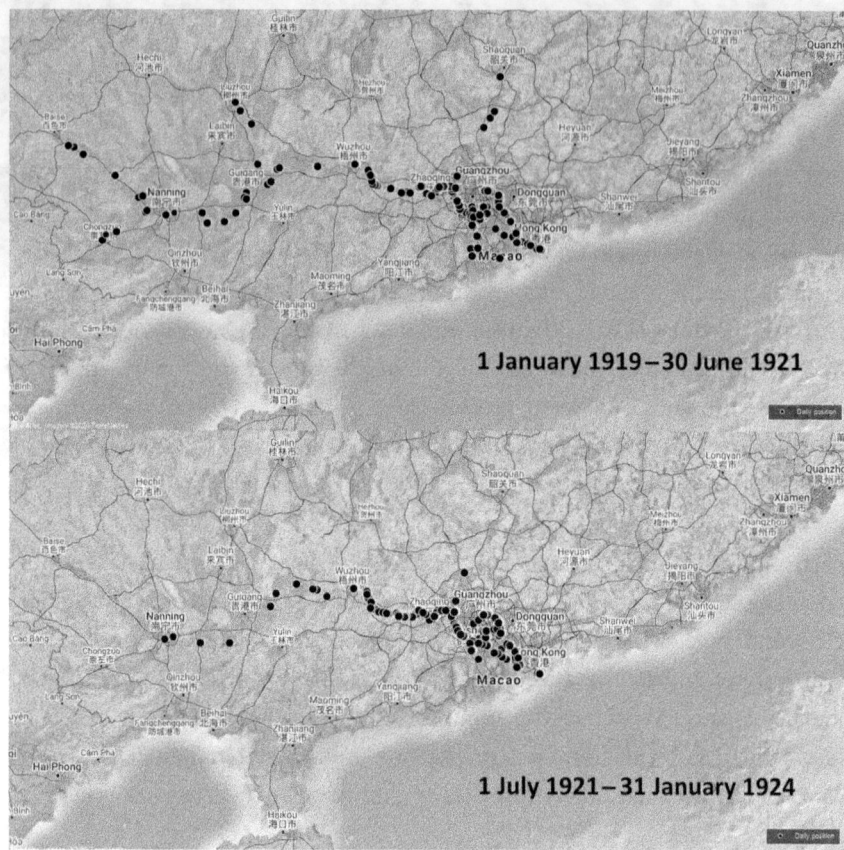

Figure 13 Patrols by HMS *Moorhen* 1919–24.
Source: Courtesy of *Journey Plotter* and *Naval-History*.net, https://www.journeyplotter.nl/index.html, last accessed 21 May 2018.

hijacking a matter for the civil authorities. Changes in the understanding of what the duties were, or at least should be, for the China gunboats started to become particularly obvious in late 1923, going into 1924.

After protection money was demanded from the British-flagged steamer *San Ming* on the West River in January 1924, HMS *Robin* sought out a suspected pirate vessel and opened fire upon it with the gunboat's main 6" gun, after the junk failed to stop. Five suspected pirates were killed in the process, after a shell hit the ship's boiler causing a large explosion. Over the course of forty minutes, a total of seventeen high-explosive shells were fired in the mid-afternoon chase.[50] Both *Robin*'s Lieutenant Commander Lionel Tudway and the Senior Naval Officer on the West River, Commander Malcolm Maxwell-Scott, argued that it was only through such firm actions that pirates would be dissuaded from attempting to attack or extort money from British merchant vessels.[51] Strong anti-piracy patrols were not in themselves unique to gunboat diplomacy as a strategy, but the consideration and use of raiding shore parties made the approach different from ordinary counter-piracy work. Through those raids, Britain was attempting to make the statement that it would ignore Chinese sovereignty to protect its interests and force local officials to do more, even if there was no effective nationwide government to take notice. Whether the tactics worked was another matter, as Tudway himself discovered four months later after he was shot through the thigh, when *Robin* was targeted by gunmen on the same stretch of river.[52]

It was shortly after those reports, during the summer of 1924, that the situation started to really change for the China Station. The Jiangsu–Zhejiang conflict and the Second Zhili–Fengtian War both brought greater risk of Britain being caught up in the fighting between warlord armies, which coincided with a surge in pirate attacks across the south of China.[53] As an indication of the threat posed by the fighting, in September 1924 an eight-thousand-strong army led by General Lu Yongxiang retreated from Shanghai and attempted to seek refuge in the International Settlement, with their weapons. As the SVC only had 1,695 men, a further 1,800 seamen and marines were landed from the warships in harbour. In addition, both the SMP and Fire Brigade were mobilized as a further impromptu defensive group. On paper that formed a total makeshift force of roughly 5,500 armed or semi-armed men, although in practice only a lower number could be relied upon. SVC records highlight that many volunteers were either not always present in Shanghai or were reluctant participants, with even the annual ceremonial parade struggling to reach one thousand attendees.[54] Nonetheless, the scale of that mobilization was unprecedented in the history of Shanghai's International Settlement, although it would soon be overtaken.

The growing combined threat from conflict and piracy precipitated a subtle change in the Royal Navy's gunboat strategy, with hawks like the commander of HMS *Robin* coming to the fore. Even as late as the previous year British gunboats had generally ignored the occasional shots aimed at them when sailing along the West River.[55] In contrast, 1924 saw a number of the China Station's gunboats using their main guns in shore bombardments against reported pirate groups, although this generally occurred when they were working in combination with forces commanded by local Chinese generals and admirals.[56] Cases of mistaken identity also crept in, with Yunnanese troops targeting *Robin* as it sailed along the West River in June, resulting in the British gunboat returning fire with its machine guns.[57] Gunboat diplomacy was no longer a passive day-to-day deterrent reinforced by odd moments of severe violence, and the first signs of its ultimate crisis were emerging.

The impact of the May Thirtieth Incident

The mid-1920s saw a return to an earlier incarnation and probably the purest form of gunboat diplomacy, in response to Britain's deteriorating position in China. The main catalyst for that decline was the May Thirtieth Incident in 1925, when British-led police shot and killed twelve protestors. With nascent concepts of nationalism in China stiffened by anti-foreign rhetoric in the aftermath of that incident, politicized groups were increasingly willing to challenge the representatives of British imperialism.[58] Even more significantly, the growing sense of commonality between cities and regions, fostered by rising nationalist sentiment, meant that potential clashes were now unlikely to pass as localized affairs. In the aftermath of the May Thirtieth Incident and subsequent clashes, anti-British protests and boycotts spread quickly across many other treaty ports.[59] Indeed, there were even small anti-imperial protests as far away as Sydney in Australia, organized in solidarity by a few unions.[60] News travelled much faster than it had done previously and could create storms far and wide.

The growing contagion effect was significant for the Royal Navy. Previously, the restricted application of force by gunboats could be used in a quasi-surgical manner to deal with issues at specific locations. In such situations, the Navy could easily achieve a localized monopoly of violence. If protests and clashes could spread nationwide as a result, however, the limited resources available on the China Station could never maintain that largely illusory threat of overwhelming force. Indeed, a June 1925 situation report to the Committee for Imperial Defence stated: 'It is unlikely that we shall be able to strengthen our naval forces commensurate with possible developments.'[61] That challenge particularly applied to the riverine ports, inaccessible by the China Station's larger warships, where the Navy might only be able to deploy a single gunboat or armed merchantman carrying a handful of marines.

The change in environment did not initially produce a fundamental reassessment of which tactics should be used by Britain's warships in China. Nor were any efforts made to transfer the Royal Navy's two remaining spare gunboats at Malta, which could have provided a modest boost to the China Station's littoral capabilities. Curiously, the Admiralty failed to acknowledge their existence during discussions with the Foreign Office, who were pressing strongly for a strengthening of Britain's riverine forces in China.⁶² That misrepresentation reflects the long-standing reluctance among senior officers to put their energy into what they saw as a peripheral imperial policing task. Indeed, the contrasting redeployment of the aircraft carrier HMS *Hermes* to Hong Kong in August suggests that the Navy's priorities lay with the major coastal ports.⁶³ Overall, there remained a belief that a few displays of Royal Navy firepower would be sufficient to remind the Chinese that Britain was the major power. Indeed, growing anti-foreign sentiment only furthered the existing trend towards a gradual hardening of gunboat tactics, with hawkish British commanders increasingly free to use their guns.

On June 23, for example, HMS *Cicala* put a landing party ashore on Shamian Island in Guangzhou, taking the lead in defending foreign possessions in the city, during anti-foreign protests resulting from the May Thirtieth Incident.⁶⁴ The island was separated by a 100-foot-wide canal, but was connected to the shore by two small bridges (see Figure 14). Photographs of the protest procession show two distinct groups, one of peaceful civilians carrying banners and umbrellas and the other of armed Whampoa Academy cadets.⁶⁵ There are conflicting accounts about what happened as they reached the western crossing, but shots were reportedly fired, which triggered a subsequent exchange of gunfire. Sir James Jamieson, the British consul general, later claimed that he had seen the Whampoa Academy cadets open fire first, but even if true the response was disproportionate.⁶⁶ That is not certain, however, as Chinese eyewitnesses swore that gunfire first erupted from Shamian Island itself, that is, the foreign forces.⁶⁷ In the violence that ensued, over fifty Chinese protestors and one French marine died, with many more injured.⁶⁸ Only after twenty minutes did Lieutenant Commander Victor Alleyne order the international forces to cease fire. Highlighting the intensity of the event, the unfortunate Petty Officer signalling the order with his whistle was shot through both hands.⁶⁹ The incident became known as the 'Shaji Masssacre'.

The British Lieutenant in charge of the Lewis machine gun party that caused many of the casualties, Cyril Faure, was instrumental in the scale of the violence. Indeed, rumours later circulated in Hong Kong that he himself pulled the first trigger to open up on the approaching crowd.⁷⁰ In the weeks before the incident, Faure had reacted very badly to criticism from the Foreign Office, for breaking the prohibition on landing British personnel on Chinese soil during a joint Anglo-Chinese anti-piracy raid near Jiangmen (Kongmoon) the previous month. While Faure also received praise, including from General Leung who commanded the raid, his behaviour changed

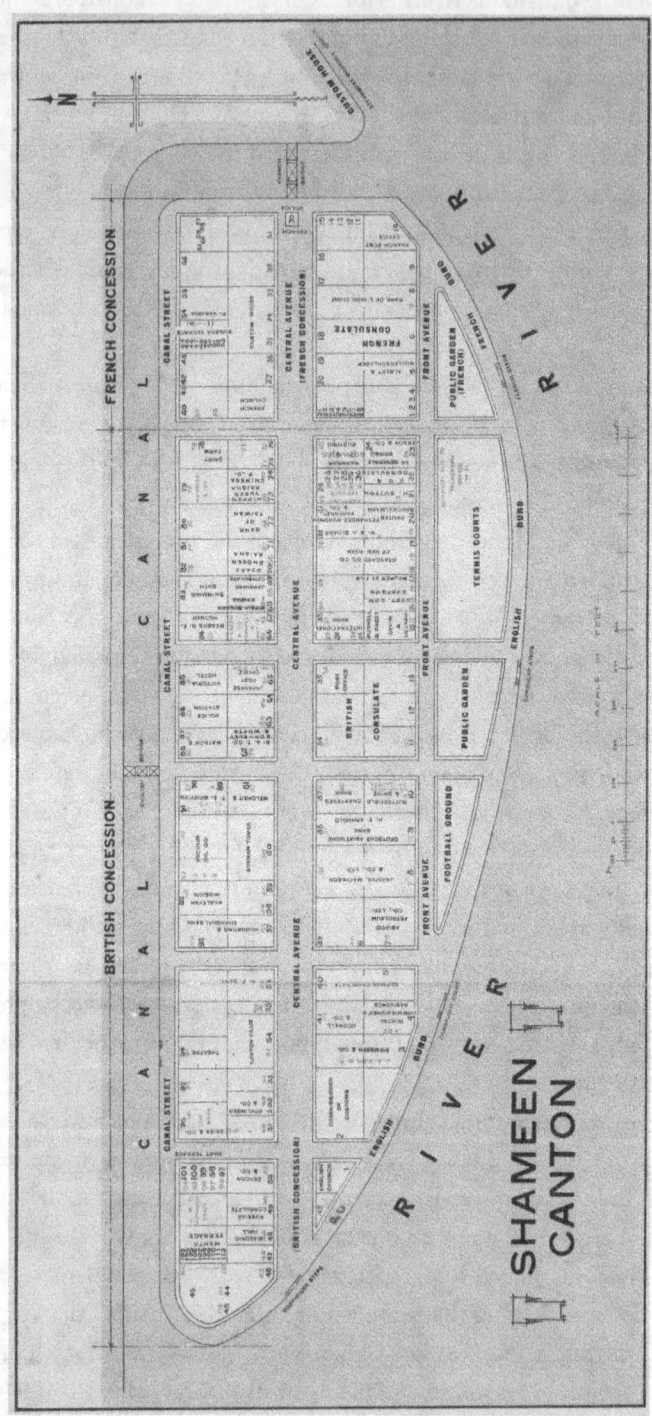

Figure 14 Shamian Island in the 1920s.
Source: Map of Shameen, Canton (Guangzhou), 1920, National Library of Australia, Braga Collection Col.67.

markedly as a result. He started getting a reputation for being drunk and disorderly on duty, with some incidents sufficiently bad to be recorded in his personnel file. This was in stark contrast to reports from previous years, when he was described as an intelligent and diligent young officer. It is worth noting that Faure had been under pressure for many weeks after he was forced to take command of HMS *Robin* when Lieutenant Commander Lionel Tudway was shot in the thigh by pirates.[71] There is no clear evidence that alcohol played a part in his actions at Shamian, but in the immediate aftermath his immediate superior Commander Maxwell-Scott recorded that Faure had become 'liable to get excited' and that a 'grievance seems to be affecting his balance'.[72] In contrast, every report about Alleyne, who had overall command at Guangzhou, indicates he was a tactful and trustworthy officer, who was skilled at calming tense situations.[73]

Despite subsequently being rotated into alternative roles, drunkenness affected Faure's actions so heavily that by 1928 he was suspended from duty and forced to retire, with Admiral Reginald Tyrwhitt simply writing 'Not recommended' on his file.[74] The following year a businessman who met Faure described him as being clearly very intelligent, but prone to drunkenness, inclined to blame his failures on others and held grudges against those he believed to have undermined him, particularly the Foreign Office.[75] Curiously, in 1934 Faure was cautiously used by the Secret Intelligence Service's Hong Kong branch. His employment was soon terminated with the assessment, 'One does not expect SIS agents to be saints, but … Lt Cdr Faure is well below the line which must be drawn'.[76] In the years after, Faure continued to live a colourful and often controversial life, later earning a reputation as a hard-line communist with strong anti-establishment views. He appears to have finally settled down into married life after the Second World War, living out his days in Hong Kong.[77]

Faure and his men's decision to open fire at Shamian reflected the Navy's increasingly aggressive stance and Alleyne would probably have reacted the same way. Alleyne had after all issued the overall order for armed men to be sent ashore, despite his reputation for calming situations. In this sense, previous descriptions of an 'atmosphere of fear' among the foreign force is at least partly accurate.[78] The high number of casualties those British sailors caused, however, was likely a tragic consequence of the rapid and sad decline in Faure's mental health. Imperialism created the situation that led to those deaths, but Faure was not a committed imperialist or motivated by such ideals.

Writing in the *Naval Review* after his retirement, Faure offered what reads as a short, half-hearted effort to restore his reputation. In it he blamed the Chinese authorities in Guangzhou, the armed volunteers under his supervision and the Foreign Office for denying him an inquiry that he felt would have vindicated his actions. Given the brevity of his argument, supported by very limited evidence and some rather grandiose claims made later in the article about his connections among China's elites, Faure does not make a particularly convincing case.[79] Indeed, with vague allusions to a conspiracy, his avoidance of taking any personal responsibility, attacks on Foreign Office Consul O'Malley's intelligence and hints at delusions of grandeur, the account adds credence to suggestions that Faure was a young man who had come off the rails.

Official guidelines, such as those Faure fell foul of, were in place to limit what the Navy's warship commanders were allowed to do in response to violence in China. In the earlier raid, British service personnel were not meant to be landed on Chinese soil, without prior express permission from Chinese officials.[80] It seems that the Foreign Office felt that General Leung was insufficiently senior to authorize the incursion, and Faure exceeded his own orders by sending men ashore, rather than simply providing naval support for the Chinese troops. Even at the treaty ports, written restrictions were imposed on when seamen or marines could be landed at times of crisis.[81]

Difficulties in defining what forms of intervention were considered acceptable, and advisable, extended up the full line of command. In August 1925, for example, Vice Admiral Edwyn Alexander-Sinclair – the new commander-in-chief – proposed a plan to the Admiralty to bombard the Taku Forts near Tianjin and the Whampoa Military Academy near Guangzhou. He felt that such strong displays in two pivotal locations would break the anti-British boycott.[82] In London, the Director of Naval Operations, Captain Ambrose Peck, suggested aircraft from *Hermes* could bombard the picket lines near Guangzhou instead, but he questioned whether such forceful action would be sensible given the reported conditions in China.[83] While ultimately Whitehall sided with Peck's caution and did not authorize Sinclair's plans, the exchange highlights the aggressive spirit developing at the head of the China Station. Sinclair sensibly chose to act in line with the guidance from London, in contrast to Faure's unfortunate decision that went beyond what he was authorized to do. For the command as a whole, however, emphasis was shifting from 'observe and coerce' to 'intervene and punish'. The Navy's culture towards command at the time also meant that most day-to-day decisions were left to Vice Admiral Sinclair, as he was the man on the spot, although he should do so 'in communication with the diplomatic and consular authorities'.[84]

It is important to note that despite the shifting mentality, the majority of cases in late 1925 where gunboats were sent to ports experiencing strikes, protests or boycotts continued to pass relatively peacefully. In his final report as the Senior Naval Officer on the Yangtze in October, Rear Admiral David Anderson commended numerous officers who had responded to such situations in a calm and restrained manner. HMS *Gnat*, for example, had shore parties ashore at Jiujiang for three weeks, during a two-and-a-half-month spell at the port, without a single clash occurring. Likewise, *Bluebell* and *Foxglove* both quietly avoided provoking violent clashes at Shantou in August, despite breaking a ferryman strike by providing cross-river transportation.[85] *Bluebell* also sent a shore party into Nanjing during fighting between Chinese armies there in October 1925, but sufficient restraint and good sense was shown that the local population reportedly gave them a friendly send-off when they departed in December.[86] Whether or not that report is true, the only physical damage done by British action during that potential crisis involved flooding the officers' bathroom aboard HMS *Concord*, due to the speed at which it steamed to *Bluebell*'s assistance. In contrast, Lieutenant Anthony Pugsley of HMS *Widgeon* was deliberately omitted from Anderson's report, despite being soundly praised by the local British officials at Chongqing. Anderson was displeased that Pugsley's uncompromising approach had come close to sparking a riot.[87] Certainly it was not an episode that Pugsley wished to mention in his memoirs, although he did discuss the difficulty involved with balancing the use of force during such incidents.[88]

The command culture of the China Station remained that of the Victorian navy, with commanders allowed considerable independence in deciding how to interpret and go about fulfilling their orders. Indeed, between mid-1925 and late-1926 the China Station was under the command of Vice Admiral Alexander-Sinclair, whose distant style of leadership meant that his thoughts on which tactics should be used remained a 'mystery' to his subordinates.[89] Indeed, Sinclair replaced Rear Admiral Allan Everett who had relinquished command in April 1925 due to ill health, having suffered a mental breakdown during his short tenure in charge.[90] In the absence of clear instructions over that two-year combined period, individual commanders were almost entirely left to follow their own instincts. That freedom, combined with the heated atmosphere in China and the growing bellicose spirit around the China Station, and Sinclair's own aggressive proposals soon contributed to the set of developments that in part led to the final crisis of gunboat diplomacy.

A double crisis: Gunboat diplomacy living up to its reputation

While the crisis that ultimately brought about a fundamental change in Britain's approach in China did not occur until late 1926, as the Northern Expedition neared the Yangtze, the tactical crisis of how the Royal Navy should conduct gunboat diplomacy began much earlier that year. Even during the tense times of 1925, most violent incidents involving the Royal Navy had tended to be reactive situations, or with some degree of official Chinese acquiescence, in particular, when gunboats or marines opened fire as a result of events ashore spiralling out of control. The Navy often played a role in the developing course of those events and threats of violence were not uncommon, but there was far more bluster than bite.

In June 1924, for example, Lieutenant Commander Ivan Whitehorn of HMS *Cockchafer* took a retaliatory attitude to the killing of an American businessman, Edwin Hawley, after the latter had been in an argument with port workers in Wanxian.[91] Amid threats by Whitehorn to bombard the port, the local Chinese commander General Lu ordered the execution of two men accused of committing the murder. During the entire incident only a single blank shell was fired in order to disperse a crowd before the landing of a small shore party to recover Hawley's body. At no point during the events did *Cockchafer* perform a main gun drill, which was normal practice when there was a possibility they might be used. Likewise, after initially being put on alert for the five hours of the evening of Hawley's killing, *Cockchafer*'s crew returned to ordinary cleaning duties the following morning.[92] Neither of those individual factors is conclusive, but when combined with the thin precedence for bombarding a city over an incident involving a non-British national, it seems likely that the threat was just a bluff, but we will never know for certain. Even then, there was pressure on the Navy from the Foreign Office for Whitehorn to face a court martial, on the grounds of grossly exceeding his orders. As no live shells were fired, and amid positive statements from the American community, no proceedings were opened into the incident. Over the following year, Whitehorn's perceived 'gamble' with his career and the Foreign Office's attitude became major talking points among the Yangtze gunboat officers.[93]

The events that unfolded two years later at Wanxian, in September 1926, provide an example of how much the interpretation of how to conduct gunboat diplomacy had shifted over the course of the 1920s. In the summer months of 1926, General Yang Sen – the warlord governor of Sichuan – and his army around Wanxian came under pressure from forces from the Northern Expedition, during their push towards the Yangtze. Faced with that threat, Yang Sen's men started to challenge the neutrality of foreign shipping by demanding that merchant vessels transport units along the river. British merchantmen had previously provided such transport in return for lucrative fees, despite strict instructions from the Foreign Office not to do so. This precipitated a crisis in September, when Chinese troops aboard the Butterfield & Swire's steamer *Wanliu* demanded transport, only to be removed with the assistance of HMS *Cockchafer*. While this was happening, a number of Chinese craft were swamped by the larger British vessels, with some of their occupants reportedly drowning. In the events that followed, Chinese troops were ordered to seize control of two other British merchantmen, *Wantung* and *Wanhsien*, by General Yang Sen.[94] During similar circumstances in 1907, the Royal Navy assembled a response force, but the officers on the scene focused on negotiating a peaceful release of the steamers, which they duly achieved.[95] At Wanxian nineteen years later, however, both the approach taken and the end result were wildly different.

While Consul General A. P. Blunt started negotiating the release of the steamers, the Royal Navy assembled a 'cutting-out' party at Hankou, intended to sail to Wanxian and take them back.[96] Within four days of the seizure of the vessels, and twenty-four hours after receiving the first official report from his subordinates on the scene, Rear Admiral John Cameron dispatched the armed merchantman *Kiawo*. Captained by Commander Frederick Darley, the *Kiawo* contained 120 sailors and marines.[97] In the words of his fictional counterpart, Jack Aubrey, it appears Cameron felt that there was 'not a moment to be lost'. Deriving its name from the process of severing a stationary vessel's anchor or mooring lines, the 'cutting-out' of large ships was an antiquated approach usually reserved for wartime. The confusion of boarding vessels held by an opposing armed force, particularly when done without the element of surprise, was a process almost certain to result in casualties. Given that Cameron knew Chinese troops were occupying the two merchantmen, and so a direct clash was likely, his decision stands out when compared with the China Station's normal reliance upon coercive threats. Cameron later reported that he had given instructions that the Chinese forces should be notified that if the British warships were fired upon from the city itself Darley was authorized to reply with the gunboats' 6″ main guns. That direct threat never reached General Yang Sen, but the associated order did reach Darley and the other gunboat commanders, with tragic consequences.[98]

Under pressure to act, Cameron's fateful decision was not made with a measured understanding of what it would mean for gunboat diplomacy in China. Indeed, his decision was based upon limited knowledge of what had actually occurred, since the report he received from Lieutenant Commander Leon Acheson aboard *Cockchafer* was highly exaggerated.[99] What Cameron did not know was that Commander Acheson and General Yang Sen did not get along well, and their attempts at negotiation amounted to little more than exchanging personal insults and making inflated demands.[100] Yang Sen had a strong personality and Acheson's personal record suggests that while a popular sportsman among his fellow officers, he was 'inclined to be obstinate ... (and) wanting in tact'.[101] Acheson had also been the officer commanding *Cockchafer* when it had assisted the *Wanliu* and so was seen by Yang Sen as responsible for the reported drownings. Subsequent negotiations led by Commander Paul Berryman of the newly arrived HMS *Widgeon* were then hampered by the profound negativity resulting from the early exchanges and occurred after Darley and *Kiawo* had already been ordered upriver.[102] Berryman had only taken up his role as Senior Naval Officer on the upper Yangtze in mid-August and his negotiations were further hampered by his lack of knowledge about what was occurring.[103] The events that unfolded as a result of Cameron's misinformed decision would force a change in the Royal Navy's tactics in China.

Despite individual displays of great bravery and later attempts to portray it as a success to the British public, the attempted cutting-out at dusk on 5 September was a catastrophic failure. Commander Darley and six other Royal Navy personnel died during the attempts to board the two vessels. A further thirteen sailors and three of the hostages were wounded during the course of events.[104] Testimony from Darley's own men outlines how the plan had been based around a complacent assumption that the Chinese troops would lay down their arms when surprised by the sudden appearance of British sailors.[105] Indeed, the boarding party were armed with wooden entrenching tool handles when they first leapt aboard the SS *Wanhsien*, such was their belief that they would be initially unopposed.[106] This was reinforced by an apparently successful ruse by the Chinese troops, with some pretending to eat dinner calmly at a table on *Wanhsien*'s deck before the attack. In reality, those troops were well aware that *Kiawo* was approaching and were prepared for a fight (Figure 15).

Darley's diligent preparation of *Kiawo* itself, including extensive makeshift armour plating, doubtless saved the lives of many of his men in the ensuing firefight. The initial melee soon burst into a pitched battle with guns flaming, bullets flying and shells bursting. While the British had been preparing for

Rear row (left to right)
Lieutenant Jack Peterson
Lieutenant Christopher Ridge (Killed)
Surgeon Lieutenant Murray (Wounded)

Front row (left to right)
Lieutenant Alfred Higgins (Killed)
Commander Frederick Darley (Killed)
Lieutenant Oliver Fogg-Elliot (Wounded)

Figure 15 Officers of the 'cutting-out' group taken on the morning of 5 September. *Source*: Photograph album of Major Frederick Burden RMLI, 1926, Royal Marine Museum, 1992/112/1.

the expedition and traveling upriver, Yang Sen had also been busy. Not only were there armed troops aboard the two steamers, but approximately a dozen field artillery pieces and numerous machine guns had been emplaced around Wanxian. After failing to seize back the steamers and coming under heavy fire from the shore, *Kiawo* and the British gunboats responded with all guns. As has been discussed in an earlier chapter, many of the shells fired landed in populated areas. Reports from both the Royal Navy and Foreign Office acknowledged that significant damage was done to Wanxian with large areas left burnt-out in the attack's aftermath.[107] At least 350 and potentially up to several thousand Chinese were killed, either directly or in the subsequent fires, with variable estimates of the proportions of military and civilians among the dead.[108] The two steamships were only later returned under diplomatic pressure and the despatch of a larger gunboat force, although the Admiralty expressly forbade its warships from firing again upon Wanxian.[109]

The casualties alone were sufficient to precipitate a fresh diplomatic crisis that fed into worsening Anglo-Chinese relations. For the Royal Navy, however, the events also represented a fundamental tactical and strategic failure. Cameron had deployed a force far stronger than those generally available to respond to such crises, and yet the Royal Navy had been made to appear both weak and brutal at the same time, despite efforts to portray the expedition as heroic.[110] The failed attempts at issuing direct threats of retribution if the vessels were not released were always tangential to the primary orders for the *Kiawo* expeditionary force to seize them back. Crucially, the instructions issued to Darley were not based upon coordinating the Navy's actions with the local consul's efforts to force Yang Sen into yielding to British demands. Indeed, *Kiawo* only possessed a short-range wireless set, intended to notify *Cockchafer* and *Widgeon* ahead of its imminent arrival and the impending raid.[111] How the slow-moving *Kiawo* was meant to achieve tactical surprise was left unanswered. While his account contains some questionable assertions, Lieutenant Pugsley later claimed that *Widgeon*, so presumably Commander Berryman, had even radioed Darley at the last minute, 'pleading' with him to change his plan as the Chinese knew of *Kiawo*'s approach.[112] In all, the rash and rushed operation was both a tactical and strategic mess. Poorly coordinated threats, followed by a naïve attempt at using force, showed neither a considered attempt at gunboat diplomacy nor military sense. As a result, what occurred at Wanxian revealed Britain's gunboat bluff and dented perceptions of the Royal Navy's power among China's regional leaders and population.

Curiously, the whole incident went against Admiralty instructions in early 1926, restricting the use of gunboats on the upper Yangtze.[113] By this point the Admiralty had already decided, in conjunction with the civil authorities, to withdraw protection from those British civilians and vessels that chose to operate in that peripheral region. The Admiralty subsequently provided retrospective approval of Cameron's decision, which had been approved by Vice Admiral Sinclair. The incident does, however, serve to highlight that the China Station's officers were taking a firm interpretation of what their responsibilities entailed. Leon Acheson's behaviour certainly adds credence to Foreign Office reports at the time that some naval officers were 'spoiling for a fight'.[114] While it might be assumed, given Cameron's pattern of strong action, that he may have been a cause of the hardening in gunboat behaviour, as shall be explored shortly, he was actually considered to be too cautious by some of his subordinates.[115]

The gunboat retreat

The final months of 1926, after the Wanxian Incident, saw a fundamental change in the Royal Navy's strategy towards and tactics in dealing with China. The strategic shift was closely aligned with the diplomatic stance taken by the Foreign Office that culminated with Austen Chamberlain's December Memorandum. Official policy changed to a withdrawal of resources from a wide range of treaty ports to focus upon the determined defence of key harbours and waterways, such as Shanghai and the lower Yangtze. The Admiralty's proposed strategy in light of the new circumstances involved the use of warships to evacuate foreign civilians from secondary treaty ports when required and to secure those of primary importance. Previously, there had been a large grey area between formal

British imperial possessions and what were seen as China's sovereign rights. After the shift in late 1926, however, a dividing line had been drawn – Whitehall had effectively told the Navy that they should consider some treaty ports as core to the British Empire and defend them accordingly.

The message sent to the warship commanders by the strategic shift was reinforced with the rapid redeployment, in September, of the aircraft carrier HMS *Hermes* and the Third Destroyer Flotilla, both from the Mediterranean.[116] That posting was largely a response to the broader environment, given the strength of anti-British rhetoric from the Guomindang in mid-1926 and the launch of the Northern Expedition. Nonetheless, while it may have been intended to show Britain's resolve to the Chinese and British expatriate communities, it had an impact upon Royal Navy personnel as well.

A subtle example of how this influenced the Navy's tactics can be seen during trouble at Hankou, soon after the Third Destroyer Flotilla arrived on the China Station. In response to anti-foreign protests after the city was seized by the Guomindang, the senior naval commander at Hankou ordered the landing of shore parties, in much the same way that the Royal Navy had behaved in years before. Unlike previous incidents, however, the decision was made to send ashore a 2-pounder quick-fire 'Pom-Pom' anti-aircraft gun.[117] That weapon could fire approximately three high-explosive shells per second at a distance of up to a kilometre and was a significant jump from the normal rifles and machine guns issued to shore parties. Prior to 1926, there are no recorded instances of the Navy landing heavy weaponry since the Boxer Uprising, nor had they requested the assistance of the treaty port volunteer corps gun batteries. The Shanghai Volunteer Corps, for example, had four 4.5″ howitzers and a battery of 2.75″ mountain guns, although the latter were antiquated and largely for show.[118]

Even in itself, having a heavy weapon ashore was a significant and explicit threat, greater in intensity than the implicit one posed by a gunboat mid-channel. Weighing 527 lb (239 kg), landing a Pom-Pom was not something ordered on a whim, and doing so showed that the shore party would not surrender their position lightly. Even mounted on a wheeled carriage, a large team was required to move the weapon around.[119] As a result, it tied the shore party into making a determined defence to avoid potentially losing a valuable piece of equipment. Using land-based heavy weapons in this way went against the very essence of gunboat diplomacy, stretching the idea that it should involve a limited application of force. By defending a fixed location there was no end-goal of trying to coerce a change in behaviour by the Chinese forces.[120]

The landing of the Pom-Pom occurred prior to the December Memorandum, signifying that gunboat diplomacy was already being abandoned prior to the official change in Britain's foreign policy towards China. This is an important distinction, as it indicates that there was a grassroots recognition within the Royal Navy that gunboat tactics were no longer effective. Existing accounts about the decision in effect to abandon Hankou in January 1927 focus heavily on the changing diplomatic situation and how that led to the decision not to defend the concession. In essence, they argue that there was a political realization after Wanxian that gunboat diplomacy was failing, which led to a shift in foreign policy towards managed imperial retreat.[121] The aggressive approach taken in early 1927 would therefore have been the Royal Navy's final gunboat hurrah, before being restrained by diplomatic pressure. The decision not to defend Hankou, however, was as much a military one as a matter of foreign policy.

In the first week of January, Britain had just three vessels stationed at Hankou – the newly arrived destroyer *Woolston*, the sloop *Magnolia* and Cameron's flagship gunboat HMS *Bee*.[122] Together with an additional detachment of marines, that only provided a force of roughly three hundred service personnel. With southern forces assembling at Jiujiang and other treaty ports, the Yangtze gunboat force was stretched thin. On paper, the Hankou Volunteer Corps (HVC) could provide a supplementary force of 130 individuals armed with a selection of small arms, passed on from SVC's larger armoury.[123] However, as many of the foreign population had already departed, the HVC was only useful for supervising the gates to the concession. Similarly, the local municipal police consisted largely of Sikhs from India, who were demoralized, not particularly committed to the British Empire and unwilling to defend the concession.[124] As it was mid-winter, water levels on the middle and upper Yangtze were also low and dropping fast, making it difficult to move *Woolston* or arrange for any additional major warships to reinforce Hankou from Shanghai. While it was subsequently discovered water levels were still sufficient to send more destroyers up to Hankou, at the critical moment no reinforcements could be expected.[125]

In contrast to the small British outpost, there was a substantial Chinese force marching on Hankou. Cameron notified Tyrwhitt on 14 January that a Chinese army numbering roughly twelve thousand men was in position around the city, with further divisions nearby around Hubei province. An earlier report, later dismissed as inaccurate and speculative, had suggested that up to forty-seven thousand troops were descending on Hankou.[126] In addition, many of the local Chinese population were involved in protests and riots against continued foreign possession of the concessions. Even allowing for the possibility that the lower figure might also have been inflated, and the potential for military assistance from other foreign powers in the port, the Hankou defence force was heavily outnumbered. Indeed, every available man was landed on 3 January just to deal with civilian protests.[127]

A subsequent assessment by Admiral Tyrwhitt suggested that an additional one thousand men, presumably referring to the 12th Royal Marine Battalion, would have evened the odds in the short term. With the Chinese army possessing a range of artillery, however, Tyrwhitt doubted whether a defence of the concession could be sustained for any period of time.[128] The shifting balance of military technology in China had changed the odds markedly from earlier decades, placing the Royal Navy in a situation where for once it was outgunned. There were also unconfirmed reports that Guomindang aircraft had been seen bombing targets around the city, adding a further potential complication to the defence.[129] Quite simply, holding the Hankou concession in January 1927 with the resources at Cameron's disposal would have been virtually impossible.

Cameron also had to keep in mind the wider situation of the middle and upper Yangtze region while choosing his course of action. There were still hundreds of British civilians at ports upriver of Hankou, who needed to be evacuated.[130] Sichuan was calmer than it had been immediately after the Wanxian Incident, but Britain was still highly unpopular. All pretence of maintaining Britain's image on the upper Yangtze had gone in the aftermath of that calamitous episode. The Navy's gunboats were forced to send small boats and ships' boys into even remote river ports to obtain supplies, due to widespread unwillingness to do business with British officials.[131] In particular, it was nearly impossible to obtain locally sourced coal to help fuel the gunboats, which were undertaking heavy duties and so consuming greater quantities than usual. Indeed, the Royal Navy's usual local coal merchant in Wanxian was arrested in late 1926 for supplying the armed steamer *Kiawo*.[132] This problem also applied at Hankou but was less acute as some foreign merchant vessels were still venturing that far upriver.

A violent clash at Hankou would therefore not only have been futile but could have endangered both the upper Yangtze gunboat force and the civilians they were attempting to evacuate. Only a reckless and bloodthirsty commander would have chosen to defend aggressively the Hankou concession in those circumstances. The decision to back down at the city does not therefore mark the end of gunboat diplomacy, which had occurred months earlier. Instead it reinforced Wanxian's lesson. Royal Navy gunboats were unable to match the challenge posed by large numbers of well-armed Chinese troops if those soldiers were no longer sufficiently in awe of British prestige and thus afraid of potential retribution.

The year 1927 would later pan out to be a year in which violent clashes between the Royal Navy and different Chinese groups occurred with a regularity and scale unlike any other part of the decade. The Northern Expedition moving along the Yangtze River and contemporary anti-foreign protests triggered a crisis for the British establishment, in its attempts to maintain many aspects of its informal imperial influence. The actions of the Royal Navy during this period have generally been assessed as a whole. This was a year unlike most others for the China Station, however, and so to understand fully the Navy's actions, we must consider the unusual nature of the force posted to the region. In the last months of 1926, the China Station was reinforced by the arrival of a destroyer flotilla and the return of HMS *Hermes* with its aircraft. That increased the number of surface fighting vessels from twenty-five to thirty-five and the total manpower on the station by roughly half. By April 1927, the number of surface warships in the region reached fifty-six, bringing with them an additional eight thousand naval personnel.[133]

The vast task force itself highlighted that the Royal Navy was attempting a different approach to dealing with the immediate challenges posed by the situation in China. That sudden influx of additional warships also brought a wave of new officers, many of whom had never served on the China Station prior to that point. As a result, few really understood the environment they found themselves in. In the case of HMS *Emerald*, for example, the first detailed official briefing the officers and crew received on the situation in China came almost three months after the warship had joined the command.[134] That presentation was made by Captain Hugh England, commanding *Emerald*, who had little additional knowledge than his crew. After a quick meeting with the commander-in-chief, shortly after arriving in China, England had few chances to discuss events with other fellow commanders, as only HMS *Caradoc* stopped at Nanjing during the intervening weeks.[135] His primary source of information was therefore from civilians living in Nanjing, particularly the British members of the Nanjing Club.[136] It seems very unlikely that England had a rounded understanding of either Britain's overall position in China or the evolving strategy for the Royal Navy to deal with the challenges it faced.

The temporary attachment of arriving warships to different commands also led to considerable variety among the crews in their loyalty to their new commanding officers. While Vice Admiral Tyrwhitt was generally highly respected, given his reputation as a hero of the First World War, his deputy

Rear Admiral Cameron, commanding the crucial Yangtze River region, was not seen in the same light. Cameron had captained the cruiser HMS *Phaeton* at the Battle of Jutland, among other warships, but the appointment to the Yangtze in 1925 was his first operational experience of senior command. As a result, Commander Louis Hamilton noted proudly in his journal that he and other officers deliberately undermined Cameron's authority and considered him to be an 'old woman' who was too willing to 'turn the other cheek to these Bolshevik swine'.[137] Given Cameron's relatively strong instructions and behaviour prior to and during the Wanxian Incident, Hamilton's statement may be more a reflection of his own attitudes and inexperience of the situation than a fair assessment of his new commanding officer. It is also possible that Wanxian's political and diplomatic repercussions took their toll on Cameron, leading to a comparatively cautious outlook. Regardless of the accuracy of Hamilton's statement, such views existed and influenced the behaviour of the officers newly assigned to Cameron's force. At the height of the crisis in the first half of 1927, it would prove to be fresh faces like Hamilton, particularly those under Cameron's command, who became heavily involved in some of the most violent and controversial incidents.

During the first two months of 1927, Cameron was tasked with evacuating the cities along the upper Yangtze, further calming the situation at Hankou and protecting Britain's interests on the middle and lower stretches of the river. The first of those tasks, conducted mostly by his existing cadre of junior officers aboard their gunboats, proved successful and largely peaceful. A total of 380 British and 200 non-British foreign civilians were safely escorted out of Chongqing, Wanxian and the surrounding areas in the first two months of the year, leaving only forty-eight remaining, many of whom were missionaries.[138] The gunboat commanders involved focused on their core assignment, with little regard for previous concerns about maintaining Britain's image or punishing Chinese transgressions. After Navy stores were stolen while being loaded aboard HMS *Mantis* at Chongqing, for example, an unarmed party of British marines who were sent to retrieve the items were beaten and forced to retire to the gunboat. An official protest was made and an apology was received from General Liu Hsiang, in command of Sichuan, but *Mantis* left the port without the stores and no one was punished for their loss.[139] Likewise, the crew of *Cockchafer* at Yichang were free to play sport ashore within a month of arriving, much in the style of earlier years, but only after calmly riding out the initial hostility to their arrival.[140] It is worth noting that the temperamental Acheson had already departed in late 1926 to recuperate from wounds sustained at Wanxian and then commanded a destroyer in home waters.[141] There was no risk that he might spark another clash in China.

There remained some superficial similarities between the Royal Navy's tactics for evacuating the upper Yangtze ports and how they had conducted their gunboat duties in previous years. During one incident at Chengling in January 1927, Lieutenant Commander Douglas Garvey aboard HMS *Woodcock* threatened to bombard the town. The message was conveyed in response to Commissioner Tung threatening to fire upon British vessels in the port and Chinese troops subsequently moved a field gun onto a hill overlooking the river. Garvey argued that as Tung represented the Guomindang his threat bordered on a declaration of war against Britain, and if *Woodcock* were fired upon a state of war would exist.[142] Formalizing the conversation led to a quick clarification by Tung that his warning was only aimed at British merchant vessels who he had not authorized to leave port. Ultimately, Tung reluctantly agreed that the port's foreign community could be evacuated aboard those steamers under the supervision of *Woodcock*. When looking in detail at the incident there are some clear differences in Garvey's tactics compared to those previously employed by the Royal Navy.

Commander Garvey appears to have been deadly serious in his threat to bombard Chengling, having kept his men at action stations by their guns throughout the drama.[143] During the full course of events, however, the gunboat remained mid-river and no parties of armed sailors were sent ashore or to the British merchant vessels. Moreover, even when picketers sank a junk in front of the British vessels and attempted to sink further boats, to prevent the steamers from departing, Garvey ordered a Jardines' tug moved to ensure there was a clear path. While he felt that Tung was bluffing, Garvey did not risk testing that theory. The local consul, Grant Jones, subsequently argued to Britain's minister to China, Miles Lampson, that a bloodbath would have been better than a surrender that had harmed Britain's image in the region. Garvey simply reported in return that his primary duty was to ensure the safety of the civilians under his care.[144] Such statements are notable in their absence from earlier accounts. Prioritizing the evacuation was different to what was expected, both tactically and emotionally, under a policy of gunboat diplomacy. While the strong defence of British possessions afloat on China's waterways did show a technical use of extraterritorial rights, in practice the Royal Navy had always considered the decks of British flagged vessels as British soil, wherever in the world they might be.[145]

Hankou may have been the core location that defined Britain's position on the upper Yangtze in early 1927, but it did not become the boundary between retreat and defence after the decision to withdraw from the concession in January. Gunboats were still supervising the official evacuation of the ports upriver, including Chongqing, Wanxian, Changsha, Yichang and Chengling. Nonetheless, on 9 January 1927, just a few days after the Hankou concessions had been effectively abandoned, the decision was made to also completely evacuate Jiujiang, a day's sailing downriver of Hankou.[146] Five thousand Chinese troops had taken up position in and around Jiujiang, presenting a threat that the Royal Navy's Yangtze flotilla was equally as incapable of countering as the twelve thousand at Hankou.[147] Against such numbers the joint parade by the entire international naval force at Jiujiang two months earlier, of just 125 sailors from Britain, America, France and Japan, appeared an ineffective and token gesture – a transparent pretence of strength and unity.[148] Anti-British rioting within the town on 7 January, in response to reports from Hankou, had led to valuables and foreign civilians already being clustered at protected properties near the waterfront.[149] Nonetheless, the final decision to abandon the concession was made due to the presence of so many well-armed troops. After evacuating Jiujiang, the confluence of the Gan and Yangtze rivers became a temporary boundary (point 3 in Figure 16). Britain had lost official direct access to the markets of Sichuan, Hunan and Hubei provinces, along with the western part of Jiangxi.

Correspondence between Cameron, Tyrwhitt and the Admiralty in January and February outlines how the Royal Navy planned to continue defending the concessions downriver of the Gan River boundary. Tyrwhitt went into considerable detail about the forces available for defending Britain's interests along the lower Yangtze and how far he could rely upon American and Japanese troops to provide support if violence ensued.[150] His official assessment sent to the Admiralty in late January also suggested that Britain should seek quietly to undermine the Chinese authorities at Hankou, rather than seize the concession back through violence. If the Guomindang were seen to have failed at Hankou, then Britain could make the case that its supervision of the treaty ports was vital for the success of China's economic hubs. Britain might then have its extraterritorial rights in Hankou restored and regain complete access to the upper Yangtze basin. Tyrwhitt included one warning – if Hankou proved a success under Chinese control, then Britain would likely lose all its possessions in China, including Hong Kong.[151] While it was a pivotal moment,

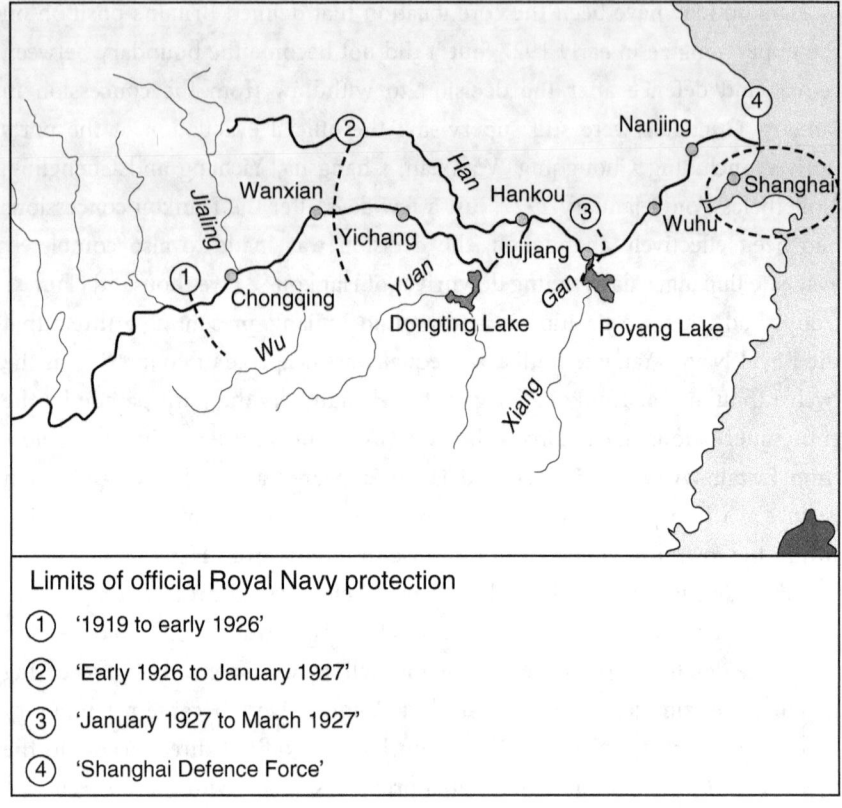

Figure 16 Extent of official Royal Navy protection on the Yangtze.

when the decision was made the withdrawal of military guarantees over British concessions at Hankou and neighbouring ports was not seen as a permanent move by the Royal Navy.

The events on the upper Yangtze between the Wanxian Incident and February 1927 meant that Britain accepted the loss of some peripheral brown-water treaty port concessions, in order to defend those of greater value. That process was not one of calculated surrender, nor was it one forced by 'vigorous popular reactions that could no longer be suppressed'.[152] Mass protests were a significant factor in triggering initial defensive preparations and some temporary evacuations. However, at both Hankou and Jiujiang in particular, but at many other ports along the upper Yangtze including Wanxian, Britain had simply been militarily outmatched. The China Station's commanders were unwilling and unable simultaneously to counter large armies at multiple locations, which were unified to some extent under Guomindang direction. Had a clash occurred between the

Royal Navy and Chinese armies, the British force would have been outnumbered and almost certainly alone, with only one Japanese and one Italian gunboat left above Hankou able to offer potential assistance.[153] These factors were made all the worse by the influx of modern weaponry.

By the end of the decade, when faced with a communist army ten thousand strong at Changsha in July 1930, the Royal Navy acknowledged that any possible attempt at gunboat bluster would have failed. Even before taking changed diplomatic priorities into account, they were heavily outnumbered and many of the Chinese troops were armed with the 'latest' machine guns and field artillery.[154] Nonetheless, the evacuations in 1926 and early 1927 did not involve complete abandonment. British gunboats, merchantmen and civilians were all still present at locations along stretches of the upper and middle Yangtze, just in lower numbers.

The lower Yangtze and other treaty ports around China remained tense during this period, but relatively calm, with protests and boycotts inspired by Wanxian and the unequal treaties in general. Those protests combined with press reports of atrocities and concern at what many felt was a significant loss of British prestige at Hankou, together creating an air of fear among the British expatriate communities, particularly at Shanghai.[155] In public, the Municipal Council issued a proclamation in January aimed at the Chinese population, stating that the SMC was happy to work with whoever controlled the Shanghai region and discussion of a possible war was premature.[156] In private, all talk was about the very real prospect of war coming to Shanghai. Tyrwhitt reported to the Admiralty on 12 January that in addition to the reinforcements already received, he needed at least an Army division to secure Shanghai. A worst-case scenario involving the evacuation of Shanghai had been discussed, but Tyrwhitt felt that not only would such an event be catastrophic for Britain's reputation, it would be virtually impossible to conduct safely. As a result, the Shanghai Defence Force was approved by Cabinet the following week, along with the immediate despatch of the First Cruiser Squadron from Malta and the hastily formed 12th Royal Marine Battalion from Britain.[157] The influx of new service personnel that started in late 1926 became a flood.

Sailing to war

Plans to defend robustly those treaty ports still considered vital to the Empire were not unique to officers on the China Station, with the new policy extending all the way to Whitehall. The First Cruiser Squadron, for example, was authorized by the Admiralty to send its midshipmen and section leaders ashore at Malta to train with the Army before departure. During the journey the warship commanders were instructed to conduct practice firing and prepare for landing shore parties.[158] Similarly, having arrived at Nanjing from the East Indies Station HMS *Emerald* practised landing its full crew, less those required to maintain the ship, in preparation for a future defence of the concession.[159] A bombardment range was also set up at Mirs Bay, so the new vessels could gain experience in firing at land-based targets.[160] All this preparatory activity may simply have been for the defence of Shanghai, except most of the new warships were subsequently spread around the treaty ports, highlighting that they were intended for a wider range of locations. Having steamed at high speed around the world, while training to fight, the new forces were prepared for action. With the Northern Expedition nearing the middle and lower Yangtze, and the existing China Station forces spread thin, the stage was set for the crisis to erupt into war.

The China Station had moved from its old approach of gunboat diplomacy, but the newly arriving crews from other stations did not know or understand that a shift had occurred. Moreover, some of the new crews arrived in a state of excitement at the prospect of action. Perhaps a portent of things to come, HMS *Emerald* was just such a ship. Captain England continued to order frequent landing drills throughout February and early March, in between social events ashore in the Nanjing concession. This included testing alternative approaches for preparing landings to improve the speed with which *Emerald* could respond in emergencies. The 'platoons' of seamen and marines intended for shore parties were split into two, for example, with alternate half-units always dressed in full kit ready for action. *Emerald* also regularly sent armed teams to intervene in disagreements involving British steamers at Nanjing, although in most cases the situation had been settled before they arrived.[161] By mid-March, a platoon of twelve personnel armed with Lewis machine guns were a regular feature on *Emerald*'s main deck, sheltering behind improvised redoubts made of sandbags and sheets of armour plating.[162] While individually none of those actions was particularly unusual, cumulatively they indicate the elevated enthusiasm of one newly arrived crew. It also highlights that Captain England did not approach his role with the same focus on calm stabilization that had become apparent among Rear Admiral Cameron's existing cadre of officers after the Wanxian Incident.

As the armies of the Northern Expedition neared Nanjing in late March, it was the enthusiastic England with *Emerald* that was on the front line. Nanjing sat inside the boundary where Britain still intended to maintain its extraterritorial possessions. In the events that unfolded, *Emerald* bombarded part of the city with its main guns, during an effort to exfiltrate British and American shore parties and civilians. Even after the initial crisis had subsided, Captain England pressed the following day for permission to punitively bombard the city.[163] Indeed, he argued so strongly that Admiral Tyrwhitt later removed England from his command and placed him in an administrative role as punishment, and Tyrwhitt himself was not shy of using violence.[164] Only a few weeks later Tyrwhitt was visibly disappointed when his flagship HMS *Hawkins* was not fired upon near Shanghai, as he was eager to see some action.[165] The overly aggressive stance taken by *Emerald* throughout the situation can therefore be partly attributed to the warship being a new arrival and an excessively enthusiastic desire to repeat the famous successes of the Boxer Uprising. That previous crisis had, after all, provided the former Admiral of the Fleet Earl Jellicoe and Admiral Roger Keyes the fame that helped launch their careers.[166]

Had it been a resident China Station cruiser posted to Nanjing the end result may have appeared broadly similar to outside observers. With a request from Allied forces ashore for an immediate supporting bombardment, it seems unlikely that any Royal Navy officer would have declined to assist their American friends. Indeed, two weeks later HMS *Carlisle* risked fresh clashes when ordered to prevent Guomindang forces from removing British-owned railway rolling stock from Nanjing by taking it across the river to Pukow.[167] Where a different course of action probably would have occurred was on the second day when Captain England threatened and vehemently demanded permission to conduct a punitive bombardment of Nanjing. While that was in keeping with what was expected from a warship conducting gunboat diplomacy, threatening or using a short violent outburst to force a change in behaviour, it was wholly at odds with Rear Admiral Cameron's orders and new policy for the Yangtze region. Admiral Tyrwhitt also explained at the time that his decision not to approve Captain England's request was ultimately because he felt it would have served no practical purpose. Again, this is not to say Tyrwhitt was against the use of violence. His biographer noted that during this period he was strongly in favour of war with China, wanting to defeat the Guomindang rather than coerce them.[168] What it does show is that neither of the two senior commanders on the China Station appears to have held the intangible longer-term focus of gunboat diplomacy in particularly high regards. While contemporary observers and later historians have been drawn to the first bombardment and its deadly collateral damage, those in the Royal Navy at the time took note of Captain England's reassignment a month after the incident.[169]

In isolation, the Nanjing incident provides a modest case showing the difference between the mentalities of newly arrived officers and those already on the station and how that influenced the tactics they adopted. When combined with other such cases a clear pattern develops. Rear Admiral William Boyle and his First Cruiser Squadron, which arrived at Hong Kong shortly after *Emerald*, certainly had a reputation for wanting to take an aggressive line with China.[170] Tyrwhitt's reluctance to share centre stage at Shanghai with another British flag officer, however, kept Boyle around Hong Kong and firmly on London's leash.[171] In contrast, newly arriving destroyers were quickly spread around the station. Commander Hamilton recorded in his diary that when dining aboard HMS *Frobisher*, after arriving at Hong Kong, he was just as keen to fight as Boyle, who he described as having a 'great blood lust on'. While Boyle was not his direct superior the discussion defined Hamilton's approach to China, with Commodore John Pearson at Hong Kong unable to provide specific orders about what the destroyers were actually meant to do.[172] While calmer than Hamilton, Commander de Winton later recalled in a similar manner how he took his ship up the Yangtze without really knowing what the situation was.[173] Enthusiastic, relatively junior officers were being fed into the Yangtze with most of their guidance coming from the war-mongering Boyle, who had no recent experience in China.

When sailing up the Yangtze, the new officers did not appear at first glance to act in a way that was far removed from the behaviour of existing China Station commanders, but there was still a difference. As might be expected in the situation, the new warships went immediately to action stations upon sighting Chinese troops, their main guns ready to fire.[174] A standing order, radioed around the station after the Nanjing Incident, stated that warships could open fire at shore targets if fired upon first.[175] The new arrivals appear to have interpreted that as 'should open fire'. HMS *Emerald*'s semi-official account of its voyage summarized the results of that confusion as events 'developed into rather a farce, as even if a little sniping took place at ships the full main armament was brought to bear'.[176]

HMS *Wanderer* under Commander Hamilton, for example, engaged Chinese troops with all the guns at his disposal after coming under relatively light, if accurate, fire near Jiangsu on 2 May 1927. Even Hamilton realized afterwards to his 'horror' that the expenditure of ammunition had been excessive and his crew too enthusiastic. *Wanderer*'s main 4.7" guns had fired off seventy-eight shells during a relatively short engagement. Hamilton had turned *Wanderer* around to make additional passes of that stretch of river to repeatedly bombard and attempt to destroy the Chinese troops' field gun, without success.[177] Similarly, HMS *Veteran* expended roughly eighty shells to flatten a field gun at Kueishing Fort near Zhenjiang in early April on its first run up the Yangtze.[178] *Veteran*'s Lieutenant Commander Henry Clanchy also ordered his ship to turn around and return past the fort to continue the bombardment, even though his destroyer had suffered no more than a few bullet scratches to its paintwork during the whole affair.[179] Both commanders had quickly expended one-sixth of their warship's total store of shells, and a much higher proportion of their high explosive ones, during single engagements against targets of negligible military value.[180]

In contrast, the China Station resident HMS *Magnolia* was fired upon on the same stretch of river in mid-April. *Magnolia*'s Commander Harold Hadley chose to make a brief reply with one Pom-Pom and Lewis guns, and ordered a ceasefire within ten minutes, once the ship moved beyond the range of the Chinese troops.[181] Similarly, the gunboat HMS *Mantis* came under fire near Nanjing in April, but only replied with its machine guns.[182] Further afield around the Pearl River Delta, dealing with groups of bandits, gunboat commanders repeatedly reported landing and talking to villagers in response to incidents of firing at passing British ships. Lieutenant Commander John Thompson on HMS *Robin*, for example, stated that he saw little value in firing as it would punish innocent civilians and the real offenders would almost certainly escape unharmed.[183] While the China Station's existing commanders were taking a pragmatic, defensive approach to dealing with gunfire from Chinese troops or bandits, the new arrivals were looking to make a statement and utilized traditional, aggressive Victorian gunboat tactics.

Given the enthusiasm with which newly arrived warships were engaging shore targets, Vice Admiral Tyrwhitt felt it necessary to relay instructions restricting his commanding officers' actions. On 18 May, orders were radioed out across the station that the expenditure of ammunition should be kept to a minimum, not only to limit the political impact but also for reasons of economy. Moreover, Tyrwhitt expressly forbade the use of the warships' main guns unless there was a clear target, presenting a threat to life and where firing would prove effective.[184]

While such orders did instil some restraint on the new arrivals, they were surprisingly resistant to softening their stance as they got to understand the situation in China better. When posted to the recently evacuated Jiujiang in mid-May, for example, Commander Hamilton was told by the local Acting-Consul Ogden that surrendering the concession had changed little in practice. While many civilians had been evacuated, and the police and other civil authorities were now under Chinese control, business largely continued as before. Ogden had even been able to get his Chinese counterpart Chen to agree to pay rent to the British consulate for using the municipal buildings. Despite that apparently favourable modus vivendi, Hamilton wrote in his journal that 'I shall not have the slightest hesitation in opening fire if they give me the opportunity.'[185]

In any event, Hamilton did not sit and wait for the opportunity. Within days of arriving at Jiujiang he sent two dozen sailors marching through the old concession in an attempt to annoy Chen and provoke a response. When visited shortly afterwards by the commander-in-chief, Hamilton felt that Tyrwhitt had been amused by the exercise, although he was subsequently taken aside by his superior and instructed to avoid creating an incident. The two officers knew and liked each other, from when Hamilton had served under Tyrwhitt during his time commanding the Harwich Force in and immediately after the First World War. Indeed, Tyrwhitt recorded that he had 'a very high opinion of this officer' after that earlier commission and played an important role in Hamilton's early career development.[186] As a result, Hamilton respected the instructions to behave himself, although only temporarily.[187]

This was one of a few recorded cases where Tyrwhitt initially gave the impression he supported such rash actions, only subsequently to request that his subordinates follow his official policy of restraint. Indeed, Tyrwhitt appears to have been conflicted between a personal desire for action and his professional sense of duty as commander-in-chief to act in Britain's best interests. On returning to Shanghai, for example, after meeting Hamilton and telling him to avoid creating incidents, Tyrwhitt was again openly disappointed that *Hawkins* had not been given an opportunity to fire.[188] This behaviour may have contributed to the aggressiveness of some newly arrived officers, who did not have time to get to understand Tyrwhitt's habits and that not all he said should have been taken as actual guidance on how to behave.

Those developments are also in contrast to earlier events, with the actions of a single gunboat commander illustrating the issue rather well. Commander Edward Jukes-Hughes was one of the first naval officers reassigned to the China Station towards the end of the First World War, as the gunboats started to be recommissioned. This was quite a change from his previous experience as Gunnery Officer aboard the armoured cruiser HMS *Minotaur*. Within weeks of taking command of HMS *Widgeon* on the upper Yangtze, the gunboat came under heavy rifle fire on 7 December 1917 after leaving the Yellow Flower Gorge near Chongqing. A later count revealed that at least a dozen bullets had hit the vessel, with one entering the officers' wardroom. Jukes-Hughes ordered his men to reply with the 6-pounder main gun, and again the following day with both the main gun and Maxim machine guns, to silence their assailants. He recorded in his journal that some of the attackers were killed. In contrast, when Widgeon came under fire on 2 July 1920 near Zhangzhou, Jukes-Hughes first ordered the firing of a blank shell, followed by a live shell aimed into the middle of an empty field. Subsequent communication then revealed a case of mistaken identity, with apologies offered by the local Chinese general, and the incident passed without injury.[189]

There was clearly some excessive enthusiasm during the former incident, but after Jukes-Hughes gained a better understanding of China he adopted the nuanced approach required with gunboat diplomacy. Admittedly the second event came almost three years later, but after that initial violent event, Jukes-Hughes's journal suggests he soon gained a taste for acting as a diplomat when dealing with potential flashpoints. This is supported by his personnel files, which are full of praise for his calm and tactful behaviour, both when commanding *Widgeon* and then after his promotion to Senior Naval Officer on the upper Yangtze. Indeed, Rear Admiral George Borrett recorded that Jukes-Hughes's actions 'materially increased the prestige of the British flag through the province of Szechuan', benefitting from having built up an 'extensive knowledge of China'.[190]

The wave of new Royal Navy commanders arriving in 1927 showed no such interest in diplomacy or getting to know the country. They arrived with and continued to maintain a desire for action and a strong willingness to take offence for perceived slights on behalf of the Navy and British Empire as a whole. That mindset went against one of the core tenets of gunboat diplomacy – the limited application of force. Curiously, while the newly arriving naval officers during this period tended to push an aggressive line, those of the 12th Royal Marine Battalion did not. Having arrived on 28 February, the marines initially took charge of defending Shanghai's International Settlement, before slowly being replaced as British Army units poured into the city. Throughout the Battalion's China war diary, the commanding officer Lieutenant Colonel Robert Carpenter repeatedly noted that given the exposed position of his men, they should focus on defusing situations and avoiding confrontation.[191] This appears to have been largely a result of the precarious situations the Royal Marines were often placed in.

Shortly after arriving in Shanghai, Colonel Carpenter proposed that those of his men tasked with defending British possessions in Pudong, in the Chinese part of the city, should be based in ships on the Bund, on the International side of the Huangpu River. That decision was based solely on the recognition that putting a small force of marines into Chinese territory, in the midst of large numbers of Chinese troops, would present a significant risk of clashes and damage to British property.[192] In a more pronounced case, in September, one company of marines was posted to defend British factories on the outskirts of Nanjing. It was hoped that those marines would provide enough protection for British businesses to retrieve valuable machinery. The expeditionary force quickly converted a factory into an improvised fort and confidently reported that they could defend it against any mob. Nonetheless, there was an underlying warning both in the orders issued to that company and the reports from it, that ten thousand Chinese troops were still positioned around Nanjing. With it came a reminder that the marines could only call upon reinforcements from a single cruiser and they were therefore badly outnumbered if the worst were to happen. As a result, the force was instructed to maintain a cordial relationship with the local Chinese commander and to avoid provoking protests.[193]

The discipline shown by the 12th RMB in strictly following Carpenter's orders is all the more unusual as it was an ad hoc unit. Newly formed from a combination of companies out of the Royal Marine depots at Chatham, Portsmouth and Plymouth, the battalion arrived at Hong Kong only six weeks after the order had been issued for its formation. Carpenter had been given little time to prepare his unit for the tasks they faced. In those circumstances, the battalion displayed a remarkable level of cohesion and unity. The challenge might have been avoided, however, had the proposals of a 1924 Admiralty committee on the 'Functions and Training of the Royal Marines' been enacted.

The 'Madden Report' as it was known, after its Chairman Admiral of the Fleet Sir Charles Madden, tendered a definition of the Marines' future role and made a series of recommendations as to how the force should be modernized. Adjutant General Alexander Hutchison stated that their primary function was as a 'landing force to preserve order, or to deal promptly with trouble in out of way places'.[194] In effect, Hutchison was arguing that the Marines were there to support the Navy's peacetime role as Britain's imperial gendarmerie. While acknowledging the financial challenges facing the Admiralty, the report proposed withdrawing the small marine contingents aboard cruisers and light warships, and the formation of four 1,600-man formations and a central reserve. Three of those units would be placed at Bermuda, Gibraltar and Hong Kong, from where they could quickly deploy to most of the likely trouble spots around the Empire. While this required 1,900 extra Marines, it was expected that savings would be made through civilians taking on some existing depot tasks, and as British Army garrisons at the three hubs could be reduced.[195] The proposal was rejected by First Sea Lord Earl Beatty on the grounds of significant initial costs.

Had the plan been enacted, the China Station would have had a force at its disposal ready for rapid deployment in response to potential threats. There have been suggestions that the essence of the proposals was still put into place, given the quick formation and deployment of the battalion to Shanghai in 1927.[196] Given Admiral Tyrwhitt's statements in January about defending Hankou if he had 1,600 marines at his disposal, however, the six weeks it took for the force to arrive from Britain was very significant.[197] Without speculating on what the end result might have been, a Royal Marine battalion at Hong Kong could have reached Hankou within a few days, with the orders issued by the commander-in-chief, not through Whitehall. The actual deployment in 1927 was hardly that of the rapid reaction force envisaged in the Madden Report. In defence of Beatty's decision, the five detachments of eighty to one hundred marines aboard each of the China Station's cruisers and smaller numbers on the sloops were probably better suited to day-to-day requirements. Apart from the 1926–7 crisis, having smaller contingents spread around the region allowed the Navy to reassure treaty port communities at very short notice during times of trouble.

The Royal Marines by nature have always been separate from their parent service. When looking just at the Royal Navy itself, there was a clear divide in mentality and tactical approach between those officers who served on and those who were attached to the China Station, throughout the core crisis period between late 1926 and mid-1927. Within the localized context, it was the arriving group of naval officers who were behaving in the unusual manner but taking the Royal Navy as a whole it was the China Station acting differently. The warships arriving in China came from all around the world; *Emerald* and *Enterprise* from the East Indies Station, the First Cruiser Squadron and Third Destroyer Flotilla from the Mediterranean Fleet, the Eighth Destroyer Flotilla from the Atlantic Fleet, and the aircraft carrier *Argus* from the Home Fleet. Sailing to the sound of the guns, those warships all came with a basic belief that aggressive gunboat tactics were effective in dealing with China and the officers were generally excited at the prospect of action. In August 1927, for example, Rear Admiral Hugh Tweedie was disappointed at being chosen to replace Cameron as commander of the Yangtze gunboats, believing himself to be the only senior officer who was not keen on getting involved in the trouble there. Tweedie lamented that prior to receiving the order sending him to China, he had been looking forward to an easier posting to spend more time with his wife.[198]

The China Station differed from the rest of the Royal Navy because of its experiences during 1925 and 1926. The Wanxian Incident demonstrated that amid growing nationalist sentiment in China, localized clusters of the populace could no longer be coerced by the appearance of a British gunboat. Violent British actions were increasingly seen as having been made against the Chinese nation and not just against regional populations. This added to the existing subtle, but deep-set, institutional reluctance within the China Station towards gunboat diplomacy as a strategy. Not only were gunboat tactics increasingly ineffective, but their demise offered the opportunity to remove the drain of mundane operations aboard cramped vessels that took men and resources away from what were seen as the 'real' duties of the Royal Navy.

Over the course of a warship's posting to any single station, its crew never remained the same for the whole commission. At regular points a portion, or indeed the entire complement, would be 'paid off' and sent back to the UK, either to rest at their home naval base or to leave the Service. In 1924, for example, both *Magnolia* and *Hollyhock* paid off their full crews at Hong Kong, taking aboard new replacements.[199] For reasons of practicality and continuity, however, this process was usually an ongoing one, with small groups of officers and men replaced when they were due for rotation or retirement. The China Station's cruisers were treated slightly differently, with the vessels sent back to Britain when a replacement cruiser arrived, such as the switch of *Cairo* with *Diomede* in 1922.[200]

While replacement crews did produce some changes in approach, for the most part newly arrived officers opted on the side of caution. There are three likely reasons why this was the case, in contrast to the more disruptive impact from the influx of new personnel in 1927. Firstly, numbers were a factor as prior to 1927, particularly during quieter months, it was entirely feasible for the one or two new commanders to call upon the commander-in-chief or the Rear Admiral commanding the Yangtze gunboats. In doing so, there was time for the senior officer to provide a detailed briefing on the assigned role as well as the general situation in China. No such luxury was available in late 1926 or 1927. Vice Admiral Tyrwhitt was busy travelling between locations trying to manage the crisis and with thirty-six new warships arriving along with further replacement commanders it was impractical to give them the same preparatory briefings. Indeed, Commander Hamilton's experience in Hong Kong, with Commodore Pearson lacking a detailed understanding of Tyrwhitt's plans, highlights that the China Station's command, control and communication structure was struggling.[201]

The second factor is the rank and general experience of the newly arriving officers and where they were being posted. During the comparatively peaceful early 1920s, most replacements were for the gunboats and sloops, which involved junior officers being given their first full command afloat. Given their inexperience of sole command, unfamiliarity with their new environment and since they were aboard quite modest warships, they were less apt to make rash decisions that could put their crews at risk or harm their career development. In contrast, destroyer commanders arriving in 1927 were generally on their second commands and the cruiser captains were seasoned officers. Captain England, for example, was 43 in 1927, his first command – the small destroyer HMS *Fawn* – was back in 1909 and he had been decorated for bravery during the First World War.[202] During the latter incident he was shot in both legs – injuries that never fully healed and led to a degree of understandable 'irascibility' to his character.[203] With years of experience, those officers were not just practised in dealing with the demands inherent with command, but they were also expected to provide decisive leadership.

Finally, it was made clear from the outset that the surge of warships heading to China were not intended to stay there permanently. Orders sent to the vessels despatched emphasized it was a short-term attachment to the China Station.[204] Likewise, First Lord of the Admiralty Viscount Bridgeman publicly stated in the House of Commons that the expeditionary force deployed to East Asia was a temporary measure.[205] As a result, there were limited consequences for the officers on attachment, compared with those permanently based in the region. A river gunboat commander, for example, may have had to continue working with his Chinese counterparts for years to come after a clash. In contrast, it was unlikely many of the newly arrived commanders would have to worry about such interactions, even if in practice one of the two destroyer flotillas later permanently joined the China Station.[206] Awareness of potential consequences did not always mean officers behaved diplomatically, as was clearly the case with Lieutenant Commander Acheson during the events preceding the Wanxian Incident.[207] The frequency with which the temporarily attached ships became involved in clashes, however, and the volume of ammunition consumed in dealing with them are clear indicators that newly arrived commanders were not worried about the long-term impact on their personal standing in China.

Against the background of debate about whether there was an anti-intellectual atmosphere within the 1920s Royal Navy, a look at the grassroots level yields some interesting results. To begin with, across all the accounts from both permanent and temporary members of the China Station, there are no records that suggest ordinary officers were dismissive of new technology in any way. This runs contrary to arguments by Arthur Marder and Jon Sumida that many officers were reluctant to adopt new equipment that mechanized existing processes.[208] Those arguments were largely made in reference to the battle fleet and wartime tactics, however, where the proposed equipment was more complicated and the consequences potentially far greater. In contrast, on the China Station the benefits of using new wireless sets, for example, were fairly obvious to all concerned. Indeed, by late 1927 Vice Admiral Tyrwhitt was putting pressure on merchant vessels to purchase and install radios, to aid the Royal Navy in its anti-piracy work.[209] Likewise, the new operational uses for HMS *Hermes*'s aircraft found between its first and second deployments to Hong Kong from display flights to scouting patrols ahead of the anti-piracy raids in Mirs Bay show not just an acceptance of new technology but an enthusiasm for employing it.[210] Together this highlights that the grand theoretical arguments about operations involving fleet vessels only illustrate what was happening within one, admittedly very important, segment of the Royal Navy. While previous reforms had much diminished its brown-water forces, the 1920s Royal Navy was still far more than just a battle fleet.

Exploring the changing tactical approaches taken by the China Station towards the challenges it faced produces a slightly different picture to that involving technology. In particular, the phase between the Wanxian Incident and late 1927 provides a range of cases where officers deliberately resisted moving away from long-established policies. Hamilton's efforts to provoke a clash at Jiujiang, for example, went completely against the new tactics proposed by Cameron and harked back to an earlier Victorian understanding of gunboat diplomacy. Outlining what he felt the situation to be in his journal, Hamilton argued that the Royal Navy was only on the Yangtze due to trade, and if China could not be trusted to ensure law and order, then Britain should do so by employing garrisons and gunboats. Moreover, Hamilton felt that any withdrawal would see British steamers having to fall back, which would severely damage British Imperial prestige.[211] While particularly vocal in his beliefs, Hamilton was not alone in holding that view, with many officers struggling to countenance alternative strategies or tactics for dealing with the situation in China, no matter how effective or not they might be.

Behind the conservatism displayed by many Royal Navy officers in China, their core mindset was tied in with a belief in the value of a Nelson Spirit, with attitude more important than tactics. This is hardly surprising when considering the early training those officers would have received as cadets or at the staff colleges. It has been suggested that the historical knowledge of many junior officers prior to the First World War amounted to 'little more than tales of heroic action and daring deed'.[212] There were some efforts at reforming the system during and after the war, but the focus remained on spirit over technical training.[213] Beyond Jutland and submarine warfare, the Cambridge University Course for Naval Officers in 1922, for example, was heavily based around lectures exhorting the bravery displayed in the time of Nelson. In the amphibious warfare section there was no mention of Gallipoli or Zeebrugge, just a few years beforehand, with the main focus on Wolfe's exploits at Quebec in 1759.[214] So pronounced was the focus upon the exploits of a few famous admirals that many cadets and junior officers regarded leadership training with a high degree of cynicism.[215]

Commander Darley's attempted cutting out of the two merchant steamers at Wanxian, against overwhelming odds, was a product of that unbalanced approach to education. Darley and his force went into action with the unwavering belief that their bravery and Nelson Spirit would leave the Chinese troops in awe, recognizing the inherent superiority of the Royal Navy and throw down their arms.[216] As retold in HMS *Despatch*'s account of the preparations: 'It was thought that ... the men on board the "Wanhsien" on seeing an armed party suddenly draw up alongside would down arms.'[217] In reality, Chinese troops were increasingly armed with weapons capable of matching those used by the Royal Navy and were also quite willing and able to use them.[218] Lieutenant Kenneth Buckley's submission to the *Naval Review* in 1930, reporting the Third Destroyer Flotilla's experiences while in China, demonstrates how the new arrivals failed to appreciate fully the significance of Wanxian. The report summarized the lesson from the incident as 'Their (the gunboats) bluff was called at Wanhsien and it was seen that, with the modern weapons of war now in China, something bigger was needed to provide security for treaty ports.'[219] Upgrading the naval deterrent from a gunboat to a destroyer at some middle Yangtze ports did provide an additional eighty sailors and two more main guns, but that changed the balance little if they were pitted against thousands of relatively well-armed Chinese troops ashore.

It was not therefore a case of anti-intellectual attitudes directly holding back the adoption of new tactics to deal with the evolving challenges faced in China, but rather a consequence of long-term inadequacies in the Royal Navy's system for educating its young officers. There was an enthusiasm for exploring new ways of using technology and for improving the way in which the Navy went about its precise tasks. When it came to dealing with the changing environment in which they operated, however, many officers displayed the hallmarks of anti-intellectualist behaviour through their weak training in objectively assessing the situation. Other factors were also at play, with racial attitudes common within the Royal Navy towards the Chinese also significant. Echoing the words of Director of Naval Intelligence Rear Admiral Gerald Dickens in 1935, the Royal Navy's patronizing and prejudiced attitude towards Asian peoples was just as problematic in its dealings with China as it would become with Japan.[220] Regarding Chinese troops as naturally inferior contributed to significant underestimations about the increasingly tenuous position Britain was in and was the underlying reason why new tactics, such as those developed by Rear Admiral Cameron in late 1926, were necessary.

Summary

Over the course of the 1920s there were numerous gradual developments in the approach taken by the Royal Navy towards China. Most notably, there was a slow and steady shift towards using greater levels of violence in providing forceful responses to threats, whether ashore or afloat. Much of that trend was catalysed by growing nationalist sentiment in China and with it the contagion impact of localized events spreading rapidly across discontiguous regions. Fundamentally, the Navy was struggling to cope with a new China, where it was dealing with numerous, increasingly well-armed groups operating in isolation, but linked by a common sense of identity. This process culminated in the violent events at Wanxian in September 1926 – the real end of the Royal Navy's purposeful use of gunboat diplomacy in China. From that point onwards, the China Station's behaviour became less about trying forcefully to coerce the local population into accepting a form of British imperial presence ashore and more about simply defending a reduced number of core ports. As events developed, it proved an impossible task to protect much more than Shanghai and Hong Kong, although the Royal Navy continued to operate far inland up the Yangtze and West Rivers. Just as the final line was drawn by the British commanders in the region, with plans to offer a sustained defence of Shanghai's International Settlement, the diplomatic situation moved on and war was avoided. Britain formally agreed to a new post-imperial relationship with China, and the Guomindang dropped its anti-foreign rhetoric to focus on battling against the Chinese Communist Party.

The cases after the Wanxian Incident where British warships employed gunboat tactics generally came as a result of the diverse force assembled during the crisis triggered by the Northern Expedition. Newly arrived officers did not generally receive enough guidance to fully understand the situation in China and tended to act in a particularly aggressive manner. A significant range of attitudes and approaches were taken by different officers. China Station warships not only appeared visibly different, with their bright white painted hulls, but the unusual circumstances in East Asia produced a specific mindset, when compared to the rest of the Royal Navy's global operations. Many newly arrived officers in 1927 were unwilling or unable to adapt to the local environment and find a solution that met Britain's interests in the region. This proved problematic when combined with those exhibiting a strong focus on the 'Nelson Spirit', putting greater emphasis on aggressive spirit and direct action, than developing more effective tactics.

The changing tactical approaches taken by the Royal Navy in China had a significant bearing upon the way events developed, even if they evolved quite slowly over much of the decade. While the Wanxian Incident represented a significant turning point, the roots of the crisis went back much further. Of all the challenges, however, that faced the China Station in its efforts to support Britain's presence in East Asia it was one completely unrelated to tactical or even strategic thought that proved the most influential. Ultimately, the lack of respect shown towards the Chinese, and the resulting failure to appreciate their greater military capabilities, undermined Britain's ability to control a measured withdrawal of informal empire. The same racially charged attitude of complacency existed towards the Japanese and would prove particularly costly for both the British Empire and Royal Navy in later years.

Notes

1 Jones, 'Towards a Hierarchy of Management', pp. 171–2.
2 de Winton, *Ships in Bottles*, p. 28. The 'CinC' referred to was Vice Admiral Tyrwhitt, with Rear Admiral William Boyle later becoming Admiral of the Fleet and 12th Earl of Cork and Orrery.
3 Robert Mandel, 'The Effectiveness of Gunboat Diplomacy', *International Studies Quarterly* 30/1 (1986), 59–61.
4 Cable, *Gunboat Diplomacy*, pp. 39–83.
5 E.g. Harry Dickinson, *Educating the Royal Navy: Eighteenth and Nineteenth Century Education for officers* (Abingdon: Routledge, 2007); C. I. Hamilton, *The Making of the Modern Admiralty: British Naval Policy-Making 1805–1927* (Cambridge: Cambridge University Press, 2011); Elinor Romans, 'Leadership Training For Midshipmen,

1919–1939', in *Naval Leadership and Management 1650–1950*, ed. Helen Doe and Richard Harding (Woodbridge: Boydell & Brewer, 2012), pp. 183–91; Bell, 'The King's English', pp. 685–716; Marder, 'The Influence of History on Sea Power', pp. 414–28; Moretz, *Thinking Wisely, Planning Boldly*, pp. 1–23.
6 Marder, 'The Influence of History on Sea Power', p. 439.
7 Mike Farquharson-Roberts, *Royal Navy Officers from War to War, 1918–1939* (London: Palgrave Macmillan, 2015), pp. 9–11; Bell, 'The King's English', p. 699; Dickinson, *Educating the Royal Navy*; Hamilton, *The Making of the Modern Admiralty*.
8 Elinor Romans, 'Selection and Early Career Education of Executive Officers in the Royal Navy c.1902–1939' (unpublished PhD, University of Exeter, 2012).
9 Roger Parkinson, *The Late Victorian Navy* (Woodbridge: Boydell & Brewer, 2008), p. 239; John Major, *Send a Gunboat* (London: Longmans, 1967), p. 145.
10 David Lyon, 'Underwater warfare and the torpedo boat', in *Steam, Steel, and Shellfire*, ed. Robert Gardiner and Andrew Lambert (London: Conway Maritime, 1992), p. 144; Major, *Send a Gunboat*, p. 161.
11 Navy List, 1897, RNM.
12 Letters from Commander Berryman to his mother, 2 September 1926, IWM, Documents. 1445.
13 Salkeld, 'Witness to the Revolution', pp. 115–21.
14 Unpublished autobiography of G. C. Dickens, undated, KCLMA, Catalogue ID 1114, Chapter two.
15 Assorted memoranda and reports from the Yangtze gunboats, 1906–07, TNA, ADM 125/127.
16 Spence, *A History of the Royal Navy*, pp. 98–100.
17 Diary of Marine W. J. Greenland, June 1926, RMM, 1978/48b.
18 Rear Admiral Cameron to Vice Admiral Tyrwhitt, 21 March 1927, TNA, ADM 116/2510.
19 Unpublished memoirs of Ordinary Seaman G. T. Weekes, IWM, Documents, 1445.
20 Interview with I. L. Wight, 1982, IWM Interview Series, Catalogue Number 6196, Reel 2, 4 minutes.
21 Lindgren, 'A station in transition', pp. 467–73.
22 Admiral Pound, Memoranda on the strategic deployment of the fleet, 23 October 1923, TNA, ADM 116/3195.
23 Farquharson-Roberts, *Royal Navy Officers from War to War*, pp. 37–38, 75.
24 Barraclough, *I Was Sailing*, p. 64.
25 Unpublished autobiography of G. C. Dickens, Chapter two.
26 Diary of Commander C. H. Drage, November 1923, IWM, PP/MCR/99, vol. 4 (1923–6).
27 Letters from Commander Berryman to his mother, August and September 1926, IWM, Documents. 1445.

Changing Attitudes, Ideas and Approaches 253

28   Unpublished autobiography of G. C. Dickens, Chapter two; Man and Lun, *Eastern Fortress*, p. 51.
29   Moretz, *Thinking Wisely, Planning Boldly*, pp. 53–4.
30   Pugsley and Macintyre, *Destroyer Man*, pp. 10–19.
31   Moretz, *Thinking Wisely, Planning Boldly*, pp. 98–9.
32   Lieutenant Commander Todd to Vice Admiral Moore, 17 July 1907, TNA, ADM 125/127.
33   Unpublished autobiography of G. C. Dickens, Chapter two.
34   Salkeld, 'Witness to the Revolution', p. 126. Salkeld notes that the initial figure reported in the newspapers and sent to London was only five dead, but the real figure was higher.
35   Unpublished autobiography of G. C. Dickens, Chapter two.
36   Konstam, *Yangtze River Gunboats*, Appendix.
37   General Letters from the China Station, 1922–4, TNA, ADM 1/8665/142.
38   Salkeld, 'Witness to the Revolution', pp. 116–35.
39   Moretz, *The Royal Navy and the Capital Ship*, pp. 258–9.
40   Farquharson-Roberts, *Royal Navy Officers from War to War*, p. 12.
41   Admiral Leveson to Admiralty, 11 October 1923, TNA, ADM 1/8665/142.
42   Instructions reissued to the commander-in-chief of the China Station, 1 February 1922, TNA, ADM 1/8727/146.
43   Unpublished memoirs of Captain Ramsbotham.
44   Diary of Commander C. H. Drage, vol. 4 (1923–6).
45   Admiral Leveson to Admiralty, 11 October 1923, TNA, ADM 1/8665/142.
46   Ship's logbooks of HMS *Moorhen* May 1919, TNA, ADM 53/49912–49938 and ADM 53/80939–80955.
47   E.g. General Letters from the China Station, 1922–4, TNA ADM 1/8665/142; Proceedings of the China Station, 1924–5, TNA, ADM 116/2262; General Letters from the China Station, 1926–7, TNA, ADM 116/2502; Proceedings of the China Station, 1929–30, TNA, ADM 116/2694.
48   Interview with A. A. Heron, 1975, IWM Interview Series, Catalogue Number 681, Reel 11, 7–10 minutes.
49   Admiral Leveson to Admiralty, 23 January 1924, TNA, ADM 1/8665/142.
50   Ship's log of HMS *Robin* January 1925, TNA, ADM 53/82919.
51   HMS *Tarantula* to Admiral Leveson, 5 March 1924, TNA, ADM 116/2262.
52   Diary of Commander C. H. Drage, 30 May 1924, vol. 4 (1923–6).
53   Jackson, 'Expansion and defence', p. 191.
54   Shanghai Municipal Council Annual Report 1924, SMA, U1-1-937; Shanghai Municipal Council Annual Report 1922, SMA, U1-1-935.
55   Admiral Leveson to Admiralty, 17 March 1923, TNA, ADM 1/8665/142.
56   Various reports from Admiral Leveson to Admiralty, 1924, TNA, ADM 1/8665/142.

57 Commodore Grace to Admiral Leveson, 10 June 1924, TNA, ADM 1/8665/142.
58 Bickers, *Empire Made Me*, pp. 164–8.
59 Fung, *Diplomacy of Imperial Retreat*, pp. 40–50.
60 Sophie Loy-Wilson, '"Liberating" Asia: Strikes and Protest in Sydney and Shanghai, 1920–39', *History Workshop Journal* 72 (2011), 74–102.
61 Summary memorandum on the situation in China, 30 June 1925, TNA, CAB 24/174/26.
62 Foreign Office memoranda on the situation in China, June 1925, TNA, FO 371/10922.
63 Ship's log of HMS *Hermes* 1925–6, TNA, ADM 53/78829.
64 Report on the events at Shamian (Shameen) Island, June 1925, TNA, ADM 1/8070/219.
65 Shaji Massacre, 1925 Collection, Historical Photographs of China, University of Bristol, Sh-s01 to Sh-s08.
66 T'ang Leang Li, *The Inner History of the Chinese Revolution* (Arlington: University Publications of America, 1975), pp. 207–8.
67 *China Mail*, 27 June 1925, p. 2.
68 Bickers, *Britain in China*, p. 4; Goto-Shibata, *Japan and Britain in Shanghai*, p. 16; Braisted, *Diplomats in Blue*, p. 52.
69 Rear Admiral Anderson to the Admiralty, 12 October 1925, TNA, ADM 1/8707/219.
70 Wright-Nooth, *Prisoner of the Turnip Heads*, p. 98.
71 Diary of Commander Drage, 30 May 1926.
72 Personnel file of Lieutenant Cyril Faure, TNA, ADM 196/122/80; Personnel file of Lieutenant Cyril Faure, TNA, ADM 196/146/649.
73 Reports about Alleyne by Commodores Bowden-Smith, Grace and Stirling, 1922–5, TNA, ADM 196/144/50.
74 Personnel file of Lieutenant Cyril Faure, TNA, ADM 196/122/80; Personnel file of Lieutenant Cyril Faure, TNA, ADM 196/146/649.
75 Character reference about Cyril Faure by G. S. Moss, 31 December 1929, TNA, WO 106/5270.
76 Letter from MI2 General Staff officer at Hong Kong, 13 September 1934, TNA, WO 106/5270.
77 Wright-Nooth, *Turnip Heads*, p. 98.
78 Goto-Shibata, *Japan and Britain in Shanghai*, p. 16.
79 C. M. Faure, 'Some Aspects of the China Situation', *Naval Review* 16/4 (1928), 659–60.
80 Admiralty correspondence regarding the use of force in China, 1925–7, TNA, ADM 116/2527.
81 Hansard, 15 July 1925, vol. 186, c. 1303.

Changing Attitudes, Ideas and Approaches 255

82 Admiral Sinclair to Admiralty, 21 August 1925, TNA, FO 371/10947.
83 Memorandum by Captain Peck, 22 August 1925, TNA, FO 371/10947.
84 Committee of Imperial Defence meeting notes on the situation in China, June 1925, TNA, CAB 24/174/26.
85 Acting-Consul Davidson to Admiral Sinclair, August 1925, TNA, ADM 1/8707/219.
86 Diary of Commander C. H. Drage, November 1923, vol. 4 (1923–6).
87 Rear Admiral Anderson to Admiralty, 12 October 1925, TNA, ADM 1/8707/219; Acting-Consul Archer to Rear Admiral Anderson, July 1925, TNA, ADM 1/8707/219.
88 Pugsley and Macintyre, *Destroyer Man*, pp. 10–19.
89 Journal of Commander Hamilton, 1927–8, NMM, HTN 214.
90 Journal of Lieutenant William Andrewes, 18 April 1925, IWM, DS/MISC/12.
91 Braisted, *Diplomats in Blue*, pp. 82–4.
92 Ship's log of HMS *Cockchafer* June 1924, TNA, ADM 53/73583.
93 Pugsley and Macintyre, *Destroyer Man*, p. 13.
94 Braisted, *Diplomats in Blue*, p. 69.
95 Unpublished autobiography of G. C. Dickens, Chapter two.
96 Tweedie, *The Story of a Naval Life*, p. 241.
97 Braisted, *Diplomats in Blue*, p. 102.
98 Rear Admiral Cameron to Admiral Sinclair, 17 September 1926, TNA, ADM 116/2509.
99 Rear Admiral Cameron to Admiral Sinclair, 17 September 1926, TNA, ADM 116/2509.
100 Consul A. E. Eastes to Sir Ronald Macleay, 7 September 1926, TNA, ADM 116/2509.
101 Personal file of Leon Stopford Acheson, TNA, ADM 196/144/741.
102 Consul A. E. Eastes to Sir Ronald Macleay, 7 September 1926, TNA, ADM 116/2509.
103 Letters by Commander Berryman to his mother, August–September 1926, IWM, Documents, 18246.
104 Braisted, *Diplomats in Blue*, p. 102.
105 Consul A. E. Eastes to Sir Ronald Macleay, 7 September 1926, TNA, ADM 116/2509.
106 Pugsley and Macintyre, *Destroyer Man*, p. 16; Allen, *With HMS Despatch to China*, p. 20.
107 Consul A. P. Blunt to Sir Ronald Macleay, 15 October 1926, TNA, ADM 116/2509.
108 Clayton, *The British Empire as a Superpower*, p. 200; Osterhammel, 'China', p. 652.
109 Rear Admiral Cameron to Admiral Sinclair, 17 September 1926, TNA, ADM 116/2509; Williamson, *Eastern Traders*, p. 210.

110 E.g. *Nottingham Evening Post*, 14 September 1926.
111 Rear Admiral Cameron to Admiral Sinclair, 17 September 1926, TNA, ADM 116/2509.
112 Pugsley and Macintyre, *Destroyer Man*, p. 17.
113 Summary of Royal Navy actions in China, 1932, TNA, ADM1/8756/137.
114 Clifford, *Spoilt Children of Empire*, p. 166.
115 Journal of Commander Hamilton, 1927–8.
116 Ship's log of HMS *Hermes* 1926–7, TNA, ADM 53/78830; Ship's log of HMS *Wild Swan* End of 1926, TNA, ADM 53/92845.
117 Interview with A. Gaskin, 1986, IWM Interview Series, Catalogue Number 9344, Reel 6, 2 minutes.
118 1921 Shanghai Municipal Report, SMA, U1-1-934; 1926 Shanghai Municipal Report, SMA, U1-1-939.
119 Photograph album of H. J. Wright, 1927, RNM, 2013/161.
120 Cable, *Gunboat Diplomacy*, pp. 36–83.
121 Fung, 'The Sino-British Rapprochement', pp. 82–8; Osterhammel, 'China', p. 653.
122 Admiral Tyrwhitt to Admiralty, 22 January 1927, TNA, ADM 116/2509.
123 Appendix to a report on the situation in China for Committee of Imperial Defence, 30 June 1925, TNA, CAB 24/174/26.
124 Rear Admiral Cameron to Admiral Tyrwhitt, 29 November 1927, TNA, ADM 116/2509.
125 January 1927 report on ship movements, TNA, ADM 116/2509.
126 Rear Admiral Cameron to Admiral Tyrwhitt, 14 January 1927, TNA, ADM 116/2509.
127 Ship's log of HMS *Bee*, 1927, TNA, ADM 53/71186.
128 Admiral Tyrwhitt to Admiralty, 7 January 1927, TNA, ADM 1/8712/154.
129 RAF intelligence report on Chinese air forces, 1927, TNA, AIR 5/865.
130 Pratt to Lampson, 14 March 1927, TNA, ADM 116/2510.
131 Intelligence reports from HMS *Widgeon*, 15 October and 31 December 1926, TNA, ADM 116/2509.
132 Rear Admiral Cameron to Admiralty, 29 January 1927, TNA, ADM 1/8712/154.
133 Hansard, 13 April 1927, vol. 205, cc. 342–3.
134 Midshipman Burnett's logbook.
135 Movements of HM Ships on the Yangtze, March and April 1927, TNA, ADM 116/2510.
136 Midshipman Burnett's logbook.
137 Journal of Commander Hamilton, 1927–8.
138 Letter from Pratt to Lampson, 14 March 1927, TNA, ADM 116/2510.
139 Letter from Pratt to Lampson, 23 March 1927, TNA, ADM 116/2510.
140 Rear Admiral Cameron to Admiral Tyrwhitt, 31 March 1927, TNA, ADM 116/2510.

141 Personal file of Leon Stopford Acheson, TNA, ADM 196/144/741.
142 Consul Jones to Lampson, 20 January 1927, TNA, ADM 116/2510.
143 Commander Garvey to Rear Admiral Cameron, 17 January 1927, TNA, ADM 116/2510.
144 Consul Jones to Lampson, 20 January 1927, TNA, ADM 116/2510.
145 Taylor, 'The Bund: Littoral Space of Empire', pp. 132–3.
146 Intelligence report by Captain Heathcote, 10 January 1927, KCLMA, within P. W. Burnett files, Catalogue ID 2243.
147 Admiral Tyrwhitt to Admiralty, 22 January 1927, TNA, ADM 116/2509.
148 Acting-Consul Ogden to Sir Ronald Macleay, 4 November 1926, TNA, ADM 116/2509.
149 Diary of Arthur Ransome, January–February 1927, Brotherton Library, BC MS 20c Ransome/1/A/9/3/3.
150 Assorted correspondence between Tyrwhitt and the Admiralty, early 1927, TNA, ADM 116/2509.
151 Memorandum on the situation in Hankou, January 1927, TNA, ADM 116/2509.
152 Clifford, *Spoilt Children of Empire*, pp. 179–83; Osterhammel, 'China', p. 653.
153 Intelligence Bulletin, 10 January 1927, KCLMA, Catalogue ID 2243.
154 Private papers of J. W. Edwards, IWM, Documents 11614, Box 01/39/1.
155 Clifford, *Spoilt Children of Empire*, p. 179.
156 'In View of Recent Occurrences in other Ports' in the *Shanghai Municipal Gazette*, 14 January 1927, SMA, U1-1-922.
157 Admiral Tyrwhitt to Admiralty, 22 January 1927, TNA, ADM 116/2509.
158 Admiral Tillard to Admiralty, January 1927, TNA, ADM 116/2510.
159 Midshipman Burnett's logbook, 20 January 1927.
160 de Winton, *Ships in Bottles*, p. 28.
161 Ship's log of HMS *Emerald*, February 1927 to February 1928, TNA, ADM 53/76701; Midshipman Burnett's logbook, 1927.
162 Photograph of HMS *Emerald*, 13 March 1927, KCLMA, Catalogue ID 2243.
163 Patterson, *Tyrwhitt of the Harwich Force*, p. 253.
164 Ship's log of HMS *Emerald*, 27 April 1927, TNA, ADM 53/76701; Captain England to Admiral Tyrwhitt, 10 May 1927, TNA, ADM 116/2527.
165 Patterson, *Tyrwhitt of the Harwich Force*, p. 262.
166 Later Admiral of the Fleet Baron Keyes. Robert Massie, *Castles of Steel* (London: Pimlico, 2005), p. 60; Man and Lun, *Eastern Fortress*, p. 51; Wright, *China's Steam Navy*, p. 117.
167 Hansard, 23 May 1927, vol. 206, cc. 1639–41; Midshipman Burnett's logbook; China Station: list of incidents and important questions 1925–32, TNA, ADM 1/8756/137. Burnett's account suggests that *Emerald* was originally chosen for this task, but it was reassigned to *Carlisle*. Given the previous events that may well have been a wise decision.

168 Patterson, *Tyrwhitt of the Harwich Force*, pp. 253–6.
169 Midshipman Burnett's logbook; Captain England to Admiral Tyrwhitt, 10 May 1927, TNA, ADM 116/2527. Captain England was assigned to organizing civilian transport for evacuating civilians from northern Chinese ports, effectively a demotion from commanding a brand-new cruiser. He did not return to commanding a front line warship until late in 1931.
170 de Winton, *Ships in Bottles*, p. 28.
171 Patterson, *Tyrwhitt of the Harwich Force*, p. 245.
172 Journal of Commander Hamilton, 1927–8.
173 de Winton, *Ships in Bottles*, pp. 28–30.
174 Ibid., p. 29.
175 Midshipman Burnett's logbook.
176 'Short Account of the Voyages and Deeds of HMS *Emerald* October 1925 to June 1928', IWM, p. 75.
177 Journal of Commander Hamilton, 1927–8.
178 Midshipman Burnett's logbook; Diary for the General Staff of Shaforce, 9 April 1927, TNA, WO 191/2.
179 K. R. Buckley, 'The Third Destroyer Flotilla in China 1926–1928', *Naval Review* 18/1 (1930), p. 107.
180 Appendix to Combined Operations Manual detailing ammunition stored on HM Ships, 1925, TNA, AIR 10/5533.
181 Ship's log of HMS *Magnolia* 1926–7, TNA, ADM 53/80211.
182 Midshipman Burnett's logbook, April 1927.
183 Lieutenant Commander Thompson to Commodore Pearson, 1 March 1927, TNA, ADM 116/2510; West River gunboat correspondence, 1927, TNA, ADM 116/2510.
184 Orders from Admiral Tyrwhitt aboard HMS *Hawkins*, 18 May 1927, TNA, ADM 116/2527.
185 Journal of Commander Hamilton, 11 May 1927.
186 Personnel file of Commander Louis Keppel-Hamilton, 1 February 1919, TNA, ADM 196/145/22.
187 Journal of Commander Hamilton, 1927–8.
188 Patterson, *Tyrwhitt of the Harwich Force*, p. 262.
189 Record of Passages made by HMS Widgeon, 1 October 1917 to 23 August 1920, NMM, JHS/5/1.
190 Personnel file for Lieutenant Commander Edward Jukes-Hughes, TNA, ADM 196/126/88.
191 War Diaries of 12th RMB on service in China, 1927, TNA, ADM 1/8709/102.
192 War Diaries of 12th RMB on service in China, 1927, TNA, ADM 1/8709/102.
193 Orders and reports from Nanjing, September 1927, TNA, ADM 1/8709/102.
194 Memorandum by Adjutant General Alexander Hutchison, 1924, TNA, ADM 1/8664/134.

195 Report on the Functions and Training of the Royal Marines, 1924, TNA, ADM 1/8664/134.
196 Clifford, *Amphibious Warfare*, pp. 16–19.
197 Admiral Tyrwhitt to Admiralty, 7 January 1927, TNA, ADM 1/8712/154.
198 Tweedie, *The Story of a Naval Life*, p. 234.
199 China Station monthly reports to Admiralty, 1924, TNA, ADM 116/2262.
200 Ship's log of HMS *Diomede*, 1922–3, TNA, ADM 53/75885.
201 Journal of Commander Hamilton, 1927–8.
202 Service record of Hugh England, TNA, ADM 196/49/69.
203 Reports on Hugh England by Admiral William Fisher, March 1934, TNA, ADM 196/91/135.
204 Admiral Tyrwhitt to Admiralty, 17 July 1927, TNA, ADM 116/2510.
205 Hansard, 2 March 1927, v. 203, cc. 358–9.
206 Hansard, 12 May 1930, v. 236, cc. 1299–300.
207 Consul A. E. Eastes to Sir Ronald Macleay, 7 September 1926, TNA, ADM 116/2509.
208 Marder, 'The Influence of History on Sea Power', p. 439; Sumida, *In Defence of Naval Supremacy*, pp. 185–265.
209 Admiral Tyrwhitt to Admiralty, 21 September 1927, TNA, ADM 116/2502.
210 E.g. Ship's log of HMS *Hermes* 1926–7, TNA, ADM 53/78830; China Station correspondence, 1926–7, TNA, ADM 116/2502.
211 Journal of Commander Hamilton, 1927–8.
212 Dickinson, *Educating the Royal Navy*, p. 212.
213 Bell, 'The King's English and the Security of the Empire', p. 699.
214 Cambridge Course for Naval Officers, 1922–3, Humphreys Files, KCLMA, Catalogue ID 1238.
215 Romans, 'Leadership Training For Midshipmen', p. 179.
216 Consul A.E. Eastes to Sir Ronald Macleay, 7 September 1926, TNA, ADM 116/2509.
217 Allen, *With HMS Despatch to China*, p. 20.
218 Chan, *Arming the Chinese*, pp. 47–114.
219 Buckley, 'The Third Destroyer Flotilla in China', p. 99.
220 Lecture on 'Japan and Sea Power' by the Director of Naval Intelligence, 15 May 1935, KCLMA, Catalogue ID 1114, Chapter two.

Conclusion

Returning to its peacetime work after the First World War, the Royal Navy's China Station found itself on the front line as the British Empire struggled to adapt to a new world environment, born out of years of conflict, revolution and turmoil. The decade of 'violent peace' that followed saw fundamental shifts in Britain's relationship with China and the Royal Navy's strategic position in East Asia. Those developments were heavily interrelated. Localized issues involving the defence of Britain's outposts of informal empire were inherently linked to matters of grand defence strategy. As a result, the China Station played a central role in maintaining the Empire and Britain's strategic planning, although not always in ways that were appreciated at the time. Fluctuations in Britain's imperial position in China influenced the strategies developed in Whitehall to counter the global spread of communism and Japan's growing military might. Events in East Asia defined the turning tide of Britain's Empire and its place in global geopolitics. Indeed, the often-overlooked 1927 Shanghai Crisis triggered one of the Royal Navy's largest peacetime deployments of naval power in its history. Britain's naval story of the interwar period involves far more than just a battle fleet preparing for a possible future decisive major engagement. The mainstream Royal Navy sustained an active operational deployment on the Chinese coast throughout the 1920s, fighting what amounted to an ongoing low-intensity conflict.

To understand Britain's imperial relationship with China we must break down the image of the Royal Navy as a wall of blue uniforms, wholly committed to imperialist ideals. A complex array of issues lay behind many of the key moments that influenced the fortunes of the British Empire in East Asia, with human and technical factors as important as ideology and instructions from the metropole. The lives and experiences of Britain's gunboat crews highlight the limited influence that senior diplomats, politicians and military commanders had upon events. Junior officers were often placed in positions with an unduly weighty responsibility for the implementation of foreign policy. Individual abilities, training, aptitude and attitudes were all just as significant as official policy. Some were brave and consummate professionals, whereas others let egos, career aspirations and racial prejudices cloud their judgement. The personality traits of key individuals played defining roles in each of the most contentious violent clashes involving the Royal Navy.

At the height of the 1927 crisis, one event in particular highlights how interconnected naval and imperial developments were during a pivotal period in Anglo-Chinese relations. At thirty-seven past three on 24 March 1927 the city of Nanjing reverberated as HMS *Emerald* and two USN destroyers hurled a salvo of shells at the city's northernmost extremities. The significance of the decisions made by *Emerald*'s Captain Hugh England, both immediately before and after that critical moment, has been misunderstood ever since. That cacophonous cannonade crowned an incident that suitably illustrates a period of momentous changes and challenges for the Royal Navy and British Empire as a whole. *Emerald* was part of a vast peacetime armada, led by officers with minimal knowledge of local circumstances who therefore adopted outdated tactics that had already been proven ineffective in a rapidly modernizing China. Throughout the Nanjing Incident, diplomats and diplomacy were sidelined as groups of armed individuals were caught in a maelstrom that led to a violent clash with lasting repercussions for the nations they represented. British imperial dominance was on the wane and the Navy's furthest outposts were already being withdrawn. As a result, the parade of naval strength that *Emerald* was a part of failed to mask that Chinese troops had already called Britain's gunboat bluff on the upper Yangtze. *Emerald* and its American counterparts may have brought Nanjing to a standstill, allowing most remaining Anglo-American personnel to be evacuated, but the violence only added momentum to the wave of change swamping Britain's extraterritorial outposts.

The Royal Navy as an organization provided the bulk of the ordinary, everyday contact between the British establishment and China's officials and population. While technology improved the Royal Navy's ability to control those interactions, events like those at Nanjing were often dictated by decisions made by relatively junior officers. Independent command was much rarer in the 1920s Royal Navy than it had been in previous decades, but the level of top-down control it was possible for senior command to exert in practice should not be overstated. The stories of those individuals who manned the China Station therefore take on a far greater significance in the broader debates of Britain's position in the interwar world. Sometimes those who made the 'great man' decisions that changed the path of events were the ordinary individuals on the scene, who have until now remained nameless and forgotten.

The China Station's anti-piracy work and implementation of gunboat diplomacy have been key features in accounts of the period. There was a remarkable degree of continuity between how the Royal Navy approached those two roles, but not always in the ways that it has been assumed. For both duties, the China Station had always been reliant upon bluff and the ability of young gunboat commanders to realize that the Navy's work could only succeed if threats of violence were sparingly executed. The Admiralty was increasingly reluctant to deploy significant resources towards tasks it saw as peripheral to the safety of the British Empire as a whole. As a result, the China Station was reinstated in 1919 with a gunboat force little different to that in place after the Boxer Uprising, twenty years earlier. China was changing rapidly in ideas, technology and international outlook, but the China Station's resources remained much the same. The Admiralty was committed to defending the Empire, but there was an institutional reluctance towards supporting peripheral informal aspects, long-established by the 1920s and which predated the corresponding changes in public and diplomatic stances.

Understanding and acknowledging that continuity and those attitudes allow us to better grasp the great significance of the task force sent out to China in 1927. Not only was it the largest peacetime deployment of Royal Navy warships east of Suez between 1901 and 1944, it also brought Britain close to partial mobilization. At no other point during the interwar period did that occur, even during the Chanak and Abyssinian crises. Shanghai is the often-forgotten crisis – a pivotal moment that played a huge role in defining the path of East Asian geopolitics in the following decade.

Fully appreciating the scale of escalation in late 1926 is vital for two reasons. Firstly, it was not just a last roll of the dice for the British Empire. As an extraordinary display of hard power in peacetime, it shows that the British government was extremely concerned about the wider significance of what was happening in China, in particular, the relationship between events in China and the global struggle against communism. The question in the minds of British officials was what impact it would have on the entire British Empire if an anti-imperialist group, supported by Soviet Russia, was seen to succeed in forcing major concessions out of Whitehall. The timing of the task force's full deployment, with many vessels despatched after the diplomatic agreements conceding extraterritorial rights on the upper and middle Yangtze, highlights that a line had been drawn, beyond which there was a genuine risk of war.

Moreover, it represented a significant statement that Britain was still the primary global naval power – no other country in 1927 had the military capabilities to sustain a similar deployment. Whether the Shanghai response represented a peak moment for British naval power projection or it occurred after the zenith had already passed is perhaps a rather academic and moot point. It does, however, represent a far more pivotal moment than any one of the new warships launched by Japan or America in the period, which has frequently been used as a crude yardstick to measure naval power. Of far greater practical significance for the years to follow, the Shanghai deployment was Britain's last serious and confident attempt at demonstrating naval supremacy, before adopting an increasingly multilateral approach towards global crises.

Secondly, the task force highlights just how exposed Britain's position in East Asia had become by the early 1920s. Following a decade of traumatic changes around the world in the 1910s, the Royal Navy faced numerous significant challenges as Britain's 'imperial gendarmerie'. The new questions being asked of the Navy in East Asia meant that China became the focus of a sustained active deployment unseen elsewhere in the world during the period. This began with the task of reining in the flourishing levels of piracy. Not only was the scale of piracy in Chinese waters a challenge, but the nature of the threat itself was relatively new.

Hostage-taking and hijacking had emerged as the predominant modus operandi among the pirate bands. Those types of attack were, and still are, difficult to prevent, detect or respond to. Britain's gunboats were also simply not designed or equipped for dealing with such low-level threats. 'Internal piracy' represented a new and difficult challenge, but there was considerable reluctance within the Royal Navy to be drawn into what many officers considered to be an issue for the local civilian port authorities. Responsibility nonetheless fell upon the China Station. That institutional disinterest and post-war financial restrictions resulted in only a small pool of pre-existing resources being assigned to dealing with the problem, further limiting the effectiveness of the Royal Navy's response.

Against that backdrop, the defence of Britain's informal imperial interests in China was conducted very efficiently, but it frequently left warships and their crews isolated and vulnerable. As surplus wartime military equipment flooded into the region, the relative safety of life aboard gunboats mid-river was taken away. Faced by those new threats, gunboat crews knew that reinforcements would take considerable time to arrive. That knowledge influenced their decisions, although not always with the same result. Most officers still had an unbridled confidence in Britain's overall naval power, but when judging their actions while conducting imperial policing we should keep in mind just how precarious the situations they were placed in were. Amid those threats human factors rose to the fore. In a few cases aggressive or unstable, generally inexperienced junior officers were placed in high-risk, high-pressure situations, culminating in truly catastrophic consequences, such as at Shamian Island and Wanxian. The violent events that ensued were symptoms of but not the cause of the collapse of Britain's Victorian approach to China. It was the extent to which crews were exposed to danger during the 1920s that led to the end of gunboat diplomacy in China, prior to the shift in official policy marked by Austen Chamberlain's December Memorandum. The outcomes of those situations were dictated by local factors, notably a lack of adequate equipment, and a failing outdated structure for controlling and supporting individual commanders.

The 1920s China Station was the Admiralty's third-largest global deployment, but the resources available were normally quite modest compared against what they were expected to achieve. The amount accomplished during its day-to-day duties demonstrates how a remarkable amount of the Royal Navy's active operational work in peacetime was done by a surprisingly small segment of the Service. Gunboat service was not generally valued as a career path. Opportunities to gain significant independent command experience and familiarity with combat pressures were overlooked in favour of training with the battle fleet. However, when compared to those capital ships, which spent the period largely dormant, the Royal Navy's small ships were busy fighting the little wars of Empire and should not be forgotten.

As it faced these new challenges, the China Station was not a constant, unevolving entity. The Admiralty promoted technology as a means of prolonging the gunboat bluff and as a means of reducing the financial cost of its work. While new technology helped the Royal Navy in that task, the impact was far outweighed by the significant improvements in equipment available to China's armies and pirate bands. As a result, the effectiveness with which British gunboats conducted their duties diminished as the safety of their crews decreased even further. Britain's military edge was not just being rapidly eroded at the top level, by major power arms races. It was being challenged by a general diffusion of deadly modern weaponry across the globe. Britain's latest warships, military aircraft and armoured vehicles were formidable threats to nations, insurgents and bandits alike, but the technological gulf was narrowing. Just as the mass availability of modern weaponry after the First World War contributed to violence and revolutionary activity in Eastern Europe, it also played a key role in changing East Asia.[1]

While the overall balance was not in the China Station's favour, technology did enable them to do more with less, prolonging Britain's ability to maintain the status quo for its outposts of informal Empire. Not all the measures were primarily intended to improve productivity, with many peacetime benefits of new equipment tangential to their wartime purpose, particularly with submarines and aircraft carriers. Radio equipment proved to be the most significant enhancement, allowing submarines to ease the burdens on the surface fleet, for example. The Silent Service is rarely thought of as having been a tool for imperial policing, but submarines played a significant role by freeing up manpower for other duties. Quietly hunting potentially pirated vessels also offered more realistic, exciting scenarios for preparing submarine crews for wartime, than pre-planned exercises with other Royal Navy warships. In this way, the operational history of the Royal Navy in peace and war is not one of two separate stories but heavily interlinked developments.

That grey scale between peace and war is particularly pertinent when looking deeper behind the employment of new technology on the China Station during the 1920s. Britain's first purpose-built aircraft carrier HMS *Hermes* was attached to the China Station nominally on imperial policing purposes, given its rapid heavy-lift capabilities. *Hermes*'s deployment to East Asia eased pressure on the China Station's surface fleet and enabled aerial patrols to help avoid unwanted violent clashes. Despite achieving successes in that role, *Hermes*'s deployment had a hidden and far more controversial motive. *Hermes* delivered supplies and aircraft to start converting Kai Tak in Hong Kong into a military airfield, in contravention of the Washington Treaty.

Hermes's secret mission emphasizes the value the British government attributed to the Washington Treaty during the early 1920s, given Whitehall's unwillingness to risk an obvious breach of its terms. There is no clear evidence whether the British government explicitly approved that decision, highlighting the sensitivity of the matter, although it seems unlikely that senior cabinet members were wholly unaware of what was happening. It was not only the Axis antagonists of the Second World War who quietly undermined the interwar peace and disarmament treaties in the pursuit of their own national interests. Additional examples are likely to be discovered in time, involving all the major powers, further emphasizing the limitations of the interwar disarmament treaties. Questions are also raised by the increasingly open ways that Britain infringed on the clause restricting the development of military bases beyond Singapore towards the end of the decade, before seeking its removal from the London Naval Treaty in 1930. All was not quite how it seemed behind the

British government's official assertions that disarmament treaties remained a cornerstone of British foreign policy and grand strategy in that key period.

While efforts to improve the efficiency with which the Royal Navy defended Britain's interests in East Asia were driven by economic necessity, wider changes in attitude towards the role of violence in imperial policing also took effect. In the aftermath of the First World War, public distaste for fresh conflict influenced decisions about how to defend Britain's imperial outposts. There were also changes in the attitudes of naval personnel towards using lethal force against those who opposed the British Empire. Moreover, concern grew within the Admiralty about negative public reactions through heavy-handed actions. While the 1926 December Memorandum marks when the British government was most concerned about violence on the ground, many of the supposedly new rules of engagement were simply restatements of those issued by the Admiralty earlier in the decade. Far from being pushed into reducing the level of violence used in enforcing Britain's foreign policy, the Royal Navy played an active role from early in the process of change.

The First World War catalysed that shift in attitude towards imperial violence, but this did not prevent the employment of violent tactics. Initially, there was an attempt to return to Victorian coercive behaviour and the threat of reprisals. Short, sharp bursts of often excessive violence could reinforce the impression of British power. However, the regular, sustained and widespread clashes by 1926 exposed the reliance of gunboat diplomacy on bluffing the Chinese population. Not even at its peak could the British Empire afford to maintain the levels of military force required, worldwide, to enforce such an approach. No single climactic incident marks the precise end of gunboat diplomacy in China, but the growing background crisis left its mark.

The pressure placed upon junior officers led to some bending the rules of engagement and others either reactively or proactively employing the weapons at their disposal. As naval fusillades became more commonplace, the China Station's gunboat flotilla slid from being a coercive force to one reliant upon the regular use of violence to achieve its aims. The Royal Navy recognized that the situation was unsustainable, but attempts to develop new strategies failed, largely due to the inability to lift the strain from the officers attempting to implement them. It was a case of too little, too late. As a result, efforts to withdraw from commitments on the middle and upper Yangtze were undermined by individual officers taking alternative paths. This was not helped by a consistent lack of clear leadership by the commanders-in-chief between 1924 and 1927. Rear Admiral Sir Allan Everett suffered a mental breakdown, Vice Admiral Sir Edwyn

Alexander-Sinclair failed to communicate effectively with his officers and Vice Admiral Reginald Tyrwhitt's mixed messages caused confusion. All three were experienced officers and the latter two were wartime heroes from battles in the North Sea, but they nonetheless struggled to coordinate their diverse and dispersed fleet. Ultimately, the disastrous attempts to update the Royal Navy's approach to China during the period reflected deep-set institutional flaws in the Service's attitude towards peacetime operations.

The near-complacency with which the Admiralty approached the 'little wars of Empire' is visible in the events leading towards the carnage at Shamian, Wanxian and Nanjing, with contradictions between official policy, strategy, personal intent and end results. This area requires greater research – the processes by which imperial policing led to mass-casualty clashes, particularly ones involving civilians. Naval bombardments may have ended with similar results, but they occurred for a variety of reasons and were influenced by a range of factors including: breakdowns in mental health (Shamian), aggressive individual officers (Wanxian), inaccurate weaponry (Nanjing), limitations of equipment (Wanxian and Nanjing) and mistaken identity (Yangtze riverside engagements). Imperial identity and beliefs were a background catalyst in almost all such clashes, but usually only as a secondary factor. Aggressive conduct did not always result from individuals intending to commit acts of violence in support of the British Empire.

The events of March 1927 provide a valuable case study for the caution required when assessing casualties resulting from politically contentious historic clashes. Captain England did not order his men to bombard Nanjing directly on the first day of the incident, as has sometimes been suggested, but instead targeted a sparsely populated area on the outskirts.[2] His belligerent behaviour the following day in threatening to punitively bombard the city and the general impression given by warships firing towards Nanjing have clouded our understanding of the incident. Looking in detail at the events of 24 March, if reports of two thousand civilian deaths that day are accurate, the majority did not result from British actions, although the numbers are likely to have been higher than British claims at the time. Captain England had the intent and opportunity, but his actions did not match his rhetoric. In contrast, while British responsibility for mass casualties at Nanjing has sometimes been overstated, the opposite is true in relation to Wanxian.

Those are relatively modest changes in our understanding of the events, but they represent valuable lessons in the need for objective and detailed assessment of such horrific incidents. Very few cases offer enough evidence for historians to say with certainty the precise number of people killed and attribute direct blame for their deaths. There is usually enough material, however, to challenge second-hand contemporary accounts, provide more accurate assessments and in doing so present nuanced explanations for who was responsible and why. With growing accusations of fake news drifting into the arena of mainstream historical study, we should return to exploring as much of the evidence as possible and come to informed judgements when dealing with divisive incidents. Not all that the Royal Navy did was honourable or brave, nor was it a pantomime villain. Acknowledging that does not undermine the tales of individual bravery, or those of great tragedy, found throughout our journeys into the past.

Amid considerable top-level wrangling between the world's major navies over arms limitation treaties, particularly between Britain, the United States and Japan, there was a different story at the operational level. On China's coastline and waterways, away from the diplomatic quarrels, foreign warships and their crews often operated quite closely. This camaraderie resulted largely from their mutually exposed location, separated by considerable distances from other warships flying the same flag. British and American crews in particular interpreted their official orders in favourable ways for their local counterparts – for their friends. Rivalry between Royal Navy and US Navy crews was tolerated, even encouraged, but regular social events built a distinct bond. There was no grand 'Special Relationship', nonetheless in times of crisis cooperation was generally given as freely as possible within the confines of official instructions and sometimes beyond them. In effect, an informal understanding was reached between the two fleets akin to the so-called 'good cop–bad cop' routine. Britain was already unpopular and so the Royal Navy could and would act aggressively to defend Anglo-American interests. Conversely, the US Navy was willing to use its neutrality as a calming influence, even if it could not promise to defend actively the civilians or property of other nations if violence erupted. That is extremely significant when assessing many events around China during the late 1920s, particularly in terms of intent and the extent to which official foreign policies were adhered to on the scene. However quickly the wartime alliance was abandoned in favour of official antagonism at a senior level, the bonds between the two institutions and their crews remained.

The Royal Navy's relationship with the Imperial Japanese Navy is also more complicated than might be assumed from top-level debates. There was a general trend of worsening attitudes between British and Japanese service personnel, in keeping with existing understanding of the period. This overall trend seems to have been driven by Japanese policy changes as the IJN's rigid command structure meant that official orders dictated end actions. In contrast, Royal Navy officers were afforded greater freedom to act on their own views. The outcomes of individual Anglo-Japanese interactions were therefore sometimes heavily influenced by strong beliefs of the British officer concerned, particularly racially charged attitudes. This does not fundamentally change our understanding of the relationship between the two powers in the period. What it does do, however, is raise the possibility that poor interpersonal relations undermined top-level cooperation, adding a human angle to the failure of joint military efforts between Britain and Japan in China.

Against that backdrop of worsening relations, the Royal Navy's planning for a potential war with Japan was heavily based around China. Familiar tales of fortifying Singapore, securing naval superiority in the South China Seas with the battle fleet and America's potential stance were all significant in Britain's grand strategy for East Asia. Nonetheless, the Admiralty believed that the most likely triggers for a war between Britain and Japan would be related to China. Given geographic considerations, the Chinese coast was also expected to play a pivotal role in the outcome of any such conflict. Existing debates surrounding the speed with which the battle fleet could be assembled at Singapore are therefore a little misaligned.

With hindsight, what happened at Pearl Harbor raises questions as to whether this China-focused strategy took too much comfort from the low likelihood of a successful surprise attack. Based on the events of 1927, Britain's intelligence capabilities in East Asia were also insufficient for the task of forewarning the China Station. The core strategic plan, however, was predicated on a reasonable assumption that major Royal Navy warships would already be heading east, before a Japanese campaign against Britain began, even if it was not the full battle fleet. The weakness in Britain's plans for countering Japan during the 1920s and early 1930s was therefore not one of timing and logistics. Instead, we should focus upon the lack of long-term planning immediately after the First World War, given that the steady growth in Japanese naval power was always going to neutralize Britain's core strategy by the mid- to late 1930s. Contemporary discussion about deflecting Japanese aggression into China and vague allusions to possible Anglo-American alliances suggest an unwillingness to confront the real challenge, and that mentality of denial requires further research.

The second stage of Britain's East Asia strategy, an attempted blockade against Japan, was similarly built around China. If the first leg was intended to prevent Britain losing the war, this phase would decide whether it could be won. This helps explain why Britain remained committed to defending Hong Kong during the period. Holding Singapore might prevent Britain from losing a war, but Hong Kong's fate would decide whether Britain could force Japan to terms. The cold, calculated decision to post a garrison was made with the belief that it might hold Hong Kong just long enough for relief against Japan and would deter Chinese aggression. The loss of that force would not compromise Britain's wider strategic position, but its potential success could lead to victory. While this strategy was ultimately driven by Admiral Herbert Richmond, often feted as one of the great naval thinkers, it is important to note the core idea was a product of his friend Admiral Arthur Leveson's imagination. Britain's continued garrisoning of its 'Exposed Outpost' was certainly unwise in the 1930s, by which point the equation had swung further in Japan's favour. During the 1920s, however, with the balance of naval power still on the Royal Navy's side, it was not an overly reckless gamble.

China was not just a potential trigger for war, nor a passive playground for the imperial powers. It also formed an integral part of the Royal Navy's plans. This went far beyond a 'deflection' strategy of encouraging Japanese expansion in Northern China. Even during the mid-1920s, when the Guomindang was the most immediate threat to Britain's informal empire in East Asia, the Royal Navy was already considering whether the same group might be able to help. In effect, key commentators within the Royal Navy had adopted the spirit of 'my enemy's enemy is my friend'. While this did not initially prompt formal discussions with the Guomindang or other factions, the Navy was planning around the belief that some degree of modest, indirect assistance was likely. This highlights that while the Admiralty was disinterested in many imperial policing duties in China, it was interested in the role China could play in a future major conflict, whether in a passive or active capacity.

That discussion about Chinese involvement in a war against Japan realigns how we approach Britain's strategic situation in the 1920s. In a search for potential allies to brace Britain's position in East Asia, there were few alternatives other than China. Britain's potential European allies no longer wielded significant clout in the region. Likewise, few Royal Navy officers felt the United States could be relied upon, given the latter's stance during the First World War and post-war isolationist policies. The lack of a clear central strategy for developing a positive relationship with China and reluctance to change the nature of Britain's informal empire therefore take on even greater significance. China was unlikely to become a full British ally, given deep-set conflicts over extraterritorial rights, the Shanghai International Settlement and Hong Kong's future. Nonetheless, the failure to update imperial priorities in East Asia contributed directly towards revealing many of the Royal Navy's shortcomings. Political disinterest in the periphery of the Empire, dismissive attitudes towards non-white nations and anti-communist paranoia undermined the Royal Navy's efforts to develop an effective long-term strategy, in favour of a forlorn hope of maintaining the status quo.

The Royal Navy's peacetime front line

The 1920s Royal Navy, its role in maintaining the British Empire, its organization and culture, and even the attitudes of its personnel all present a complex picture, not easily reduced to a straightforward narrative. The Admiralty and many of its officers were nominally dismissive of its peacetime work in imperial policing, particularly using gunboats. Nevertheless, the Royal Navy and those same individuals threw men, materiel and energy into the task. Gunboat service itself was generally mundane and likely to hinder an officer's career, and yet it increasingly put those crews in the path of extreme danger, in circumstances where decisions made by a young lieutenant could have a significant impact on the future of the British Empire in East Asia.

In contrast to efforts made in understanding what civilian officials thought, how that affected their decisions and how it contributed to clashes with Chinese protesters, Royal Navy personnel have not been treated as individuals. Inspector Everson and the other leading actors in the Louza shooting, for example, have been assessed as humans with all their flaws, whereas Lieutenant Faure, Lieutenant Commander Acheson, Captain England and all their colleagues have been hidden by their uniforms.[3] They were all very different individuals and their actions came with personal as well as diplomatic consequences. Alcoholism, drug addiction, chronic injuries, forced retirement and demotion affected those key protagonists in the immediate aftermath of their actions.

For all those cases, what is remarkable is how most officers and enlisted men somehow successfully navigated the immense challenges they faced on the China Station, or at least found redemption for their mistakes. Admiral Cameron erred in his response to events at Wanxian, but his cool head played a key role in avoiding what could have been an even more catastrophic scene at Hankou. Likewise, while Captain England does not come across as a particularly likeable character, one does have sympathy for what he suffered in the First World War and great respect for his later contributions to the liberation of Europe in 1944. This was not a one-way process and we should remember that many peaceful outcomes came as a result of effective, if sometimes robust, communication with Chinese officials whose own attitudes were just as pivotal.

The 1920s Royal Navy could and often did adapt quickly, readily and logically in the face of opportunities and challenges, but at times it was also guilty of complacency and resistance to change. Anti-intellectualist sentiment was a contributing factor to some failures, along with factional friction between networks of officers. Indeed, many existing debates over anti-intellectualism in the interwar Navy have elements of truth. A diverse range of attitudes were displayed across the Service, with personal views and loyalties influencing the willingness of individual officers to adapt to new proposals and tactics. There were unifying elements, however, common to most officers, including a consistent lack of urgency to make changes, which stemmed in part from dismissive assumptions about Asia itself. Some officers were overtly racist and many displayed subtler orientalist attitudes, although they were far from universal. Of particular importance, however, was the way almost all Royal Navy officers failed to appreciate how quickly East Asia was modernizing.

Perhaps the core conclusion is that the interwar Royal Navy involved considerably more than just the much-studied battle fleet. That may seem an obvious statement, but the Royal Navy's smaller warships were heavily employed maintaining the British Empire, even if contemporary and subsequent debate has focused upon its capital ships. Gunboat life in China generally involved a rather dull existence, but at times it placed servicemen in positions as dangerous as those in wartime. Peace was not always peaceful for Britain's armed forces. Indeed, the 1927 crisis pushed the Royal Navy close to a war footing.

The Royal Navy was not a uniform and blunt tool of empire. The China Station played a complicated part in the British Empire's evolving relationship with China. In return, China itself had a significant impact upon Britain's grand strategy for East Asia. The slow evolution of the China Station during the 1920s was central to how long the British Empire's informal interests in East Asia could be maintained and to the viability of the Empire's strategic defence. Those priorities were not always aligned, but they were interlinked. By the end of that process, moving into the 1930s, the Royal Navy had gone from clashing with the Guomindang to training its Navy, in the hope they might join forces against mutual threats. One British officer involved in that work asked a friend about what the future might hold as a result. His response brings us back to events in the present day:

'Realise that in due course China will be a super-power in the world. It is no small thing to lay the foundations of its future navy ... You may well be starting something that will have a world importance later on.'[4]

Notes

1. Gerwarth, *The Vanquished*, p. 9.
2. E.g. Fung, *Diplomacy of Imperial Retreat*, p. 138; Goto-Shibata, *Japan and Britain in Shanghai*, p. 50.
3. Bickers, *Empire Made Me*, pp. 164–72; Bickers, *Britain in China*, p. 4; Clifford, *Spoilt Children of Empire*, pp. 166–71; Fung, *Diplomacy of Imperial Retreat*, pp. 40–2; Osterhammel, 'China', p. 652.
4. Letter from W. F. Tyler to Captain Harold Baillie-Grohman, 23 January 1931, NMM, GRO/1.

Appendix 1

Examples of key warship types

Battlecruiser – HMS *Hood* (Special Service Squadron Flagship)

Length: 860 feet
Displacement: 41,200 tons
Armament: 8 × 15″ main guns, 12 × 5.5″ guns and 4 × 4″ AA guns
Maximum design speed: 31 knots
Full complement: 1,430

Aircraft carrier – HMS *Hermes* (China Station 1925–6 and 1926–8)

Length: 600 feet
Displacement: 10,850 tons
Armament: 6 × 5.5″ guns, 4 × 4″ AA guns and 15 aircraft (in the 1920s)
Maximum design speed: 25 knots
Full complement: 565 (excluding aircrew)

Heavy cruiser – HMS *Hawkins* (China Station Flagship 1919–27)

Length: 605 feet
Displacement: 12,110 tons
Armament: 7 × 7.5″ main guns, 8 × 3″ AA guns and 2 × 2 pdr 'Pom Pom' AA guns
Maximum design speed: 30 knots
Full complement: 732

Light cruiser – HMS *Carlisle* (China Station 1919–28)

Length: 451 feet
Displacement: 5,240 tons
Armament: 5 × 6″ main guns, 2 × 3″ AA guns, 4 × 3 pdr guns, and 2 × 2 pdr 'Pom Pom' AA guns
Maximum design speed: 29 knots
Full complement: 375

Destroyer – HMS *Wanderer* (China Station 1926–8)

Length: 300 feet
Displacement: 1,110 tons
Armament: 4 × 4.7″ main guns and 2 × 2 pdr 'Pom Pom' AA guns
Maximum design speed: 32 knots
Full complement: 134

Pre-First World War destroyer – HMS *Otter* (China Station 1900–14)

Length: 214 feet
Displacement: 335 tons
Armament: 1 × 12 pdr (3″) main gun and 5 × 6 pdr guns
Maximum design speed: 30 knots
Full complement: 70

Sloop – HMS *Bluebell* (China Station 1922–7)

Length: 262 feet
Displacement: 1,200 tons
Armament: 2 × 3″ main guns and 2 × 3 pdr AA guns
Maximum design speed: 17 knots
Full complement: 77

River (heavy) 'Insect class' gunboat – HMS Cockchafer (China Station 1920–37)

Length: 237 feet
Displacement: 645 tons
Armament: 2 × 6″ main guns and 2 × 3″ AA guns
Maximum design speed: 14 knots
Full complement: 53

Upper Yangtze gunboat – HMS Woodlark (China Station 1900–28)

Length: 145 feet
Displacement: 150 tons
Armament: 2 × 6 pdr (2.2″) guns
Maximum design speed: 13 knots
Full complement: 25

West River 'Heron class' gunboat– HMS Robin (China Station 1900–28)

Length: 108 feet
Displacement: 85 tons
Armament: 2 × 6 pdr (2.2″) guns
Maximum design speed: 9 knots
Full complement: 25

Submarine – L20 (China Station 1919–29)

Length: 239 feet
Displacement: 890 tons (surfaced)
Armament: 1 × 4″ gun and 6 torpedo tubes
Maximum design speed: 17 knots (surfaced)
Full complement: 38

Submarine depot ship – HMS *Titania* (China Station 1919–29)

Length: 350 feet
Displacement: 5,250 tons
Armament: 2 torpedo tubes
Maximum design speed: 14 knots
Full complement: 239

Appendix 2

Timeline of senior officers

Commander-in-chief

1919–22 – Admiral Sir Alexander Duff
1922–4 – Admiral Sir Arthur Leveson
1924–5 – Vice Admiral Sir Allan Everett
1925–6 – Vice Admiral Sir Edwyn Alexander-Sinclair
1926–8 – Vice Admiral Sir Reginald Tyrwhitt
1928–30 – Vice Admiral Sir Arthur Waistell
1930–3 – Admiral Sir Howard Kelly

Rear Admiral Yangtze

1919–20 – Captain Alfred Ellison
1920–1 – Rear Admiral George Borrett
1921–3 – Rear Admiral Crawford Maclachlan
1923–5 – Rear Admiral David Anderson
1925–7 – Rear Admiral John Cameron
1927–9 – Rear Admiral Hugh Tweedie
1929–31 – Rear Admiral Colin MacLean

Commodore Hong Kong

1918–20 – Commodore Victor Gurner
1920–2 – Commodore William Bowden-Smith
1922–4 – Commodore Henry Grace
1924–6 – Commodore Anselan Stirling
1926–8 – Commodore John Pearson
1928–30 – Captain Richard Hill
1930–2 – Commodore Arthur Walker

Bibliography

Archive sources

China

Shanghai Municipal Archives, Shanghai

Shanghai Volunteer Corps papers.
Shanghai Municipal Council papers.
The Municipal Gazette.

United Kingdom

Brotherton Library Archive, Leeds

Unpublished memoirs of Lieutenant Commander* Edward Barraclough.
Diary of the journalist Arthur Ransome.
Lieutenant Commander Meredith Spalding papers.
Mr Frank Turner papers.
*Ranks at time of writing.

Hansard

Imperial War Museum, London

Lieutenant William Andrewes papers.
Commander Paul Berryman papers.
Sub Lieutenant Douglas Claris papers.
Diary of Lieutenant Charles Drage.
Unpublished memoirs of Lieutenant Commander Brian Dean.
Lieutenant J. W. Edwards papers.
Unpublished memoirs of Ordinary Seaman G. T. Weekes.
Diary of Paymaster Commander Hugh Miller.
Lieutenant Commander Reginald Ramsbotham papers.
Leading Seaman William Roberts papers.
Oral History Interview Series.
Commander Cecil Talbot papers.
Diary of Petty Officer Herbert Page.

Liddell Hart Centre for Military Archives (King's College London), London

Midshipman Philip Burnett papers.
Unpublished memoirs of Captain Francis De Winton.
Captain Sir Gerald Dickens papers.
Midshipman Lawrence Humphreys papers.
Journal of the Royal United Service Institution.

National Maritime Museum, London

Admiral of the Fleet Earl David Beatty papers.
Commodore Harold Baillie-Grohman papers.
Journal of Commander Edward Jukes-Hughes.
Commander Louis Keppel Hamilton papers.
Commander Cedric Holland papers.
Commander Arthur Peters papers.
Admiral Herbert Richmond papers.
Royal Navy War College, Greenwich papers.
Navy Lists.

National Museum of the Royal Navy, Portsmouth

Diary of Chief Petty Officer Douglas Poole.
Midshipman Leonard Sheppard papers.
Photograph album of H. J. Wright.
Assorted Royal Navy official paperwork.

Royal Marines Museum, Southsea

Diary of Marine William J. Greenland.
Photograph album of Marine W. S. Phillips.
Photograph album of Major Frederick Burden.

School of Oriental and African Studies, London

China Association Collection.
Papers of Sir Guy Francis Acheson.

The National Archives, London

Admiralty (ADM): 1, 53, 116, 125, 137, 196.
Air Ministry (AIR): 5.
Cabinet (CAB): 2, 23, 24.
Foreign Office (FO/FCO): 93, 141, 228, 371, 373.

Government Code and Cypher School (HW): 12.
Maps (MR): 1.
Security Service (KV): 3.
Treasury (T): 1, 162, 225, 265.
War Office (WO): 33, 106.

Online

Hathi Trust Digital Library (Originals held by University of Michigan): Annual Reports of the Navy Department (USN).
National Library of Australia – https://catalogue.nla.gov.au/: Braga Special Map Collection.
Naval History and Heritage Command – www.history.navy.mil/our-collections: Photography collection of C. E. Winslow USN.
Perry-Castañeda Library Map Collection – https://legacy.lib.utexas.edu/maps/: Historic maps of China.

Newspapers

China Mail
Gloucester Citizen
Hong Kong Daily Press
Hong Kong Telegraph
New York Times
North China Herald
Nottingham Evening Post
Western Morning News

Contemporary publications

Allen, W. T. (ed.), *With HMS Despatch to China 1925–1927*. Shanghai: Willow Pattern Press, 1927.
Anonymous, 'China, Its Past and Present Situation, April 1928', *Naval Review* 16/3 (1928).
Anonymous, 'Imperial Defence', *Naval Review* 14/1 (1926).
Anonymous British naval officer, 'An Incident in China', in *The Anatomy of Neptune*, ed. Brian Tunstall. London: Routledge, 1936.

Beauchamp, R. R., 'Piracy in the South China Seas', *Naval Review* 13/4 (1925).
Beauchamp, R. R., 'Piracy in the South China Seas II', *Naval Review* 14/1 (1926).
Buckley, K. R., 'The Third Destroyer Flotilla in China 1926-1928', *Naval Review* 18/1 (1930).
Buesst, Tristan, 'The Naval Base at Singapore', *Pacific Affairs* 5/4 (1932), 306-18.
Callwell, Charles, *Military Operations and Maritime Preponderance: Their Relation and Interdependence*. London: Blackwood, 1905.
Clegg, John H. K., 'The Yangtze and the Situation in China', *Naval Review* 15/1 (1927).
Edwards, William, *British Foreign Policy 1815-1933*. London: Methuen, 1934.
Faure, Cyril M., 'Some Aspects of the China Situation', *Naval Review* 16/4 (1928).
Flux, A. W., 'British Export Trade', *Economic Journal* 36/144 (1926), 551-62.
Hutchison, Colin, 'Notes from a Yangtze Diary – November 1927 to February 1929', *Naval Review* 17/3 (1929).
Liddell-Hart, Basil, *When Britain Goes to War*. London: Faber & Faber, 1935.
May, Edward, *Principles and Problems of Imperial Defence*. London: Sonnenschein, 1903.
Teichman, Eric, *Affairs of China: A Survey of the Recent History and Present Circumstances of the Republic of China*. London: Methuen, 1938.
Tweedie, Hugh, *The Story of a Naval Life*. London: Rich & Cowan, 1939.
Unattributed, *Short Account of the Voyages and Deeds of HMS Emerald October 1925 to June 1928*. Devonport, 1928.

Secondary sources

Aizawa, Yoshio, 'The Path towards an "Anti-British" Strategy by the Japanese Navy between the Wars', in *The History of Anglo-Japanese Relations, 1600-2000; Volume III: The Military Dimension*, ed. Ian Gow, Yoichi Hirama and John Chapman. Basingstoke: Palgrave Macmillan, 2003, 139-50.
Aldcroft, Derek, *From Versailles to Wall Street 1919-1929*. London: Allen Lane, 1977.
Alderson, G. L. D., *History of RAF Kai Tak*. Hong Kong: Royal Air Force, 1972.
Aldrich, Richard, 'Britain's Secret Intelligence Service in Asia during the Second World War', *Modern Asian Studies* 32/1 (1998), 179-217.
Andrew, Christopher, 'The British Secret Service and Anglo-Soviet Relations in the 1920s Part I: From the Trade Negotiations to the Zinoviev Letter', *Historical Journal* 20/3 (1977), 637-706.
Asada, Sadao, *From Mahan to Pearl Harbour: The Imperial Japanese Navy and the United States*. Annapolis: Naval Institute Press, 2006.
Babij, Orest, 'The Royal Navy and the Defence of the British Empire: 1928-1939', in *Far Flung Lines*, ed. Keith Neilson and Greg Kennedy. London: Cass, 1996, 171-89.
Barnett, Correlli, *The Collapse of British Power*. Gloucester: Sutton, 1984.
Beaumont, Roger, *Joint Military Operations: A Short History*. London: Greenwood, 1993.
Bell, Christopher, *Churchill and Sea Power*. Oxford: Oxford University Press, 2013.

Bell, Christopher, '"How Are We Going to Make War?" Admiral Sir Herbert Richmond and British Far Eastern War Plans', *Journal of Strategic Studies* 20/3 (1997), 123–41.

Bell, Christopher, '"Our Most Exposed Outpost": Hong Kong and British Far Eastern Strategy, 1921–1941', *Journal of Military History* 60/1 (1996), 61–88.

Bell, Christopher, *The Royal Navy: Sea-Power and Strategy between the Wars*. Basingstoke: Macmillan, 2000.

Bell, Christopher, 'The "Singapore Strategy" and the Deterrence of Japan: Winston Churchill, the Admiralty and the Dispatch of Force Z', *English Historical Review* 116/467 (2001), 604–34.

Bell, Christopher, 'The King's English and the Security of the Empire: Class, Social Mobility, and Democratization in the British Naval Officer Corps, 1918–1939', *Journal of British Studies* 48/3 (2009), 695–716.

Bell, Christopher, 'Thinking the Unthinkable: British and American Naval Strategies for an Anglo-American War, 1918–1931', *International History Review* 19/4 (1997), 789–808.

Bickers, Robert, *Britain in China: Community, Culture and Colonialism 1900–1949*. Manchester: Manchester University Press, 1999.

Bickers, Robert, 'The Colony's Shifting Position in the British Informal Empire in China', in *Hong Kong's Transitions 1842–1997*, ed. Judith Brown and Rosemary Foot. Basingstoke: Macmillan, 1997, 33–61.

Bickers, Robert, *Empire Made Me: An Englishman Adrift in Shanghai*. London: Penguin, 2004.

Bickers, Robert, 'Ordering Shanghai: Policing a Treaty Port, 1854–1900', in *Maritime Empires: British Imperial Maritime Trade in the Nineteenth Century*, ed. David Killingray, Margarette Lincoln and Nigel Rigby. Woodbridge: Boydell, 2004, 173–94.

Bickers, Robert, *The Scramble for China: Foreign Devils in the Qing Empire 1832–1914*. London: Penguin, 2012.

Bickers, Robert, 'Shanghailanders: The Formation and Identity of the British Settler Community in Shanghai 1843–1937', *Past and Present* 159 (1998), 161–211.

Bittner, Donald F., 'Britannia's Sheathed Sword: The Royal Marines and Amphibious Warfare in the Interwar Years – A Passive Response', *Journal of Military History* 55/3 (1991), 345–64.

Black, Jeremy, *The British Seaborne Empire*. Yale: Yale University Press, 2004.

Black, Nicholas, *The British Naval Staff in the First World War*. Woodbridge: Boydell & Brewer, 2009.

Bond, Brian, *British Military Policy between the Two World Wars*. Oxford: Oxford University Press, 1980.

Bond, Brian, *War and Society in Europe, 1870–1970*. Stroud: Sutton, 1998.

Boot, Max, 'Pirates, Then and Now: How Piracy Was Defeated in the Past and Can Be Again', *Foreign Affairs* 88/4 (2009), 94–107.

Boyd, Andrew, *The Royal Navy in Eastern Waters: Linchpin of Victory*. Barnsley: Seaforth, 2017.

Boyle, William, *My Naval Life: 1886–1941*. London: Hutchinson, 1942.

Braisted, William, *Diplomats in Blue: U.S. Naval Officers in China, 1922–1933*. Florida Scholarship Online, 2011.

Brown, David, *Nelson to Vanguard: Warship Design and Development 1923–1945*. London: Chatham, 2006.

Butler, Lawrence, 'The British Empire, 1918–1945: Interwar Change and Wartime Pressures', in *Crises of Empire: Decolonisation and Europe's Imperial States, 1918–1975*, ed. Lawrence Butler, Bob Moore and Martin Thomas. London: Bloomsbury, 2008, 17–46.

Cable, James, *Gunboat Diplomacy: Political Applications of Limited Naval Force*. Basingstoke: Macmillan, 1981.

Cain, Peter, and Hopkins, Antony, *British Imperialism: 1688–2000*. Harlow: Longman, 2002.

Campbell, J., 'Naval Armaments and Armour', in *Steam, Steel, and Shellfire*, ed. Robert Gardiner and Andrew Lambert. London: Conway Maritime, 1992, 161–7.

Cannadine, David, *History in Our Time*. Yale: Yale University Press, 1998.

Chan, Anthony B., *Arming the Chinese*. Vancouver: University of British Columbia Press, 1982.

Chapman, John W. M., 'Britain, Japan and the "Higher Realms of Intelligence", 1900–1918', in *The History of Anglo-Japanese Relations, 1600–2000; Volume III: The Military Dimension*, ed. Ian Gow, Yoichi Hirama, John Chapman. Basingstoke: Palgrave Macmillan, 2003, 71–87.

Chen, Zhongping, 'The May Fourth Movement and Provincial Warlords: A Re-examination', *Modern China* 27/2 (2011), 135–69.

Chesneau, Robert (ed.), *All the World's Fighting Ships 1922–1946*. London: Conway, 1992.

Cheung, Ting-yan, and Tsoi, Pablo Sze-pang, 'From an Imported Novelty to an Indigenized Practice: Hong Kong Cinema in the 1920s', in *Early Film Culture in Hong Kong, Taiwan, and Republican China: Kaleidoscopic Histories*, ed. Emilie Yueh-yu Yeh. Ann Arbor: University of Michigan Press, 2018, 71–90.

Ch'I, Hsi-Sheng, *Warlord Politics in China 1916–1928*. Stanford: Stanford University Press, 1976.

Chi, Madeleine, 'Bureaucratic Capitalists in Operation: Ts'ao Ju-lin and His New Communications Clique, 1916–1919', *Journal of Asian Studies* 34/3 (1975), 675–88.

Chow, Phoebe, 'British Opinion and Policy towards China, 1922–1927'. Unpublished PhD, LSE, 2011.

Clayton, Anthony, *The British Empire as a Superpower 1919–1939*. Basingstoke: Macmillan, 1986.

Clayton, Anthony, 'Deceptive Might: Imperial Defence and Security 1900–1968', in *The Twentieth Century: Oxford History of the British Empire*, ed. Judith M. Brown and William R. Louis. Oxford: Oxford University Press, 2001, 280–305.

Clements, Jonathan, '23 August 1914: Japan Declares War on Germany', in *June 28th: Sarajevo 1914 – Versailles 1919: The War and Peace That Made the Modern World*, ed. Alan Sharp. London: Haus, 2014, 146–50.
Clifford, Kenneth, *Amphibious Warfare Development in Britain and America from 1920 to 1940*. New York: Edgewood, 1983.
Clifford, Nicholas, 'A Revolution Is Not a Tea Party: The "Shanghai Mind(s)" Reconsidered', *Pacific History Review* 59/4 (1990), 501–26.
Clifford, Nicholas, *Spoilt Children of Empire: Westerners in Shanghai and the Chinese Revolution of the 1920s*. Hanover: University Press of New England, 1991.
Coble, Parks, *The Shanghai Capitalists and the Nationalist Government 1927–1937*. Cambridge, MA: Harvard University Press, 1984.
Cohen, Paul, 'The Boxer Uprising', in *China: Adapting the Past, Confronting the Future*, ed. Thomas Buoye, Kirk Denton, Bruce Dickson, Barry Naughton and Martin Whyte. Ann Arbor: University of Michigan Press, 2002, 62–74.
Cole, Bernard, *Gunboats and Marines: The United States Navy in China, 1925–1928*. Newark: University of Delaware Press, 1983.
Dahl, Eric, 'Naval Innovation: From Coal to Oil', *Joint Force Quarterly* 2 (2000), 113–15.
Darwin, John, 'The Chanak Crisis and the British Cabinet', *History* 65/213 (1980), 32–48.
Darwin, John, 'Imperialism and the Victorians: The Dynamics of Territorial Expansion', *English Historical Review* 112/447 (1997), 614–42.
Daunton, Martin, 'How to Pay for the War: State, Society and Taxation in Britain, 1917–1924', *English Historical Review* 111/443 (1996), 882–919.
Daunton, Martin, 'The Sea and the Economic Slump, 1919–1939', in *The Sea in History: The Modern World*, ed. N. A. M. Rodger. Woodbridge: Boydell & Brewer, 2017, 594–604.
Dickinson, Harry, *Educating the Royal Navy: Eighteenth and Nineteenth Century Education for Officers*. Abingdon: Routledge, 2007.
Dockrill, Michael, and Goold, J. D., *Peace without Promise: Britain and the Peace Conferences 1919–1923*. London: Batsford, 1981.
Dunnaway, Cliff, *Wings over Hong Kong: An Aviation History 1891–1998*. Hong Kong: Pacific Century, 1999.
Edgerton, David, *Warfare State: Britain 1920–1970*. Cambridge: Cambridge University Press, 2006.
Eldridge, C. C., *Victorian Imperialism*. London: Hoddern and Stoughton, 1978.
Elleman, Bruce, 'China Turns to the Sea, 1912–1990', in *The Sea in History: The Modern World*, ed. N. A. M. Rodger. Woodbridge: Boydell & Brewer, 2017, 319–28.
Elleman, Bruce, *Modern Chinese Warfare, 1795–1989*. London: Routledge, 2001.
Elliot, Peter, *The Cross and the Ensign: A Naval History of Malta 1798–1979*. London: Granada, 1982.

Elman, Benjamin A., 'Naval Warfare and the Refraction of China's Self-Strengthening Reforms into Scientific and Technological Failure, 1865–1895', *Modern Asian Studies* 38/2 (2004), 283–326.

En-han, Lee, *China's Recovery of the British Hankow and Kiukiang Concessions in 1927*. Perth: University of Western Australia, 1980.

Everest-Phillips, Max, 'The Pre-War Fear of Japanese Espionage: Its Impact and Legacy', *Journal of Contemporary History* 42/2 (2007), 243–65.

Farquharson-Roberts, Mike, *A History of the Royal Navy: World War I*. London: Tauris, 2014.

Farquharson-Roberts, Mike, *Royal Navy Officers from War to War, 1918–1939*. London: Palgrave Macmillan, 2015.

Fedorowich, Kent, '"Cocked Hats and Swords and Small, Little Garrisons": Britain, Canada and the Fall of Hong Kong, 1941', *Modern Asian Studies* 37/1 (2003), 111–57.

Felton, Mark, *China Station: The British Military in the Middle Kingdom 1839–1997*. Barnsley: Pen and Sword, 2013.

Fenby, Jonathan, *The Penguin History of Modern China: The Fall and Rise of a Great Power 1850 to the Present*. London: Penguin, 2013.

Ferris, John, *The Evolution of British Strategic Policy 1919–1926*. Basingstoke: Macmillan, 1989.

Ferris, John, 'The Greatest Power on Earth: Great Britain in the 1920s', *International History Review* 13/4 (1991), 726–50.

Ferris, John, 'The Last Decade of British Maritime Supremacy: 1919–1929', in *Far Flung Lines*, ed. Keith Neilson and Greg Kennedy. London: Cass, 1996, 124–70.

Ferris, John, 'Treasury Control, the Ten Year Rule and British Service Policies, 1919–1924', *Historical Journal* 30/4 (1987), 859–83.

Field, Andrew, *Royal Navy Strategy in the Far East 1919–1939: Preparing for War against Japan*. London: Frank Cass, 2006.

Fieldhouse, David, *Western Imperialism in the Middle East 1914–1958*. Oxford: Oxford University Press, 2006.

Fisher, John, 'British Forward Defence in Asia during World War I', *Journal of Asian History* 37/1 (2003), 70–102.

Foppiani, Oreste, 'The World Cruise of the US Navy in 1907–1909', *Il Politico* 71/1/211 (2006), 110–40.

Forty, George, *British Army Handbook 1939–1945*. London: Dreadnought Books, 2000.

Foster, Anne, 'Secret Police Cooperation and the Roots of Anti-Communism in Interwar Southeast Asia', *Journal of American-East Asian Relations* 4/4 (1995), 331–50.

Friedman, Norman, 'Electronics and Navies', in *The Eclipse of the Big Gun*, ed. Robert Gardiner. London: Conway Maritime, 1992, 192–7.

Fung, Edmund S. K., *The Diplomacy of Imperial Retreat: Britain's South China Policy, 1924–1931*. Oxford: Oxford University Press, 1991.

Fung, Edmund S. K., 'The Sino-British Rapprochement, 1927–1931', *Modern Asian Studies* 17/1 (1983), 79–105.

Gallagher, John, and Robinson, Ronald, 'The Imperialism of Free Trade', *Economic History Review* 6/1 (1953), 1–15.

Gerwarth, Robert, *The Vanquished: Why the First World War Failed to End, 1917–1923*. London: Penguin, 2017.

Goto-Shibata, Harumi, *Japan and Britain in Shanghai 1925–31*. London: Macmillan, 1995.

Gow, Ian, 'The Royal Navy and Japan, 1921–1941', in *The History of Anglo-Japanese Relations, 1600–2000; Volume III: The Military Dimension*, ed. Ian Gow, Yoichi Hirama and John Chapman. Basingstoke: Palgrave Macmillan, 2003, 109–26.

Gowen, Robert, 'Great Britain and the Twenty-One Demands of 1915: Cooperation versus Effacement', *Journal of Modern History* 43/1 (1971), 76–106.

Grainger, John, *The British Navy in the Mediterranean*. Woodbridge: Boydell & Brewer, 2017.

Gray, Steven, *Steam Power and Sea Power: Coal, the Royal Navy and the British Empire, c.1870–1914*. London: Palgrave Macmillan, 2017.

Grove, Eric, *The Royal Navy*. Basingstoke: Macmillan, 2005.

Guogi, Xu, 'China and Empire', in *Empires at War: 1911–1923*, ed. Robert Gerwarth and Erez Manela. Oxford Scholarship Online, 2014, 214–33.

Hamilton, C. I., *The Making of the Modern Admiralty: British Naval Policy-Making 1805–1927*. Cambridge: Cambridge University Press, 2011.

Harland, Kathleen, *The Royal Navy in Hong Kong*. Hong Kong: Royal Navy, 1985.

Harrington, Ralph, '"The Mighty Hood": Navy, Empire, War at Sea and the British National Imagination, 1920–60', *Journal of Contemporary History* 38/2 (2003), 171–85.

Havens, Thomas, 'Japan's Enigmatic Election of 1928', *Modern Asian Studies* 11/4 (1977), 543–55.

Headrick, Daniel, and Griset, Pascal, 'Submarine Telegraph Cables: Business and Politics, 1838–1939', *Business History Review* 75/3 (2001), 543–78.

Hezlet, Arthur, *Aircraft and Sea Power*. London: Davies, 1970.

Higham, Robin, *Armed Forces in Peacetime*. London: Foulis, 1962.

Hirama, Yoichi, 'The First World War and Japan: From the Anglo-Japanese Alliance to the Washington Treaty', in *The Sea in History: The Modern World*, ed. N. A. M. Rodger. Woodbridge: Boydell & Brewer, 2017, 412–25.

Hobbs, David, *Aircraft Carriers of the Royal and Commonwealth Navies*. London: Greenhill, 1996.

Hone, Thomas, and Hone, Trent, *Battle Line: The United States Navy 1919–1939*. Annapolis: Naval Institute Press, 2006.

Hone, Thomas, Friedman, Norman and Mandeles, Mark D., *American and British Aircraft Carrier Development 1919–1941*. Annapolis: Naval Institute Press, 1999.

Howard, Michael, *The Continental Commitment: The Dilemma of British Defence Policy in the Era of the Two World Wars*. London: Ashfield, 1989.

Hunt, Barry, *Sailor-Scholar: Admiral Sir Herbert Richmond, 1871–1946*. Waterloo: Wilfred Laurier University Press, 1982.

Hyam, Ronald, 'The British Empire in the Edwardian Era', in *The Oxford History of the British Empire: Volume IV: The Twentieth Century*, ed. Judith M. Brown and William R. Louis. Oxford: Oxford University Press, 1999, 47–63.

Ion, Hamish, 'The China Squadron and the Boxer Uprising', in *British Naval Strategy East of Suez, 1900–2000: Influences and Actions*, ed. Greg Kennedy. Abingdon: Frank Cass, 2005, 35–61.

Iriye, Akira, *The Origins of the Second World War in Asia and the Pacific*. Harlow: Longman, 1987.

Ismay, Hastings, *The Memoirs of Lord Ismay*. London: Heinemann, 1960.

Jackson, Isabella, 'Expansion and Defence in the International Settlement at Shanghai', in *Britain and China, 1840–1970: Empire, Finance and War*, ed. Robert Bickers and Johnathan Howlett. Abingdon: Routledge, 2016, 187–204.

Jeffrey, Keith, *The British Army and the Crisis of Empire 1918–22*. Manchester: Manchester University Press, 1984.

Jianguo, Zhang, and Junyong, Zhang, *Weihaiwei under British Rule*, trans. Alec Hill. Jinan City: Shandong Pictorial, 2006.

Jones, Mary, 'Towards a Hierarchy of Management: The Victorian and Edwardian Navy 1860–1918', in *Naval Leadership and Management, 1650–1950*, ed. Helen Doe and Richard Harding. Woodbridge: Boydell & Brewer, 2012, 157–72.

Jordan, John, *Warships after Washington: The Development of the Five Major Fleets 1922–1930*. Barnsley: Seaforth, 2011.

Kagan, Robert, 'From Revolutionary Iconoclasm to National Revolution: Ch'en Tu-hsiu and the Chinese Communist Movement', in *China in the 1920s: Nationalism and Revolution*, ed. F. G. Chan and Thomas Etzold. New York: F. Watts, 1976, 69.

Kanya-Forstner, Alexander, 'The War, Imperialism, and Decolonization', in *The Great War and the Twentieth Century*, ed. Jay Winter, Geoffrey Parker and Mary Habeck. New Haven, CT: Yale University Press, 2000, 231–62.

Keller, Wolfgang, Li, Ben and Shiue, Carol, 'Shanghai's Trade, China's Growth: Continuity, Recovery, and Change since the Opium Wars', *IMF Economic Review* 61/2 (2013), 336–78.

Kennedy, Greg, 'British Sea Power and Imperial Defence in the Far East: Sharing the Seas with America', in *Sea Power and the Asia-Pacific: The Triumph of Neptune?*, ed. Geoffrey Till and Patrick Bratton. London: Routledge, 2012, 195–213.

Kennedy, Greg, 'Britain's Policy-Making Elite, the Naval Disarmament Puzzle, and Public Opinion, 1927–1932', *Albion* 26/4 (1994), 623–44.

Kennedy, Paul, *The Realities Behind Diplomacy: Background Influences on British External Policy, 1865–1980*. London: Fontana, 1985.

Kennedy, Paul, *The Rise and Fall of British Naval Mastery*. London: Macmillan, 1983.

Kershaw, Ian, 'War and Political Violence in Twentieth-Century Europe', *Contemporary European History* 14/1 (2005), 107–23.
Kier, Elizabeth, *Imagining War: French and British Military Doctrine between the Wars*. Princeton, NJ: Princeton University Press, 1997.
Kiernan, Victor, *Colonial Empires and Armies 1815–1960*. Stroud: Sutton, 1998.
Killingray, David, '"A Swift Agent of Government": Air Power in British Colonial Africa, 1916–1939', *Journal of African History* 25 (1984), 429–44.
Kinghorn, Jonathan, *The Atlantic Transport Line, 1881–1931*. Jefferson, NC: McFarland, 2012.
Kirby, William, 'The Internationalization of China: Foreign Relations at Home and Abroad in the Republican Era', *China Quarterly* 150 (1997), 433–58.
Kitchen, Martin, *Europe between the Wars: A Political History*. London: Longman, 1988.
Kitching, Carolyn, *Britain and the Geneva Disarmament Conference*. Basingstoke: Palgrave Macmillan, 2003.
Kitching, Carolyn, *Britain and the Problem of International Disarmament: 1919–1934*. London: Routledge, 1999.
Konstam, Angus, *Yangtze River Gunboats 1900–49*. Oxford: Osprey, 2011.
Kuramatsu, Tadashi, 'Britain, Japan and Inter-War Naval Limitation, 1921–1936', in *The History of Anglo-Japanese Relations, 1600–2000; Volume III: The Military Dimension*, ed. Ian Gow, Yoichi Hirama and John Chapman. Basingstoke: Palgrave Macmillan, 2003, 127–38.
Lai, Sherman X., 'Nationalistic Enthusiasm versus Imperialist Sophistication: Britain from Chiang Kai-shek's Perspective', in *Britain and China, 1840–1970: Empire, Finance and War*, ed. Robert Bickers and Jonathan Howlett. Abingdon: Routledge, 2016, 205–21.
Lambert, Nicholas, 'Admiral Sir Francis Bridgeman-Bridgeman (1911–1912)', in *The First Sea Lords*, ed. Malcolm Murfett. Westport: Praeger, 1995, 55–74.
Lambert, Nicholas, 'Strategic Command and Control for Manoeuvre Warfare: Creation of the Royal Navy's "War Room" System, 1905–1915', *Journal of Military History* 69/2 (2005), 361–410.
Lautenschlaeger, Karl, 'The Submarine in Naval Warfare, 1901–2001', *International Security* 11/3 (1986), 94–140.
Lautenschlaeger, Karl, 'Technology and the Evolution of Naval Warfare', *International Security* 8/2 (1983), 3–51.
Li, T'ang Leang, *The Inner History of the Chinese Revolution*. Arlington: University Publications of America, 1975.
Liddell-Hart, Basil, *The Liddell Hart Memoirs, Vol. 1*. London: Cassell, 1965.
Liddle, Peter, *Men of Gallipoli: The Dardanelles and Gallipoli Experience*. London: Allen Lane, 1976.
Lindgren, Scott, 'A Station in Transition: The China Squadron, Cyprian Bridge and the First-Class Cruiser, 1901–1904', *International Journal of Maritime History* 27/3 (2015), 460–83.

Linge, John, 'The Royal Navy and the Irish Civil War', *Irish Historical Studies* 31/121 (1998), 60–71.

Lipkin, Zwia, *Useless to the State: 'Social Problems' and Social Engineering in Nationalist Nanjing 1927–1937*. Cambridge, MA: Harvard University Press, 2006.

Liu, Chang, 'Making Revolution in Jiangnan: Communists and the Yangzi Delta Countryside, 1927–1945', *Modern China* 29/1 (2003), 3–37.

Louis, William R., *British Strategy in the Far East 1919–1939*. Oxford: Clarendon Press, 1971.

Louis, William R., *Ends of British Imperialism: The Scramble for Empire, Suez and Decolonization*. London: Tauris, 2006.

Lovell, Julia, *The Opium War: Drugs, Dreams, and the Making of China*. London: Picador, 2011.

Loy-Wilson, Sophie, '"Liberating" Asia: Strikes and Protest in Sydney and Shanghai, 1920–39', *History Workshop Journal* 72 (2011), 74–102.

Lyon, David, 'The Destroyer and Torpedo Boat', in *The Eclipse of the Big Gun*, ed. Robert Gardiner. London: Conway Maritime, 1992, 80–95.

Ma, Debin, 'Economic Growth in the Lower Yangzi Region of China in 1911–1937: A Quantitative and Historical Analysis', *Journal of Economic History* 68/2 (2008), 355–92.

MacGregor, David, 'The Use, Misuse, and Non-Use of History: The Royal Navy and the Operational Lessons of the First World War', *Journal of Military History* 56/4 (1992), 603–16.

Maiolo, Joe, 'Anglo-Soviet Naval Armaments Diplomacy before the Second World War', *English Historical Review* 123/501 (2008), 351–78.

Maiolo, Joe, *The Royal Navy and Nazi Germany, 1933–1939*. Basingstoke: Macmillan, 1998.

Major, John, *Send a Gunboat*. London: Longmans, 1967.

Man, Kwong Chi, 'Anglo-Japanese Alliance, the First World War, and the Defence of Hong Kong: The Emergence of the First Landward Defence Line in Hong Kong, 1898–1918', *Journal of the Royal Asiatic Society Hong Kong Branch* 54 (2014), 7–32.

Man, Kwong Chi, and Lun, Tsoi Yiu, *Eastern Fortress: A Military History of Hong Kong 1840–1970*. Hong Kong: Hong Kong University Press, 2014.

Mandel, Robert, 'The Effectiveness of Gunboat Diplomacy', *International Studies Quarterly*, 30/1 (1986), 59–76.

Marder, Arthur, 'The Influence of History on Sea Power: The Royal Navy and the Lessons of 1914–1918', *Pacific Historical Review* 41/4 (1972), 413–43.

Marder, Arthur, *From the Dardanelles to Oran: Studies of the Royal Navy in War and Peace 1915–1940*. London: Oxford University Press, 1974.

Marder, Arthur, *Portrait of an Admiral*. London: Cape, 1952.

Massie, Robert, *Castles of Steel*. London: Pimlico, 2005.

Maurer, John, and Bell, Christopher, 'Introduction', in *At the Crossroads between Peace and War: The London Naval Conference in 1930*, ed. John Maurer and Christopher Bell. Annapolis: Naval Institute Press, 2014, 10–14.

Mazower, Mark, 'Violence and the State in the Twentieth Century', *American Historical Review* 107/4 (2002), 1158–78.

Millett, Allan, 'Assault from the Sea, the Development of Amphibious Warfare between the Wars: the American, British and Japanese Experiences', in *Military Innovation in the Interwar Period*, ed. Williamson Murray and Allan Millett. Cambridge: Cambridge University Press, 1996, 50–95.

Mockaitis, Thomas, *British Counter-Insurgency: 1919–1960*. London: Macmillan, 1990.

Montgomery-Hyde, Harford, *British Air Policy between the Wars 1918–1939*. London: Heinemann, 1976.

Moretz, Joseph, *The Royal Navy and the Capital Ship in the Interwar Period*. London: Frank Cass, 2002.

Moretz, Joseph, *Thinking Wisely, Planning Boldly: The Higher Education and Training of Royal Navy Officers, 1919–39*. Solihull: Helion, 2014.

Morgan, Kenneth, 'England, Britain and the Audit of War: The Prothero Lecture', *Transactions of the Royal Historical Society* 7 (1997), 131–53.

Murdoch, Michael, 'Exploiting Anti-Imperialism: Popular Forces and Nation-State-Building during China's Northern Expedition, 1926–1927', *Modern China* 35/1 (2009), 65–95.

Murfett, Malcolm, '"Are We Ready?" The Development of American and British Naval Strategy, 1922–1939', in *Maritime Strategy and the Balance of Power: Britain and American in the Twentieth Century*, ed. John Hattendorf and Robert Jordan. Basingstoke: Palgrave Macmillan, 1989, 214–42.

Murfett, Malcolm, *Naval Warfare 1919–1945: An Operational History of the Volatile War at Sea*. London: Routledge, 2009.

Murphy, Hugh, and Johnman, Lewis, *British Shipbuilding and the State since 1918*. Exeter: Exeter University Press, 2002.

Murray, Williamson, and Millet, Allan (eds.), *Military Innovation in the Interwar Period*. Cambridge: Cambridge University Press, 1998.

Nathan, Andrew, *Peking Politics 1918–1923*. London: University of California Press, 1976.

Neidpath, James, *The Singapore Naval Base and the Defence of Britain's Eastern Empire 1919–1941*. Oxford: Clarendon Press, 1981.

Neilson, Keith, 'Japan, Maritime Power and British Imperial Defence', in *British Naval Strategy East of Suez, 1900–2000: Influences and Actions*, ed. Greg Kennedy. Abingdon: Frank Cass, 2005, 62–89.

Nish, Ian, 'An Overview of Relations between China and Japan, 1895–1945', *China Quarterly* 124 (1990), 601–23.

O'Brien, Philips P., *British and American Naval Power: Politics and Policy 1900–1936*. Westport: Praeger, 1998.

O'Brien, Philips P., 'The Titan Refreshed: Imperial Overstretch and the British Navy before the First World War', *Past & Present* 172 (2001), 146–69.

O'Brien, Philips P., 'The Washington Treaty Era, 1919–1936: Naval Arms Limitation', in *The Sea in History: The Modern World*, ed. N. A. M. Rodger. Woodbridge: Boydell & Brewer, 2017, 500–9.

O'Hara, Glen, '"The Sea Is Swinging into View": Modern British Maritime History in a Globalised World', *English Historical Review* 125/510 (2009), 1109–34.

Osterhammel, Jürgen, 'China', in *The Oxford History of the British Empire: Volume IV: The Twentieth Century*, ed. Judith Brown and William R. Louis. Oxford: Oxford University Press, 1999, 643–66.

Osterhammel, Jürgen, 'Imperialism in Transition: British Business and the Chinese Authorities, 1931–37', *China Quarterly* 98 (1984), 260–86.

Overlack, Peter, 'The Force of Circumstance: Graf Spee's Options for the East Asian Cruiser Squadron in 1914', *Journal of Military History* 60/4 (1996), 657–82.

Padfield, Peter, *Rule Britannia: The Victorian and Edwardian Navy*. London: Routledge & Kegan Paul, 1981.

Parkinson, Johnathan, *The Royal Navy, China Station: 1864–1941*. Kibworth: Matador, 2018.

Parkinson, Roger, *The Late Victorian Navy*. Woodbridge: Boydell & Brewer, 2008.

Patterson, Alfred, *Tyrwhitt of the Harwich Force*. London: Macdonald, 1973.

Phimister, Ian, 'Foreign Devils, Finance and Informal Empire: Britain and China c. 1900–1912', *Modern Asian Studies* 40/3 (2006), 737–59.

Platt, Desmond, 'The Imperialism of Free Trade: Some Reservations', *Economic History Review* 21/2 (1968), 296–306.

Platt, Stephen, *Autumn in the Heavenly Kingdom: China, the West, and the Epic Story of the Taiping Civil War*. London: Atlantic Books, 2012.

Porter, Bernard, *The Absent Minded Imperialists*. Oxford: Oxford University Press, 2004.

Porter, Bernard, *The Lion's Share: A History of British Imperialism 1850 to the Present* (5th edn). Harlow: Longman, 2012.

Pugh, Philip, *The Cost of Seapower*. London: Conway, 1986.

Pugsley, Anthony, and Macintyre, Donald, *Destroyer Man*. London: Weidenfeld and Nicolson, 1957.

Qianping, Chen, 'Foreign Investment in Modern China: An Analysis with a Focus on British Interests', in *Britain and China, 1840–1970: Empire, Finance and War*, ed. Robert Bickers and Jonathan J. Howlett. Abingdon: Routledge, 2016, 148–65.

Redford, Duncan, 'Collective Security and Internal Dissent: The Navy League's Attempts to Develop a New Policy towards British Naval Power between 1919 and the 1922 Washington Naval Treaty', *History* 96/1 (2011), 48–67.

Redford, Duncan, and Grove, Philip, *The Royal Navy: A History since 1900*. London: Tauris, 2014.

Reynolds, David, 'The Origins of the Two "World Wars": Historical Discourse and International Politics', *Journal of Contemporary History* 38/1 (2003), 29–44.

Robinson, Ronald, Gallagher, John and Denny, Alice, *Africa and the Victorians: The Official Mind of Imperialism*. London: Macmillan, 1981.
Romans, Elinor, 'The Internal Economy of the Royal Navy in the Twentieth Century', *Mariners Mirror* 94/1 (2008), 79–88.
Romans, Elinor, 'Leadership Training for Midshipmen, c.1919–1939', in *Naval Leadership and Management, 1650–1950*, ed. Helen Doe and Richard Harding. Woodbridge: Boydell & Brewer, 2012, 173–92.
Romans, Elinor, 'Selection and Early Career Education of Executive Officers in the Royal Navy c.1902–1939'. Unpublished PhD thesis, University of Exeter, 2012.
Roskill, Stephen, *Hankey, Man of Secrets, Vol. 2: 1919–1931*. London: Collins, 1972.
Roskill, Stephen, *Naval Policy between the Wars. Vol. 1, the Period of Anglo-American Antagonism 1919–1929*. London: Collins, 1968.
Rowe, Laura, *Morale and Discipline in the Royal Navy during the First World War*. Cambridge: Cambridge University Press, 2018.
Ruger, Jan, *The Great Naval Game: Britain and Germany in the Age of Empire*. Cambridge: Cambridge University Press, 2007.
Sabahi, Houshang, *British Policy in Persia 1918–1925*. London: Cass, 1990.
Salkeld, Kim, 'Witness to the Revolution: Surgeon Lieutenant Bertram Bickford on the China Station 1910–12', *Journal of the Royal Asiatic Society Hong Kong Branch* 51 (2011), 115–42.
Satia, Priya, 'The Defense of Inhumanity: Air Control and the British Idea of Arabia', *American Historical Review* 111/1 (2006), 16–51.
Schofield, Brian, *British Sea Power*. London: Batsford, 1967.
Sheridan, James, *China in Disintegration: The Republican Era in Chinese History 1912–1949*. New York: Free Press, 1975.
Shih Shu-Mei, 'Gender, Race, and Semicolonialism: Liu Na'ou's Urban Shanghai Landscape', *Journal of Asian Studies* 55/4 (1996), 934–56.
Spence, Daniel O., *Colonial Naval Culture and British Imperialism 1922–67*. Manchester: Manchester University Press, 2015.
Spence, Daniel O., *A History of the Royal Navy: Empire and Imperialism*. London: Tauris, 2015.
Stevens, Keith, '"Duncan Force" – the Shanghai Defence Force in 1927, & the Career of Captain Ronald Spear', *Journal of the Royal Asiatic Society Hong Kong Branch* 48 (2008), 151–74.
Stoker, Donald, *Britain, France and the Naval Arms Trade in the Baltic 1919–1939: Grand Strategy and Failure*. London: Routledge, 2012.
Sturtivant, Ray, *British Naval Aviation: The Fleet Air Arm, 1917–1990*. Annapolis: Naval Institute Press, 1990.
Sumida, Jon T., 'British Naval Operational Logistics, 1914–1918', *Journal of Military History* 57/3 (1993), 447–80.

Sumida, Jon T., 'British Naval Procurement and Technological Change, 1919–1939', in *Technology and Naval Combat in the Twentieth Century and Beyond*, ed. Philips P. O'Brien. London: Routledge, 2001, 128–47.

Sumida, Jon T., *In Defence of Naval Supremacy: Finance, Technology, and British Naval Policy, 1889–1914*. London: Routledge, 1993.

Sumida, Jon T., ' "The Best Laid Plans": The Development of British Battle-Fleet Tactics, 1919–42', *International History Review* 14/4 (1992), 681–700.

Sutton, Donald S., *Provincial Militarism and the Chinese Republic*. Ann Arbor: University of Michigan Press, 1980.

Tawney, Cyril, *Grey Funnel Lines: Traditional Song & Verse of the Royal Navy 1900–1970*. London: Routledge, 1987.

Taylor, Alan J. P., *The Origins of the Second World War*. London: Hamilton, 1969.

Taylor, Jay, *The Generalissimo: Chiang Kai-shek and the Struggle for Modern China*. Cambridge, MA: Harvard University Press, 2009.

Taylor, Jeremy, 'The Bund: Littoral Space of Empire in the Treaty Ports of East Asia', *Social History* 27/2 (2002), 125–42.

Tenney, Warren, "A Disturbance Not of Great Importance': The Tientsin Incident and U.S.Japan Relations in China, 1919–1920', *Journal of American-East Asian Relations* 3/4 (1994), 325–44.

Thomas, Martin, *Violence and Colonial Order – Police, Workers and Protest in the European Colonial Empires 1918–1940*. Cambridge: Cambridge University Press, 2012.

Thompson, Julian, *The Royal Marines*. London: Pan, 2000.

Till, Geoffrey, *Air Power and the Royal Navy 1914–1945*. London: Jane, 1979.

Till, Geoffrey, *Seapower: A Guide for the Twenty-First Century*. London: Routledge, 2013.

Tsai, Wen-Hui, *Patterns of Political Elite Mobility in Modern China 1912–1949*. Hong Kong: Chinese Material Centre, 1983.

Van de Ven, Hans J., *War and Nationalism in China 1925–1945*. London: Routledge, 2003.

Van der Vat, Dan, *Standard of Power – The Royal Navy in the Twentieth Century*. London: Pimlico, 2000.

Van Dijk, Kees, *Pacific Strife: The Great Powers and Their Political and Economic Rivalries in Asia and the Western Pacific 1870–1914*. Amsterdam: Amsterdam University Press, 2015.

Waldron, Arthur, *From War to Nationalism: China's Turning Point, 1924–1925*. Cambridge: Cambridge University Press, 1995.

Wasserstrom, Jeffrey, *Global Shanghai, 1850–2010: A History in Fragments*. London: Taylor & Francis, 2008.

Watts, Barry, and Murray, Williamson, 'Military Innovation in Peacetime', in *Military Innovation in the Interwar Period*, ed. Williamson Murray and Allan Millett. Cambridge: Cambridge University Press, 1996, 369–416.

Wells, Anthony, 'Naval Intelligence and Decision Making in an Era of Technical Change', in *Technical Change and British Naval Policy 1860–1939*, ed. Bryan Ranft. London: Hodder and Stoughton, 1977, 123–46.
West, Nigel, *MASK: MI5's Penetration of the Communist Party of Great Britain*. London: Routledge, 2005.
Wilbur, Clarence, *The Nationalist Revolution in China: 1923–1928*. Cambridge: Cambridge University Press, 1984.
Williamson, Albert, *Eastern Traders*. Jardine: Matheson, 1975.
Wise, Jon, *The Role of the Royal Navy in South America, 1920–1970*. London: Bloomsbury, 2014.
Woodward, David, *Lloyd George and the Generals*. London: Associated University Presses, 1983.
Wright, Richard, *China's Steam Navy*. London: Chatham, 2000.
Wright-Nooth, George, *Prisoner of the Turnip Heads*. London: Leo Cooper, 1994.
Zarrow, Peter, *China in War and Revolution 1895–1949*. London: Routledge, 2005.

Index

1927 task force 2, 115–25, 135–6, 206, 263

Acheson, Sir Archibald 97
Acheson, Leon 184–90, 226–8, 233, 247, 272
Africa Station 46
Alexander-Sinclair, Sir Edwyn 22, 115, 179–80, 222–3, 228, 267–8
Alleyne, Victor 111, 219–21
Amery, Leo 129
Anderson, Sir David 75, 77, 223
Anderson Jr, Edwin 155
Andrewes, Sir William 173–4
Anglo-American relations 41–4, 73–83, 112–13, 117, 134, 160, 191, 224, 269
Anglo-Chinese cooperation 63–6, 82, 98, 104, 110–12, 169, 212, 217, 219, 223, 242–4, 247
Anglo-French relations 42, 45, 63, 123, 134, 151, 160
Anglo-Japanese alliance 22, 26, 42–5, 66
Anglo-Japanese cooperation 66–71, 113, 134, 175, 270
anti-intellectualism 9, 29–30, 207, 249, 273
anti-imperial displays 32, 50, 65–8, 75, 101, 113, 120, 124, 130–1, 168, 175, 190–2, 218–19, 227–31, 234–5, 263
Arab nationalism 3, 32
Araki, Jirō 191–2
Archangelsk 32
Arcos Affair 124, 136
Armitage, Arthur 48
arms trade 122, 158–61, 168, 214, 249, 264–5
Asiatic Petroleum Company 108
Australia 22–3, 27, 55, 218

Baillie-Grohman, Harold 65
Baldwin, Earl Stanley 100
banditry (*see* piracy)
Barraclough, Edward 211

Beatty, Earl David 44, 61, 123, 245
Beijing 31, 97–8, 120, 133, 169, 171–2, 178
Beiyang 31, 97
Berryman, Paul 212, 226, 228
blockade 60–2
Boer War 54, 133
Borrett, George 243
Boxer Uprising 31, 98, 109, 113, 117, 119, 125, 133, 158, 210–11, 229, 239
boycotts 64–5, 113–14, 120, 190, 218–23, 234
Boyle, Earl William 107, 205, 240
Bridge, Sir Cyprian 45, 211, 215
Bridgeman, Viscount William 119, 167, 247
Bristol, Mark 155
British Army 31, 46, 52, 63, 68–73, 79–80, 118–21, 128, 134, 150, 158, 180, 237–8, 244
British domestic politics 95, 100, 115, 125–6, 267
budget cuts (*see* defence expenditure)
Buckley, Kenneth 249
Burnett, Philip 173–4, 188
Butler, Smedley 79–80

Cam Ranh Bay 74
Cameron, John 132–3, 189, 225–39, 245, 250, 272
Caplain, Roger 185, 188
Carnarvon Commission 208
Carpenter, Robert 243
Chamberlain, Sir Austen 68, 100, 129, 166, 194, 206, 228, 265
Chanak Affair 2, 32, 119, 263
Changsha 235–7
Chengdu 115, 131
Chengling 234–5
China Association 77, 103
China Salt Administration and Custom Service 24, 102

Chinese Communist Party 32, 96, 122, 125, 250
Chinese nationalism 75, 96, 98, 124, 132, 214, 218, 246
Chinese navy/navies 51–2, 65, 110–12, 157, 189, 273
Chinese troops 43, 64–70, 79, 111–13, 120–2, 130–2, 156, 167–8, 174, 177, 181–90, 222–6, 230–7, 241, 244, 249, 262
Chongqing 78, 115, 129, 156, 173, 194, 223, 233–5, 242
cinemas 15–16, 76
civilian casualties 8–9, 69, 98, 111, 128–34, 182–90, 213, 219–21, 226–7, 268
civilian evacuations 72, 78, 120, 126–7, 183–9, 228, 233, 235, 237, 241
Clanchy, Henry 241
Clementi, Sir Cecil 113, 128, 160
command culture 7–9, 61, 77–8, 82, 104, 153, 194, 205, 212–14, 223, 228, 240–9, 264–7
command structure 23–4, 67, 71, 75–7, 170–8, 193–4, 205–7, 222, 241, 246, 262
Commander-in-Chief 49, 68, 169, 193, 214
Committee for Imperial Defence 50, 67, 134, 218
Communism – British fears of 8, 32, 45, 66, 122–5, 135, 263
conditions afloat 20
Coolidge, Calvin 78
Curzon, Lord George 104
cutting-out expeditions 170, 182–4, 225–6

Darley, Frederick 225–8, 249
Daya Bay 73, 106, 112, 151, 161, 176, 179–80, 215
De Winton, Francis 205, 240
December Memorandum 59, 68, 129, 135, 194, 206–7, 228–30, 265, 267
defence expenditure 3, 28–30, 53, 68, 109–10, 116, 125–6, 134–5, 149–51, 159, 170
Dickens, Sir Gerald 63, 170, 210, 212, 250
diplomatic events 20, 172, 210
disaster relief 20, 171–2
Drage, Charles 66–7

Duff, Sir Alexander 155
Duncan, Sir John 73, 79–80, 177
Dutch East Indies 48

East Indies Station 22, 46, 50, 53, 59, 118, 238, 245
Egypt 115, 209
Eighth Destroyer Flotilla 245
England, Hugh Turnour 168, 185–92, 232, 238–9, 247, 262, 268, 272
entertainment ashore 17–18, 58, 76–7, 81, 169, 210–11, 233
Everett, Sir Allan 223, 267
extra-territorial rights 24, 59, 64, 99–100, 105, 208, 210, 229, 234–8

Faure, Cyril 111, 219–22, 272
Fifth Light Cruiser Squadron 47, 52, 155
First Cruiser Squadron 237–40, 245
First Shandong Expedition 69
First World War 2, 7, 19, 25–31, 45–52, 95–108, 112, 116, 123–6, 131–5, 150–4, 161, 166, 171, 210–14, 232, 242, 247–9, 261, 264–72
Fisher, John 'Jackie' 22, 153, 160, 168
food supplies 21, 56, 82, 231
Foreign Office 27, 29, 50, 58, 69–70, 97–8, 102, 105, 108–16, 124–7, 151, 169, 171–7, 191, 214, 218–28, 234
France 99, 102, 133, 161
France, Marine Nationale 71–4, 112, 156, 167, 219, 235
Franks, Ivan 48
French Concession 79
Fuel 54–9, 74, 181, 231
Fuzhou 54, 67

Gallipoli campaign 2, 184, 192, 248
Garvey, Douglas 234
Gaskin, Arthur 168
Geddes' cuts 6, 28
Germany 42–3, 47, 49, 61, 103, 135
Germany's East Asia Squadron 22, 95, 153
Gibraltar 244
Giichi, Baron Tanaka 27, 65, 69
Giles, Lancelot 109
Great Kantō earthquake 20, 171
Greece 151
Greenland, William 20, 58

Index

Guangzhou 50–1, 100–1, 104, 110, 149, 160–2, 167–8, 176, 215
Guangzhou, Shaji Massacre 111, 115, 127, 173, 219–21, 265, 268
Guangzhou, other incidents 65–6, 106, 113, 155–6, 170, 180
Guomindang 31, 50, 64–9, 78–82, 97–8, 105–6, 110–13, 118, 120, 130, 132, 136, 160–4, 167, 174, 189–91, 229, 234–6, 239
Guomindang reconciliation with Britain 115, 125, 271–3
Guomindang schism with communists 75, 122–5, 250

Hadley, Harold 241
Halahan, Frederick 176
Hamilton, Sir Louis 71, 158, 190–1, 233, 240–2, 246, 248
Hankey, Baron Maurice 123
Hankou 21, 23, 43, 68, 73, 122, 127, 132–3, 154, 168, 172–3, 194, 211, 225, 229–37, 245
heavy weaponry 52, 155–8, 184, 190–1, 194, 214, 227, 229–31, 237, 241, 249
Heron, Albert 166
hijacking 107–10, 180, 215, 264
HM Treasury (*see* defence expenditure)
HM Ships
    aircraft carriers 8, 116, 160–7, 179–81, 218, 222, 229, 232, 245, 248, 266
    capital ships 4, 20, 25–6, 46, 53, 57, 117, 152
    cruisers 20, 29, 45, 57, 68, 117, 120, 130, 132, 153–5, 162, 166, 172–3, 179–92, 210, 215, 223, 232–3, 238–49, 262
    destroyers 71, 78, 154, 158, 162, 170, 174, 180, 190–1, 230, 240, 247
    gunboats 17, 20–3, 45, 51, 65–6, 95, 106–10, 129, 131, 156–7, 179, 183–90, 210–30, 233–4, 241–3
    minesweepers 23
    sloops 30, 51, 57, 66–7, 76, 114, 126–7, 132–3, 154, 157, 171–82, 214, 223, 230, 241, 246
    submarines 21, 61, 66, 117, 173–6, 215
Holland, Cedric 18, 99

Hong Kong 15, 65–6, 95, 106–8, 113, 120, 126–8, 161–2, 169–70, 172–3, 176, 178, 180, 215, 219, 221
Hong Kong, defence of 6, 46, 49–51, 59–64, 74, 82, 118, 125, 161, 235, 244, 250, 270–1
Hong Kong facilities 58–9, 150, 163–7, 181, 211, 266
Hong Kong, governor 105, 113, 211
Hong Kong, naval presence 4, 23, 41, 54–7
Hong Kong, social events 21, 67, 240
Hough, Henry 191
House of Commons 54, 100, 119, 124, 153, 166–7, 247
Howard, Ronald 179
HSBC 113
Hsiang, Liu 233
Hutchison, Sir Alexander 244

imperial policing 3, 31–2, 70, 107, 113, 117, 128, 131–6, 152–3, 158, 165–8, 173, 193, 206–13, 222–3, 231, 241–6, 250, 263–7
Imperial Japanese Navy 22, 27, 42–4, 49, 51, 66–71, 74, 112, 118, 136, 154, 191, 235, 237, 269
imperial violence 15, 32, 64, 66, 113, 120, 126–36, 183–93, 206–10, 213–14, 219–33, 239–47, 262, 267–8
India 42–8, 123, 230
Indian troops 33, 67, 73
inter-service rivalry 30
international finance 31, 44, 97, 101–3
Iraq 33, 134
Ireland 4
Italy 42, 63, 72–3, 103, 121, 134, 237

Jamieson, James 161, 219
Japan 65, 77, 103, 160, 164
Japan, Britain's plans for war with 4, 42, 46–53, 57–62, 82–3, 116, 164–5, 270–1
Japanese imperial expansion 47–9, 61, 65, 98, 135
Japanese interests in China 101–3, 121, 175
Jardine Matheson 101, 106, 113
Jellicoe, Earl John 239
Jerram, Sir Martyn 171

Jiangjiu 162
Jiangmen 115, 219
Jiangsu 240
Jiangsu-Zhejiang War 122, 217
Jiangyin 158, 174, 191
Jiujiang 54, 65, 101, 223, 230, 235–6, 242, 248
Jukes-Hughes, Edward 242
Jutland, 233

Kai Shek, Chiang 124, 191
Kelly, Sir Howard 65, 74
Kenworthy, Joseph 119, 153
Keyes, Roger 212, 239
Kirke, Cecil 114
Knox, John 167
Kobayashi, Seizo 67

Lampson, Sir Miles 70, 98, 104, 234
language 16
League of Nations 33
Leshan 169
Leveson, Sir Arthur 49, 62–6, 82, 109, 155, 171–2, 215, 271
life afloat 56, 76, 150, 210–11, 215, 246, 272–3
London 17, 20, 43, 67, 102, 169, 175
London Naval Conference 165, 266

Macau 160
MacKinnon, Lachlan 181
Maclachlan, Crawford 109
Macleay, Sir Ronald 109
MacMurray, John 75
Madden Committee 9–10, 244
Malta 33, 46, 110, 116, 164, 181, 218, 237–8
Manchuria 26, 61
Maxwell-Scott, Malcolm 110, 216, 221
May Forth Movement 99
May Thirtieth Incident 32, 64, 75, 113, 115, 120–1, 127, 129, 162, 167–8, 173, 175, 210, 218–19, 272
McEuen, James 123
McNeill, Ronald 124
McVay Jr, Charles 75, 77–8
Mediterranean 3, 26, 46, 57, 76, 116–19, 160, 167, 213, 229, 245
mental health 221–3, 247, 267–8, 272

Mexico 115
Middle East 127, 133–6, 163, 181, 213
Miles, Roderick 114
Mirs Bay 46, 58, 238, 248
Missionaries in China 32, 233
Moore, Sir Arthur 169–70
Mosul 33

Nanjing 21, 65, 72, 100–6, 122, 128, 157, 172–4, 223, 232, 241, 244
Nanjing incident (1927) 8, 69, 79, 130–2, 162, 167–8, 182–92, 205, 238–40, 262, 268
Nanning 215
naval aviation 26, 129, 151–2, 160–7, 181, 192, 222, 266
naval intelligence 151, 174–8
Naval Review 123, 221, 249
naval shore bombardments 111, 130–2, 157–8, 162, 182–92, 206, 214, 217–26, 234, 238–40, 242–3, 268
Netherlands 44, 71–2, 118, 160
New Zealand 27
newspapers 15–16, 32, 69, 124, 131, 133, 160–2, 168, 173–4, 185, 189
Nishihara loans 103
Northern Expedition 57, 68–9, 75, 100, 103–4, 115, 118, 120–2, 130, 132, 189, 192, 224, 229–32, 238, 250

one-power standard 27
Onion, Henry 156
Opium Wars 5, 64, 100, 149

Pacific Station 23, 118
Page, Herbert 156
Palariet, Sir Michael 161
Pearl River 51, 105, 110, 156–7, 160, 194, 215, 241
Pearson, John 176, 240, 246
Peck, Ambrose 222
Peifu, Wu 173
piracy 25, 31, 56, 63, 105–16, 120, 125, 134–5, 153–6, 168, 176–82, 192–4, 214–19, 241, 248, 263–5
Plan Red 47
Poland, Allan 176
Poole, Douglas 19, 67
Port Arthur 59

Porter, Harold 124
Portsmouth 165, 181, 244
Portugal 45, 71–2, 103, 121
Pound, Sir Dudley 62, 211
power projection 26, 41, 57–9, 74, 96, 135, 167, 206–8, 217–19
Powlett, Frederick 171
Pudong 17, 80, 120, 243
Pugsley, Anthony 21, 129–30, 212, 223, 228

Qing collapse 25, 96–7, 155
Qing Dynasty 51, 65, 100, 105, 108, 126–7, 149
Qinhuangdao 173, 175

racial issues 63, 66–7, 71, 98–9, 103, 131, 175, 250–1, 262, 270, 273
radio (*see* wireless)
railways 101–3, 149, 191, 239
Ramsbotham, Reginald 77, 164, 214
Republic of China 25, 96
Richmond, Sir Herbert 3, 50, 59–64, 271
Roberts, William 15, 19, 58
Royal Air Force 30, 52, 97, 118, 127, 133–6, 162–5
Royal Fleet Auxiliary 56, 58
Royal Marines 18, 20, 156, 168, 173, 180, 192, 210, 217–18, 225, 238
Royal Marines, 12th Battalion 10, 70, 80, 118, 128, 173, 181, 231, 237, 243–5
Royal Navy reserves 118–19, 150
Royal Navy War Colleges 48, 65
Russian Revolution 3, 103, 135
Russian Pacific Fleet 22, 42, 95
Russian troops in Persia 133
Russo-Japanese War 95

Schurman, Jacob 75
secret intelligence 42, 44, 51, 70, 106, 177
Secret Intelligence Service 176, 221
security service 124
Second Zhili-Fengtian War 217
Sen, Yang 21, 183–6, 224–7
Shandong 47, 99
Shanghai 17–21, 44, 52, 101–4, 155, 172, 237, 242
Shanghai crisis 2, 7, 57, 68, 72–5, 78–80, 115–19, 122, 134, 151, 238, 245, 261–3

Shanghai Defence Force 29, 68–73, 79–80, 118–19, 136, 181, 237, 250
Shanghai International Settlement 17, 73, 78–9, 100, 103, 114, 217
Shanghai Municipal Police 18, 32, 64, 108–9, 120–3, 179, 217
Shanghai night life 19–21, 211
Shanghai, Royal Navy presence 56–8, 95, 127, 178
Shanghai St John's University 80–1
Shanghai Volunteer Corps 121–2, 158–9, 190, 217, 229–30
Shanghailanders 17, 98, 103, 113, 121, 237
Shantou 114, 157, 223
Shaokuan, Chen 65
Sheppard, Leonard 68
Shidehara, Kijuro 67
shore parties 31, 63, 110–11, 128–9, 132–3, 180–2, 206, 215–24, 229, 235, 238–9, 242, 244
signals intelligence 67, 174–8
Singapore 15, 22–4, 29, 46–9, 52–4, 61, 74, 153
Singapore, defence of 59–60, 165
Singapore, facilities 53, 57, 150
Singapore, naval presence 24–6, 178
Singapore strategy 3, 41, 83, 270
Smithwick, Algernon 66
smuggling 108–9, 160, 225
Songshi 111
South China Sea 74
Soviet Union 32, 45, 48–9, 63, 68, 104, 118, 121–4, 131, 136, 161, 263
Spain 71–3, 75, 118
Special Service Squadron 26, 152–4
sport 21, 152, 210–11, 233
Stewart, Gershom 166
Stirling, Anselan 111
Strauss, Joseph 77
Stubbs, Reginald 67, 105
Submarine warfare 29, 60, 116, 176, 248, 266
Sykes, Sir Frederick 30

Taiping Rebellion 31
Talbot, Cecil 164–6
Telegraph 169–70, 173–4, 208
Ten Year Rule 3, 123
Third Destroyer Flotilla 229, 245, 249

Thompson, John 241
Tianjin 77, 100, 120, 149, 171, 222
Todd, George 153, 169–70
trade 5, 29, 31, 44, 60, 100–1, 106–8, 114, 208, 225, 235, 249
Trenchard, Viscount Hugh 30, 166
Tsushima, Battle of 42
Tweedie, Sir Hugh 107, 125, 184, 190, 207, 245
Twenty-One Demands 47, 99
two-power standard 27
Tudway, Lionel 216–17, 221
Tucker, Colin 109
Tyrwhitt, Sir Reginald 71, 74, 79, 82, 118, 131, 191–2, 205, 221, 230–48, 268

United States 1–4, 26, 55, 60–3, 68, 72, 135, 162–4, 186
United States interests in China 101, 103, 121, 224
United States Marine Corps 75, 78–80, 121, 183
United States Navy (USN) 26–8
USN actions at Nanjing 130, 183–91, 262
USN Asiatic Fleet 67, 74–83, 118, 154–5, 167–8, 174, 210, 269
USN Yangtze Patrol 69, 75, 112, 155, 235

Waistell, Sir Arthur 74
Walker, Arthur 210–11
Wallace, Thomas 166
Wangtong 111
Wanxian Incident 8, 73, 78, 105, 122, 130, 170, 182–90, 212, 224–37, 246–51, 265, 268, 272

Washington Treaty 8, 27, 163–6, 266
Weihai 6, 23, 41, 47, 51, 54–8, 82, 120, 126, 150, 163, 172–5
Wenzhou 214
West River 24, 51, 110, 170, 215–17, 250
Whampoa Military Academy 65, 219–22
Whitehorn, Ivan 224
Whitney, Ernest 168
Wight, Ian 168
Williams, Clarence 78–80, 155, 191
Winsloe, Alfred 45
wireless 8, 20, 151, 170–9, 191–4, 205, 241, 248, 266
Wuchang Uprising (*see* Xinhai Revolution)
Wuhan 96
Wuzhou 215

Xiamen 54, 66
Xinhai Revolution 25, 30–1, 43, 65, 95–101, 105, 108, 116, 126–7, 135, 155, 214
Xinjiang 42

Yantai 57, 66, 77, 126
Yat-sen, Sun 72
Yellow Sea 51–2, 56, 74
Yichang 210, 233, 235
Yongxiang, Lu 217
Yǒurén, Chén 105

Zhangzhou 243
Zhenjiang 78, 241
Zongchang, Zhang 97
Zuolin, Zhang 161